JOURNAL FOR THE STUDY OF THE OLD TESTAMENT
SUPPLEMENT SERIES
87

Editors
David J A Clines
Philip R Davies

JSOT Press
Sheffield

THE BIBLE IN THREE DIMENSIONS

Essays in celebration of
forty years of Biblical Studies
in the University of Sheffield

edited by
**David J.A. Clines,
Stephen E. Fowl,
Stanley E. Porter**

Journal for the Study of the Old Testament
Supplement Series 87

Copyright © 1990 Sheffield Academic Press

Published by JSOT Press
JSOT Press is an imprint of
Sheffield Academic Press Ltd
The University of Sheffield
343 Fulwood Road
Sheffield S10 3BP
England

Printed in Great Britain
by Billing & Sons Ltd
Worcester

British Library Cataloguing in Publication Data

The Bible in three dimensions: essays in celebration
of forty years of biblical studies in the
University of Sheffield
1. Theology
I. Clines, David J.A.   II. Fowl, Stephen E.
III. Porter, Stanley E.
230

ISSN 0309-0787
ISBN 1-85075-227-3

CONTENTS

Part 2

*Studies in the Social World
of Israel and Early Christianity*

Part 3

Questions of Method

ABBREVIATIONS

AB	Anchor Bible
ANRW	*Aufstieg und Niedergang der römischen Welt,* ed. H. Temperini and W. Haase (Berlin: de Gruyter, 1972–)
ASTI	*Annual of the Swedish Theological Institute*
BETL	*Bibliotheca ephemeridum theologicarum lovaniensium*
Bib	*Biblica*
BJRL	*Bulletin of the John Rylands University Library of Manchester*
BTB	*Biblical Theology Bulletin*
BWANT	Beiträge zur Wissenschaft vom Alten und Neuen Testament
BZ	*Biblische Zeitschrift*
CB	Coniectanea Biblica
CBQ	*Catholic Biblical Quarterly*
CTM	*Concordia Thological Monthly*
EB	Echter Bibel
ÉBib	Études bibliques
ÉglTh	*Église et Théologie*
EQ	*Evangelical Quarterly*
ExpTim	*Expository Times*
FRLANT	Forschungen zur Religion und Literatur des Alten und Neuen Testaments
FS	Festschrift
HBT	*Horizons in Biblical Theology*
HeyJ	*Heythrop Journal*

HTR	*Harvard Theological Review*
HUCA	*Hebrew Union College Annual*
ICC	International Critical Commentary
Interp	*Interpretation*
JANES	*Journal of the Ancient Near Eastern Society of Columbia University*
JBL	*Journal of Biblical Literature*
JETS	*Journal of the Evangelical Theological Society*
JHS	*Journal of Hellenic Studies*
JJS	*Journal of Jewish Studies*
JR	*Journal of Religion*
JSNT	*Journal for the Study of the New Testament*
JSNTSup	*Journal for the Study of the New Testament, Supplement Series*
JSOT	*Journal for the Study of the Old Testament*
JSOTSup	*Journal for the Study of the Old Testament, Supplement Series*
JTS	*Journal of Theological Studies*
KHAT	Kurzer Hand-Commentar zum Alten Testament
MeyerK	Meyer Kommentar
NCB	New Century Bible
N.F.	Neue Folge, new series
NICNT	New International Commentary on the New Testament
NICOT	New International Commentary on the Old Testament
NIGTC	New International Greek Testament Commentary
NLC	New London Commentary
NovT	*Novum Testamentum*
ns	new series
NTAbh	Neutestamentliche Abhandlungen
NTD	Das Neue Testament Deutsch
NTS	*New Testament Studies*
OTL	Old Testament Library
RNT	Regensburger Neues Testament
SBL	Society of Biblical Literature
SBT	Studies in Biblical Theology
SEÅ	*Svensk Exegetisk Årsbok*

SNTSMS	Society for New Testament Study Monograph Series
SNTU	Studien zum Neuen Testament und seiner Umwelt
SPDSOE	*Studies in the Period of David and Solomon and Other Essays* (ed. T. Ishida; Tokyo: Yamakawa-Shuppansha, 1982)
ST	*Studia theologica*
TDNT	*Theological Dictionary of the New Testament,* ed. G. Kittel and G. Friedrich, tr. G.W. Bromiley (10 vols.; Grand Rapids: Eerdmans, 1964-76)
TQ	*Theologische Quartalschrift*
TRE	*Theologische Realenzyklopädie*
TS	*Theological Studies*
TynB	*Tyndale Bulletin*
VC	*Vigiliae Christianae*
VT	*Vetus Testamentum*
VTSup	*VT* Supplements
WBC	Word Biblical Commentary
WMANT	Wissenschaftliche Monographien zum Alten und Neuen Testament
ZAW	*Zeitschrift für die alttestamentliche Wissenschaft*
ZNW	*Zeitschrift für die neutestamentliche Wissenschaft*
ZTK	*Zeitschrift für Theologie und Kirche*

PREFACE

This volume, *The Bible in Three Dimensions*, has something of the character of a *Festschrift*, an anniversary volume to celebrate forty years of academic biblical studies in the University of Sheffield. But its appearance does not in the least signify that we regard the department's task as complete; rather, it is a dedicatory volume by current and former teaching staff and students in anticipation of further years of productive teaching and research. The figure of forty is of course richly laden symbolically; sometimes indeed we have all feared that our progress has been imitating the circularity of the forty years of the wilderness journeyings—even if the forty years did eventually lead to the brink of Canaan. At other times, it has seemed more like forty days and nights of testing in the wilderness. And latterly we have begun to wonder whether the department should not expect to find forty a dangerous age and prepare itself for a collective mid-life crisis. In the end, whether we have arrived, or whether we have made progress, or whether we have been travelling in any direction at all, is for others to judge. For ourselves it was enough that we are here, and have been here, for a cause of celebration to exist.

The discipline of academic biblical studies in Great Britain, as well as in the rest of the Western world, has undergone profound changes in the last forty years, since F.F. Bruce founded the department of Biblical History and Literature soon after the end of World War II. The department was the first biblical studies department in Great Britain to be located in a faculty of arts rather than divinity. This significant origin has helped to shape its orientation toward academic study of the Bible during the post-war burgeoning of the discipline, opening up biblical studies to those not theologically or eccle-

siastically inclined in traditional ways. Not only has the
department been on the forefront of this democratization of
biblical studies, a position jealously guarded to this day, but it
has been instrumental in developing several important methodological approaches which have come to typify the discipline
as a whole in the latter part of the twentieth century. It is to
these approaches that this book is devoted.

Three of the newer areas where Sheffield continues to make
its presence felt world-wide form the three sections of this
book. Of course, the department is engaged in traditional biblical studies as well, but these three have come to represent
Sheffield's most concentrated activity and they continue to
attract faculty and post-graduate students from Great Britain
and abroad. We have a horror of being typecast as one-dimen-
sional in our interests, of adopting only one approach to our
study. We dare to hope that the three dimensions represented
in this volume constitute a distinct solidity.

Literary readings of the final form of the biblical text comprise the first area of interest. Sheffield was a pioneer in this
area through the work of David M. Gunn (now at Columbia
Theological Seminary and Emory University, Atlanta, Georgia) on the stories of King Saul and King David and of David
J.A. Clines on the Pentateuch. One recent handbook on interpretation of the Bible indeed refers to followers of the final-
form approach as members of the 'Sheffield School', but of
course, whatever the influence of Sheffield publications in this
area, we take no proprietorial responsibility for what others
have done of their own free will! Although it has been work on
the Old Testament that has led the way along this methodological path, recent work of this kind on the New Testament,
in particular the Gospels, is pushing forward. The present
collection of essays includes six examples of final-form readings of the biblical text, ranging from close readings of individual passages to re-readings of entire books. David Clines
offers readings of the Esther story from formalist, structuralist, feminist, materialist and deconstructionist perspectives,
illustrating as well how the critical questions asked are instrumental in governing the answers received. David Gunn
offers a critique of the concept of the reliable narrator, whose
presence is generally taken for granted in biblical literature.

Barry G. Webb (now at Moore College, Sydney) offers an integrated reading of the book of Isaiah on the basis of the concept of remnant as pointing to the ultimate transformation of Zion. Laurence A. Turner (now at Avondale College, New South Wales) reads Genesis 18–19, two troublesome chapters, in light of their noteworthy fascination with questions of sex and violence. Andrew Lincoln offers a reading of the Gospel of Matthew focusing upon the literary characterization of the disciples as developing, authoritative teachers. And Stanley E. Porter (now at Biola University, La Mirada, California), examining one particular Gospel pericope—Luke's parable of the unjust steward (Luke 16.1-13)—enters the claim that irony affords the best understanding of it.

The social world of Israel and early Christianity provides the second major area of interest. Sheffield's important contribution here was first established through the work of Bruce D. Chilton (now at Bard College, Annandale-on-Hudson, New York) and Philip R. Davies. This area of exploration is the broadest represented. The six essays in this collection range from interpretations of individual texts to conceptual and developmental studies in light of social and historical conventions of the ancient world. K. Lawson Younger (now at Le Tourneau University, Longview, Texas) explores the degree to which figurative and contextual features of writing bear upon the issue of historicity, with special reference to 1 Kings 1–11. David J. Chalcraft (now in Oxford) explores the concept of social deviance in the book of Judges, noting how practices depicted are related to the social standards created by the several societies represented. Ronald E. Clements (now at King's College, London) utilizes the notion of the routinization of charisma to account for the development of traditions in the book of Jeremiah. Loveday C.A. Alexander, in a wide-ranging study, discusses the preference evinced by both Christian and non-Christian writers of the first centuries of our era for the 'living voice' over the written word. Colin J.A. Hickling raises the question whether baptism was a requirement for first-century church membership. And Bruce Chilton treats the well-known passage of the coin in the fish's mouth (Mt. 17.24-27) in the light of different social and literary realms, including the early church, Judaism and the Jesus movement.

The question of method in biblical interpretation is the
third area of exploration. Sheffield's most important contribution has been developed through the work of Anthony C. Thiselton (now principal of St John's College, University of
Durham) and John W. Rogerson. Research in biblical interpretative method continues to pose important questions about
the presuppositions and purposes of modern biblical criticism.
Six such essays are included in this collection, with several
focusing on the nature of interpretation itself, several on the
language of interpretation, and another on the question of application. John Rogerson introduces the work of J. Habermas,
with his notion of the 'communicative life-world', as a contribution to central questions of Old Testament theology. Gerald
O. West (now at the University of Natal, South Africa) contrasts two South African interpretations of the Cain and Abel
story to probe their different applications of this text in a context of liberation. Philip Davies challenges the standard
vocabulary used by biblical scholars, calling for a recognition
that this vocabulary is coloured by an admixture of theological
as well as critical concerns. Anthony Thiselton considers some
methodological questions of contexts and goals in interpretation. Mark G. Brett (now at Lincoln Theological College),
using distinctions from the social sciences, differentiates several questions one might have when approaching interpretation of any text, including a biblical text. And Stephen E. Fowl
(now at Loyola College, Baltimore) examines some of the ethical issues arising from the quest for textual meaning.

Each of these areas is a continuing interest of the Department of Biblical Studies in the University of Sheffield. No
claim is made for the enduring quality of each of the individual essays included, although each is offered in the spirit of
continuing discussion of topics which promise to be on the
cutting edge in academic biblical studies. Students and staff
of the department are not certain whether it was their
common interests which attracted them to the department or
whether the communal spirit fostered by the weekly
staff/student seminar and various less formal consultations
encouraged these interests in their individual work. But the
department attracts students who gather from various
contexts and with divergent backgrounds to pursue with those

in residence the major questions in biblical studies. These essays are offered to their readers in token of the excitement their authors feel for biblical studies as an academic discipline, their enthusiasm for the future development of the subject as the focus of many humanistic and religious concerns, and their hope for a continuing and lively contribution to it by the Sheffield department.

For the last twenty-five years, David Hill has given freely to the Department of Biblical Studies in the University of Sheffield through his devoted teaching, perceptive supervision of research, trenchant scholarship, and genuine Christian good-will. David has now, at the end of September, 1989, retired. Those of us who have known him, whether as colleagues or students, will never forget his profound and lasting contribution to the department. It is to him that we formally dedicate this volume.

The Editors

BIBLICAL STUDIES AT SHEFFIELD

John W. Rogerson

The Department of Biblical Studies at Sheffield University was established in 1947, under the name of Department of Biblical History and Literature.

That it took over 65 years for any teaching of a subject allied to theology to be admitted on an official basis (the University dates its beginnings to the foundation of Firth College in 1880) is a reflection of the secular attitudes that prevailed, and which to some extent still prevail, in Sheffield. Before 1947 the major breach in the University's secular attitude came from a private venture, the establishment in 1912 of the Sir Henry Stephenson Church Hostel. The Hostel was intended to provide residence for candidates for ordination in the Church of England who wished to study for degrees at Sheffield, and its wardens were able to do some teaching in the University, particularly in the area of adult evening classes for members of the general public. The first warden, from 1912 to 1915, was the Revd Edwyn Hoskyns, later to become the famous New Testament scholar, translator of Barth's *Epistle to the Romans*, and author of the incomplete commentary on St John's Gospel. Two of Hoskyn's successors, the Revd E.H. Ward and the Revd G. Inglis, provided, on a temporary basis, such teaching in the general area of Theology as was possible before the permanent closure of the Sir Henry Stephenson Hostel in 1939. Ward lectured in the field of Church History in the Department of History. Strong pleas from Christian educationalists in the 1930s, endorsed by powerful figures such as Archbishop William Temple, that the University should establish a Department of Theology, were dismissed on the grounds of the parlous economic situation facing the country and the University.

The impetus for establishing the Department of Biblical History and Literature in 1947 came from the passing of the Education Act of 1944. This act of Parliament enabled the State to absorb the sizeable Church of England sector in primary and secondary education, in return for which the state guaranteed that religious instruction would be a compulsory subject for all pupils in the State sector of education, and that every day would begin with an act of worship. Provisions for parents to withdraw their children from assembly and religious instruction lessons were made, but the assumption was that the great majority of children would not be withdrawn. The University of Sheffield felt that it had a duty to provide courses for future teachers for the one compulsory subject in the State sector of education, and because the Agreed Syllabuses for use in RI courses were biblically based, it was felt that the need could best be met by the establishment of a Department of Biblical History and Literature in the Faculty of Arts. Surprisingly, Religious Instruction was not one of the subjects available for third-year specialization at that time in Training Colleges, not even in those maintained by the Church of England. No other teaching of theology or religions seems to have been envisaged in Sheffield, and the department became unique in English universities in being a biblical studies department without the support or cooperation or the teaching of any other form of theology or religious studies. This remains the situation today.

The first Head of Department to be appointed was F.F. Bruce who, in 1957, became the first professor. An Honours School was established in 1949, and soon after, the department began to produce graduates at M.A. and Ph.D. level. Today, the department admits around 20 students each year to the Single Honours School of Biblical Studies and the Dual Schools with English, German, Linguistics, Music and Philosophy. It also admits about 15 students each year to the programme for the M.A., M.Phil., Ph.D. and Diploma.

Although the rationale in 1947 for establishing the Department was that this would help the University to meet one of the requirements of the 1944 Education Act, the present members of the Department sees its rationale as lying essentially in its engagement in research, teaching and publication in the field of Biblical Studies. In practice, a majority of graduates enters the teaching profession, but the Department has not felt a need to adjust to the changing trends in the field of Religious Education throughout the past 40 years. Had it done so, it would no doubt have ceased to be a Department of Biblical studies, and would have become a Department of Religion, offering a 'phenomenological' approach to religion in general and certain religions in particular. As it is, by maintaining its distinctive identity, the Department has been in the forefront of developments in biblical studies in a way made easier by the fact that its programme does not have to fit in with a broader spectrum of theological or religious studies.

Being placed as it is in a Faculty of Arts within a secular university, the department has to operate within certain constraints. The university statutes make only one concession to religious convictions, and that it is to allow that no student be compelled to take examinations on a day of religious obligation. Otherwise, the statutes guarantee to staff and students alike freedom from religious tests, and some members of the University Senate have been known to interpret the statutes so narrowly as to argue that the University is not entitled even to assist religious denominations to mount privately funded chaplaincy work. On the question of admissions, the Department conforms to the standards laid down for all university admissions, giving greatest priority to academic potential.

While many may think it is a disadvantage to study the Bible in the absence of supportive courses in theology or religious studies in general, the Department takes the view that, on the whole, it is a distinct advantage to have a Department of Biblical Studies alone. In Theology departments, the Old Testament may be regarded as simply preparatory to the New Testament, and the subject to which the department is devoted may be thought only to begin properly with Patristic Theology and Systematic Theology. Many students in Theology devote only a small fraction of their time to the Old Testament in their final examinations with the result that the teachers are tempted to cram in too much basic material, dissatisfied by the enormous gaps in coverage that nonetheless remain. There can sometimes be an unhealthy gap between the biblical courses, with their concentration on the historical-critical method, and the theological courses, some of whose teachers see little or no relevance in the historical criticism of the Bible.

In the Sheffield department, there is no question of the Bible being seen as preparatory to something else. Even in the relation of Old Testament studies to New Testament studies, the former is not seen as the poor relation of the latter. Both Testaments are studied in their own right, as collections of texts that have distinctive histories, literary forms and religious witnesses. Although the majority of the members of the Department, staff and students alike, are Christians who necessarily approach the Old Testament from the standpoint of their own religious connections, no formal attempt is made to teach Biblical Theology in a way that assumes some form of unity of Old and New Testaments.

The result of concentration upon the body of texts that make up the Bible is that a broad view of Biblical Studies can be taken. In addition to requiring all students specializing in Biblical Studies to study sufficient Greek and Hebrew for them to make effective use of these languages, as well as grounding students in the basics of the historical-critical method, the syllabus is able to cover areas not commonly found in university courses on the Bible. Sheffield has been among the pioneers of the new literature approaches to the Bible, and of the application of philosophical hermeneutics to biblical interpretation. It has also made notable contributions to more traditional areas such as the Jewish and Hellenistic matrix of early Christianity, the Dead Sea Scrolls, and the history of biblical interpretation, as well as producing many volumes of commentaries on the Biblical text of both Testaments. The Department has also kept a watching brief on new developments, such as structuralism both anthropological and literary, sociological approaches to Old and New Testament studies, liberation theology, the use of the Bible in modern ethical discussions. All these interests are reflected in the syllabus and the teaching.

At the time of writing (October, 1989) the Department of Biblical Studies is, like other university departments in Britain, involved in formulating an academic plan for its teaching and research up to 1995. We hope and expect the department to be a noticeably different place by then, its student body, its teachers, its curriculum in its details. But we hope and expect no less that it will be recognizeably the same place, in 1995 and beyond, playing its own distinctive and vigorous place in the development of the academic study of the Bible.

THE DEPARTMENT OF BIBLICAL STUDIES
The Early Days

F.F. Bruce

The Department of Biblical History and Literature (as it was then called) in the University of Sheffield was inaugurated on October 1, 1947. My qualification to speak about its early days lies in my appointment as Senior Lecturer in charge of the Department with effect from that date. Since before that I was on the teaching staff of another university, I have no firsthand knowledge of events and debates leading up to the establishment of the Department. Some influential members of the University (I gather from oral tradition) thought the setting up of such a Department to be an undesirable development. One or two feared that it might give the Bishop of Sheffield a foothold in university affairs beyond what he already had as a member of the Council of the University. Perhaps it was not by accident that there was no Anglican on the short list for the appointment, nor yet that the one layman among the short-listed candidates secured the post.

This, however, I can say from personal experience: once the Department was set up and the appointment made, those who might previously have had misgivings about its establishment were as helpful and encouraging to the first head of the new Department as any one could desire.

For the first year I was the only member of the departmental teaching staff, but the duties were not onerous. There were half a dozen first-year students, to whom I had to give a few lectures a week on the Old and New Testaments in English— mainly introductory, with (as I recall) more special study of Judges and Acts.

From the beginning of the second year an additional lecturer was provided—a young Oxford scholar, Dr Aileen Guilding (who in 1959 succeeded me in the Chair). Once she was installed, the time seemed ripe for instituting an Honours School, and this was done in time for the admission of our first honours student, David Payne, in October 1949. When the institution of the honours school was debated in the Faculty of Arts, one faculty member complained that it might encourage a type of student that we didn't particularly want (I supposed he meant aspirants to the ministry, though he didn't say so explicitly). However, David Payne did not represent that type. The Department was fortunate in securing him as its first honours student: if anything was lacking for establishing its academic credibility, his achievement supplied it, for when he graduated in 1952 he was awarded the Gibbons Prize as the most distinguished honours graduate of his year in the Faculty of Arts. Seven years later he was added to the departmental teaching staff; I looked forward to having him as a colleague, but this was not to be, for as soon as his appointment was confirmed, I was called away to Manchester.

At an early stage we began our modest intake of graduate students. Our first M.A. was Frank Glendenning, the Precentor of Sheffield Cathedral. Among our Ph.D.s I recall Percival Hadfield, Maurice Barnett, Cyril Powell and David Mowbray. Ronald Clements was registered for the Ph.D. course under my supervision: I recall that when his subject—'The Dwelling-Place of God in the Old Testament'—was reported to the Faculty of Arts, someone asked if he shouldn't rather have been registered in the Department of Architecture. By the time he submitted his thesis, I had left; I was called back as an adjunct internal examiner. He was by far the most distinguished Ph.D. produced by the department up to that time. His external examiner, Norman Snaith, who could be quite fierce on such occasions, had nothing but praise for his thesis.

Nor should James Atkinson, our first Stephenson Fellow, be overlooked. Having gained the Durham M.Litt. with a thesis on Origen's commentary on John, he was registered in our Department for a research project on Luther's work on the Fourth Gospel. Luther captivated him from the moment he began this study. When it was completed, it was not to Sheffield University that he submitted it, but to the University of Münster, from which he gained a doctorate in Theology. Later he became our third Professor of Biblical Studies, and what the Department owes to him can scarcely be computed.

Among the many colleagues whose help and encouragement proved so valuable in the early days of the Department, Dr Sidney Peyton, university librarian at that time, deserves special mention. From his modest budget he immediately allocated £200 to lay the foundation for a biblical section in the Library. £200 did not go very far, but books were less costly forty years ago than today. And from then until his retirement he was a tower of strength to the Department on the library side.

Another valiant supporter was Maurice Bruce, Director of Extramural Studies. He was tireless in making our Department, and its subject, well known throughout the wider area served by the University. After the discovery of the Dead Sea Scrolls, the demand for extramural lectures on them became almost too great to be met; I think we just managed to meet it.

These were small beginnings, but at least they were beginnings. Those who sponsored the founding of the Department could never have envisaged the strength and prestige which it has acquired since then. When I look at the three journals, the publishing house, and now the projected *Dictionary of Classical Hebrew*, I am tempted to make a response in words which would be strangely out of keeping with the self-consciously secular spirit in which the Department was conceived and launched: *a Domino factum est istud; hoc mirabile in oculis nostris.*

Part 1

LITERARY READINGS

READING ESTHER FROM LEFT TO RIGHT
Contemporary Strategies for Reading a Biblical Text

David J. A. Clines

The first episode of the Biblical book of Esther concerns Vashti, the Persian queen who (to speak briefly) refused to come to the king's banquet when bidden, and was subsequently deposed. Those are the barest bones of her story, and there are no two ways about reading it. But when the bone structure is fleshed out with the language, focalization, characterization and pacing of the Biblical narrative, varieties of readings become possible, and readers have to begin adopting strategies for how they will read, that is, how they will approach, grasp, and handle the episode as a whole.

Reading the story of Vashti from right to left, reading in classical Hebrew, that is to say, and reading according to the social and sexual conventions of the time, we are likely to read Vashti's story as a whole as a satire on the Persian king. He is, in Vashti's story, a monarch of absolute power, a showy entertainer, and a sovereign in masterful control—on every front but the domestic. To be unable to command his queen's obedience makes him an object of fun to the first Jewish readers of the book; and Vashti, for her part, owes both her presence and her significance in the story to little other than the way she holds the king up to ridicule.

Reading the story from left to right, however, not just in English but in our own cultural context, we cannot help seeing Vashti not just as a Persian queen but even more as a woman. As a woman she becomes a character in her own right, not just a foil to Ahasuerus, and as a woman she earns our applause for resisting the king's intention to display her as a sex object before his drunken cronies. Since she is regarded by the male as significant only for her body, and since she depends on no argument or principle or precedent to excuse her non-compliance to his sexist demands, but simply asserts her human right to say no, we find ourselves hailing her as the first (perhaps the only) radical feminist in the Bible.

Now Vashti the Persian queen and Vashti the woman are the same Vashti, and we do the story no violence by insisting on reading it in our context, not only its, or hers. Living as and when we do, we are bound to read from left to right, bound to resist the author's intention as the only possible meaning, and bound to enrich the story by reading it in different modes, or dimensions, or contexts.

The Vashti story in its double significance I take to be paradigmatic for reading any part of the Bible today. It remains open to us, of course, to read forever reconstructively, reading our way toward a determinate goal of discovering the author's meaning or hypothesizing how the work was heard in its own time—and resting content with that. But alternatively (or, as well), we may approach the text with the reading strategies of our own time, not indeed to corrupt the text into saying whatever it is we want it to say but to hear whatever it may have to say on matters we are, out of our own convictions and interests, concerned about.

In this paper I will explore how adopting some of the reading strategies available to readers of our own age can prove fruitful for understanding a familiar ancient text. I shall approach the text from the standpoints of five different strategies, formalism, structuralism, feminism, materialism and deconstruction.

1. *Formalism*

It is perhaps arguable whether formalism constitutes a reading strategy—at least in the same sense that feminism, materialism and deconstruction certainly do, and that structuralism most probably does—in that with formalism there is no overt philosophical foundation or commitment from which the strategy draws its strength. Nevertheless, because it is a way of approaching reading that scholars and readers of a former age did not have available to them, at least not explicitly, I think it is appropriate to regard it as one of the resources, and thus strategies, contemporary readers can avail themselves of. There is also a practical value in beginning this essay with a formalist consideration of the text, in that it compels us to focus upon the shape of the work as a whole before we engage in more self-regarding readings.

Among the range of formalist concerns over which one might spend time,[1] I choose here only one: plot, its structure and development.

Esther has, structurally speaking, a conventional plot, with beginning, middle, and end clearly marked out

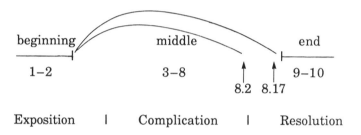

If we analyse plots as typically consisting of exposition, complication, resolution, and coda, in the Book of Esther chs. 1–2 are evidently Exposition. These chapters enclose seven distinct scenes portraying circumstances anterior to the plot proper. The Complication begins only in ch. 3, with Mordecai's refusal of obeisance to the newly elevated Haman, and with Haman's reaction. That is the point at which the destruction of the Jews is determined upon, which decision constitutes the base-point for two arcs of tension which will reach as far as the Resolution. At the end of ch. 8, at the point when the second imperial decree is issued, we know the moment of Resolution has arrived, for the Jews can relax and make holiday. Thereafter, the last two chapters, at least from 9.20

---

1 See for example Ann Jefferson, 'Russian Formalism', in *Modern Literary Theory. A Comparative Introduction* (ed. Ann Jefferson and D. Robey; London: B.T. Batsford, 1982), p. 22.

onward, form a Coda projecting the discourse beyond the time-frame of the narrative proper.[1]

Two points of interest emerge from this analysis. The first is that the Exposition is unusually long, suggesting that the story is not so naive as its simple style might tempt us to think. What is being delivered in the Exposition is not the mere details of time, place and personages of the story—which is all an Exposition needs. Rather, we are presented with a mass of background, on the symbolism of power, the character of the king, the battle of the sexes, the relationship of Esther and Mordecai, which must be held in mind in the course of the subsequent narrative and cross-fertilized with the matter of the action. So for example, when we read the response of Ahasuerus to Haman in 3.11, 'do with them as seems good to you'—which may sound, taken by itself, like a brisk imperial efficiency—we are obliged to recall, on the contrary, that we know from the Exposition that this king is a man who can make no decision of his own accord, like how to handle the disobedience of Vashti or what to do when he finds he is missing her, but has always to rely on the advice of his courtiers. When someone comes to him with a concrete proposal like the extermination of an anonymous race of deviants, the king is only too glad to have someone else to do the troublesome business of decision-making for him and cheerfully consigns the people to Haman to do with them as he likes.

The second point concerns the resolution of the tension. At first sight the Resolution is the death of Haman (7.10), author of the decree for the extermination of the Jews. But to stay with that perspective is to have failed to notice that the moment of complication of the plot is not precisely the threat of 3.13 against the Jewish people, but the fact that the threat has the form of a law of the Persians and Medes (which the Exposition in 1.19 has forewarned us is unalterable). So it will be no final resolution of the plot when Haman is unmasked as

---

1   See W. Labov, *Language in the Inner City. Studies in the Black English Vernac-ular* (Conduct and Communication, 36; Philadelphia: University of Pennsylvania Press, 1972), used by Adele Berlin, *Poetics and Interpretation of Biblical Nar-rative* (Bible and Literature Series, 9; Sheffield: Almond, 1983), pp. 101-102, 107-109.

involving even the queen in his scheduled genocide, or when he is hoist on his own stake (to the height of 75 feet), or even when Mordecai the Jew is made vizier in Haman's place (8.2). For even when those resolutions have come about, the Complication is not yet resolved, for the unalterable law which has decreed the Jews' destruction still stands—as the king reminds Esther when she begs for the decree to be revoked (8.8). The intellectual problem of how to alter the unalterable is solved, and the tension of the plot therewith resolved, only by Mordecai's brilliant idea of a *supplementary* law of the Persian and Medes requiring the Jews to defend themselves against any attempt at genocide (8.11-12). Since the first law had thoughtlessly failed to require any particular persons to carry out the genocide, no one, in the event, could be blamed for failing to obey it; and clearly Jews and non-Jews alike throughout the empire read the situation as a (bloodless) victory for the Jews (8.15-17), without a whiff of criticism for the doctrine of the Persian law's unchangeability. As against that resolution, the bloodletting of 9.5-6 is a concretization of the new-found Jewish supremacy; it purges the empire of anti-Jewish elements, which is good news for the future. But it does not resolve anything, for there is nothing still needing to be resolved. Mordecai's drafting of the second edict has already done that. So to analyse the plot, even along the quite unsophisticated lines here sketched, is not simply to perceive the subtlety of the narrator's art but to touch base already with the narrative's own specific attitudes to power, violence, law.

2. *Structuralism*

In using a structuralist strategy for reading, we are explicitly seeking—below the surface of the text—relationships, especially of opposition and contrast, which manifest themselves on the level of the text. In the discipline of literary structuralism there are several different procedures that stand ready-made as grids on which the narrative may be laid out. Two of these may be of service here, an actantial and a semantic analysis.

a. *Actantial analysis*

An analysis of the actants in the Esther narrative is quite
straightforward, but it reveals two interesting realities. The
actantial pattern, in the style of A.J. Greimas, may be set out
thus:

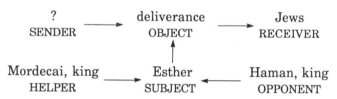

The first interesting aspect of this analysis is that, if we designate the Object as *deliverance* for the Receiver, the Jews, we
are left with a question as to the identity of the Sender. The
Sender is the person or circumstance that endeavours to communicate the Object to the Receiver. Now the Sender in any
narrative (or, performance, in Greimasian language) can of
course be, *faute de mieux*, the Story itself, or Fate; but in this
particular narrative, in its Biblical context, we are tempted to
designate the sender as God, even though God does not actually appear in the story as a character nor is any allusion
made to him. Outside the Hebrew Bible, other versions of the
Esther Story—such as the elaboration it receives in the Greek
Bible—make it entirely explicit that the story is essentially a
narrative of God's action. The crucial coincidences of the plot
(e.g. the presence of a Jewish girl on the Persian throne, the
reading of the chronicle of Mordecai's deliverance of the
king's life at the very moment when Mordecai's own enemy
has arrived to seek *his* life) unmistakably point to the hand of
God, despite the absence—for whatever reason—of God from
the explicit action. A structural analysis, then, dealing solely
with the evidence of the text, registers the text's lack of identification of the Sender as a crucial distinctive of the story.

Secondly, we observe that the position of the king in the
actantial grid is ambiguous. Inasmuch as he authorizes the
plan of Haman, he belongs with him as Opponent; but inasmuch as he commands Haman's death and signs Mordecai's
edict bringing deliverance to the Jews he is Helper. This ambiguity in the role of the Persian king, which the actantial

ysis reflects, corresponds with the ambiguity of the book's stance towards the Persian government, which is experienced by the Jews both as threat and as protection—an experience consequently inscribed in the book.

b. *Semantic analysis*
Another tactic from the structuralist strategy that can be profitably employed for Esther is a semantic analysis of codes, the groupings of terms distinctive of our text.[1] The result of such an analysis will be that each of the several codes we examine here will turn out to be a manifestation of the theme of power, a central concern of the writing.

We can look first at the *alimentary code*. There is a good deal of data relating to this code, for there are nine banquets (*mishteh*, lit. drinking-parties) in the book. The first and second are displays of the king's wealth and munificence (1.1-4, 5-8). The third is Vashti's all-female counterpart to the king's all-male banquet (1.9), and the fourth is Esther's, given by the king to celebrate Esther's accession to the throne (2.18). Fifth is the drinking of the king and Haman when the plot against the Jews has been hatched (3.15). Sixth and seventh are Esther's banquets at which Haman is unmasked (5.5-8; 7.1-8). Eighth is the banquet held by the Jews in every city after the 23rd day of the third month, celebrating the arrival of the edict of Mordecai (8.17), and ninth are the empire-wide Jewish banquets of the 14th and 15th of the twelfth month, celebrating the 'rest' achieved by the pogroms of anti-Semites on the previous day(s) (9.17-19).

Since banquets celebrate success, it is appropriate that the first five should be Persian banquets, and the last four Jewish banquets, for the story represents the movement of power from Persians to Jews. The first pair, given by the king in a vulgar display of wealth and power, contrast with the last pair, which celebrate, by contrast, survival and honour (though they, of course, may be not so very different, albeit in another key, from wealth and power!). The third and fourth,

---

1 A paradigm for the present study is provided by David Jobling, *The Sense of Biblical Narrative. Three Structural Analyses in the Hebrew Bible. I* (2nd edn; JSOTSup, 7; Sheffield: JSOT, 1986), pp. 26-62.

given by and for the Persian queens (Vashti and Esther), contrast with the sixth and seventh, given by the Jewish-Persian queen (Esther). The fifth and central banquet is shared by the Persian Ahasuerus and his supporter Haman the Agagite: in celebrating the decree that has been just now issued against the Jews it marks the point at which Persian success will begin to be overshadowed by Jewish success.

Beside the banquets, there is a negative mode of feasting—which is fasting. Persian power, as expressed in the first edict, is responded to by the spontaneous Jewish fasting of 4.3, a symbol of powerlessness. Esther's further demand for a fast of unparalleled severity, no food or water for three days or nights (4.16), conveys how absolute is Jewish powerlessness. She herself, ironically, while maintaining this extreme Jewish fast with her maids, has been preparing a Persian-style banquet for the king (5.4, on the third day; cf. 4.15 and 5.1). She is the only Jew who is in the position to do anything about the edict, because she is the Jew who is also a Persian. She must fast and feast simultaneously therefore, bravely preparing her victory banquet in the very moment of experiencing intense powerlessness.

The *code of clothing* is significant also. There are distinctions here between normal and deformed clothing, between workaday clothes and celebratory clothing, between the clothes of the powerless and the clothes of the powerful. The issuance of the edict against the Jews has its effect in Mordecai's tearing his usual clothes and putting on charmless sackcloth (4.1)—as if he were already dead and enfeebled like the inhabitants of the underworld, wearing clothes for no more than decency's sake in a world where aesthetic sensibilities no longer apply. Esther, who does not yet know of the edict, sends out replacement normal garments to Mordecai 'so that he might take off his sackcloth' (for she knows of nothing to mourn about), but he sends them back to her (4.4). She herself, even when she hears of the edict, cannot of course wear sackcloth within the palace (cf. 4.2), though she can fast. For the sake of the Jews in sackcloth this Jewess must show herself a Persian, dressed in her 'royal robes' (5.1) for the king's presence. Clothing will become conspicuous ultimately when Mordecai leaves the king's presence in royal robes of blue and white, fine linen and purple (colours and materials all recalling the imperial colours of the pavilion hangings in 1.6). That will proclaim his identity as Persian—as Persian as it is possible for a Jew to be. He has already had a foretaste of that identity in his temporary elevation as 'the man whom the king delights to honour' (6.7-11), paraded through the city in 'royal robes which the king himself has worn' (6.8). Clothing then is a conspicuous code signalling where one stands on the power axis.

The *topographical code* is another coding for power; its significance bcomes transparent in the manner in which it relates to *areas* of power. There is in the narrative a simple disjunction between inside and outside, in which Jews begin by being outside (Mordecai walking daily outside the harem, 2.11; sitting at the king's gate, 2.19, 3.2; unable to enter the king's gate in sackcloth, 4.2). It is a given that acts of power originate in the inside and are despatched outwards (3.12-13; 8.9-10). Esther is an outsider who gains power when she becomes an insider (ch. 4); she is an unusual figure in that she does not loosen her links with the outside world even when she is in the court. Haman, who is to begin with very much of an insider, after the first banquet prepared by Esther innocently 'goes out' of the king's presence and 'goes home' (5.9, 10); but we know that this exit from the centre of power is symbolically unwise. For when he comes again in the morning he has been displaced by Mordecai (6.6). And when he goes home the second time it is only to have his outsider status confirmed by his wife (6.13). Now that he has become an outsider, even when he enters the king's presence once more (ch. 7), he comes as a disempowered person who will hear at the centre of power nothing to his own advantage but only the pronouncement of his own death sentence; and he exits directly from the court to the gallows (7.9-10). The disjunction between inside and outside, constitutive of the story, and fatal to Haman, but privately circumvented by Esther, is ultimately abolished in the appointment of Mordecai: in going out of the king's presence clad in royal robes, he manifests that the imperial power is now no longer located within the throne-room, but is concentrated in his person. His co-religionists, whose welfare he seeks (10.3), are therefore no longer to be regarded as outsiders; in ch. 9, any town where they may happen to find themselves, and especially any place where they are 'gathered' in a show of solidarity, becomes a centre of power which no one can resist (9.2).

There is also a further disjunction within the 'inside' sphere, that is, between the king's presence and the rest of the palace: the king's presence is so 'inside' that even the rest of the palace is 'outside' by comparison. This disjunction is manifested in the law, known not just in the palace but throughout the whole empire, that to enter the king's presence unbidden is to risk death (4.11). The king's presence, as the focus of the greatest power, is evidently the most dangerous place. And that is true not just in an obvious sense. For Vashti has discovered that not to enter it when bidden is nearly as dangerous as entering it unbidden (1.11f., 19).

These codes signal the narrative's concern with power, where it is located, and whether and how it can be withstood or manipulated by others.

3. Feminism

A feminist criticism is concerned with 'the way the hypothesis of a female reader changes our apprehension of a given text, awakening us to the significance of its sexual codes'.[1]

The feminist issue in the Book of Esther is, it may be suggested, whether power truly resides in the males, as the conventional wisdom both Persian and Jewish would have it. In the case of the Vashti episode, we are being invited to consider the question, Where does power truly lie? Is it with the king, who has well-nigh universal power, but of whose power it becomes plain at the first opportunity that it is always open to resistance? Or does it not rather lie with Vashti, who knows how to take the power she needs for her own self-determination—which is to say, all the power that matters? He can be thwarted; she, however, provided she stands her ground, cannot. Her power is all the more evident when we ask, What

---

1 Elaine Showalter, 'Towards a Feminist Poetics', in *Women Writing and Writing about Women*, ed. Mary Jacobus (London: Croom Helm, 1979), pp. 22-41 (25).

exactly is Vashti resisting? It is not, apparently, any demands of Ahasuerus that she appear naked, adorned by nothing more than her crown (though some rabbinic commentators thought so, reading 1.11). Nor is it his drunkenness, even though it is true that his 'heart is merry with wine' (1.10). It is simply his demand. And the strength of her resistance lies in the very absence of a reason for refusing his demand. She doesn't need to have a reason, for she is under no obligation. Her power lies in her freedom to choose for herself.

As if to underline the fact that the issue is not one of legality but of power, the king's response is simply one of anger; that can only mean that she has done nothing illegal but has only made him lose face (cf. 7.7). His appeal to his wise men to tell him what, 'according to the law', is to be done to her for her disobedience (1.15) conspicuously fails to elicit any existing law, though they can invent an edict intended, *post eventum,* to punish her (1.19). But in this they seem to wrongfoot themselves, since the punishment they prescribe (not to come before the king) is evidently Vashti's dearest wish (it was 'coming before the king' that she had declined in 1.11-12). The issue of power, that is to say, is still in the forefront: even when the king and princes believe they are exercising power over her, by preventing her entering the king's presence, they are achieving no more than what she herself has desired.

The issue of power in sexual politics is further explored in the response of the princes of Persia to the news of Vashti's disobedience. They unhesitatingly assume that throughout the empire it will be the signal for wives, long suppressed, to start rising in rebellion against their husbands, and 'there will be contempt [on the wives' part] and wrath [on the husbands' part] in plenty' (1.18). This truly hysterical assumption can only mean that the men feel threatened, and that male supremacy is being depicted as resting on the flimsiest of foundations. It can only be ironical that their recipe for maintaining the sexual hierarchy is to spread the news of Vashti's recalcitrance throughout the empire, and it can only be satire on males that a multilingual decree needs to be issued throughout the 127 provinces asserting that every man should be master in his own house (1.22). It should be observed, incidentally, that this satire is, no doubt, from the

author's perspective, at the expense of the Persian king and
his courtiers, not of males generally. It corresponds to the
critique of Persian power that is characteristic of the book as a
whole. But because the princes fear the consequences of
Vashti's defiance upon 'all women' and foresee not political
dangers but purely domestic difficulties we are bound to read
in this scene not only that, but, even more tellingly, a satire
against any male power that apes the Persian style.

The issue of power underlies the portrayal of Esther also,
even if less obviously. Esther is an altogether different type of
woman from Vashti, a 'traditional' woman and no radical
feminist but a beauty queen, a charmer. In the narrative
about Esther herself there is not the open satire we have met
with in ch. 1. But we are not supposed to forget that her king is
a shallow and nervous male chauvinist and that it is he who
sets the style for the relation between the sexes in Persia. The
regimen of twelve months' beauty preparation for potential
bedfellows of the king (2.12) is a rather unpleasant sample of
male psychology, as though there were something distasteful
about women in their natural state. The king of course needs
no such preparation himself; he must be beautiful and fra-
grant enough already. The text itself subverts the Persian theory about female beauty when we find that Esther's success
with the king apparently results in large measure from her
rejection of all the artificial beauty aids that his palace admini-
strators have devised (2.15). Nevertheless, the fact remains
that she owes her place on the Persian throne to nothing but
her good looks, her only other great asset being her cookery.
She herself falls in with the prevailing sexual politics when she
does not hesitate to use her female charm as a bargaining
counter. For when in ch. 8 she pleads for the decree against
the Jews to be revoked, her last and climactic argument is her
own sexual attractiveness: 'If I be pleasing in his [the king's]
eyes' (8.5) is the argument she thinks will linger most effica-
ciously with him.

So Esther is a conventional beauty queen who wins favour
and status both in the harem and with the king on the basis of
her charm (2.9, 15, 17). Equally conventionally, she is also the
dutiful adopted daughter, who does everything Mordecai tells
her to: she does not divulge her ancestry because Mordecai

has charged her not to (2.10, 20); and even in the palace she 'obeyed Mordecai just as when she was brought up by him' (2.20).

Yet there is another dimension to the image of Esther. The scene between her and Mordecai in ch. 4, in which they communicate across the boundary between the inside and the outside, is crucial in establishing her as the central figure through whom deliverance for the Jews must come if it is to come at all. Mordecai in this chapter treats her for the first time as an adult in a sentence that in the same moment underlines her alienation from her people and her identity with them: 'Think not that in the king's palace you will escape any more than all the other Jews' (4.13). She is indefeasibly an outsider, but with a chance to operate as an insider, that is, with power. Esther rises to the occasion, and the narrator signals, with the scene's concluding sentence, that Esther has taken charge: 'Mordecai went away and did everything *as Esther had ordered him*' (4.17), so reversing the language of 2.10 and 2.20.

Thereafter, though weighty matters like the fate of her people, and the disposal of half of the kingdom or Haman's life are in the king's gift, Esther is the one who is in confident command: her ingenious play with the two banquets proves that. For she does not blurt out at once or at the first banquet what she wants, since it may be dangerous to take your sovereign's masterful 'half of the kingdom' *au pied de la lettre* when it is the head of his prime minister you want (who knows whether that might be more than is on offer?); it is safer to make the king's acceptance of the second invitation a pledge to do whatever Esther wants without quantifying fractions, and at the same time to represent her own request as nothing other than 'doing what the king has said' (5.8).

There is another aspect to Esther's role that a feminist perspective alerts us to. If we ask how the danger to the Jews comes about, the answer is plainly: through Mordecai's intransigence. And how is the danger averted? Mordecai has no hand in that, except to alert Esther to the facts and to put pressure on her. It is she who makes all the running, and picks up the pieces that male honour has threatened to make of her people. Mordecai, to be sure, solves the intellectual puzzle in ch. 8 neatly enough, but he has not had the wit to protect himself in the fight for power that constitutes life at the Persian court. Esther represents effective action over against Mordecai's somewhat gauche integrity.

The book as a whole purports to portray a triumph for a woman. For its name is Esther's, and it is the story of her success as a woman over her upbringing as a traditional woman and over the expectations of her as a woman at the Persian court. Even so, the ending of the book raises some doubts about how thorough a success hers is. For some sexual-political struggle between the figures of Esther and Mordecai seems to be going on in ch. 9. We observe that it is *Mordecai* who writes the letter to the Jews throughout the empire enjoining observance of the 14th and 15th of Adar as days of celebration in commemoration of the victory achieved (9.20-22). And the Jews do what *Mordecai* has written to them (9.23). But in 9.29 'Esther the Queen' is writing 'with full authority this second letter about Purim in order to make its observance obligatory', because her power needs to be safeguarded literarily. The struggle is not yet over, however, for subsequently, it seems, some scribe, breaking grammatical concord,[1] finds it necessary to add 'and Mordecai' because he (it must be a he) does not care for the flavour of the politics. And then finally Esther is lost sight of altogether, and the book itself peters out with wishy-washy generalities about *Mordecai* (10.1-3), for all the world as if the story had really been about him all the time.[2]

The ultimate victory in the sexual politics of the Book of Esther comes not in the Hebrew book, however, but in the Greek version with its expansions. Here the whole story becomes framed by narratives of the dream of Mordecai and its interpretation (A 1-11=11.2-12; F 1-10=10.4–11.1). The whole chain of events is thus represented as divinely foreseen and foreordained, and, more to the present purpose, as portraying the conflict of the narrative as a struggle between *Mordecai* and Haman. We know that the male has finally edged Esther out of her triumph when in 2 Maccabees we hear the day of celebration (which had come into being pri-

---

1 The verb וכתב is feminine singular, but the subject in the text as it stands is both Esther and Mordecai.
2 For details see David J.A. Clines, *Ezra, Nehemiah, Esther* (New Century Bible; London: Marshall, Morgan and Scott, 1984), pp. 329-30.

marily through Esther's courage and shrewdness) being referred to as 'Mordecai's Day' (15.36).[1]

4. *Materialism*

A materialist criticism approaches the text in terms of the material, i.e. socio-economic, conditions that produce it, especially the condition of antagonistic social classes.

The Book of Esther professes itself the product of an oppressed group; and the Jews of the time it depicts are unquestionably a subject people. Their story satirizes the Persian claim to absolute power, and claims power for themselves. The Jews cannot of course deny that the king possesses the power—the wealth, the provincial organization, the military force (cf. 1.3; 8.11), and the means of communication (the imperial postal system, 3.13-14 and 8.9-14). They find power exercised against them (and the other subject peoples), for example, when the king can appoint officers in all the imperial provinces to gather all beautiful young virgins to the harem in Susa (2.3). But what it really means to be subject or oppressed becomes evident chiefly in the fact that the ultimate power, over life or death, is firmly in the hands of the Persians, who are in the position to formulate decrees, not just for individuals' deaths, but for genocide.

Yet this story, however sincerely it represents the position of a subject race, self-evidently does not originate from the masses. However much they too may be affected by the imperial edict, this is a court-tale, told by habitués of the seat of power, reflecting the intrigue typical of the palace and the harem. For this reason the narrative must be described as reactionary rather than progressive. For it tolerates Persian power in every respect except in the ultimate area, that is, over life and death, and it commends co-operation rather than resistance. In accord with such a stance, the ideal state of affairs for the Jews of the book of Esther is not that the Persian government should be overthrown, but that a co-religionist of theirs should be 'next in rank' to the king (10.3) and should

1 See further David J.A. Clines, 'The Additions to Esther', *Harper's Bible Commentary* (ed. James L. Mays; San Francisco: Harper and Row, 1988), pp. 815-19.

wield the 'power and might' of the Persian empire (10.2). The important thing is not that Persian power should be eliminated but that Mordecai the Jew should grow 'more and more powerful' (9.4). Infiltration of the Persian court by a Jewish woman is not for the sake of sabotaging the power base of an alien authority but in order to swing Persian power behind a Jewish cause at a time of need. And once the Jews become influential at the Persian court, they are not shy of pressing the imperial means of maintaining control (the means of communication) into the service of the Jewish deliverance (8.9-14).

Moreover, as if to prove how reactionary they can be, once the Jews have thrown in their lot with the Persian system, they adopt some of the less charming manners of the Persian court: they set about exterminating those who seek their hurt (9.2), doing 'as they pleased to those who hated them' (9.5)— that 'as they pleased' being elsewhere the sign of godless licence (as in Dan. 8.4). They seek no change in the structure of society; it is accepted as given, as itself one of the 'laws of the Persians and the Medes'. The Jewish ambition is solely to position themselves at the centre of power in that society. Having once decided that if you can't beat them you should join them, they now determine as well to have their cake and eat it. They want to be Persian citizens and cultural outsiders at the same time. They support the government but they support Jewishness no less.

Such a blurring of identities and shovelling underground of the ultimate divergence of interests of Jews and Persians is pragmatic rather than principled. A materialist perspective points up the fragility of the stance toward power adopted by the book. Some might call it realist, of course, but the underlying tension is too strong for the compromise position to last.

5. Deconstruction

'To deconstruct a discourse', says Jonathan Culler, 'is to show how it undermines the philosophy it asserts, or the hierarchical oppositions on which it relies'.[1] I see two points at which the narrative of Esther is open to deconstruction in these terms.

The first is the issue of identity. It can be taken for granted that it is quintessential to the standpoint of the narrative that Jews should maintain their racial identity. It is true that, until the edict against them they are, at least from the official point of view, a group without strong coherence: they are 'a certain people scattered abroad and dispersed among the peoples in all the provinces' (3.8), many of them exiles cut off from their homeland, carried away from Jerusalem by Nebuchadnezzar (2.6). But once the edict for their annihilation is delivered, we see the reality of Jewish solidarity: they act only and everywhere in concert. 'In every province, wherever the king's command and his decree came, there was great mourning among the Jews, with fasting and weeping and lamenting' (4.3); all the Jews in Susa gather themselves at Esther's command for a communal fast (4.16); and when the second edict arrives, 'in every province and in every city, wherever the king's command and his edict came, there was gladness and joy among the Jews, a feast and a holiday' (8.17). In ch. 9 also the Jews of the empire act unitedly on the fateful 13th of Adar. And once the hostility has been eliminated, they pledge themselves to perpetuate the memory of their common action: 'they ordained and took it upon themselves and their descendants that without fail they would keep these days, that these days should be remembered and kept throughout every generation, in every family, province, and city, and that these days should never fall into disuse among their descendants' (9.27-28, abbreviated). All of which is to say that the narrative sees itself as promoting racial identity, stressing collective action, experience, and memory.

What it celebrates, however, is a deliverance achieved through *denying* one's Jewishness. Esther not only contracts a marriage with a Gentile—which is the quickest and surest way of denying one's Jewishness—but keeps secret her ancestry, deliberately, in response to her guardian's injunction (2.10, 20). Of course she does reveal her racial identity when it

---

1   Jonathan Culler, *On Deconstruction. Theory and Criticism after Structuralism* (London: Routledge and Kegan Paul, 1983), p. 86.

will be advantageous, but we cannot get over the fact that it is only by denying it that she can use it profitably. And, as if to reinforce the idea that Jewish identity has its drawbacks, the narrative reminds us that the threat of genocide against the Jews arises only because Mordecai divulges his Jewishness (3.4) and acts on Jewish principle so rigorously as to deny his superior the conventional courtesies (3.2). Which is to say: the Jewish people find themselves under a death sentence because one Jew acts like a Jew and tells his people he is a Jew; they escape through the good offices of another Jew who has pretended she is not a Jew. If being Jewish is being Esther-like no tragedy need be expected; if it is being Mordecai-like, no saviour in high places can be counted on. This is a very confusing message from a narrative that purports to sustain Jewish identity.

The second issue is the function of writing. In this narrative, reality—from the Persian point of view—always tends towards inscripturation, and attains its true quality only when it is written down. Only what is written is valid and permanent. We have first been alerted to the value of writing in Persian eyes at 1.19 where it is not enough that the recalcitrant Vashti be deposed; her loss of office only becomes a reality when it is 'written among the laws of the Persians and Medes'. Next, the social order of 'each man master in his own house' can only be assured by 'letters to all royal provinces, to every province in its own script and every people in its own language' (1.22). Then, the deepest reality about the plan for Jewish annihilation is not that Haman wills it or the king assents to it, but that it stands written. Writing is what makes the threat real to every Jew, that ferrets them out in every corner of the empire and confronts them with their fate; it is wherever this royal edict comes—the written text, that is— that there is great mourning among the Jews (4.3). The writing itself, and not just its content, is the threat.

Between chs. 4 and 7 there is (of course) no writing, because nothing there is settled or finalized. Only when the flux of dialoguing, negotiating, and executing has come to an end will the secretaries be summoned again (8.9) and the imperial pleasure be set down in the diverse scripts of the empire. The very act of writing—quite apart from the fact that it is irreversible Persian law that is being written—makes matters certain and makes royal decrees everywhere effectual. The deliverance itself is depicted as the result of the writing: 'in every province and in every city, wherever the king's command *and his edict* came, there was gladness and joy among the Jews, a feast and a holiday' (8.17).

Now there are two moments of disequilibrium or decon-struction over this matter of writing. The first deconstruction manifests itself in the Jewish adoption of Persian writing. It is one thing to use the imperial chancellery and the royal post for dispatching the second edict; that is a matter of convenience, and clearly advantageous to the Jewish people. It is another matter that the upshot of the whole sequence of events should be that Mordecai 'recorded these things, and sent letters to all the Jews who were in all the provinces of King Ahasuerus' (9.20). For that means to say that the story of Esther and Mordecai is now written into the Persian record (as indeed was the story of Mordecai's discovery of the eunuchs' plot, 2.23), as well as being circulated in written form to his kinsfolk. Jews as well as Persians apparently need to have the realities of the Haman affair permanently enshrined in written form.

This is in its own small but deeply symbolic way, a crisis for Jewish identity, though the narrative does not perceive it. Persian writing is a symbol of Persian bureaucracy, which is a manifestation of empire with its conglomerate of 127 pro-vinces and who knows how many ethnic groups. But Jews, though dispersed, are 'one people' (3.8), with one language and possessed of a folk memory. In the terms of this narrative, they should not need writing. It is a betrayal of ethnicity to adopt the administrative machinery of an alien empire in the hope of preserving the national memory. Are the threat of genocide and the amazing deliverance from it so impotent, have they stirred the Jewish imagination so little, that the only way of retaining the memory of them is to give them the Per-sian treatment, recording them in chronicles of such dismal banality that they will be read only to put people to sleep (6.1)?

We see in 9.24-25 what the Persian treatment of the events is. In this capsule entry for the imperial chronicles what we find is the true story cruelly denatured, Esther written out of the record, and no less than seven mistakes made about the course of events (including, incidentally, the novel information that the king 'gave orders in writing' for the death of Haman, which he certainly did not according to the narrative).[1] The Jewish story pays a high price for being abstracted into the Persian chronicles.

And as the end of ch. 9 makes patent, in almost laughable fashion, once the memory of the event has been committed to the scriptorium, the paperwork never stops. Not only must Mordecai draft a minute for the chronicles and a circular to Jews everywhere, but Esther too must write to them a 'second letter' (9.29) supporting or extending the letter of Mordecai. For, it appears, the Jewish people had instituted on their own initiative a ritual of fasting and lamenting in commemoration of the danger. But for that institution to attain full reality there needs to be a 'command of Queen Esther' that 'fixed these practices' and was 'recorded in writing' (9.32). She has undeniably become the (Persian) Queen Esther.

The second point of deconstruction concerns the validity of writing. Writing in this book is primarily the writing of law, law that not only has the authority of the king behind it but, in the society of the Medes and Persians, is informed by its own tradition of irreversibility. This is the law that the Jews in ch. 9 assimilate to themselves as a guarantor of the memory of their deliverance and of the correct observance of its rituals.

But what the narrative has also told us, *sotto voce*, is that the concept of the irreversibility of Persian law is a myth. Everyone pretends that it cannot be altered, but if you are determined enough, you can beat an unmovable object over the head with an irresistible force. Mordecai undid the effect of the first edict: that is the heart of the narrative. Writing is thereby proclaimed—against the grain of the whole narrative—to be not permanent; its validity is challengeable. What price then Jewish commitment to writings that concern them? What future is there for the Book of Esther? Has it not become a self-consuming artifact?

---

1 For the details, see David J.A. Clines, *The Esther Scroll. The Story of the Story* (JSOTSup, 30; Sheffield: JSOT, 1984), pp. 52-53.

A deconstructive reading removes certainties and dismembers dogmas. It casts a quizzical eye over what has been passing for truths. And in so doing it draws our attention to the fact that texts are not transcripts of the way the universe is, nor tape-recordings of what actually happened. It need make no mock of the sincerity of the text, not turn us against the text as flimsy or fallible. If anything, it can sometimes happen that a text shorn of the bogus claims of its reverers can become more effectual, indeed attractive. Seeing the emperor has no clothes might sometimes be the best way of recognizing what a fine figure of a man he truly is.

Observations in Conclusion

1.   I am impressed in this study by the value of as many strategies as possible for reading a text. As a critic of the text, I should hate to be restricted by a methodological purism. What I have noticed is that different strategies confirm, complement or comment on other strategies, and so help develop an integrated but polychromatic reading.

2.   I say as many strategies 'as possible' since there must be texts where certain strategies are inappropriate. I did not, for example, see what could be made of a psychoanalytical approach to this text—though I could see some interesting psychological angles to it.

3.   I did not see any methodological difficulties in reading an ancient text, which is also a simple text, not to say a naive one, using contemporary strategies. The readings are inevitably not so coruscating as readings of intricate and self-conscious texts such as are often chosen by contemporary literary critics. No doubt that is largely my fault, but I do think the text itself is in part the cause of the deficiency.

4.   I did not feel well served, as a critic, by current exponents of critical theories. I did not, for example, though I do not know the scholarly literature very well, find any critic doing—for any text—what I have attempted to do here.[1] And

---

1   Since this paper was first written, I have come across the volume *Literary Theory at Work. Three Texts* (ed. D. Tallack; London: B.T. Batsford, 1987), in which nine contributors read three works (Joseph Conrad's *Heart of Darkness*, Henry James's *In the Cage*, and D.H. Lawrence's *St Mawr*) from their own theoretical

I found that those who wrote about strategies tended to be rather defensive, protective and uncritical of their own favoured strategy—though eager enough to polemicize. Among structuralists and deconstructionists, for example, I saw an unwillingness to blow the whistle on members of the same guild with febrile imaginations and an inability to communicate.[1] Why do theorists not realize that they are not in *show-business* but in the business of *persuasion*? But then, since Socrates at least, the sophist has often been mistaken for the entertainer.

perspective. This is still not quite the same as having *one* critic perform different theoretical operations on the *same* text.

1   I know about the 'tyranny of lucidity', and accept that 'To challenge familiar assumptions and familiar values in a discourse which, in order to be easily readable, is compelled to reproduce these assumptions and values, is an impossibility' (Catherine Belsey, *Critical Practice* [London: Methuen, 1980], pp. 4-5). I am talking about mystification.

READING RIGHT
Reliable and Omniscient Narrator, Omniscient God, and Foolproof Composition in the Hebrew Bible*

David M. Gunn

How curious it is that Meir Sternberg's book about ideological literature, *The Poetics of Biblical Narrative: Ideological Literature and the Drama of Reading*,[1] should have so little to say about ideological readers. Yet perhaps not so strange. Sternberg is reading for closure—reading, that is, for the right meaning. Meaning, on this view, is located in the text, which is to say that meaning is essentially a matter of reading competence. The ideology of the text is stable and recoverable, the ideology of the reader variable and discardable. Inculcate competence (by learning '*the* poetics'), eschew ideology, and you will take the 'point of it all' (p. 51; 'the moral point' [p. 234]); in short, you will read the Bible right.

Foolproof composition

Lest we underestimate his determination on the subject, Sternberg formulates an hypothesis of 'foolproof composition'. 'By foolproof composition', he writes, 'I mean that the Bible is difficult to read, easy to underread and overread and even misread, but virtually impossible to, so to speak, counterread' (p. 50).

* An earlier version of this paper was presented to the Structuralism and Exegesis Seminar at the Annual Meeting of the Society of Biblical Literature, Boston, December 1987.
1 Indiana Literary Biblical Series; Bloomington: Indiana University Press, 1985.

The terms employed ('difficult', 'easy', 'under', 'over', 'mis-' and 'counter-') are, of course, all relative—to Sternberg's point of view. But having an idea where he might stand on some issues, I can easily respond that within even recent decades readings which would have to count as counter-readings from his (and my) points of view have been perpetrated, by 'believers' (to use Sternberg's term) in the name of faithful reading of Scripture. One has only to think, for example, of the Dutch Reformed Church in South Africa on the question of apartheid.

There is no need to press the point. It seems to me to be so obvious; for the history of biblical interpretation is full of what are for me counter-readings, some of them devastatingly perverse. Let me merely reiterate that 'under', 'over', 'mis-' and 'counter-' are relative terms, all assuming a norm, a benchmark, in short, a 'right reading'. And in context it is hard to avoid concluding that this norm must be either Sternberg's reading plain and simple or else a set of readings in a dogmatic (believing) tradition for which he is an apologist. Acknowledging reluctantly that there are and have been 'controversies among exegetes, spreading to every possible topic' (pp. 50-51), he attempts to salvage his point by laying blame for much wrong reading at the door of those readers—Jewish and Christian religious leaders included—who have read in 'ignorance, willfulness, preconception, tendentiousness'—who have read, in a word, in 'bad faith'. The observation leads inexorably back to reading in 'good faith', Sternberg's faith.

But to speak of that further would be perhaps to touch him(self) a little closely. So the argument veers away from the reader's faith, which is to say the reader's ideology. No, faith, on this view, has little to do with the business of biblical reading. For Sternberg (at least on the surface of his text), right reading is essentially a matter of poetics—observe carefully the mechanics of composition and all will go well. This is because, in his view, biblical ideology and biblical poetics mirror each other. Biblical poetics is a unique and sublime invention to propagate a unique and sublime ideology.[1]

---

1 Given the criticism Sternberg levels at them (see esp. ch. 1), Robert Alter (*The Art of Biblical Narrative* [New York: Basic Books, 1981]) and Herbert N. Schneidau

For this mirror view of the relation between ideology and poetics to work in biblical narrative, given an absolutist notion of ideological truth (Sternberg's view—'the whole truth'?), it is necessary to have a narrator who is both 'reliable' (in the literary sense[1]) and 'omniscient'. In this case the narrator has a clear view and understanding of everything in the story world, sees and knows all. Accordingly all is, in principle, discernible by the discerning reader. The two notions of reliability and omniscience are therefore close associates. Moreover, the reliable narrator assumes divine authority, since the narrator's omniscience is ultimately in symmetry with that of God, for God, too, is omniscient according to this account of biblical poetics. Indeed, it really ought to be the case that Sternberg's narrator be also omnipotent, but this is a point at which the theorist's theological nerve fails, and he backs down: God is the maker, and the narrator only the shaper, of the plot.

My view of what is going on when we read biblical narrative is rather different. Meaning, I take it, lies (at least) between text and interpreter.[2] To assert this position is to assert that readers may validly read a text differently. Readers really are in significant part responsible for creating the meaning of a text. It is also to assert that no amount of 'competence' is going to settle substantial questions of meaning.

In particular, the notions of reliability and omniscience in biblical narrative look to me suspiciously like postulates of convenience, devices to lend credence to the idea that the 'point of it all' is indeed transparent, out there in the text, merely awaiting competent recovery by the objective interpreter. Let me develop this suspicion.

(*Sacred Discontent: The Bible and Western Tradition* [Berkeley: University of California Press, 1977]) might find some satisfaction in the fact that in this regard at least Sternberg is singing but a version of their own theme song.

1 See, e.g., Wayne C. Booth, *The Rhetoric of Fiction* (2nd edn; Chicago: University of Chicago Press, 1983), esp. ch. 7.

2 For introduction to the relevant hermeneutical discussion as it touches biblical texts see, e.g., J. Severino Croatto, *Biblical Hermeneutics: Toward a Theory of Reading as the Production of Meaning* (Maryknoll: Orbis Books, 1987) or Edgar V. McKnight, *Post-Modern Use of the Bible: The Emergence of Reader-Oriented Criticism* (Nashville: Abingdon, 1988).

The reliable narrator

'The Bible', claims Sternberg, 'always tells the truth in that its narrator is absolutely and straightforwardly reliable' (p. 51). Such a claim, however, cannot be sustained without significant modification.

First, one needs to restrict reading within boundaries that look much like source-critical divisions in order to avoid major disjunctions in the text—temporal, spatial and simply factual—regarding the actions of characters.

Second, one needs to ignore the possibility that a narrator so attuned to deploying irony against characters might deploy it against readers, for example by intruding ironic as well as 'straightforward' evaluative comment. Sternberg effectively follows both strategies for avoiding raising difficulties with his poetics.[1]

As far as irony is concerned, the treatment of Solomon in 1 Kings may suffice to make my point. 'Solomon', we are told in 1 Kgs 3.3, 'loved the Lord, walking in the statutes of David his father; only he sacrificed and burnt incense at the high places'. But when we view the closing phase of his story, contemplate the multiplication of his foreign brides and calculate some seven hundred (and more) altars set up to foreign gods, replete with sundry 'goings after' and an angry condemnation by God, then we may choose to read that apparently innocuous 'only' (*raq*) as packing quite a punch. An ironic reading of the 'only' clause can turn the narrator's evaluation from laudatory to condemnatory in a stroke. The possibility of irony is therefore inherently destabilizing where the relationship between narrator and reader is concerned. It precludes any possibility of simple 'straightforward' or literal reading being an infallible reading strategy. Sternberg claims, 'The reader cannot go far wrong even if he [*sic*] does little more than follow the statements made and the incidents enacted on the narrative surface'. I beg to differ. Protestant Christianity has been bedevilled by that kind of literalism for

---

1 On the following points (ironic evaluation and 'factual' contradiction) see also David M. Gunn, 'New Directions in the Study of Biblical Hebrew Narrative', *JSOT* 39 (1987), pp. 65-75, esp. 70-72.

centuries and I see no reason to embrace it now just because it assumes the garb of a sophisticated poetics.

Where facticity ('what actually happened' in the story world) is concerned, one need only cite the case of David and Goliath—who *did* kill Goliath? Or just when did which tribes take possession of the land (Joshua and Judges)? Historical critics have not been entirely beside the mark in identifying 'inconsistency' or 'contradiction' in these biblical texts. The mention of Elhanan (2 Sam. 21.19) really does disturb convictions of reliability, whether we are talking in historical or literary categories. Perhaps it is no accident that Sternberg condemns 2 Sam. 21–24 as a 'sorry stretch of discourse' (p. 42), a 'hodgepodge' which 'has the least pretensions to literariness and... hardly coheres as more than an appendix' (p. 40). The condemnation comes as little surprise, given that this text not only undermines his claim that variants are neutralized by being sequenced, but also contains material that undermines his fundamental (and fundamentalist?) premise of strict narratorial reliability.

The omniscient narrator

Of course it is easy to see that by the same token the Elhanan passage destroys the notion of narratorial omniscience also. What are the alternatives? That the narrator knows who killed Goliath but is not letting on? So much for reliability! Or is it that the narrator who seems to know so much, doesn't actually know everything, not even something as fundamental for a literal, 'straightforward' reading as whether David's encounter with the Philistine is fact or fiction, so to speak? Is the narrator, perhaps, wishing to stave off our idolatry, wishing to remind us that narrators, too, are human, fallible? That thought ought to please Sternberg, given his sensitivity to a biblical doctrine of the transcendence of God, but it is not one that he can live with and still maintain his theory of the mutual mirroring of poetics and ideology. So the data that lead to it are rejected or ignored.[1]

1 My own reading of these chapters (2 Sam. 21–24) discovers both the levelling of the narrator and a summary ironic treatment of David. The latter works principally by juxtaposing the utterance of the righteous psalmist whose ego lies at the centre of

Such a reminder of the narrator's humanity is little different in principle from Homer's intrusion into the beginning of
the *Iliad* (through invocation of the Muse), despite Sternberg's
aggressive insistence that biblical poetics and the poetics of
other ancient narratives are radically different on this score
(cf., e.g., pp. 117-21).

Indeed, in some respects the biblical narrator outdoes
Homer in narratorial intrusion. Frame-breaks are, I think,
more common in biblical narrative and through them the
narratorial voice may, for example, remind us periodically of
its time-boundness (as with 'to this day'). Moreover, much
more so than with Homer, the narrator's human status is also
discernible though the cumulative effect of narratorial point
of view, which is to say, a human point of view. The first
chapters of Genesis and of Job must count as among the few
exceptions to the general practice of narrating from the
human situation. Though the narrator periodically claims
knowledge of God's mind and emotions, such information is
always related to a focal interest in the predicament of the
human character. It is humankind that does most of the
acting and talking in biblical narrative. And even Genesis and
Job cannot sustain a divine focus for long. Finally, Mosaic
exhortations to remember and retell the stories of God and
people, or pedantic indications of further literary sources, such
devices serve the same function—they suggest that the telling
of the tale is the business of humans, a human responsibility
even, a craft open to all (and not just the child of the Muse).
They cut a seemingly 'know-all' narrator down to size.

Can omniscience, then, be said to be a characteristic of the
narrator? That is only obviously true in a very restricted
sense. In a story like Genesis–2 Kings it becomes clear that the

a boldly geometrical arrangement—'the most conspicuous and large-scale
instance of chiasm in Samuel' (Sternberg p. 40, though he sees no significance in
it)—with texts of another discourse (e.g. 23.8-39), the reminders of a world where
self-serving pragmatism, aggression, and deception hold sway. The juxtaposition redefines righteousness as self-righteousness. The irony of 2 Sam. 21–24 is
then like the irony of Judges 17–21. And like that material it is, on my reading, a
prime candidate for 'misreading' or indeed 'counterreading'. See further, David
M. Gunn, 'In Security: The David of Biblical Narrative', in J. Cheryl Exum (ed.),
Signs and Wonders: Biblical Texts in Literary Focus (Semeia Studies; Atlanta:
Scholars, 1989), pp. 133-51.

narrator narrates from the point of view of the end of the story. What happens is, in that sense, known in advance. Yet Sternberg advocates something much more sweeping than that. The narrator knows everything about the narrated world, he claims, including the hearts and minds of God and the human characters.

But what is the evidence for this assertion? What, for that matter, is the evidence that the character God is omniscient in the particular story we are looking at, the Story of Creation to Exile, Genesis–2 Kings? And for Sternberg these are no idle questions; for this material is the proving ground of his poetics and narratorial omniscience is one of the undergirding assumptions of his theory. What is the evidence regarding the latter? Not too much, I would say, and none of it strong. When, in the Samson story, Robert Polzin discerns a narrator who 'undercuts his own omniscience',[1] Sternberg takes him to task for 'creat[ing] problems where none actually exist' (p. 182). Because we are not told all that a narrator knows, says Sternberg, we must not assume that the narrator knows no more than is narrated. Indeed, 'if a narrator shows himself qualified to penetrate the mind of one of the characters and report his secret activities—a feat impossible in everyday life—he has established his competence to do so in regard to all other inaccessibles as well. The superhuman privilege is constant and only its exercise variable' (p. 183).

But this, of course, is sheer dogmatism. Most of us indulge in the creative adventure of mind-probing but we tell of our discoveries with varying degrees of conviction. To lay claim to privileged knowledge is not necessarily to lay claim to omniscience, unless omniscience is to mean something other than 'knowing all'. No, to assign omniscience to the narrator (and so to exclude in any given case alternatives such as partial knowledge, ignorance, confusion, or agnosticism) is to opt for merely one of several possible and reasonable assumptions. It is an assumption, moreover, that runs up against all sorts of

---

1 *Moses and the Deuteronomist: A Literary Study of the Deuteronomic History. Part One. Deuteronomy, Joshua, Judges* (New York: Seabury, 1980), p. 189; cf. p. 191: 'For in addition to the voice which names and explains events, there is the voice which cries out to Yahweh for understanding' (quoted by Sternberg, p. 182).

problems. And so we come back to that simple question of fact:
Who killed Goliath?

The problem with the notion of narratorial omniscience,
however, goes beyond the problems of gaps, ambiguity, factual
fudging or plain contradiction. It also involves the limitations
evident in the implication of readership—the implied reader
of Genesis–2 Kings is evidently somewhere in exile (or early
post-exile?). Beyond that the narrator can perhaps see, as in a
vision, but clearly does not know. The book as a whole is an
invitation to belief and to action—and the narrator plainly
narrates at a particular threshold in time, looking back to the
known (or, I would want to say, the partially known[1]) and
looking forward to the unknown. The narrator is not all-
knowing and makes no claim to be so. The narrator's future
and the implied reader's future are open.

The omniscient God

By the same token I would challenge—and not be the first to
do so—Sternberg's even more basic claim that God in 'biblical
narrative' is omniscient. In Hebrew narrative, Sternberg
asserts, 'the omniscience of divinity assumes the greatest
importance, both as an article of faith and as a concomitant of
absolute powers of action and judgment'. Yet divine omniscience is not, I believe, a category readily drawn from Hebrew
Bible narrative. Like the narrator, God may have insights into
the future, God may have visions; but in some respects the
future lies hidden to God as it does to the people of the story.

The notion of divine omniscience mocks the humans and
makes a cynic of God in those stories of intercession by Abraham or Moses. Warming to another theme (the link between
knowledge of God and God's wonder-making—which in my
perspective Sternberg has counter-read), he observes how
Moses 'dissuades' God from wiping out the seemingly hopeless
Israelites (p. 102). But one can only dissuade someone when
that other genuinely intends to do something. Or again Sternberg observes that wonder-working does not always bring

---

1 On the narrator as 'partially or selectively omniscient', cf. Danna Nolan Fewell,
Circle of Sovereignty: A Story of Stories in Daniel 1–6 (Bible and Literature, 20;
Sheffield: Almond, 1988), p. 24.

success 'and God at times yields to despair. "How long will
they not believe in me", [God] rages... "despite all the signs
which I have wrought among them? I will strike them with
pestilence" (Num. 14.11-12). Only with difficulty (and partial
success) does Moses manage to avert the catastrophe'
(p. 109). One is hard pressed to read God's question here as
rhetorical and Sternberg appears not to do so. So then to
interpret such a passage (both the biblical discourse and
Sternberg's) in terms of an omniscient and omnipotent God
would tax a Calvin beyond his limits. Why bother? Neither of
those categories seems to me to belong with this text. Why
import them?

The narrator, the plot and God-as-character

I do not propose to examine the category of omnipotence further here. Suffice to say that it, too, seems to me not to be a
useful one when talking of God in Hebrew narrative, whereas
for Sternberg it, along with omniscience, is fundamental. God
makes, the narrator merely shapes, the plot. But as the example just cited makes clear, Moses also makes the plot. In other
words, such a claim is only true in a strictly qualified sense, for
example, as a way of talking about the way divine grace
extends the story of Genesis–2 Kings (although the exercise of
that plot-extending grace depends upon the people's rejection
of it!).

But of course common sense tells us that the narrator is
making the plot, and behind the narrator the author. To claim
that God-as-character in the Bible is not the creature of the
author/narrator is, in my view, perverse. For the reader to
whom this narrative is Scripture the question then is, what is
the relation between God-as-character and the God of faith?
What is the relation between the world-inside-Scripture and
the world-outside-Scripture? Sternberg appears not to distinguish between God-as-character and the God of faith. That
lack of distinction is perhaps one of the biggest sources of confusion in his work, and a matter of significant neglect for
someone so insistent on epistemological discrimination. And
ironically that neglect, together with his absolutist, authoritar-

ian hermeneutics, aligns him most closely with modern fundamentalism.

Blurring and lucidity

I say 'ironically' because Sternberg's own theory and practice is rich in an appreciation of ambiguity and gapping—features of reading generally shunned by fundamentalists and literalists. Yet in the end the ambiguities and gaps and shadows count for little. He has a wonderful maxim. The greater the ambiguity in the presentation of the material the plainer the plain sense or moral judgment (the message or ideological evaluation). The more opaque the evaluation the fewer the ambiguities (pp. 54-55). Hence it is that readers will have no difficulty in arriving at the 'right' attitude. In a nutshell, whatever we may be tempted to think of Saul and David (for example) throughout their chequered careers, we will come to recognize the one as a bad guy and the other as a good guy. 'Initial blurring' will inevitably give way to 'retrospective lucidity' (p. 99).[1] As so often, I find myself reading in counterpoint to Sternberg. Abram? Jephthah? Saul? Jonah? Job? In most of these cases, what seemed to me fairly clear at the beginning is by the end wrapped in complexity if not mystery.

Sternberg's one extended reading of material in 1 Samuel is an account of the rejection of Saul, entitled 'Ideology, Rhetoric, Poetics' (ch. 13). It has not led me to alter significantly my own, very different, reading.[2] Yet his is an essentially conventional or 'consensus' position, which I recognize as a possible, if not compelling, reading. So why do we diverge? Is it just that I am an incompetent reader—I and others who have heard the story in more sardonic tones than Sternberg has done?[3] Obvi-

1 On this concept of 'retrospective lucidity', see pp. 98-99 (on Noah, Abram and Joseph) and also ch. 13, on Saul. As Danna Fewell has wryly observed to me, one might be tempted to wonder at the reliability of a narrator who needs so tortuously to mislead us in order to have us arrive at such an obvious goal.

2 See David M. Gunn, *The Fate of King Saul: An Interpretation of a Biblical Story* (JSOTSup, 14; Sheffield: JSOT, 1980).

3 See especially Peter Miscall's many-sided reading of 1 Samuel 15 (*1 Samuel: A Literary Reading* [Indiana Studies in Biblical Literature; Bloomington: Indiana University Press, 1986); cf. Lyle Eslinger, *Kingship of God in Crisis: A Close Reading of 1 Samuel 1-12* (Bible and Literature, 10; Sheffield: Almond, 1985).

ously, I doubt that this is really the reason. In other words, let me repeat what I said at the beginning: I doubt that we can settle the matter by appeal simply to the text. *Pace* Sternberg, there is too much for us to disagree about. We can disagree about reading strategy, for example, because our poetics are divergent, and I'm not prepared to accept his dictate on this subject. We can disagree over the opacity of the text for another—for me it really *is* dense with enlivening ambiguities, gaps, and disjunctions. And the 'plain sense' of what the narrator stands for is not nearly so plain as our theorist wants us to think.

Divergent standpoints

But more than that, I think we are reading from significantly divergent psychological and ideological standpoints. And this shapes *both* our understanding of biblical poetics *and* our particular interpretations of biblical texts. That Sternberg can read Genesis–2 Kings as proposing a necessary bond between Israel's knowledge of God and God's wonder-working (pp. 102, 115 and n. 22) is to me to turn the text on its head, a wonderful counter-reading. But that's a theologically significant difference—it comes from a Sternberg who also seeks interpretational security through a foolproof poetics. For me the challenge is to live with interpretational insecurity and the threat of a relativist hermeneutic. For me, too, the wonder-working stories are in the end impoverished without those mundane stories, of Ruth and Esther, for example—Esther which Sternberg, like Luther, seems to wish had never made it into the canon (pp. 105-106). For their world—the worlds of Ruth and Esther—and my world merge so much more readily than the grandiose world of parting seas and tumbling walls and floating axe-heads. Nor is Sternberg's diffidence about Esther particularly surprising: if all biblical texts are about knowing God (Sternberg's view), then perhaps texts that present God in an ambiguous light, let alone texts that present God barely or not at all, will automatically become problems for Sternberg.[1]

---

1 The observation is Danna Fewell's (private communication).

Sternberg invokes omniscience and omnipotence. God can do what God wishes. Self-limitation can be undone at will (p. 181). But to me that is to view God merely in terms of absolutes and power, contextless. Rather I read in Biblical narrative of a God (a character) who from the beginning of the story chooses to be defined in terms of relationship and responsibility and once so defined is no longer 'free' simply to appeal to divine right. That in turn places humanity's freedom in the context of responsibility in relationship, as well as rights.

But now I have shifted gear and begun to talk again as though our differences were simply rooted in different interpretation. Rather I see a fundamental ideological difference between us. It is a difference rooted in our understanding of human and divine authority. It is, I suspect, also a difference rooted in our personalities. It is unlikely to dissolve through the application of much rational argument. I might characterize him as absolutist; he might see me as relativist. Both those labels would be inadequate and perhaps divisive, though not, I think, altogether misleading.

The ideology of biblical poetics

Labelling, however, can be invidious and is not my point. Rather my purpose has been to draw attention to some ideological implications of Sternberg's book. It is not simply that Sternberg reads from an ideologically distinctive position, whether acknowledged or not. What I have been trying to say is more than that. 'Poetics' may sound such a neutral term; determining the 'mechanics of composition' may seem such an objective activity. But it is not so. The propagation of 'poetics' is an ideological enterprise. 'Reliable', 'omniscient', and 'foolproof' are heavily loaded terms.[1] *Caveat emptor!*

---

1 A further, feminist, critique of the notion of 'foolproof composition' and the androcentric values it masks in Sternberg's reading is forthcoming in Danna Nolan Fewell and David M. Gunn, 'Tipping the Balance: Sternberg's Reading and the Rape of Dinah' (presented to the Biblical Criticism and Literary Criticism Section at the Annual Meeting of the Society of Biblical Literature, Chicago, November 1988).

ZION IN TRANSFORMATION
A Literary Approach to Isaiah

Barry G. Webb

The subject of this essay is the book of Isaiah as a whole. This is an objectively given entity with a very long history and therefore no justification is needed for taking it as an object of study.[1]

The approach taken is literary as opposed to historical or sociological. That is, the way in which the various elements of the text interact with one another to produce meaning for the present reader is studied without reference to the putative background and development of the text. The text itself of course makes frequent reference to historical persons and events, and to sociological phenomena, but my concern here is solely with how these function within the text. No attempt is made to reconstruct them.

The approach is subjective in the sense that the meaning which emerges is the product of my personal interaction with the text. Such subjectivity is an essential part of interpretation and requires no apology.[2] The subjective judgments involved in constructing a hypothetical text or context are absent, however, and therefore the interpretation has an objective basis.

1 Quotations are from the RSV with reference to the underlying MT where required to elucidate the argument.
2 It is important to recognize that since the biblical message is conveyed through literary expression the discipline of biblical interpretation belongs essentially to the humanities rather than to the sciences. This of course does not in any way diminish the role of the critical faculties, but it does recognize that a subjective element is entirely appropriate. On the other hand the approach is objective in the sense that the phenomena appealed to in the interpretation are at every point directly observable in the given text.

To the extent that such an interpretation succeeds in persuading others of its validity it creates a community of understanding in relation to the text, but it never achieves the status of an objectively true or final statement of the text's meaning. The task of interpretation never ends.

While the type of literary criticism I have been describing here has been fashionable in biblical studies for a number of years now, the interpretation of biblical books as such from this perspective is still in its infancy. This is particularly so in the case of the book of Isaiah. Brevard Childs in his *Introduction*[1] was of course more concerned with the canonical shaping of the Isaiah tradition than with the purely literary features of the book as such. His canonical criticism has an historical dimension which distinguishes it from the type of literary criticism I have in mind here. But to the extent that he did draw attention to the canonical shape and theological unity of the text, he provided a major stimulus for renewed interest in the structural and thematic unity of the book itself. Since that time a sprinkling of articles has appeared which have approached the book from a more thorough-going literary perspective. The most significant of these in my judgement are those of W.J. Dumbrell,[2] C.A. Evans,[3] and E.W. Conrad.[4] But the offering to date is meagre considering the major significance of the book in the canon. The recent two-volume work by John Watts[5] represents the first attempt, to my knowledge, to apply the insights of the new literary criticism to a full-length commentary on the book. This is a stimulating and pioneering work, and Watts has made a major contribution to the interpretation of the book. But the literary approach of the commentary is significantly qualified, as the writer himself makes clear (p. xliv), by a concern to relate the interpretation of the text to a particular historical setting. Watts regards the book in its finished form as a fifth-century work

1   B.S. Childs, *Introduction to the Old Testament as Scripture* (London: SCM, 1979).
2   'The Purpose of the Book of Isaiah', *TynB* 36 (1985), pp. 111-28.
3   'On the Unity and Parallel Structure of Isaiah', *VT* 28 (1988), pp. 129-47. Evans expands on a thesis put forward tentatively by W.H. Brownlee in 1964.
4   'The Royal Narratives and the Structure of the Book of Isaiah', *JSOT* 41 (1988), pp. 67-81.
5   J.D.W. Watts, *Isaiah* (2 vols; WBC; Waco, Texas: Word, 1985/87).

addressing fifth-century issues.[1] The gap between the text and the modern reader is bridged by some attention to the history of interpretation at the appropriate points in the commentary. In its fundamental orientation, therefore, Watts's commentary is more closely aligned with Childs's canonical approach than with the new literary criticism.

The germ for my own thinking in the present study was supplied by Dumbrell's article, and my indebtedness to him and others will be acknowledged where appropriate below. My principal aim however is not to review or critique the work of others but to advance a thesis which I believe has the capacity to integrate many of their best insights. The thesis is that the transformation of Zion is the key to both the formal and the thematic structure of the book as a whole. Only preliminary justification for the thesis can be advanced in an essay of this length, but sufficient groundwork can be laid, I believe, to demonstrate its fruitfulness.

1. *Initial indicators of formal and thematic unity*

Even a cursory reading of the text, observing how it begins, how it ends, and how it is structured (in the very broadest sense), brings to light a number of indicators that what we have before us is a conceptual whole. Some of these indicators are of a formal nature, relating to the structure of the text, and some are of a material nature, relating to its content. Together they constitute a prima facie justification for the kind of unitary interpretation of the text which will be developed in the body of the article.

The first such indicator is the title in 1.1. It is, as it stands, a superscription to the book as a whole and subsumes it all under the rubric, 'the vision of Isaiah'.[2] This title, therefore,

---

1 '[The vision] develops and presents fifth-century issues by presenting materials from eighth-, seventh-, sixth-, and fifth-century settings' (p. xliii).

2 While דבר 'word(s)', and משא, 'burden', also occur as genre terms (e.g. 2.1; 13.1), חזון is the term which is used comprehensively for the book as a whole. This is rare in the OT prophetic literature. Only Obadiah opens in precisely the same way as Isaiah, but compare Nahum 1.1, 'The book of the vision of Nahum...' Precise definition of חזון as a literary genre in this comprehensive sense is not possible. For a discussion see Watts, *Isaiah*, I, pp. xliv-xlv. In my judgment Watts gives the concept of חזון as drama too large a part in his interpretation.

does not simply attach the contents of the book to a particular prophet or to a particular setting, but at once orients us to the whole as a conceptual unity. The whole is to be read as one vision.

This title is picked up and partially repeated at the beginning of the second chapter. Here 'word' replaces the more comprehensive term 'vision' and the temporal note, 'in the days of Uzziah...', is dropped, but the rest of 2.1 follows closely the wording of the opening title, with the expression 'which Isaiah... saw' (חזה) providing the specific link to the vision of 1.1. This echo of the opening title introduces an eschatological passage (2.1-4) in which 'in the latter days', the temple mount of Zion is raised above the surrounding hills and all nations flow to it to acknowledge and submit to Yahweh's universal rule.

The effect of this repetition is to alert us at the outset of the book to the comprehensive nature of the vision which it contains. Taken together, the title in 1.1 and its echo in 2.1 indicate that while the vision concerns Judah and Jerusalem in particular and takes its rise during the reigns of certain kings in the eighth century BCE, it includes within its scope all nations and reaches to the very eschaton itself. Temporally, the vision moves between the twin poles of 'the days of Uzziah...' (1.1) and 'the latter days' (2.1). Notionally, it is centred on 'Judah and Jerusalem'.

The second indicator is the way in which the book begins and ends. It begins with heaven and earth being called to witness the word which Yahweh speaks (1.2). It ends with the heavens and earth being themselves directly affected, indeed so radically affected that they are transformed into a new heaven and a new earth (66.22; cf. 65.17). But this transformation of the cosmos is directly related to the transformation of Jerusalem/Zion[1] as the threefold repetition of 'create' (ברא) in 65.17-18 makes clear:

---

1 In their usage in Isaiah both terms refer to the city as a whole. Compare for example, vv. 1 and 27 of ch. 1, and vv. 14 and 16b of ch. 28. The two stand parallel to one another in 2.3; 31.9; 33.20; 40.9; 41.27; 52.1; 62.1; 64.10. Cf. also 4.3, 4; 30.19; 51.16-17; 52.8-9. Functionally, therefore, the two terms are synonymous and the variation in their usage is not, in itself, semantically significant. Unlike 'Jerusalem', however, 'Zion' is frequently nuanced by the addition of one or more

> I *create* new heavens and a new earth...
> But be glad and rejoice forever
>   in that which I *create*;
> For behold I *create* Jerusalem a rejoicing,
>   and her people a joy.

The eschaton towards which the book as a whole moves is a new cosmos centred on a new Jerusalem/Zion (cf. 2.1-4). As ch. 1 makes clear, however, the transformation of Zion will involve radical judgment on the rebels within her. This note is struck at the very outset of the chapter (1.2) and underscored at its climax (vv. 27-28):

> Zion shall be redeemed by justice,
>   and those in her who repent, by righteousness.
> But rebels and sinners shall be destroyed together,
>   and those who forsake the Lord shall be
>   consumed.

The book ends with a grim reminder of this threat and of the certainty of its execution (66.24):

> And they shall go forth and look on the dead bodies of the
> men that have rebelled against me...

So the scope and focus of the vision as indicated by the title and its repetition in 2.1 are confirmed by the way the end of the book picks up major motifs from its beginning.

The third indicator is the role that the Hezekiah narrative in chs. 36–39 plays in the overall structure of the book. This compositional unit lies close to the centre of the book. It is quite distinct stylistically from the poetic material which immediately precedes and follows it, but structurally and conceptually it is closely integrated into its wider context.

First, it depicts the climax and the decisive resolution of the Assyrian threat which has largely dominated chs. 1–35. In particular it has numerous, striking connections of both style and substance with the Ahaz narrative of ch. 7,[1] and the

---

qualifiers, e.g. 'mount Zion' (4.5), 'daughter Zion' (1.8), 'virgin daughter Zion' (37.22).

1 These have been detailed by Conrad in 'The Royal Narratives', pp. 67-81. Compare especially 7.1 ('Rezin... came up') with 36.1 ('Sennacherib... came up'), 7.3 ('the conduit of the upper highway to the Fuller's Field') with 36.2 (where the identical expression occurs), and 7.14 ('the Lord himself will give you a sign')

destruction of the Assyrian in ch. 37 is the fulfilment of the war oracle of ch. 10 (vv. 24-27). But if chs. 36 and 37 are integrally related to what precedes, chs. 38 and 39 are just as intimately connected with what follows. They in fact provide the transition to the Babylonian crisis which will so largely dominate the second part of the book.[1] Hezekiah's sickness in ch. 38 becomes the occasion for the visit of Merodach-baladan's envoys in 39.1-2, and this leads to the prediction of the deportation to Babylon in 39.3-8 which provides the transition to what follows.

Now this transitional function of the larger unit, chs. 36–39, is made possible by a particular ordering of the material within it, as has been pointed out afresh by Walton and Smelik in recent articles.[2] The temporal indicator, 'in those days', of 38.1 sets the events of chs. 38–39 in the same general period as those which have preceded without specifying the relationship more precisely.[3] As the narrative develops from this point a radical temporal disjunction soon surfaces in the text. In 38.6 the deliverance of Jerusalem from the Assyrian is still in prospect, but this has already been accomplished decisively in the previous chapter. In other words the events of chs. 36–37 and 38–39 respectively stand in inverted chronological sequence in the text[4] and it is precisely this ordering of the text which allows the unit as a whole, chs. 36–39, to function as it does within the book. In terms of the book's overall structure it

with 36.30 ('this shall be the sign for you'). Both narratives contain a war oracle delivered to the king by Isaiah (7.4-9; cf. 10.24-27; 37.6-7), and both end with the threat of a worse catastrophe to come (7.15-17, 20; 39.6-7).

1 This is certainly so in chs. 40–55, but it continues to surface at many points in chs. 56–66 also. See, e.g., 57.14-18; 62.1-5; 64.8-12.

2 J.H. Walton, 'New Observations on the Date of Isaiah', *JETS* 28 (1985), pp. 129-32, and K.A.D. Smelik, 'Distortion of Old Testament Prophecy: The Purpose of Isaiah xxxvi and xxxvii', *Oudtestamentische Studiën* 24 (1986), pp. 70-93. The observation in itself is not new, as both authors acknowledge. Both, however, proceed to argue on this basis for the primacy of Isa. 36–39 over its parallel in 2 Kings, and Walton for an eighth-century date for the book as a whole.

3 Compare, in Judges, the contrast between the precise ordering of the judge-narratives of chs. 3-16, and the assignment of the events of chs. 17–21 to the same general period by the repetition of the phrase, 'in those days...' (17.6; 18.1; 19.1; 21.25).

4 Confirmatory evidence of an historical nature is given by Walton in 'New Evidence', p. 129, and in most of the commentaries.

functions as a pivot effecting the transition from the 'Assyrian' first half of the book to its 'Babylonian' second half.[1] The final indicator is the sustained focus on Jerusalem/Zion throughout the book in all its parts. This has been thoroughly documented, if proof is necessary, in the article by Dumbrell mentioned earlier.[2] This focus is particularly clear at the beginning and end of the book as we have seen, but it is also abundantly clear in chs. 36-39 which we have just identified as a major structural pivot. There is a fine interplay in these chapters between the certainty of Yahweh's commitment to Zion on the one hand (37.33-35; 38.6) and the very real consequences of human faith (ch. 37) or faithlessness (ch. 39) on the other.[3] But the concern with Zion and its fortunes is all-pervasive. Even in chs. 13–23, which are given over almost entirely to oracles against foreign nations, the underlying concern is with the security of Zion. The nations on view in these chapters have all, like Judah, come under Assyrian pressure and are all actual or potential partners with Judah in anti-Assyrian activity.[4] The recurring theme is that Zion's security is to be found not in foreign alliances, but in reliance upon Yahweh[5] (see especially 20.1-6; 22.8-11). The vision of the book moves, in fact, from the historical Jerusalem of the eighth century (under judgment) to the new Jerusalem of the eschaton, which is the centre of the new cosmos and symbol of the new age.[6] To this new Jerusalem the nations come (66.18-21; cf. 60.1-22) so that ultimately the nations find their salvation in Zion and not vice versa. It is this sustained focus on the

---

1   The distinction is not absolute, of course. Anticipatory Babylonian material surfaces at certain points in chs. 1–36, notably at 13.1-14, 23; 21.1-10 and, by implication, 35.1-10. It is possible, however that 21.1-10 refers to a defeat in the Assyrian period; see J.N. Oswalt, *The Book of Isaiah, Chapters 1–39* (NICOT; Grand Rapids: Eerdmans, 1986), pp. 389-90.

2   'Purpose of Isaiah'.

3   This is a further important point of connection between the royal narratives of chs. 7 and 36–39. From faithless Ahaz we pass, via the ideal king figure of 9.6-7, to the faithful Hezekiah of chs. 36–37, but he too finally proves to be a disappointment, and by his failure puts Zion at risk again (ch. 39). See Conrad, 'The Royal Narratives', p. 74. I shall argue below that the ideal figure of ch. 9 is in fact a metaphor for the eschatological remnant.

4   See S. Erlandsson, *The Burden of Babylon. A Study of Isaiah 13:2–14:23* (CB OT Series, 4; Lund: Gleerup, 1970), pp. 102-105.

5   Cf. Dumbrell, 'Purpose of Isaiah', p. 119.

6   Cf. Dumbrell, 'Purpose of Isaiah', p. 129.

significance of Zion that gives the vision its theological cohesion.

In this section, then, we have looked at four initial indicators of the formal and thematic unity of the book. Taken together, they demonstrate a sufficient degree of cohesion, in my judgment, to justify a unitary reading of the text at a deeper level.

2. *The remnant concept and the structure of the book*

The key to the transformation of Zion is purifying judgment. This is at once apparent in the movement from the indictment of Zion in ch. 1 (vv. 2-23) to the vision of the eschatological Zion in ch. 2 (vv. 1-4), a movement which anticipates the movement of the book as a whole, as we have seen. This movement is effected via the purifying judgment of 1.24-25:

> Therefore the Lord says...
> I will turn my hand against you
> and will smelt your dross as with lye
> and remove all your alloy.

The result is the production of a purified remnant which becomes the nucleus of the new Zion of the eschaton. The term 'remnant' itself (שאר/שארית) is not used in ch. 1, but the concept is clearly present. The purifying judgment of v. 25 results in a radical separation between 'those who repent' and 'rebels and sinners' (vv. 27-28). The former are redeemed and the latter destroyed, and it is from here that we pass to the vision of the eschatological Zion of 2.1-4. After the brief exhortation of 2.5 the same sequence is then repeated in 2.6–4.6, namely, indictment of Zion (2.6-11a), then the announcement of judgment (2.11b–4.1), followed by a second vision of the eschatological Zion (4.2-6). Here remnant terminology is introduced for the first time, making explicit what was implicit in chs. 1 and 2:

> In that day... he who is left (שאר) in Zion... will be called holy... when the Lord shall have washed away the filth of the daughter of Zion and cleansed the bloodstains of Jerusalem from its midst by a spirit of judgment and a spirit of burning (4.2-4).

The fundamental importance of the remnant motif to the theology of chs. 1–39 is well recognized.[1] But given the programmatic significance of 1.1–2.4 we may justifiably expect to find that the remnant concept has more comprehensive significance. It certainly surfaces at a crucial point in the transitional unit, chs. 36–39 (see 37.31-32). It surfaces again in 46.3, where the exiles in Babylon are addressed as 'all the remnant (שְׁאֵרִית) of the house of Israel', and the concept, if not the term itself, is present at the end of the book where a sharp distinction is made between Yahweh's 'servants' who are comforted in the new Jerusalem (66.13-14) and the rebels whose bodies are exposed outside it (66.24; cf. 64.8-25).

Clearly, however, remnant is not a static concept with a single stable semantic content throughout the book. It is variously nuanced, and the changes are rung on it as the book progresses through the various sub-units which comprise the whole.

In chs. 1–12 the remnant is variously 'a few survivors' who are left after a devastating invasion of Judah (1.9), 'those in her [Zion] who repent' (1.27), 'the righteous' with whom it will be well (3.10), 'the survivors of Israel' who inhabit the eschatological Zion (4.2-3), 'the holy seed' which remains in the stump after Judah has been felled by God's judgment, 'everyone left in the land' after Assyrian depredation (7.22), chastened survivors who lean now on Yahweh and no longer on Assyria (10.10-21), and surviving Israelites of various lands whom Yahweh will finally gather into their own land again (10.11-12, 16). The text oscillates between intermediate and ultimate forms of the remnant concept, but finally comes to rest on the ultimate with the song of praise in ch. 12. What the remnant is *finally* is the community of the new, eschatological Zion that will emerge on 'that day' (12.1) beyond judgment.

In chs. 13–27 the remnant idea at first assumes a more negative aspect as the focus shifts temporarily to the nations. Remnant language is used of the last vestige of Babylon to be

---

1 See especially G.F. Hasel, *The Remnant. The History and Theology of the Remnant Idea from Genesis to Isaiah* (2nd edn; Michigan: Andrews University Press, 1974), pp. 216-72.

destroyed by Yahweh, signalling her complete demise (14.22),
of the Philistine survivors of one Assyrian attack, destined to
perish in another (14.30), of the survivors of Moab who are
destined to be devoured by lions (15.9) or who are in any case
few and feeble (16.4), of the enfeebled remains of Syria, comparable to the pitiful remains of the northern kingdom of
Israel (17.3), of the surviving few of Kedar's archers and
mighty men (21.17), and finally of the remnants of the nations
after the cataclysmic, all-embracing, final judgment (24.13).
Plainly the cosmic judgment of ch. 24 is climactic with respect
to the particular judgments of chs. 12–23. Hence, chs. 24–27,
often regarded as a distinct unit, properly belong with chs. 13–
23 so far as the logical development of the text at this point is
concerned. Compositionally, chs. 13–27 are a single unit
within the overall structure of the book. But the purpose of the
judgments announced here, and of the cosmic judgment of
ch. 24 in particular, is to establish Yahweh's rule in Jerusalem/
Zion, as 24.23 makes clear:

> Then the moon will be confounded,
> and the sun ashamed;
> for the LORD of hosts will reign
> on Mount Zion and in Jerusalem
> and before his elders he will manifest his glory.

These elders are presumably the leaders of the community
which inhabits the new Zion.[1] As this major unit draws to its
climax the focus shifts back from the nations to Zion, and the
cocncept of the remnant in its ultimate, theological sense
returns. This unit, like the previous one, ends with an eschatological song of praise (or, to be more precise, two songs) sung
by the saved remnant in Zion[2] (chs. 26–27; cf. ch. 12).

In chs. 28–35 there is no use of the remnant idea with
respect to surrounding nations. It is used, however, of
Jerusalem/Judah in both its intermediate and ultimate
aspects. In 30.17 it is used, in a manner reminiscent of 1.8-9, of

1 Cf. Rev. 4.4, 9-11, and contrast the way the leaders of the old Zion, including the
   elders, were indicted at the outset of the book (1.23; 3.14).
2 This eschatological remnant is variously 'the righteous nation which keeps faith'
   (26.2), simply 'the righteous' (singular, the community personified, 26.7), and
   'those who were lost' or 'those who were driven out' but who are restored to Zion
   (27.12-13).

the pathetic remainder of Judah after a devastating invasion, the end result of relying on Egypt instead of on Yahweh (see 30.1-3). But flanking this, near the beginning and again at the very end of the unit, are two uses of the idea in its final sense. In 28.5 the eschatological remnant will enjoy, 'in that day',[1] the perfect, just rule of Yahweh in place of the corrupt rule of the leaders of Samaria and Jerusalem (vv. 1-4, 14-22) which brought the two kingdoms to ruin. As v. 16 indicates, it is in Zion that this perfect rule of Yahweh will finally come to realization. In 35.10 'the ransomed of the Lord' returr to Zion with singing, there to experience 'everlasting joy'[2] and the banishment of all ills. Again the consummation is reached in Zion and 'the ransomed of the Lord' are the eschatological remnant. The reference to their singing here echoes the references to eschatological singing in chs. 12 and 26–27, so that this major unit ends on the same note as the previous two.

In chs. 36–39 the remnant idea occurs only in its intermediate sense. In 37.4 Hezekiah asks Isaiah to pray for the remnant of Judah which is presently confined in besieged Jerusalem. In vv. 31-32 of the same chapter Isaiah assures him that 'a remnant' will survive and 'go forth' from the city. The 'sign' of renewed agricultural productivity in v. 30 becomes a metaphor for renewed community life in v. 31. But the whole has reference to the immediate threat posed by the Assyrians and its removal (see vv. 33-35). Beyond this lies another, very different kind of egress from the city, as the following two chapters indicate. The unit as a whole closes with no remnant ('nothing left') of the royal treasury, and the remnants of the Davidic house ('some of [Hezekiah's] sons') not 'going forth' but being 'taken away' from the city to Babylon (39.5-8).

---

1 As so often in this book, the text moves between the twin poles of the present (judgment) and the eschaton (salvation). The eschatological sense of the expression 'in that day' is established at the outset of the book (see 2.2, 11, 12, 17, 20; 4.1) and reaffirmed in the chapter immediately preceding the present one (see 27.1, 2, 12, 13; cf. 26.1).

2 There is a nice contrast here with the smoke of Edom's destruction which goes up 'forever' in the previous chapter (v. 10). The final salvation of Zion and the final destruction of her enemies (symbolized by Edom) stand back-to-back in chs. 34 and 35. The logical connection is made in 34.8.

This virtual destruction of Jerusalem and apparent demise of the Davidic house[1] at the end of the unit stand in tension with the earlier promise of Yahweh to 'defend this city to save it for my own sake and for the sake of my servant David' (37.35). A resolution is called for but none is forthcoming at this point and so the unit ends on a note of unresolved tension.

In keeping, then, with the transitional nature of these chapters there is no finality to the remnant concept here and no movement to an eschatological climax. Chs. 36–39 simply close one major division of the book and open another in the progress towards that climax.

Chapters 40–55 are commonly taken together as the next major unit within the book as we have it. Attention to the formal and logical arrangements of the material in these chapters, however, indicates that they should be seen as consisting of two compositional units, namely 40.1–51.11 and 51.12–55.13.

In 40.1–51.11 the remnant idea is sustained in two ways. The first is by the transference of the remnant concept to the exiles. This is done explicitly in 46.3 (the exiles are the addressees):

> Harken to me O house of Jacob,
>> all the remnant of the house of Israel,
> who have been borne by me from your birth,
>> carried from the womb.

The second is by the exact repetition in 51.11 of the climactic words of 35.10:

> And the ransomed of the LORD shall return,
>> and come to Zion with singing;
> everlasting joy shall be upon their heads;
>> they shall obtain joy and gladness,
>> and sorrow and sighing shall flee away.

This shift of the remnant concept to the exiles, therefore, is not unexpected. The way has already been prepared for it by ch. 35, immediately preceding the central pivot (chs. 36–39). But what was implicit there is now made explicit. Together with this shift comes the reapplication of the refining meta-

---

1   Cf. Dumbrell, 'Purpose of Isaiah', p. 122.

phor of 1.25 to the exilic situation. The Babylonian exile now becomes the 'furnace of affliction' in which Israel is refined and from which a purified remnant emerges (48.10). At the end of this unit the intermediate and ultimate senses of the remnant idea converge. The return of the exiles is viewed in eschatological terms, and the unit ends, like those in the first half of the book, with the inhabitants of the new Zion singing Yahweh's praise (51.11).

There is no explicit use of remnant language in 51.12–55.13, but, as we have seen, the identification of the exiles as 'the remnant of the house of Israel' has already been made in 46.3. The same identification holds, implicitly, in the present unit, which opens in a way strongly reminiscent of ch. 40. 'I, I am he that comforts you' in 51.12 recalls 'Comfort, comfort my people, says your God' in 40.1. The reference to 'the son of man who is made like grass' in 51.12 recalls 40.6, 'all flesh is grass'. The command to say to Zion, 'You are my people', in 5.16 recalls 'Comfort, comfort my people... speak tenderly to Jerusalem' in 40.1-2. The declaration to Jerusalem that she has 'drunk at the hand of the LORD' the cup of his wrath 'to the dregs' in 51.17 recalls the similar statement in 40.2 that Jerusalem 'has received from the Lord's hand double for all her sins'. The subsequent declaration on the mountains of the good tidings of Yahweh's reign and of his return to Zion in 52.7 recall the strikingly similar passage in 40.9-10. So after the climax that is reached in 51.11 the text then reverts to the point from which the previous unit has set out in ch. 40. This new unit subsequently reaches its own climax at the end of ch. 55 where, once again, the saved remnant returns to Zion with singing (55.12-13). This time the whole creation responds to the joy of the returnees with singing of its own. The 'everlasting joy' of 51.11 is here developed in terms of the 'joy' (and peace) with which the exiles return (55.12) and the 'everlasting' sign[1] of the transformed environment (55.13). So 40.1–51.11 and 51.12–55.13 are closely related conceptually, but are nevertheless distinct compositional units.

---

1 That is, the transformation envisaged here is permanent, and a testimony to Yahweh's covenant faithfulness. Compare Gen. 9.8-17 where the same terminology is used of the rainbow.

In chs. 56–66, as the book draws to a close, one final development in the remnant concept takes place. In the previous two
units the exiles were viewed corporately as the remnant and
their return to Zion as the dawning of the new eschaton. But
with ch. 56 a distinction begins to be drawn within the restored
community between the righteous and the wicked, and a gap
opens up between the return and the eschaton.

This development begins from the very outset of ch. 56. In
56.1, where the imperatives are in the plural, the community[1]
is charged 'to keep justice and do righteousness', and the
eschaton is relegated to the future, albeit the near future:

> for *soon* my salvation shall come,[2]
> and my righteousness will be revealed.

The next verse, 56.2, personalizes the exhortation of v. 1 and
by implication draws a distinction between those who will
heed it and those who will not:

> Blessed is the man who does this...
> and keeps his hand from doing any evil.

This distinction is then made explicit in ch. 57 where 'the
righteous' (v. 1) stand in stark contrast to 'the wicked' (vv. 20-
21).[3] The righteous within the community are those who 'take
refuge in Yahweh' (57.13b) and 'those in Jacob who turn
away from transgression' (59.20). They call themselves
Yahweh's 'servants' (63.17) and are so owned by Yahweh
himself in 65.8-9. There then follows in 65.13-16 a series of
five antithesis in the form 'my servants... but you...' in which
Yahweh pronounces blessing on those who are his servants
and curses on those who are not. This litany of blessing and
curse leads significantly to an eschatological climax in 65.17-
25 where the new order comes to fruition in a new creation

---

1   That is, the *restored* community. The shift in perspective is not explicit at this
point but becomes so at v. 8: 'I will gather yet others to him *besides those already
gathered*' (my italics). The restored community is to be further augmented (by
further returnees and by proselytes), but the initial gathering or return is viewed
as past. Cf. C. Westermann, *Isaiah 40–66. A Commentary* (OTL; London: SCM,
1969), p. 315.
2   Literally 'for near (is) my salvation to come' with קרובה ('near') standing emphatically before the noun.
3   The contrast is developed progressively through the chapter (see vv. 1a, 3, 13b,
20a).

centred on a new Zion inhabited by those whom Yahweh owns
as 'my people' (v. 19). So in this closing unit of the book there is
a final sifting of the *restored* remnant to produce the
eschatological remnant, described distributively as Yahweh's
'servants' and collectively as his 'people' (עם singular), with
the climax of this process reached in 65.17-25.

But another, complementary process is also discernible in
chs. 56–66, namely, the opening of the community to outsiders
who are willing to acknowledge and submit to Yahweh's rule.
This process is not dwelt upon in such detail as the previous
one, but our attention is forcibly drawn to it at the outset and
again at the end of this final section of the book. In ch. 56
'foreigners' who join themselves to the Lord are numbered
among Yahweh's 'servants' (v. 6), eunuchs[1] who display
covenant loyalty are accorded an honoured place in the community (vv. 4-5, thus bringing to an end the ban of Deut. 23.1),
and the restored temple is declared to be a 'house of prayer for
all the peoples' (v. 7). In ch. 60 the converted nations make
their pilgrimage to Zion, there to 'proclaim the name of the
LORD' (v. 6) and to make reparation for past wrongs by serving their Jewish brethren (v. 10). Their sacrifices are accepted
on Yahweh's altar as a token that they themselves are
accepted (v. 7b). The climax of this process is reached in 66.18-
23 where representatives of 'all nations and tongues' (v. 18),
having been told of Yahweh's glory, come to Zion bringing the
last of the dispersed Israelites with them (v. 20), and Yahweh
is worshipped in Zion by 'all flesh' (v. 23). As in 65.17-25, the
arrival of the eschaton is announced in new creation language.

In this final unit, then, the remnant idea is both contracted
and expanded. This is reflected formally in the double climax
of 65.17-25 and 66.22-23. In the end the remnant is not
defined in national or ethnic terms, but in confessional and
behavioural terms. Being Israelite does not guarantee inclusion in the remnant, and being foreign does not entail exclusion from it. But the final verse of the book stands as a grim

---

1 The eunuchs in view here are almost certainly those referred to in 39.7, namely,
those who accepted this condition on entering official employment in exile (R.N.
Whybray, *Isaiah 40–66* [NCB; Grand Rapids: Eerdmans, 1981], p. 198).

reminder that while the remnant may be inclusive it is not universal. The remnant is a remnant still. It is not everyone. Salvation and judgment are both final realities and not merely temporal ones.[1]

Chapters 56–66, then, are set off from what precedes by the shift of perspective in ch. 56, and by the final development of the remnant idea which takes place in them. They are also marked off formally by the inclusion created by the occurrence of the significant expression 'my holy mountain' (= Jerusalem/Zion) at 56.7 and 66.20, in the opening and closing passages respectively. At the same time, these chapters are also closely integrated, both conceptually and formally, into what has gone before. The final climax to which this unit comes in 66.22-23, namely, perfected worship in the new Zion, is fully congruent with the climax towards which all the previous units have come. They all, with the exception of the central transitional unit, chs. 36–39, have climaxed in eschatological singing either in, or en route to, Zion. In this final unit the motif of singing appropriately gives way to the more inclusive idea of worship (66.23), but conceptually this climax matches perfectly all those which have preceded. In addition, the inclusive note which is struck here, with the expansion of the remnant to embrace foreigners, has been anticipated earlier (see e.g. 44.5). Furthermore, the distributive plural 'servants', which is so central to the final development of the remnant concepts in this unit, was first introduced in the previous unit at 54.17.[2] Finally, this unit rounds off, as we have seen, the 'vision of Isaiah' programmatically presented in 1.1–2.4, by picking up and repeating a number of its key motifs from there, particularly the pilgrimage of the nations to Zion (66.18-23; cf. 2.1-4) and the final putting down of rebellion (66.24; cf. 1.2, 5). The perfect worship with which the book ends is the final answer to the corrupt worship with which it began.[3]

---

1 Contrast the 'all flesh' of v. 23 with its negative counterpart in v. 16, and compare, finally, the 'all flesh' of v. 24.
2 The plural 'servants' has occurred previously in 14.2; 36.9, 11 and 37.5, 24, but this is its first use of Israelites in a theological sense.
3 Cf. Dumbrell, 'Purpose of Isaiah', p. 128.

To summarize, then, our study thus far has revealed that the book has a balanced, seven-part structure. A central pivot (chs. 36–39) is structured in such a way as to provide the transition from the first half of the book, which is dominated by the Assyrian crisis, to the second half, which is dominated by the Babylonian crisis. This central transition unit is preceded by three units (chs. 1–12, 13–27 and 28–35) each of which ends with the praises of Yahweh being sung in or en route to the new Zion. It is followed by three units (40.1–51.11; 51.12–55.13 and chs. 56–66) which end in the same way. Furthermore, our survey of the remnant concept and its development has also revealed the all-pervasive presence and central importance of this concept to the vision which the book encapsulates. The transformation of Zion is the key to the transformation of the cosmos, and the emergence and eventual perfection of a faithful remnant is the key to the transformation of Zion.

We are now in a position to take our inquiry one step further by asking how the remnant concept is related to other theological motifs such as the holy seed, the Immanuel child, the foundation stone, the messianic figure and the servant.

3. *The remnant concept and other theological motifs*

The process by which the eschatological remnant is finally produced is represented in the book by a variety of metaphors. One which we have already noted in passing is that of metal refining. The affliction through which the nation, and Jerusalem/Zion in particular, is made to pass is the intense heat of a furnace. The inhabitants of the old Zion are the gross ore, and the eschatological remnant that will inhabit the new Zion is the pure, refined metal. This metaphor is used in both the 'Assyrian' and 'Babylonian' sections of the book (see e.g. 1.24-26 and 48.10).

Birth is another metaphor used for this same process. The mother is Jerusalem/Zion, the afflictions she suffers as a result of Yahweh's historical judgments on her are her labour pains, and the faithful remnant which is formed through the process is the child or children to which she gives birth. A striking example, which comes near the climax of the book, is 66.7-9.

All the elements of the metaphor are present, but they are presented in riddle form:[1]

The riddle: (v. 7)	Before she was in labour
	        she gave birth
	before her pain came upon her
	        she was delivered of a son.

The answer: (v. 8b)	As soon as Zion was in labour she brought forth her sons.

In retrospect, the pains of labour will be insignificant. They are as nothing compared with the glorious outcome.[2] The 'sons' which Zion brings forth here are the 'servants' of v. 14, that is, the remnant in its final sense. The process is being viewed here retrospectively from the point of eschatological fulfilment.

The same metaphor is used in chs. 7 and 8 in the first half of the book with reference to an earlier stage in the process. Given the situation (Jerusalem beset by foes, 7.1) and the fact that Isaiah is pointedly told to take his son Shear-jashub ('a remnant shall return') as he goes to confront the faithless Ahaz (7.2), there can be little doubt that 7.14 refers metaphorically to the emergence of a faithful remnant.[3] The young woman who is about to give birth is Zion.[4] Her son, symbolically called Immanuel, is the small community of believers who gather around the prophet, his 'disciples' or 'children' (8.16-18).[5] They are the remnant in the immediate sense anticipated by the name Shear-jashub. They are ones who have 'returned' in repentance to the Lord. But they are also 'signs and portents in Israel from the LORD of hosts who dwells on Mount Zion' (8.18), and hence harbingers of the eschatological remnant. They are the earnest of the new Zion which is yet to be.

1 See E.C. Webster, 'A Rhetorical Study of Isaiah 66', *JSOT* 34 (1986), pp. 96-97, who notes that this riddle is similar in form to that of Samson in Jgs 14.14.
2 Cf. Paul's perspective on his own very real afflictions in 2 Cor. 4.17.
3 Cf. G. Rice, 'A Neglected Interpretation of the Immanuel Prophecy', *ZAW* 90 (1978), pp. 220-27.
4 Cf. 'the daughter of Zion', that is, 'the daughter (בת), Zion' in 1.8. The change to 'the young woman' (העלמה) in 7.14 is appropriate in view of the association in this context with conception and birth.
5 The context leaves little doubt that the 'children' of v. 18 are the 'disciples' of v. 16. Cf. Rice, 'A Neglected Interpretation', p. 222.

A third metaphor is the re-growth of a plant, especially a tree. The tree is Judah with its capital Jerusalem/Zion and its Davidic dynasty. The cutting down of the tree is the historical judgments visited upon the nation by Yahweh. The stump that remains in the ground is the remnant in the immediate sense. The new tree or forest that grows from the stump is the remnant in the final sense.

The programmatic significance of this metaphor is apparent from its occurrence in 6.13 at the end of the account of Isaiah's call in which both the immediate and long-term prospects for the nation are being canvassed. It occurs in the transitional pivot of the book, at 37.31-32, where remnant in an immediate sense is on view.[1] In the concluding unit of the book (chs. 56–66) it occurs at 61.3 with reference to the remnant in its final sense. In this passage, which is clearly eschatological,[2] the remnant who inhabit the new Zion are called 'the oaks (אילים) of righteousness, the planting of the LORD'. Here is the final regrowth from the felled oak (אלה) of 6.13.

Finally, it is likely that the precious corner stone, laid in Zion as a sure foundation in 28.16, is also a metaphor for the believing remnant associated with the prophet,[3] although this metaphor is not developed eschatologically as the others are.

Both the birth and re-growth metaphors have a secondary messianic application. After the promise of the Immanuel child in ch. 7 and its development in terms of the faithful remnant in ch. 8, a royal figure appears in ch. 9, introduced by the words, 'to us a child is born, to us a son is given' (v. 6). He is clearly an ideal, Davidic figure. Related passages, such as 11.1-9, use the re-growth metaphor for the emergence of this figure: 'There shall come forth a shoot from the stump of Jesse, and a branch shall grow out of his roots' (11.1). Interestingly, what finally emerges at the end of the book is not an eschatological Davidic ruler in a personal sense but an eschatological royal community. It is upon this community that the blessings

---

1   That is, survivors of the immediate crisis, but not necessarily repentant.
2   Note the 'everlasting joy' of v. 7b and the banishment of all sorrow in v. 3, as in 35.10 and 51.11.
3   I take it that the inscriptional sentence, 'he who believes . . .', is generic and gives the hallmark of the community represented by the stone. For the various alternatives that have been proposed see Oswalt, *Isaiah 1–39*, p. 578.

once promised to David are conferred (55.3), and it is this community which rules the nations and receives their tribute (66.12-14). In terms of the book's overall development, then, the royal figure of the messianic passages in chs. 1–35 is to be seen not in individual but in corporate terms as a metaphor for the eschatological remnant.[1]

A similar development is evident with respect to the suffering servant figure of chs. 40–55. The servant is the true Israel, elect from his mother's womb (49.1-3). He is also a young plant, and a shoot that comes up out of dry ground (53.2). This servant is finally glorified and divides the spoils as a conqueror (53.12). But what emerges at the end of the book is not a glorified individual servant figure, but a glorified servant community (66.13-19). So again, in terms of the overall development of the book, the servant figure of chs. 40–55 is to be seen in corporate terms as yet another metaphor for the remnant— elect, faithful, suffering and glorified.

I conclude therefore that the holy seed, the Immanuel child, the foundation stone, the messianic figure and the suffering servant figure are all metaphors for the faithful remnant.[2] It is the emergence of this remnant which is the key to Zion's transformation, and hence to the transformation of the cosmos.

---

1   The ultimate background for such a concept is Exod. 19.6 where Israel theologically is a royal nation.
2   Cf. A.E. Skemp, 'Immanuel and the Suffering Servant of Yahweh: A Suggestion', *ExpTim* 44 (1932/33), pp. 94-95. The identification of the messianic figure and the suffering servant figure helps to explain the royal elements in the so-called Servant Songs to which Westermann has drawn attention in his *Isaiah 40–66*.

LOT AS JEKYLL AND HYDE
A Reading of Genesis 18–19

Laurence A. Turner

Genesis 18–19 forms the longest sustained story in the Abraham cycle. While numerous analyses of parts of the story have been undertaken, my intention here is to read chs. 18–19 as one unit in order to ascertain the narrative's portrayal of Lot. While Lot appears only in the latter chapter, Abraham's actions in the former chapter provide the immediate context for reading the account of Lot's rescue from the destruction of Sodom. Two recent studies illustrate the lack of consensus concerning the presentation of Lot in ch. 19. In his short article, Desmond Alexander argues that Lot is consistently presented as righteous; nothing in ch. 19 detracts from this.[1] In direct opposition to such an assessment, S.P. Jeansonne sees in the Sodom story a damning indictment of Lot.[2] In this study I will attempt yet another analysis of his character.

Lot has been present in the Abraham story from the outset, and a review of how the story so far has presented who he is and what he does will help place the story of chs. 18–19 in its larger context.[3] There seems little doubt, to my mind, that at the time Abraham receives his divine call he considered Lot to

---

1 T. Desmond Alexander, 'Lot's Hospitality: A Clue to his Righteousness', *JBL* 104 (1985), pp. 289-91.
2 Sharon Pace Jeansonne, 'The Characterization of Lot in Genesis', *BTB* 18 (1988), pp. 123-29.
3 Space prohibits a full treatment of this here. I would refer the reader to my analysis elsewhere: L.A. Turner, *Announcements of Plot in Genesis* (Ph.D. thesis, University of Sheffield, 1988), pp. 42ff. Forthcoming from JSOT Press.

be his surrogate son[1] and the one through whom the promise of 12.2a would be fulfilled. This can be seen by the fact that his wife is barren (11.30). Yahweh has not yet promised her fertility (this does not happen until 17.15), and Abraham is not promised that he will be the literal biological father of a son until 15.4. In this light, it is important to note that on being told to leave behind his kindred and father's house (12.1), Abraham *takes Lot with him*. Lot is the son of Abraham's deceased brother Haran and as such belongs to Abraham's kindred. In taking Lot, therefore, Abraham has not left behind his kindred, and has not gone 'as the Lord has told him' (12.4a).[2] However, I would suggest that Abraham thought that he was being obedient to Yahweh's call, but that he did not consider Lot merely to be his 'kindred' or simply part of his 'father's house'. He must have thought Lot was someone far more important—none other than the one through whom the 'great nation' would come. There is no other reason why Abraham should take Lot.[3] Abraham was willing to leave his father in Haran,[4] but not Lot. His hopes are clearly invested in his nephew. Lot's importance to Abraham at that stage can be seen in Abraham's reaction to Yahweh's promise in 12.7, 'To your descendants ($l^ezar^ak\bar{a}$) I will give this land'. Knowing that the land of Canaan is to be his descendants' possession,

---

1 Cf. L.R. Helyer, 'The Separation of Abram and Lot: Its Significance in the Patriarchal Narratives', *JSOT* 26 (1983), p. 82.

2 G.W. Coats (*Genesis: With an Introduction to Narrative Literature* [Grand Rapids: Eerdmans, 1983], p. 108) fails to see the inherent contradiction in his statement, 'Abram executed the instructions [of 12.1-3] as received and took Lot along'. Cf. *idem*, 'The Curse in God's Blessing: Gen. 12,1-4a in the Structure and Theology of the Yahwist', in J. Jeremias and L. Perlitt (eds.), *Die Botschaft und die Boten* (Neukirchen-Vluyn: Neukirchener Verlag, 1981), p. 31.

3 The narrative does not support the view that Lot was a minor who needed his uncle's protection. No sooner has Lot returned with Abraham and Sarah from Egypt—a brief interlude in the story—than Abraham suggests that the two of them live separately (13.8), because the servants of *both of them* are in dispute. Lot is obviously of a mature age. Such an understanding would tend to be further supported by the note in 12.5, which strongly suggests that both Abraham *and Lot* had many possessions and slaves when they set out from Haran.

4 A comparison of the chronologies provided by 11.25, 32 and 12.4b shows that Terah lived for at least sixty years after his son left him in Haran. Cf. U. Cassuto, *A Commentary on the Book of Genesis* (trans. I. Abrahams; Jerusalem: Magnes Press, 1964), vol. 2, pp. 310, 317; G. von Rad, *Genesis: A Commentary* (rev. edn; trans. J.H. Marks; Philadelphia: Westminster Press, 1972), p. 158. Most assume, impossibly, that 11.32 is chronologically prior to 12.1.

Abraham offers part of that land to Lot (13.9)—which
suggests that, as far as Abraham is concerned, Lot is his
'descendant'.

Up to this point in the story Lot has been a passive character, merely accompanying his uncle on his travels. Lot exer-
cises some initiative for the first time when, in response to
Abraham's offer, he chooses the fertile Jordan valley for himself (13.8-10). The selfishness of Lot in choosing the more prosperous area is clear enough but in this narrative he is not necessarily being contrasted with Abraham.[1] While Abraham
shows some generosity in this incident, the immediately preceding story has shown that Abraham himself can act just as
selfishly. In Egypt, as a ploy to save his own skin, Abraham has
told the lie that Sarah is his sister[2] and has happily seen her
enter into an adulterous relationship with the Pharaoh
(12.12-15). Lot's choice of the best land for himself suggests
that he is learning from Abraham's example. (I am tempted to
say, 'Like *father*... like *son*'.) He is not perfect, but he does not
form a contrast to his uncle.

Despite the fact that they are now living separately, Lot
maintains his importance for Abraham. This is clearly
demonstrated in ch. 14 where Abraham risks his life on the
battlefield to rescue Lot (14.13ff.). When in Egypt Abraham
had not risked his life for Sarah; but he does here for Lot. His
nephew is obviously of more importance to him than his wife.

This is the background information concerning Lot that the
reader brings to the story of chs. 18–19. Many elements in
ch. 18 are echoed in ch. 19, and our understanding of the narrative's presentation of Lot in ch. 19 will be facilitated by noting the contents of the former chapter. Divine visitors appear
to Abraham while he sits by the door of his tent (18.1-2a). On
seeing them Abraham shows them great deference (18.2b-3)
and offers them lavish hospitality of rest (18.4) and food (18.5-

---

1 This is the usual line taken by commentators. Cf. J. Skinner, *Genesis* (ICC;
Edinburgh: T. and T. Clark, 1930), p. 253; von Rad, *Genesis*, p. 166.

2 Some take the position, on the basis of 20.12, that Abraham spoke the truth here—
Sarah being his half-sister. However, 11.29 informs us that Nahor married
within the family, his wife Milcah being his brother Haran's daughter. The same
verse tells us that Abraham married Sarah. Given what we are told regarding
Nahor's marriage, if Sarah, like Milcah, had also been a close relative, we would
surely have been told.

8). Yahweh then announces that the purpose for their visit is to inform the couple that Sarah is to have a son (18.10). This news is greeted with a private laugh of unbelief from Sarah (18.12), who is rebuked by Yahweh (18.13-15). The visitors depart and Abraham accompanies them 'to set them on their way' (18.16). The narrative allows the reader to be privy to Yahweh's intentions regarding Sodom and Gomorah (18.17-21), which leads to the crucial discussion between Abraham and Yahweh concerning the fate of the cities (18.22-33).

Any interpretation of the story of chs. 18–19 must come to grips with the significance of this human-divine dialogue. Scholars have arrived at no consensus over the function of these verses. While many suggestions have been made,[1] it should be obvious that in its present form this pericope functions as part of the larger episode of chs. 18–19, which itself forms part of the Abraham story as a whole. It goes without saying, therefore, that the dialogue between Abraham and Yahweh can only be understood in its present form and place, if the reader takes it not as *self-contained* philosophical discourse concerning theodicy[2] but as an integral part of the larger plot. When this is done some obvious questions arise. Why should Yahweh feel it necessary to divulge to Abraham on this particular occasion 'what he is about to do' (v. 17)? Most commentators suggest that Abraham's status as the one chosen by God 'raises Abraham to a level of importance and honor such that he is deemed worthy to share in God's plan'.[3] But such a view fails to explain why Yahweh does not take Abraham into his confidence every time he acts, nor does it give an adequate explanation for everything Yahweh says in

1   Cf. the various suggestions made by Coats, *Genesis*, p. 142; J.L. Crenshaw, 'Popular Questioning of the Justice of God in Ancient Israel', *ZAW* 82 (1970), p. 380; C.S. Rodd, '"Shall not the judge of all the earth do what is just?" (Gen 18.25)', *ExpTim* 83 (1972), p. 137; W. Brueggemann, 'A Shape for Old Testament Theology, II: Embrace of Pain', *CBQ* 47 (1985), pp. 409-10; *idem*, *Genesis: A Biblical Commentary for Teaching and Preaching* (Atlanta: John Knox, 1982), p. 167; J. Blenkinsopp, 'Abraham and the Righteous of Sodom', *JJS* 33 (1982), p. 129.

2   As is done for example, by G.F. Hasel, *The Remnant: The History and Theology of the Remnant Idea from Genesis to Isaiah* (Berrien Springs, Michigan: Andrews University Press, 1974), p. 148.

3   C. Westermann, *Genesis 12–36: A Commentary* (tr. J.J. Scullion; Minneapolis: Augsburg, 1985), p. 288. Cf. Driver, *Genesis*, pp. 194-95; von Rad, *Genesis*, pp. 209-10; E.A. Speiser, *Genesis* (AB; Garden City, NY: Doubleday, 1983), p. 135.

18.17-19, particularly in the initial part of Yahweh's musings, 'Shall I hide from Abraham what I am about to do, seeing that Abraham shall become a great and mighty nation... ?' I would suggest that Yahweh draws a connection between divulging his intentions concerning Sodom on one hand, with Abraham's destiny of becoming a great nation on the other, for a specific reason. If, as I have argued, Abraham is putting his (partial) trust in Lot as his descendant, then in Abraham's eyes there is a very specific and important connection between the possible destruction of Lot's dwelling place and Abraham's destiny as a great nation. It is from this perspective that Abraham stands before the Lord (18.22) and engages him in debate. The reader will recall the fact that the last time Abraham intervened on Sodom's behalf he was likewise motivated by a desire to rescue Lot: 'When Abraham heard that his kinsman had been taken captive, he led forth his trained men...' (14.14). We have just seen Ishmael dismissed by Yahweh as the son of promise, together with Abraham's protest at this decision (17.18, 19). Isaac has not yet been born. It is true that Lot has previously been eliminated from contention (with Yahweh's promise of a biological son in 15.4), but if he should die in the destruction of Sodom it would leave Abraham feeling exposed. Before the birth of Isaac—should he ever be born—Abraham has two 'half-chances' for a descendant in Ishmael and in Lot, and he wishes to preserve them at all costs. This explains why he willingly circumcises Ishmael (17.25-26) and pleads for Sodom. I would suggest that Abraham's plea to save the whole city on ethical grounds is motivated largely by a desire to save his nephew and potential heir.[1]

It should be carefully noted that Abraham does not ple₍ 1 for the salvation of a righteous remnant from the destruction of Sodom,[2] because, like the reader, he has entertained some misgivings about Lot since being worsted by him in the real estate transaction of ch. 13. In addition, Abraham has met the Sodomites first-hand (ch. 14), which has surely made him aware of the information divulged to the reader in 13.13,

---

1 One of the few to see this is J. Baldwin, *Genesis 12–50*, pp. 73, 77.
2 While the tone of Abraham's speech suggests that 'the destruction is just only if it strikes the malefactors alone' (Westermann, *Genesis 12–36*, p. 291), this result is *not* what Abraham pleads for. Cf. von Rad, *Genesis*, p. 213.

'Now the men of Sodom were wicked, great sinners against the Lord'. Knowing this, he may well wonder what corrupting effect they have had on Lot. As a result, Abraham pleads for the salvation of the *whole city*, on the basis of the vicarious righteousness of a minority of ten. In his pleading, Abraham divides the inhabitants of Sodom into two mutually exclusive groups: the righteous (*ṣaddîq*) and the wicked (*rāšā'*). Abraham's plea for the vicarious salvation of the whole city means that regardless of whether Lot is deemed to be righteous or wicked, he will be saved along with the rest of the city, *if* there are ten righteous Sodomites.[1]

The scene now moves to Sodom. Chapter 19 opens with strong echoes of the introductory verses of ch. 18, which invites the reader to make comparisons between the two. There, Abraham had been sitting at the opening of his tent in the heat of the day when three visitors approached, to whom he offered hospitality (18.1ff.). Here, Lot is sitting at the gate of Sodom at evening time when two visitors approach to whom he offers hospitality (19.1ff.). It is commonplace for commentators to remark on the way in which the narrative of ch. 18 emphasizes Abraham's service to the strangers. He 'ran' (*wayyāroṣ*), 'bowed' (*wayyištaḥû*) to the earth (18.2), 'hastened' (*wayᵉmahēr*, 18.6), etc. The contrast between the understatement of his speech, 'a little water... a morsel of bread' (18.4-5), and the lavishness of the feast he prepares which includes 'cakes' (*'ugôt*), curds, milk and meat (18.6-8), also serves to underline that Abraham is the ideal host.[2] Abraham's hospitality, like Job's, is an expression of his righteousness (Job 31.31-32; cf. Ps. 37.21, 25-26; Prov. 21.26).

There is a tendency on the part of some scholars to see Lot's treatment of his angelic guests as forming a contrast to that of his uncle's. Speiser considers that Lot's demeanour before his guests is not only servile compared with the 'simple dignity' of

1   G.W. Coats ('Lot: A Foil in the Abraham Saga', in J.T. Butler, *et al.* (eds.), *Understanding the Word: Essays in Honor of Bernhard Anderson* [JSOTSup, 37; Sheffield: JSOT Press, 1985], pp. 120, 130 n. 20) believes that the discussion between Abraham and Yahweh *in itself* demonstrates that there were not even ten righteous in Sodom, and thus the city was doomed to destruction from the start. This understanding is totally unjustified regardless of whether one reads the dialogue as it occurs in the story so far or if one reads with hindsight.

2   Cf., e.g., Speiser, *Genesis*, p. 129; Westermann, *Genesis 12–36*, pp. 276-79.

Abraham (which is based on the statement in 19.1 that Lot bowed down 'with his face to the ground'), but also lacks the spontaneity of the former. Lot offers a simple everyday meal of 'flat cakes' (*maṣṣôt*, 19.3), in contrast to the gourmet fare of 'semolina biscuits' ('cakes') in 18.6.[1] More recently Jeansonne has made a more detailed attack on Lot. She argues that whereas Abraham 'ran' to meet his guests, Lot merely 'rose' (18.2; cf. 19.1). Abraham *requests* his visitors to accept his hospitality but Lot's speech lacks the former's humility (18.3; cf. 19.2). Abraham's *direct address* to the visitors offers them both rest and food, but Lot's *words* mention rest alone (18.4-5; cf. 19.2). Like Speiser, she too sees a contrast between Abraham's elaborate meal and Lot's simple unleavened bread, a contrast which she believes is underlined by the narrative's comparatively detailed description of Abraham's feast and the hasty outline of Lot's meal. Finally, she argues, the response of the visitors to their host's initial invitations forms a contrast: with Abraham, they agree immediately to his suggestion, but initially they refuse Lot's offer (18.5; cf. 19.2).[2] In addition, some have seen in Lot's addressing his visitors as 'my lords' (*ᵃdōnay*) a contrast to Abraham's words, where the MT has 'my Lord' (*ᵃdōnāy*).[3] Such arguments lead to the conclusion that Lot in 19.1-3 is depicted as a contrast to righteous, hospitable Abraham.

It can readily be seen that most of these points are rather forced attempts to condemn Lot. Some of the 'contrasts' brought forward are in my opinion nothing more than the kind of slight differences one would expect in a sophisticated narrative that wanted to portray similarity without recourse to verbatim repetition. Other points require more detailed consideration. One should note that the two angels arrive in Sodom in the evening (*bā'ereb*, 19.1). There is therefore little time for the preparation of a sumptuous repast, in contrast to Abraham's situation where the visitors arrived much earlier, during the heat of the day (*kᵉḥōm hayyôm*, 18.1). Secondly, the text does not indicate that the angels received only unleav-

---

1 Speiser, *Genesis*, pp. 138-39, 143.
2 Jeansonne, 'Characterization of Lot', p. 126.
3 E.g. W. Vogels, 'Lot, père des incroyants', *ÉglTh* 6 (1975), p. 146.

ened bread from Lot: 'he made them a feast *and* baked unleavened bread' (*wayya'aś lāhem mišteh ûmaṣṣôt*, 19.2); bread was only part of the meal. The term 'feast' (*mišteh*) is used in other contexts to indicate a substantial meal[1] (e.g. Est. 5.6; Dan. 1.5; Jer. 16.8; Job 1.5, etc.), and it will shortly be used to describe the meal at the celebration of the weaning of Isaac (21.8), which was surely not a simple affair of unleavened bread.

To argue from the different responses of the visitors to the initial invitations of Abraham and Lot that a contrast is being made between these human characters, is to fail to see the two passages in their narrative contexts. The visitors went to Abraham's tent for the express purpose of announcing to him and his wife that Sarah would soon have a son. Acceptance of Abraham's hospitality in itself, *in this context*, cannot be taken as a positive (or negative) assessment of Abraham. When the two visitors continue to Sodom, they do not go with the express purpose of finding Lot. They go to discover just how wicked the city is and whether the outcry which has come to Yahweh is justified or not (18.20-21). Prior to the angelic visit to Sodom, Yahweh does not know how wicked the city is and has not decided whether he will destroy it or not.[2] Yahweh's statement in 18.17, contrary to the assumption of most scholars, does not say that Yahweh has already decided to destroy the city.[3]

---

1 F. Brown *et al.*, *A Hebrew and English Lexicon of the Old Testament* (Oxford: Clarendon Press, 1907), p. 1059; L. Koehler and W. Baumgartner, *Lexicon in Veteris Testamenti Libros* (Leiden: Brill, 1958), p. 581. Cf. S.R. Driver, *The Book of Genesis* (10th edn; London: Methuen, 1916), p. 198.

2 This is in keeping with the narrative's general presentation of the divine visitors who display both 'divine' knowledge and 'human' ignorance. For example, they know the name of Abraham's wife without having been introduced, but they do not know where she is (18.9). They know Sarah's *thoughts* (18.13, 15), but do not know whether the Sodomites' actions are truly wicked or not (18.21). When the angels go to Sodom, they have the ability to strike the mob with supernatural blindness (19.11), yet do not know the exact size of Lot's extended family (19.12).

3 E.g. Driver, *Genesis*, p. 194; Skinner, *Genesis*, p. 303; von Rad, *Genesis*, p. 210; Westermann, *Genesis 12–36*, pp. 285, 288. I can find no justification at all for Westermann's contention that 'Abraham, for all his questioning, is aware from the start that God will go through with his decision to punish Sodom' (p. 291). Cf. Gibson, *Genesis*, 2:81; Blenkinsopp, 'Righteous of Sodom', pp. 129-30. Klein ('Que se passe-t-il', pp. 82, 92) notes correctly that the text so far has not stated that Yahweh will destroy Sodom. Blenkinsopp ('Righteous of Sodom', p. 120) notes the

What Yahweh is 'about to do' (v. 17) is to investigate the
degree of Sodom's sinfulness (vv. 20-21). Abraham *assumes*
that the purpose of such an investigation is to decide to destroy,
and his dialogue with Yahweh in 18.22-23 shows his assumption to be correct. This precise motivation for the angel's visit
to Sodom makes possible a plausible reason for their initial
refusal of Lot's hospitality. It may be seen as a test, designed to
judge whether his offer is purely perfunctory or genuine. Lot's
insistence on opening his home to them shows him to be a true
host, no less than Abraham.

Furthermore, Lot's addressing his visitors as 'my lords'
rather than using Abraham's 'Lord' is hardly sufficient reason for questioning Lot's righteousness. Even putting aside the
difficulties in reading the MT of 18.3,[1] it is quite obvious that
Yahweh does not go in person to Sodom. Of the three visitors
who came to Abraham only two 'angels' (*mal'ākîm*) proceed
to the city (19.1), while Yahweh remains in conversation with
Abraham (18.22). Therefore, Lot *could not* have addressed his
visitors as Abraham had his. This is a point confirmed by the
angels' reference to Yahweh as having *sent* them (19.13).

I would suggest, therefore, that on the matter of hospitality,
Lot is being compared favourably rather than contrasted with
Abraham.[2] (The contrast with Abraham's hospitality is provided later by the Sodomites, not by Lot.[3]) Since giving hospitality to strangers is a feature of righteousness, then Lot has
demonstrated that, *on this particular point*, there is at least
one righteous person in Sodom. As Alexander says,

> By caring for the needs of others he resembles Abraham,
> and since Abraham is commended for his generosity Lot is

usual understanding of 18.17, but suggests that the verse 'could just as easily
[refer to]. . . the destiny of Abraham's descendants'.

1 For discussion see Driver, *Genesis*, p. 192; Skinner, *Genesis*, pp. 299-300; Speiser,
   Genesis, p. 129; von Rad, *Genesis*, p. 206; Westermann, *Genesis 12–36*, p. 278.

2 The contention that Lot's invitation to his guests lacks humility is hardly tenable.
   He addresses them as 'my lords' (cf. Abraham's 'my Lord'); entreats them, 'I
   pray you' (cf. Abraham's 'if I have found favour') and invites the pair to 'your
   servant's house' (cf. Abraham's 'your servant'). He compares *favourably* with
   Abraham. Even Jeansonne ('Characterization of Lot') concedes that although Lot
   offers the angels rest only, he *provides* food as well (and thus hardly contrasts
   with Abraham's offering of both).

3 Cf. Blenkinsopp, 'Righteous of Sodom', p. 119.

therefore also to be viewed in a favourable light. Lot's hospitality is a mark of his righteousness.[1]

No sooner has Lot served his evening meal than the visitors discover the rest of the Sodomites are not so kindly disposed to strangers. The piling up of descriptive epithets in 19.4 emphasizes that the *entire city* surrounded Lot's house, '...the men of the city, the men of Sodom, both young and old, all the people to the last man...' In this one act the visitors discover the extent of the city's sin; there are not even ten righteous to be found. Lot, as the righteous host, comes to the aid of his guests. His action in leaving his house to speak to the townspeople not only reinforces the reader's positive assessment of him gained from 19.1-3, but also contrasts him explicitly to the crazed mob: 'I beg you, my brothers, do not act so wickedly' (*tārĕʿû*, 19.7). The *righteous* host condemns the *wickedness* of the entire city. In the episode so far, Lot has acted consistently as a truly righteous man and stands alone in marked contrast to the rest of wicked Sodom.

However, from now on the reader must make significant modifications to this initial assessment of Lot. Lot's offer to the mob, giving them licence to do to his daughters whatever they please (19.8), has been interpreted in several different ways. Some have defended his action, claiming that as host Lot had to protect his guests and that his offer is 'recorded to his credit',[2] or that 'Lot's predicament calls for a sympathetic understanding',[3] and in no way diminishes his righteousness. Others have felt some difficulty in giving such an optimistic assessment, but have not gone as far as outright condemnation. They suggest that Lot was 'less than heroic'[4] or indulged in 'a compromise'.[5] But are such benign judgments really possible? We must not allow Lot's initial gentlemanly behaviour to blind us to the real horror he proposes for his daughters. To have offered *himself* to be homosexually abused in place of his guests would have maintained his high standing in the reader's eyes. But, rather than self-sacrifice, he chooses to

1   Alexander, 'Lot's Hospitality', p. 290.
2   Skinner, *Genesis*, p. 307.
3   Alexander, 'Lot's Hospitality', p. 291.
4   Coats, 'Lot: A Foil', p. 121.
5   Von Rad, *Genesis*, p. 218.

offer his *virgin daughters*. (We see here Lot's penchant for
self-interest, previously displayed in 13.10-13.) To my mind
there is no room for quibble. Lot's offer of his daughters is an
act of wickedness, and I would agree with the small minority
of scholars who have been willing to judge him in this way.[1]
We have just seen the analogy between Abraham's and Lot's
acts of hospitality, but the careful reader is reminded also of
how Lot's offer here compares with Abraham's charade in
Egypt (12.10-20). Abraham, feeling himself to be in a life and
death situation, had been willing to surrender Sarah to the
Pharaoh's bed. By no stretch of the imagination can this be
said to be recorded to Abraham's credit. We must pass the
same judgment on Lot, who in a desperate situation was likewise willing to offer members of his own family to satisfy the
lusts of strangers.

The increasingly complex nature of Lot's character is confirmed in the next development, where the angels, after being
convinced of the depravity of the whole city (19.13), tell Lot to
give the news of the city's destruction to his relatives so that
they too might be saved. At first sight Lot seems to stand in
contrast to his debauched sons-in-law,[2] who in response to
Lot's words, 'Up, get out of this place; for the Lord is about to
destroy the city' (19.14), think that their father-in-law is joking. However, it could well be that they so judge him because
they fail to hear the ring of conviction in Lot's voice; for in the
morning Lot shows that he himself does not take the angels'
word seriously. He 'lingers' (*wayyitmahmāh*, 19.16) in
Sodom, even while the warning of imminent destruction is on
the angels' lips. He feels comfortably at home and, like his
sons-in-law, cannot be persuaded to leave. He has to be
dragged outside the city. His lingering hardens into outright
disagreement with his saviours over his place of sanctuary.
On being told to flee to the hills, he replies 'Oh, no, my lords'
(19.18). His pleading for Zoar shows his extraordinary attraction to the cities of the Jordan valley. Finally, the sordid episode

1   E.g. Jeansonne, 'Characterization of Lot', p. 126.
2   The stress in 19.4 that *every* man in Sodom was in the mob outside Lot's house
    would seem to indicate that his sons-in-law were among their number. The text of
    19.14 simply says that Lot 'went out' (*wayyēṣē*) to speak to them—possibly just
    outside his door.

with his daughters in the cave (19.30-38) shows that those who were saved from the overthrow of the city have sunk to the level of those who were exterminated.

As we look back on this chapter it can be seen that the characterization of Lot goes through several stages of development. At first he is presented as being righteous—he is the ideal host. This assessment has to be modified when we see him attempting to protect his guests (admirable in itself) by offering his daughters. The reader's assessment of Lot becomes increasingly critical as we witness him procrastinating in his exit, naming his own refuge just a short distance away, and finally being seduced into an incestuous union with the same daughters he had previously though to be expendable. (The reader can hardly fail to see in this last incident an ironic comment on Lot's previous attempt to sacrifice his daughters. Lot receives due recompense for his previous actions.) The deterioration of Lot is highlighted by the contrast between the narrative's introduction where Lot offers hospitality to *two angels* and its conclusion where he is plied with wine by his *two daughters*.[1]

As the reader reviews the account of Sodom's destruction, certain basic similarities with the Flood narrative (chs. 6–9) come to mind. Both narratives describe the destruction of a wicked human community (although ch. 19 is not so broad in scope), and in each a remnant is saved. Each narrative mentions a specific sin anticipating the judgment (6.1-4; cf. 19.5-11). This is followed by a general statement regarding the wickedness of the doomed community (6.5-8; cf. 19.13). Next, provisions for the salvation of a remnant are outlined (6.11ff.; cf. 19.15-23), and finally the destruction comes (7.6ff.; cf. 19.24-28).

The close similarities between the stories of the Flood and of Sodom justify a more detailed comparison between their central characters, Noah and Lot, even though a complete comparison between them is not possible, since Noah is for the most part only a 'type', while Lot becomes a fully-fledged

---

1 Cf. D.A. Aycock, 'The Fate of Lot's Wife: Structural Mediation in Biblical Mythology', in E. Leach and D.A. Aycock, *Structuralist Interpretations of Biblical Myth* (Cambridge: Cambridge University Press, 1983), p. 114.

'character'.[1] From the start Noah is presented in a positive light. He finds favour in God's eyes (6.8); he is deemed to be righteous (6.9b); he walks with God (6.9b). Gen. 6.8-12 contrasts Noah with the corruption of his world. In the Flood narrative as a whole, with the possible exception of 9.20-27, Noah is the ideal righteous man. Despite the restricted characterization of him, we see that when Noah takes the initiative, it is the right choice (e.g. 8.20-22). Out of all the characters mentioned, Noah is the one who takes the lead; others accompany him (e.g. 7.7-9, 13, 15, 23b; 8.1a, 18).

Alternatively, in the Abraham cycle, Lot is either the passive, used individual, or else when he does take the initiative, he invariably makes the wrong choice. At the beginning of the cycle other people *take* Lot, or he merely *accompanies* them (11.31; 12.4, 5; 13.1, 5); the kings *take* Lot (14.12), while Abraham *brings* him back (14.16). In Sodom the angels *drag* him indoors (19.10); his procrastination results in his *being taken* again by the angels (19.16). Finally, it is appropriate that passive Lot should last appear in the narrative in an act of utter passivity: 'he did not know when she lay down or when she arose' (19.33, 35). With the one exception of his offer of hospitality, in the only significant occasion where Lot takes the initiative, he makes the wrong choice; in ch. 13 he decides to move toward wicked Sodom, and when there offers his virgin daughters to the mob.

Throughout the Flood narrative Noah is entirely silent. He acts, reacts, obeys, but does not speak until it is over—immediately before his obituary notice. In contrast, Lot is almost verbose in his speech to the angels, the townspeople and his sons-in-law. Yet in the final episode of the sexual sin of 19.30-38 he becomes silent. Our last image of Lot is that of him in a drunken stupor in a cave. The contrast between Lot's speech and Noah's silence is suggestive. Even the silent Noah is compelled to speak up at the outrage of his son's (sexual?) offence (9.20f.), his first words in the whole narrative marking the heinous nature of the deed. Lot's silence in 19.30-38, in contrast to his previous speech and protests, is witness to the way

---

1   See A. Berlin, *Poetics and Interpretation of Biblical Narrative* (Sheffield: Almond Press, 1983), pp. 23-32, for a discussion of these terms.

in which he has fallen from his status at the beginning of the
story, where he resolutely objected to the wickedness of the
homosexuals' attempted gang rape. By the end of the story, he
not only raises no moral objections to incest,[1] but is totally
unaware of what has happened. His ignorance does not
absolve him of blame,[2] but again suggests a contrast to Noah.
On awaking, Noah *knows* what has taken place; as far as we
know Lot never does.

Even those people associated with Lot and Noah display
similar contrasts. Noah's wife, sons and daughters-in-law all
obey him unquestioningly, as witnessed in the repeated 'his
sons and his wife and his son's wives with him' (e.g. 6.18; 7.7;
8.18; see also 7.13). On the other hand Lot's family are his
worthy accomplices. His sons-in-law (with some justification)
think he is joking (19.14); his wife looks back and is turned
into salt (19.26); his daughters' incestuous seduction (19.30-
38) suggests that they too had imbibed Sodomite morality. At
almost every step of the way the reader can see in Lot an
inversion of Noah. In contrast to Noah's obedience, 'Noah did
this; he did all that God commanded him' (6.22; cf. 7.5), we
read of Lot's procrastination: 'They said, "Flee..." And Lot
said to them, "Oh, no, my lords"' (19.17-18). In the light of
Noah's behaviour it is understandable why he 'found favour
(*ḥēn*) in the eyes of the Lord' (6.8). Lot's behaviour, apart from
his act of hospitality and protection of his guests, recommends
him to no one, and the reader is tempted to hear a tone of
incredulity in Lot's voice when he says to the heavenly

---

1 Some scholars see no stigma attached to this incident, maintaining that the
   actions of Lot's daughters are laudable: e.g. Speiser, *Genesis*, p. 145; Brueggemann, *Genesis*, p. 176. Westermann (*Genesis 12-36*, p. 314) believes that if the
   reader attaches the label 'incest' to the incident, then one cannot understand what
   the story is trying to say. However, since ch. 19 is concerned with distinctions
   between wickedness and righteousness, salvation and judgment, the reader is
   surely being invited to make some judgment about the incident.
2 As argued by J.R. Porter, 'The Daughters of Lot', *Folklore* 89 (1978), p. 128. Cf.
   Coats, *Genesis*, p. 147: 'To be seduced by one's own daughters into an incestuous
   relationship with pregnancy following is bad enough. Not to know that the seduction had occurred is even worse. To fall prey to the whole plot a second time is
   worse than ever.'

visitors, 'your servant has found favour (*ḥēn*) in your sight' (19.19).[1]

One additional comparison crystallizes the chapter's presentation of Lot. At the structural centre of chs. 6–9 we read the salvific statement, 'God remembered (*wayyizkōr*) Noah' (8.1). By comparison, God's act at Sodom is summarized in 19.29: 'God remembered (*wayyizkōr*) *Abraham* and sent Lot out of the midst of the overthrow'. The contrast could hardly be greater. Noah preserves humanity and his family because of his righteousness. Poor Lot cannot even save himself. He has to be dragged out of the city by the angels, and is saved through his association with Abraham. He is certainly not saved because of his righteousness.[2]

When the reader assesses the presentation of Lot in ch. 19, informed as it is by analogies drawn from chs. 18 and 6–9, it emerges that Lot is a complex character. In comparison with Noah, the focal hero of the flood in chs. 6–9, Lot is not being depicted as the consistently righteous man saved from the destruction of a sinful community. Reading ch. 19 in the light of ch. 18 shows in more detail exactly how he is being depicted. The reader's assessment of Lot becomes increasingly critical as the narrative moves from its introductory scene of Lot's hospitality in his home to its conclusion of incest in the cave. Between these two points we witness Lot's insensitivity to his daughters and his lack of desire to obey Yahweh's messengers. Is Lot righteous? At the beginning of the story (in his offer of hospitality), yes, he is. Is Lot wicked? At certain points in the story (e.g. in his offer of his daughters), yes, he is. Taking ch. 19 as a whole, Lot emerges as being neither entirely righteous nor entirely wicked. He exhibits both qualities—he is a Jekyll and Hyde character.

This view of the characterization of Lot has implications for reading, this time from hindsight, the crucial dialogue

---

1 While *ḥēn* is not uncommon in the OT, being used more than fifty times, and is found on Abraham's lips in the preceding chapter (18.3), its ironic intention in this account seems guaranteed by the many close affinities between chs. 19 and 6–9.

2 Contra Crenshaw, 'Popular Questioning', p. 385; Coats, *Genesis*, p. 143 (though he notes that Lot's 'righteousness differs from that of Noah or Abraham' [p. 144], and remains somewhat equivocal on the whole issue of Lot's righteousness [see especially p. 145]); Brueggemann, *Genesis*, pp. 166, 170; Speiser, *Genesis*, p. 135.

between Abraham and Yahweh (18.22-33). Two major observations must be made. First, when Abraham starts to plead
with Yahweh he asks, 'Wilt thou indeed destroy the *righteous*
(*ṣaddîq*) with the *wicked* (*rāšāʿ*)?' (18.23), and these two terms
are juxtaposed explicitly in v. 25 and implicitly in the rest of
the dialogue, in which Abraham succeeds in getting Yahweh
to agree to a remnant of ten righteous being sufficient to save
the whole city. Abraham assumes that each inhabitant of
Sodom belongs to one of two mutually exclusive groups. However, the way in which Lot is presented in ch. 19 shows that
the moral world is more complicated than Abraham assumes.
While no Sodomites were righteous, and almost all were irre-
deemably wicked, one character, Lot, will not fit entirely into
either category. W. Brueggemann has recently suggested, on
traditio-historical grounds, that 18.22-33 forms a theological
critique of the conventional retributive theology reflected in
ch. 19.[1] However, the final form of reading I have presented
here sees the relationship as the reverse of this. Chapter 19
may be seen as a critique of the 'conventional theology' reflected in 18.22-33, that all people belong to one of two classifications—righteous or wicked.

The second point that must be made concerns the relationship between the agreement struck between Yahweh and
Abraham in ch. 18 and the subsequent turn of events in ch. 19.
Yahweh had agreed to spare the entire city if ten righteous
could be found. The investigation carried out by the angels
revealed that not even this minimal righteous remnant was
present. In keeping with the previous conditions, Yahweh
destroyed the city. He did, however, rescue Lot and his daughters. This was not in agreement with the conditions set out in
Abraham's debate with Yahweh, according to which Lot and
his family should have perished in the flames. This should
have been their fate *even if* one judges them to have been
righteous, for Abraham did not plead for the rescue of the
righteous, but for the rescue of the entire city (including Lot),
if ten righteous could be found. Genesis 19.29 suggests quite
strongly that Yahweh was not hoodwinked by Abraham's
pious posturing and gave Abraham what he really wanted—

---

1 Brueggemann, *Genesis*, pp. 167ff. (cf. *idem*, 'Embrace of Pain', pp. 409ff.).

Lot—when he consigned Sodom to the flames: 'So it was that, when God destroyed the cities of the valley, *God remembered Abraham*, and sent Lot out of the midst of the overthrow'. One wonders whether Abraham would have pled for the salvation of Sodom at all if he had known that this would be the result.

In reviewing the characterization of Lot in Gen. 18–19, I conclude that he is presented as a complex character. Just as in the Abraham cycle as a whole Abraham acts in seemingly contradictory ways, Lot himself does not fit neatly into one category. He is not presented as occupying a compromised position, straddled between wickedness and righteousness, but as exhibiting both traits, even though there is a definite movement from the positive to the negative end of the spectrum as ch. 19 moves towards its conclusion. I believe that most previous analyses of Lot have committed the error of assuming that the narrative presents a monochrome picture of Lot's character, with Lot acting consistently as either righteous of unrighteous. While such a view of a human character is the assumption underlying Abraham's discussion with Yahweh, the depiction of Lot in ch. 19 reveals how wrong Abraham was.

Looking at the story with hindsight we can see, perhaps, that it carries an implicit warning about the dangers of engaging Yahweh in debate, and that Yahweh's granting a human his or her wishes can be a mixed blessing. As a result of Abraham's pleading, Lot is rescued (cf. 19.29). However, we are left wondering whether this was a better fate than that which would otherwise have overtaken him. To have perished in the flames of judgment which visited his wicked neighbours, or to have died an heroic death defending his guests from their hands, is arguably preferable to losing one's dignity and moral sense as one is dragged reluctantly to some refuge. Further, the rescue of Lot is also hardly unmitigated good news for Abraham. His rescued nephew is seduced into incestuous unions which produce the progenitors of two nations, the Moabites and Ammonites, who will subsequently harass Abraham's descendants. Human beings may certainly question and accuse Yahweh, and cause him to alter his course of action. But there is a price to pay.

MATTHEW—A STORY FOR TEACHERS?*

Andrew T. Lincoln

Introduction

From a primarily redaction-critical perspective G.N. Stanton could write, 'Matthew is undoubtedly the supreme literary artist among the evangelists'.[1] It is curious, therefore, that when one looks at literary approaches to the Gospels and Acts, one might well be forgiven for forming the impression that the work that has so far been done on Matthew is not on the whole as exciting, convincing or fruitful as that done on other narratives, and that perhaps Matthew's story has proved to be the least fertile soil for a narrative analysis.

If both Stanton's judgment and this impression about current literary analyses are basically correct, there are three possible explanations. First, some might be inclined to a negative conclusion about narrative criticism of the gospels. If it is unable to do justice to the literary quality of *this* gospel, then perhaps the whole approach is of limited value.

Secondly, it could be that Matthew's literary artistry is not *narrative* artistry. It might lie rather in skilful working with and elaboration on sources and traditions and in a clever arrangement of these for the writer's own purposes.[2] It might

---

* This venture into a Gospel on which David Hill has done so much invaluable work is dedicated to him in appreciation of his friendship and help while he was my senior New Testament colleague in Sheffield.

1 'The Origin and Purpose of Matthew's Gospel: Matthean Scholarship from 1945 to 1980', *ANRW* II.25.3 (1984), p. 1906.

2 Note the title of R.H. Gundry's redaction-critical commentary—*Matthew: A Commentary on His Literary and Theological Art* (Grand Rapids: Eerdmans, 1982).

be the case that, for all this, the end product simply lacks sufficiently attractive features as a story. It does not have, for
example, the narrative style, the extensive thematic unity and
literary patterning of Luke–Acts, the ironies of the Fourth
Gospel or the vivid yet enigmatic qualities of Mark. In comparison with Mark especially, it fills in the gaps in Mark's
story-line about Jesus that involve the reader, providing
answers to many of the questions raised for the reader by
Mark's narrative. This greater completeness, together with a
pruning down of episodes to their essentials, makes for less
engagement of the reader's imagination and less involvement
by the reader in Matthew's story of Jesus.[1] Problems are
caused also by the five major sections of teaching material
which break the flow of the narrative and slow down the
action. One of the stumbling-blocks in narrative analysis of
Matthew has been a lack of consensus about how to account
for these. How do they fit the development of the plot? Do they
have an integral role in the narrative?[2]

Thirdly, it could be that our initial impression about a literary approach to Matthew involves a premature judgment. It
is still relatively early days in narrative criticism of the
gospels, and perhaps the type of scholarship that has been at
the forefront of the attempt to popularize this approach to
Matthew has had its own particular problems. Sometimes it
appears to have been too dependent on the work previously
done on Mark, where the literary approach first began to
thrive, and to have proved to be not only derivative but also
second-best in comparison. The best known exponent of the
narrative approach to Matthew is J.D. Kingsbury whose early
literary analyses,[3] despite their merits, fall into this category.
In addition, they are marred by being too concerned with

---

1 Cf. also R.T. France, *Matthew* (Leicester: IVP, 1985), p. 22, who, while noting the
   careful construction of the gospel, concedes that 'the effect is that Matthew is less
   immediately attractive as a story-teller'.
2 For a survey of the debate, see D.R. Bauer, *The Structure of Matthew's Gospel*
   (Sheffield: Almond Press, 1988), pp. 21-55, and for his own discussion, see pp. 129-
   34; cf. also W. Wilckens, 'Die Komposition des Matthäus-Evangeliums', *NTS* 31
   (1985), pp. 24-38, who places the discourses at the heart of five of his six main divisions in the gospel.
3 'The Figure of Jesus in Matthew's Story: A Literary-Critical Probe', *JSNT* 21
   (1984), pp. 3-36; *Matthew as Story* (Philadelphia: Fortress, 1986).

christological titles and with establishing positions arrived at
by other methods, primarily redaction-critical; by attempting
to privilege God's point of view within the narrative as if it
were distinct from the narrator's or Jesus' point of view; by
neglecting the discourses; and by being too schematic and not
paying enough attention to the flow of the story and the gaps
in the narration.[1] It may well be, therefore, that further work
will be able to reveal qualities of Matthew's gospel as a narrative that have not yet received sufficient attention. This essay
is offered as a contribution to that further work.

I wish to suggest in outline form that, before we relegate
Matthew to fourth place in the literary stakes, it is possible
that solutions to some of the above problems may be forthcoming and greater justice to the potential impact of Matthew's
story may be done, if, instead of concentrating immediately
and so much on the role of the central character, Jesus, more
attention is paid first of all to the role of the disciples in the narrative. Through focusing on the disciples, attention can also be
paid to the implied readers.[2] Although they are expected to
share the point of view of Jesus, the implied readers' situation
is most similar to that of the disciples, not to that of Jesus.
Therefore, their identification with characters in the story is
more with the disciples, whose portrayal includes develop-

1 Cf. the debate with D. Hill, 'The Figure of Jesus in Matthew's Story: A Response to
   Professor Kingsbury's Literary-Critical Probe', *JSNT* 21 (1984), pp. 37-52, and
   Kingsbury's further contribution, 'The Figure of Jesus in Matthew's Story: A
   Rejoinder to David Hill', *JSNT* 25 (1985), pp. 61-81; cf. also R.A. Edwards' review
   of *Matthew as Story* in *CBQ* 49 (1987), pp. 505-506. Other analyses have had their
   problems. For example, F.J. Matera, 'The Plot of Matthew's Gospel', *CBQ* 49
   (1987), pp. 233-53, takes a fresh look at Matthew's plot in the light of S. Chatman's
   categories of kernels and satellites (*Story and Discourse* [Ithaca: Cornell University Press, 1978]), but there must be doubts about how convincing his analysis is,
   when neither the episode of Jesus' death nor that of his resurrection figures as a
   kernel, and about the value of these categories for plots which are episodic in
   nature and whose progression is not always in terms of cause and effect. R.A.
   Edwards' *Matthew's Story of Jesus* (Philadelphia: Fortress, 1985), although a
   brief, non-technical treatment, pays more attention to the impact of the flow of the
   narrative and of its gaps on the reader.
2 This is to attempt to carry further the suggestive, though sketchy, approach of R.A.
   Edwards, 'Uncertain Faith: Matthew's Portrait of the Disciples', *Discipleship in
   the New Testament*, ed. F.F. Segovia (Philadelphia: Fortress, 1985), pp. 47-61. Cf.
   also H.J.B. Combrink, 'The Structure of the Gospel of Matthew as Narrative',
   TynB 34 (1983), pp. 88-90.

ment and uncertainty, than with Jesus, who is in many ways more static and fulfils his narrative role or task in a fairly straightforward and unambiguous fashion.[1] The notion of identification does not mean that the implied readers can be substituted for the disciples at all points in the narrative but allows for both attraction and repulsion, involvement and distancing in the relationship.[2]

Disciples as Authoritative Teachers

I shall argue that the story of the disciples with their developing understanding yet uncertain faith is a story of those who are being prepared to teach with authority among all nations. The implied author highlights this throughout the narrative and in a number of ways, but nowhere more clearly than through the words of Jesus at two climactic points—the first at the close of the major period of public ministry in 16.13-20 and the second at the ending of the narrative as a whole in 28.16-20.

The Promise of 16.13-20
16.13-20 is to be seen as the climax of the first half of the account of Jesus' ministry in the narrative.[3] But what is often neglected or ignored is that this episode is climactic not only in regard to the disciples' identification of Jesus in Simon Peter's reply, 'You are the Christ, the Son of the living God', but also in

---

1 Cf. also Edwards, 'Uncertain Faith', pp. 50-53, who claims that the gaps in the narrator's exposition are primarily in connection with the disciples, not with Jesus. 'The disciples, not Jesus, are the mystery... The process of hypothesis formation, re-evaluation, and confirmation about the disciples in Matthew is more intense than it is for Jesus because there is less basic information to begin with'. By contrast, 'Jesus' character is already rather firmly fixed, and although the specifics of his program have yet to be detailed, the question that confronts the reader is how people will react to him as he proceeds'.

2 Cf. J.D. Kingsbury, 'Reflections on "the Reader" of Matthew's Gospel', *NTS* 34 (1988), pp. 457-58; also Edwards, 'Uncertain Faith', p. 52 on the 'both/and' technique of the narrator in regard to the disciples. Contrast this to the formulation of e.g. P.S. Minear, *Matthew: The Teacher's Gospel* (London: Darton, Longman and Todd, 1984), pp. 11, 12: 'The twelve disciples correspond to the prophets, wise men, and scribes who were leaders in the churches of the second generation'.

3 Cf. also e.g. Combrink, 'The Structure', pp. 70, 83; Kingsbury, *Matthew as Story*, pp. 38, 76; Bauer, *Structure*, pp. 93-95.

regard to the disciples' own role.[1] In fact, the bulk of Jesus' statement of approval, which brings the narrative to a temporary halt on a positive note, is devoted to the role of Jesus' followers as represented by Peter, the first among equals (cf. also 18.18-20).[2]

In order to appreciate the force of this statement, we should remind ourselves of the disciples' role in the third section (12.15–16.20) of the narrative of the public ministry for which this episode provides the conclusion. The disciples are depicted in a positive light as the true family of Jesus, for whoever does the will of Jesus' Father is his brother, sister and mother (12.46-50). Towards the beginning of the teaching discourse which contains the parables of the kingdom (13.1-52) the disciples are again evaluated favourably as those, who, over against the crowds, have been given to know the secrets of the kingdom of heaven (13.11). In fact, in 13.16, 17 they are complimented with a beatitude (anticipating the beatitude of 16.17-19) in which they are placed in a privileged position as over against, not just the crowds, but also previous prophets and righteous men because of what they now see and hear. And at the end of the discourse (13.51, 52), when, in reply to Jesus' question, they tell him that they have understood all the parables, it is significant that Jesus can respond by depicting them as scribes, learned teachers[3] who have been trained or discipled (μαθητευθείς) not for the Torah but for the kingdom

---

1   E.g. both Kingsbury, *Matthew as Story*, p. 76, and Bauer, *Structure*, pp. 93-95, ignore this element of the climax; but cf. E. Schweizer, *The Good News According to Matthew* (London: SPCK, 1975), p. 344.

2   Cf. J.D. Kingsbury, 'The Figure of Peter in Matthew's Gospel as a Theological Problem', *JBL* 98 (1979), pp. 67-83; also M.J. Wilkins, *The Concept of Disciple in Matthew's Gospel* (Leiden: Brill, 1988), pp. 193, 198, 215.

3   For the purposes of this essay the notions of the disciples as teachers and of the disciples as scribes overlap. For a detailed treatment of the scribes in this gospel, see D.E. Orton, *The Understanding Scribe* (JSNTSup, 25; Sheffield: JSOT Press, 1989), esp. pp. 15-38, 137-63. He claims that Matthew conforms disciples to his picture of the ideal scribe who has wisdom and understanding, is an authoritative and righteous teacher, and shares the mission and creative inspiration of the prophets (cf. pp. 161-62). For a discussion of 13.51-52, see pp. 137-53, 171-74. Cf. also Wilkins, *Concept*, pp. 53-91, who argues that the training of prophets, scribes and wise men provides the background for the master-disciple relationship in Matthew. In addition to prophet, wise man and scribe, righteous man (cf. 10.41; 13.17; 23.29) may also be a reference to one who functions as a teacher; cf. D. Hill, 'Δίκαιος as a Quasi-Technical Term', *NTS* 11 (1965), pp. 296-302.

of heaven. Like a householder who can bring out of his treasure what is new and what is old, they have in their treasury of understanding not only the old—insight into the law and the prophets—but also the new—insight into the secret of the kingdom of heaven, announced by Jesus and fulfilling the old, insight producing freshness and creativity in interpretation.[1] But despite the successful discipling that has been done and that could lead to such a description, the narrative reveals that further training is necessary before the disciples are ready to *act* as scribes of the kingdom. In the walking on the water episode in 14.22-33 Peter's faith in Jesus lapses temporarily and he is seen by Jesus as a man of little faith who doubts, although when Peter and Jesus are both in the boat the narrator tells us that the disciples then worship Jesus as Son of God. Again in 15.10-20 Peter, on behalf of the other disciples, asks for an explanation of a parable, revealing that not only the disciples' faith but also their understanding is not yet complete (cf. Jesus' rebuke in v. 16, 'Are you also still without understanding?'). When the disciples have forgotten to take bread (16.5-12), once more both their little faith and their lack of complete understanding are highlighted. But the episode concludes with the narrator informing the implied reader in 16.12 that after Jesus' rebuke the disciples did understand what he had meant about the leaven of the Pharisees and Sadducees. So immediately before the episode at Caesarea Philippi a positive evaluation of the disciples' understanding has been made.[2] This is then reinforced in the following verses.

Peter's confession of Jesus as Messiah and Son of God distinguishes the disciples' understanding from that of the general populace and it is greeted with the beatitude and promises of 16.17-19. Jesus declares Peter blessed, because he, the

---

1   In the context of reflections on the thought of Derrida and Foucault, G.A. Phillips ('History and Text: The Reader in Context in Matthew's Parables Discourse', *Semeia* 31 [1985], pp. 11-38) shows how this chapter, and especially its final parable, involves and transforms the reader, claiming that 'Matthew 13 is a manual for scribal or interpretative self-development, a working template of how to be a competent scribe oneself' (p. 136).

2   The narrative's positive emphasis on the disciples' understanding, despite their little faith, is to enable the implied reader to realize that for the most part they have actually comprehended Jesus' teaching and therefore will themselves be in a position to teach this when the time comes.

leader and representative of the twelve, in contrast to the so-called wise and understanding Jewish teachers from whom these things have been hidden (cf. 11.25, 26), has been the specially chosen recipient of revelation from the Father. The faith and understanding expressed in his confession are to be seen as totally a gift from God. On the basis of what the Father has already revealed, Jesus now bestows promises expressed in the images of vv. 18, 19. In v. 18, in exchange for the titles conferred on Jesus, Peter now receives the title 'Rock' in the well-known play on words (Πέτρος, πέτρα). He is the firm, unshakable rock on which Jesus will build his church, and though the floods of death flow forth from the gates of Hades, sweeping all before them, they will not prevail against this church built on Peter. Already this announcement with its future tense points the implied reader to the end of the narrative and the appearance of the risen Lord to his disciples, because it is only after his own death and resurrection, which defeat the powers of death (cf. 27.51-53; 28.2-7), that Jesus will be in a position to found a church which, when faced with persecution and martyrdom, is secure against the threatening abyss of death and the dark powers associated with it. In such a church Peter will be given the keys of the kingdom. The implied reader, who has been alerted by the implied author on numerous occasions, and particularly through the formula quotations, to note links between this story and the Scriptures, might well be expected to recall at this point the similar imagery of Isa. 22.22 where God says of Eliakim, 'I shall place the key of the house of David on his shoulder; when he opens, no one shall shut, when he shuts no one shall open'.[1] Peter is to be

---

1 Cf. also O. Cullmann, *Peter: Disciple, Apostle, Martyr* (London: SCM, 1953), p. 203; J.A. Emerton, 'Binding and Loosing: Forgiving and Retaining', *JTS* ns 13 (1962), pp. 325-31; P.F. Ellis, *Matthew: His Mind and His Message* (Collegeville: Liturgical Press, 1974), pp. 130-31; J.P. Meier, *The Vision of Matthew* (New York: Paulist, 1979), p. 113. To posit knowledge of such an allusion by the implied reader is to work with the sort of definition of the implied reader usefully summarized by Kingsbury, 'Reflections', p. 456: '. . . because the implied reader is a construct inferred from the text, he or she will always be imagined to respond to the text with whatever knowledge, understanding, or emotion the text calls for at any given juncture. The implied reader, then, is the one in whom the intention of the text achieves its realization. In this sense, the implied reader may also be said to be the ideal reader.' For fuller exposition of such a view of the implied reader,

seen as the chief steward in the royal household of the church
to whom similar authority has been delegated. The nature of
this delegated authority of the keys is illumined by contrast for
the implied reader later in the narrative in the negative
evaluation of Jewish teachers and rabbis, the scribes and
Pharisees, who receive a curse rather than a blessing because
in their missionary teaching they shut the kingdom of heaven
against people, neither entering themselves nor allowing those
who want to enter to go in (23.13, 15). The power of the keys of
the kingdom given to Peter, then, appears to involve the sort of
authoritative teaching which is the means whereby people
can enter the kingdom of heaven. It was by his teaching that
Jesus himself had opened and shut the kingdom for people (cf.
e.g. 5.3, 10; 5.20; 7.21). Jesus, the true teacher about the kingdom, the true interpreter of Torah in the light of that kingdom, will delegate his interpretative authority to Peter, who
will also take over Jesus' role in superseding the teaching
office of the rabbis.

This is spelled out further in the statement about binding
and loosing, technical terms referring to a rabbi's power to
declare particular acts permissible or forbidden, and in association with this to exclude a person from the community or to
readmit that person.[1] Peter is promised, then, that he will give
authoritative teaching in the church and will have the disci-
plinary power to make that teaching effective. In fact, his
authority will be such that whatever he declares lawful on
earth, God will declare lawful in heaven. Though the confess-

---

see W. Iser, *The Implied Reader* (Baltimore: Johns Hopkins University Press,
1974), pp. 101-20.

1 Cf. Meier, *Vision*, pp. 113-14. For a bibliography and survey of the literature on
these terms, see D.C. Duling, 'Binding and Loosing: Matthew 16.19; Matthew
18.18; John 20.23', *Forum* 3/4 (1987), pp. 3-32, though Duling's own focus is on the
issue of authenticity. The interpretation taken here of the meaning of the terms in
their Matthean context is the consensus one; cf. e.g. D. Hill, *The Gospel of
Matthew* (London: Oliphants, 1972), p. 262; Schweizer, *Matthew*, p. 343; Gundry,
Matthew, pp. 334-36; J.D.M. Derrett, 'Binding and Loosing (Matt 16.19; 18.18;
John 29.23 [sic])', *JBL* 102 (1983), pp. 112-17; G. Bornkamm, 'The Authority to
"Bind" and "Loose" in the Church in Matthew's Gospel', *The Interpretation of
Matthew*, ed. G. Stanton (London: SPCK, 1983), pp. 88, 93, 94; R.H. Hiers, '"Bind-
ing" and "Loosing": The Matthean Authorizations', *JBL* 104 (1985), pp. 249-50;
Orton, *The Understanding Scribe*, p. 160, who sees the terms as a reference to 'the
proper authorization of a scribe'.

ing Peter is the foundation of the church, this promise is not just for him. This is made clear in Jesus' next teaching discourse, in a passage (18.15-20) whose audience in the narrative is the disciples but which reaches out to the time of the implied readers. In the context of a problem of discipline in the church, the same authority to bind and loose is promised to all the disciples.[1] The judgments of these disciples again have heavenly sanction, because where two or three of them are gathered in Christ's name, Christ himself is present in the midst. Jesus promises to the disciples, who will be teaching and disciplining, not only his delegated authority but also his powerful presence. The implied reader is again pointed forward to the similar pronouncement to the disciples that closes the entire story in 28.20—'Lo, I am with you always, to the close of the age'. Although both 16.13-20 and 18.15-20 point the reader towards the narrative's closure, the closing verse of 16.13-20 with its command to silence about Jesus' identity as the Christ, particularly since it comes after such a statement of approval about Peter's insight and his teaching role, has a jarring effect, making the reader stop and ask why it is that the disciples are not yet ready to fulfil their task and pass on the insight they have been given.[2]

The Commissioning of 28.16-20

If 16.13-20 is of crucial importance as the climax of the first part of the narrative, then there can be no doubt about the significance of 28.16-20 as the ending of the whole narrative.[3] It provides an effective closure for the main elements of the plot and makes a final and decisive impact on the implied readers. Again the focus of that impact is through the role of the disci-

---

1 Cf. the discussion in W.G. Thompson, *Matthew's Advice to a Divided Community* (Rome: Biblical Institute Press, 1970), pp. 188-202, who sees the particular focus of the authority in this context as binding or releasing the guilt of sin.

2 Cf. also D. Patte, *The Gospel according to Matthew* (Philadelphia: Fortress, 1987), p. 233.

3 On 28.16-20 as the climax of the gospel, see Bauer, *Structure*, pp. 109-28. Cf. also B.J. Hubbard, *The Matthean Redaction of a Primitive Apostolic Community: An Exegesis of Matthew 28.16-20* (Missoula, MT: SBL, 1974), pp. 98-99, 135; Ellis, *Matthew*, pp. 19-25; O. Michel, 'The Conclusion of Matthew's Gospel: A Contribution to the History of the Easter Message', *The Interpretation of Matthew*, pp. 30-41.

ples in the ending.[1] What had been promised in 16.13-20 is now set in motion in 28.16-20.[2] This internal prolepsis, the evoking in advance of an event that will take place later in the narrative, has served to create tension within the plot by raising the questions of how and when the future event will take place.[3] How and when will the disciples be ready to teach with authority?

Once more the alternating positive and negative evaluations of the disciples in the preceding narrative should be noted. I shall take this up in the second part of the long section, 16.21–28.20, which begins with the entry to Jerusalem in 21.1. The disciples here are seen in a positive light primarily because of the future role they will have as Jesus' representatives in the narrative world beyond the end of the story. They are those whom Jesus is sending out with his delegated authority as prophets, wise men and *scribes* to meet persecution and death at the hands of Jewish scribes and Pharisees (23.34; cf. also 10.40-42; 13.52).[4] For his name's sake they will experience tribulation, death and hatred by all nations (24.9). They will be involved in preaching the gospel of the kingdom throughout the whole world, as a testimony to all nations (24.14). They will represent Christ among these nations (25.31-36). In this period they will need to endure (24.13), watch (24.42; 25.13), be ready (24.44) and act as faithful servants (24.45-51; 25.14-30). In the story itself they share a Passover meal with Jesus in which they are invited to associate themselves with his death in such a way that they will receive forgiveness of sins, and they are promised participation in the feast with Jesus in God's final kingdom (26.26-29). But on the negative side the disciples fail to see the appropri-

---

1 Cf. also Minear, *Matthew*, p. 141; Edwards, *Matthew's Story*, p. 94.

2 M. Torgovnick (*Closure in the Novel* [Princeton: Princeton University Press, 1981], p. 13) uses the term 'parallelism' for this sort of link between the middle and the end of a narrative.

3 Cf. G. Genette, *Narrative Discourse* (Ithaca: Cornell University Press, 1980), pp. 40-76; S. Rimmon-Kenan, *Narrative Fiction* (London: Methuen, 1983), pp. 48, 126: 'In order to increase the reader's interest . . . the text will delay the narration . . . of the event the reader is now curious to learn about, or of the event which will temporarily or permanently close off the sequence in question'.

4 For a discussion of 23.34, see F.W. Burnett, *The Testament of Jesus-Sophia* (Lanham, MD: University Press of America, 1981), pp. 35-57, 172-81; Orton, *The Understanding Scribe*, pp. 153-59.

ateness of the woman's anointing of Jesus' head (26.6-13). Judas betrays Jesus (26.14-16, 20-25, 46-50; 27.3-5). The failure of the rest of the disciples is predicted (26.31-35), Peter, James and John prove unable to watch with Jesus in Gethsemane (26.26-46), all forsake him and flee (26.56), and Peter denies him three times (26.69-75). These disciples are then absent from the narrative during the trial before Pilate, the crucifixion, burial and resurrection. After the resurrection both an angel and the risen Jesus tell the women to pass on the message to the disciples about a meeting in Galilee, with Jesus calling his disciples brothers (28.7, 10). Although there are now only eleven disciples who go to Galilee and see Jesus, they are portrayed for the reader in the same way as the earlier narrative's positive and negative assessment of the twelve, because here also there is a mixture of worship and doubt among them (28.17). But because of what has happened to Jesus, their role is now to be a changed one.

What has happened to Jesus makes possible his announcement that all authority in heaven and on earth has been given to him (28.18). In his public ministry Jesus had taught with authority (7.28), he had had authority to cast out unclean spirits and to heal diseases (cf. 10.1), and on occasion authority over the wind and sea (8.27); and as Son of man he had authority on earth to forgive sins (9.6) and authority over the sabbath as its Lord (12.8). But now as the vindicated Son of man, seated at the right hand of Power (26.64), he has full and universal authority[1]—in heaven and on earth—and therefore over the nations (cf. Dan. 7.13, 14).[2] As in the climactic statement of 16.13-20, however, this Christological affirmation is subservient to what is to be said about the disciples' role. Despite still being a group of doubting worshippers, they are now, because of the risen Jesus' full authority and commissioning, in a position to make disciples of all nations, baptizing

---

1 On Jesus' authority in the narrative, see also Bauer, *Structure*, pp. 115-21.

2 Cf. also Michel, 'Conclusion', p. 36; G. Barth, 'Matthew's Understanding of the Law', in G. Bornkamm, G. Barth, H.J. Held, *Tradition and Interpretation in Matthew* (London: SCM, 1963), pp. 133-34; Hill, *Matthew*, p. 361; Schweizer, *Matthew*, pp. 531-32; Hubbard, *Matthean Redaction*, p. 82; Ellis, *Matthew*, pp. 22-24; Meier, *Vision*, pp. 37-38, 212; J. Schaberg, *The Father, the Son and the Holy Spirit* (Chico, CA: Scholars Press, 1982), pp. 111-340.

and teaching them. Readers are not allowed to miss the focus on the disciples' teaching role, because it is referred to twice. In discipling others they have obviously now become the teachers (v. 18) and this activity and its content are underlined in the closing verse (v. 20).[1] Because all has been accomplished (cf. 5.17) and through Jesus' death and resurrection a new and decisive stage in history has been inaugurated (cf. especially 27.52-54; 28.2-7),[2] the disciples through this appointment in Galilee with the risen Lord can be considered to have had their previous training completed. They are now to participate in the new situation by discipling or training others. The new situation is indicated also by the fact that it is not just others who are to be discipled, but all nations.[3] In marked contrast to the limited scope of the disciples' earlier mission from which the Gentiles were excluded (10.5, 6), their activity now is to be universal.[4] There is also a contrast with the content of the previous commissioning. The disciples had at that time been given authority to cast out unclean spirits and to heal diseases (10.1) and to preach the message, 'The kingdom of heaven is at hand' (10.7). Now they are to baptize (and thereby to admit into the church) and to teach with the full authority of the risen Jesus with them (28.19, 20). Previously only Jesus had been the teacher with authority, the disciples had not been commissioned to teach,[5] but only, as we have seen, promised that they would have Jesus' authority to teach when he built his church (16.18, 19; 18.18-20). Now that time has come.

---

1 Ellis (*Matthew*, pp. 136-37) suggests that the apostles' mission to teach is akin to Moses' mandate to teach in Deut. 5.30-33.

2 Cf. Meier, *Vision*, pp. 33-36, 204-10; D. Senior, *The Passion of Jesus in the Gospel of Matthew* (Wilmington, DE: Michael Glazier, 1985), pp. 38, 141-50, 182-84; D.C. Allison, *The End of the Ages Has Come* (Edinburgh: T. and T. Clark, 1987), pp. 40-50, though the arguments of e.g. R.D. Witherup ('The Death of Jesus and the Raising of the Saints: Matthew 27.51-54 in Context', *SBL 1987 Seminar Papers*, ed. K.H. Richards [Atlanta, GA: Scholars Press, 1987], pp. 574-85) should make one wary of pressing this perspective too hard.

3 This reading follows J.P. Meier, 'Nations or Gentiles in Matthew 28.19?', *CBQ* 39 (1977), pp. 94-102, rather than D.R.A. Hare and D.J. Harrington, 'Make Disciples of all the Gentiles', *CBQ* 37 (1975), pp. 359-69.

4 For discussion of the way this universal emphasis also takes up previous indications of universalism, see Bauer, *Structure*, pp. 121-24.

5 Cf. also Edwards, 'Uncertain Faith', p. 59.

And what are they to teach? Jesus informs them (28.20) that the nations are to be taught to keep not the commandments of the Torah but 'all that I have commanded you'. The disciples are to pass on what they have been taught by the supremely authoritative interpreter of the Torah, Jesus himself. Where have they received this teaching? Above all, in the five great teaching discourses, which can now be seen to have been integral to the completion of the narrative's plot.[1] Knowing all Jesus' teaching, the disciples are also now in fact able to be the sort of teachers who meet with Jesus' approval according to the very first mention of their teaching task in the Sermon on the Mount in 5.19—those who teach and do even one of the least of his commandments.

Disciples, Implied Readers and the Teaching Discourses
Although they seemed to disrupt the flow of the narrative and to have little to do with advancing the action, the five teaching discourses were in fact all the time preparing the disciples to be authoritative teachers of all that Jesus commanded them, the climactic commissioning to which the narrative builds up in its major two-part movement (cf. 16.17-19; 28.16-20). This slowing down of the narrative had been a deliberate ploy on the part of the implied author, but the reasons for it and its full implications are not revealed until the narrative's close when those who were being taught become teachers. If closure is one of the features on which the quality of the narrative is most often judged,[2] then this story provides a strong and satisfying sense of closure for the reader.[3]

The implied readers of this story identify mainly with the disciples as the characters whose situation is most analogous to their own. The implied readers are followers of Jesus who live between the resurrection and the end (cf. 24.14, 15). At the end of the narrative, therefore, they can envisage themselves

---

1   Cf. also Bauer, *Structure*, p. 133.
2   Cf. Rimmon-Kenan, *Narrative Fiction*, p. 18.
3   This strong sense of closure involves what B.H. Smith (*Poetic Closure* [Chicago: University of Chicago Press, 1968], p. 119) calls retrospective patterning, 'that is, connections and similarities are illuminated, and the reader perceives that seemingly gratuitous or random events, details and juxtapositions have been selected in accord with certain principles'.

in the role assigned to the disciples between the resurrection and the end of the age. The implied readers also now know for sure what they had sensed previously, namely, that the teaching discourses were meant for them. It becomes clear that in those discourses Jesus was addressing the implied readers and their present situations as much as the disciples in the narrative. A number of features had already hinted that the implied readers were to see themselves as addressed by the discourses and to treat these discourses as in many ways transparent for the present.[1] There is sometimes ambiguity about the audience of a discourse and about its relation to the surrounding narrative. In the case of the Sermon on the Mount (5.1–7.27), for example, 5.1, 2 state that it is addressed to the disciples. But which disciples? Only the four who have been mentioned at this stage of the narrative (cf. 4.18-22)? The narrator chooses not to mention the twelve until 10.1, 2. But at the end of the sermon further questions are raised, because there when the audience is described it is the crowds and not the disciples who are mentioned. It is as if the audience within the narrative itself is secondary; the teaching for the implied readers is what really counts. In that teaching Jesus speaks of those who claim him as lord but who are in fact false prophets (cf. 7.21-23), a phenomenon unknown to either the disciples or the crowds at this point in the narrative but familiar to the implied readers. Further, the teaching discourse of 10.5-42 is not tied in with the surrounding narrative. The disciples are sent out and given instructions for their mission. But, unlike in Mark's story (cf. Mk 6.7-13, 31, 32), in this one the implied readers are left to assume that the disciples actually went on this mission and they are told neither what happened on it nor that they came back. 11.1 speaks neither of the disciples' departure nor of their return. The narrator is interested only in the instructions given, and in the second half of these, particularly in 10.17-22, the situation addressed is clearly that

---

1 Cf. especially U. Luz, 'The Disciples in the Gospel According to Matthew', in *The Interpretation of Matthew*, pp. 98-128, on the notion of transparency. Although there are overlaps between the phenomenon of transparency and the discussion of implied readers, Kingsbury helpfully points out some of the ambiguities and problems in the former notion, arising from its use in redaction criticism and the historical interests of that approach; cf. 'Reflections', pp. 445-59.

of the time of the reader and the mission to the Gentiles rather than that of the time of the disciples in the narrative and their exclusive mission to Israel (cf. 10.5, 6).[1] Similarly the parable of the weeds of the field in 13.24-30, 36-46 is addressed to the time of the Son of man's kingdom up until the close of the age, 18.15-20 speaks explicitly to the situation of the future church (cf. 16.18, 'I will build my church'), and 24.1–25.46 depicts ahead of time the period of universal mission between the resurrection and the parousia. All of these are different ways of talking about the period in which the implied readers live. So, by the end of the narrative, when the implied readers find themselves sharing the commission of the eleven to disciple and teach all nations that which Jesus commanded, they too come to the full realization that those sections of teaching were preparing them not simply for their own discipleship but for their vital task of teaching others with authority.

The discourses have another effect on the implied readers. At the same time as slowing down the action, they have actually involved the readers more in the story. Instead of the readers only being told by the narrator what Jesus is like, the direct address involves them more immediately in deciding whether to accept the narrator's perspective on Jesus' teaching.[2] Because the content of the teaching is often disturbing and demanding, the implied readers need to be assured of the teacher's reliability. By the end of the narrative they are more fully able to share the narrator's point of view about Jesus' trustworthiness, and the resurrection in particular confirms the authority of Jesus' teaching.[3]

Lowly Teachers with Authority

To focus only on the promise to and commissioning of the disciples to be teachers with authority would be to provide a distorted picture of the narrative's projection of their role. There are various qualities expected of disciples in this story, such as righteousness and forgiveness, but perhaps that which is most

---

1 Cf. also Kingsbury, *Matthew as Story*, pp. 37-38, 110.
2 *Pace* Edwards, *Matthew's Story*, p. 10, the readers' evaluation is not independent of what they have been told by the narrator. After all, it is the narrator who reports and formulates the speeches.
3 Cf. also Patte, *Matthew*, p. 400.

essential in providing a balance to their authoritative teaching role is the quality of lowliness. It is made clear in ch. 23 that those to whom Jesus will delegate teaching authority, unlike Jewish teachers, will not be called rabbi. These future teachers know that in fact they have only one teacher or master (cf. also 10.24, 25) and that they are simply a community of brothers, amongst whom greatness is to be measured in terms of lowly service (23.7-12; cf. also 20.25-27). It is well-known that in this story disciples are often designated as 'little ones' (οἱ μικροί).[1] Disciples and little ones are equated in the mission discourse in 10.42, but this description receives greater prominence in the discourse of ch. 18. This begins with Jesus talking about childlike behaviour as the condition of entrance into the kingdom of heaven: 'unless you turn and become like children, you will never enter the kingdom of heaven'. But then in 18.6 the terminology for those who believe alternates from 'children' to 'these little ones', and this is repeated in 18.10, 14. What makes children and little ones appropriate figures for disciples? According to 18.4 it is the attitude of lowliness, the action of humbling oneself. Those to whom teaching authority has been promised are the lowly, those who know themselves to be nothing in themselves. In the words of the first teaching discourse they are the poor in spirit (5.3), the meek (5.5), those who accept their emptiness before God. The narrative indicates that those who accept such a role are in fact following in the footsteps of *the* authoritative teacher,[2] because he is depicted in the words of the Scripture not only as the servant who will not wrangle or cry aloud (12.18, 19) and the humble king (21.5), but also as the Son of man who came not to be served but to serve (20.28) and the wisdom-teacher who is lowly in heart (11.29). Future teachers must learn from Jesus the teacher, and their training can be summed up in the words of 11.29: 'Learn from me; for I am gentle and lowly in heart'.

---

1 Cf. especially G. Barth, 'Matthew's Understanding of the Law', pp. 121-25.
2 On the continuity between the role of Jesus and that of the disciples, see also Bauer, *Structure*, pp. 57-63.

Disciples and the Story-line about Israel and the Gentiles

One of the main elements in Matthew's plot is Israel's response to Jesus, the hardening of that response into rejection and the consequent change of recipients for Jesus' message from Israel to the nations.[1] This movement of the plot is anticipated in a number of places, but especially in Jesus' saying, in response to the centurion's faith, that 'many will come from east and west and sit at the table with Abraham, Isaac and Jacob in the kingdom of heaven, while the sons of the kingdom will be thrown into the outer darkness' (8.10-12); in the parable of the wicked tenants with its message to the chief priests and the Pharisees that 'the kingdom of God will be taken from you and given to a nation producing the fruits of it' (21.33-46); and in the programmatic statement of 24.14, that 'this gospel of the kingdom will be preached throughout the whole world, as a testimony to all nations; and then the end will come' (cf. also 26.13). The closure of the narrative in 28.16-20 has made clear that the disciples have a key role to play in this movement of the gospel from Israel to the nations, as they are commanded to make disciples of, baptize and teach all nations. Again this had been anticipated earlier in the narrative, as we have seen, when the prediction in the mission discourse that 'you will be dragged before governors and kings for my sake, to bear testimony before them and the Gentiles' (10.18) transcends the original command about an exclusive mission to the lost sheep of the house of Israel (10.5, 6). The issues that emerge in this shift from an exclusive mission to Israel to a universal mission, such as Jesus' attitude to the law and his evaluation of Israel's religious leaders, will be instructive for the implied readers in their own confrontation with the synagogue in their continuing mission to Israel (cf. 10.23) as part of their broader mission to all nations. Not only so, but the importance of the characterization of the disciples as teachers is highlighted by the contrast with the depiction of Jesus' opponents, who are seen as scribes or teachers who abuse their

---

1 Cf. especially Matera's summary in 'Plot', p. 243: 'In the appearance of Jesus the Messiah, God fulfils his promises to Israel. But Israel refuses to accept Jesus as the Messiah. Consequently, the Gospel passes to the nations.'

teaching authority, acting as blind guides.[1] In this way the Jewish leaders function as negative models of discipleship activity.[2]

But it is significant that in the 'parable' of the sheep and the goats in 25.31-46, the disciples are given the clearest preview of what will be involved in their mission of being lowly teachers with authority among the nations. Here the criterion of judgment for all nations in regard to entry into or exclusion from the kingdom is their attitude to the King's representatives, his brothers. The five great teaching discourses, we have claimed, have been preparing the disciples to be delegated to authority to teach the nations, and so it should not be surprising that the final part of the final discourse should reflect some of the consequences of accepting this role.

The Son of man is pictured as coming in his glory to judge all the nations and to separate the sheep from the goats. As the king upon his throne, he invites the righteous to inherit the kingdom, while to the wicked he says, 'Depart from me, you cursed, into the eternal fire prepared for the devil and his angels'. But how is this verdict reached? The Son of man has been present among the nations all the time, but he has been hungry, thirsty, a stranger, naked, sick and in prison. The righteous are those who have ministered to him in his affliction, while the wicked have ignored him in his time of need. When neither group is aware that these things have happened, the king explains: 'As you did it to one of the least of these my brothers, you did it to me' (25.40), or, 'As you did it not to one of the least of these, you did it not to me' (25.45). The implied reader knows that these brothers with whom the Son of man so closely identifies himself and who have undergone such privations are the disciples. It is they who are designated

1   On the characterization of the Jewish leaders in Matthew's story, see J.D. Kingsbury, 'The Developing Conflict between Jesus and the Jewish Leaders in Matthew's Gospel: A Literary-Critical Study', *CBQ* 49 (1987), pp. 57-73. On the repeated contrast between Jesus' disciples and the Jewish leaders, see S. van Tilborg, *The Jewish Leaders in Matthew* (Leiden: Brill, 1972), pp. 99-141. Cf. also Orton, *The Understanding Scribe*, pp. 15-38, who argues that because Matthew has a positive ideal of the scribe in mind, he characterizes the opposition to Jesus not just as scribes but primarily as scribes and Pharisees, i.e. Pharisaic scribes.
2   Edwards (*Matthew's Story*, p. 79) sees scribes and Pharisees as 'the antitype of the disciple'.

by Jesus as his brothers (cf. 12.46-50; 28.10) and who as a consequence form a community of brothers (cf. 23.8; also 5.22-24;
7.3-5; 18.15, 21, 22, 35). In addition, the term ἐλάχιστος, 'least',
is the superlative of μικρός, 'little', and this escalation in terminology intensifies the humiliation attached to such brothers.
As has been seen, in ch. 18 the believing followers who are
called brothers are also called little ones, and the relationship
between Jesus and a little one in 18.5, 6, where whoever
receives such a one receives him, is the same as that posited
between Jesus and the least of his brothers in 25.31-46. In fact,
in 10.40, 42, this receiving of disciples as little ones, which is
also a receiving of Jesus, includes giving them a cup of cold
water to drink when they are thirsty. So the brothers of the
Son of man, the least of these, are the disciples who have been
commissioned to teach all that Jesus commanded.[1] Correspondingly, the group being divided into sheep and goats is
precisely all the nations (25.32), the same group that the disciples are commissioned to teach at the end of the narrative.
These nations are to be judged on the basis of their response
not only to the teaching but to the teachers, on the basis of how
they have acted towards the Son of man's authorized representatives on earth.

The force of this for the implied readers is striking. Where
are they in this parable? As the disciples they are the hungry,
the thirsty, strangers, naked, sick and in prison. They are
deprived and oppressed, lowly and suffering. It is not that they
are being called on to help the poor and the outcast, but that in
the completion of their task of authoritative teaching of the
nations they should themselves expect to be the poor and the
outcast.

---

1 For this reading of the passage, see e.g. J.R. Michaels, 'Apostolic Hardships and
Righteous Gentiles. A Study of Matt. 25.31-46', *JBL* 84 (1965), pp. 27-37; L. Cope,
'Matthew xxv. 31-46—"The Sheep and the Goats" Reinterpreted', *NovT* 11 (1969),
pp. 37-41; G.E. Ladd, 'The Parable of the Sheep and Goats in Recent Interpreta-
tion', *New Dimensions in New Testament Study*, ed. R. Longenecker and M.
Tenney (Grand Rapids: Zondervan, 1974), pp. 191-99; D.R. Catchpole, 'The Poor
on Earth and the Son of Man in Heaven. A Re-Appraisal of Matthew xxv. 31-46',
BJRL 61 (1979), pp. 355-97; J. Lambrecht, *Once More Astonished: The Parables of
Jesus* (New York: Crossroad, 1981), pp. 196-235; Gundry, *Matthew*, pp. 511-16; J.R.
Donahue, 'The "Parable" of the Sheep and the Goats: A Challenge to Christian
Ethics', *TS* 47 (1986), pp. 3-31; J.R. Donahue, *The Gospel in Parable*
(Philadelphia: Fortress, 1988), pp. 109-25.

Disciples and the Story-line about Jesus

Having isolated some of the major factors in the implied author's point of view about the task of his implied readers, we are now in a position to look briefly at his story-line about Jesus, on which more work has previously been done, and to attempt to examine it in the light of its significance for such implied readers.

When one views the narrative as a whole, what is primary and most pervasive in the portrayal of its central character is not a particular title but his role as teacher.[1] Of course the amount of teaching material bears witness to this, especially the five great discourses interspersed throughout the narrative with their fivefold repetition of some variation on the concluding formula, 'when Jesus had finished all these words'. The implied author makes Jesus' teaching activity the warp and woof of his story. The summary of Jesus' activity in Galilee near the beginning of the public ministry puts his teaching first (4.23). The same is true of the summaries in 9.35 and 11.1. The three chapters which contain the opening Sermon on the Mount begin by emphasizing that Jesus 'opened his mouth and taught them' (5.2), and conclude both by stressing the necessity of hearing and doing his words (7.24-27) and by underlining the astonishment of the crowd at this teaching, 'for he taught them as one who had authority, and not as their scribes' (7.28, 29; cf. also 22.33). Through the teaching of this opening discourse Jesus is presented as the authoritative interpreter of Torah ('But I say to you...'), the supreme instructor in what is the will of the Father. He sees his relationship to his followers as that of teacher to disciples (10.24, 25), inviting them to take on the yoke of his wisdom teaching (11.25-40).[2] He is the teacher par excellence, the one teacher (23.8, 10). He can sum up the last part of his ministry in Jerusalem in the words 'day after day I sat in the temple teaching' (26.55), and, as we have seen, the narrative closure singles out his teaching activity with its reference to 'all that I commanded you' (28.20).

---

1   Cf. also e.g. Meier, *Vision*, pp. 45-51. *Pace* Bauer, *Structure*, p. 35.
2   On this passage, see especially C. Deutsch, *Hidden Wisdom and the Easy Yoke* (JSNTSup, 18; Sheffield: JSOT Press, 1987).

But the implied author makes clear that Jesus' unique teaching raises further questions about his identity. What is the source of such wisdom and authority (cf. 13.54-56; 21.23-28)? And while other characters in the narrative address Jesus as 'teacher' or 'rabbi' (cf. 8.19; 9.11; 12.38; 17.24; 19.16; 22.16, 24, 36), full disciples, with the significant exception of Judas (cf. 26.25, 48), do not. They are those who, in line with the point of view already set out by the implied author in his prologue (1.1–4.16), come to recognize the true identity of the teacher and why his teaching carries unique authority. But it is not enough for them to understand that this teacher is the Messiah in the line of David and the Son of God. It is on the basis of such recognition that they are promised their future role as authoritative teachers (cf. 16.13-20), but they will not be ready for the costly nature of this role until they have also seen that their teacher is the sort of Son of God and Son of man who is himself the lowly Servant who must experience humiliation, rejection and death before being vindicated on the third day. The second part of the narrative of the ministry from 16.21 onwards makes clear to the initially resistant disciples and to the implied readers that this is what has to happen to their teacher. In fact, it is immediately underlined that while Peter misunderstands the necessity of his teacher's suffering and death, not only is he not ready to use the keys, but he is not the rock for the church but a stone of stumbling (σκάνδαλον) for Jesus, one who does the work of Satan and whose point of view is not aligned with God's but is merely human (16.22, 23).

The story-line about Jesus' life, death and resurrection must be completed before the disciples are ready to embark on their mission, because it forms an integral part of the gospel of the kingdom that they are to proclaim and teach among the nations (cf. 24.14). But there is also another reason why this story-line must be completed before the disciples are ready to be teachers with authority among the nations. They need to experience Jesus as the living God with them. The implied author has indicated that this is who Jesus is in the first formula quotation in the birth narrative ('Emmanuel', God with us; cf. 1.22, 23). And the look ahead to the disciples' authoritative teaching ministry in the church in 18.18-20 had promised the experience of the divine presence in Jesus as a resource. But the completion of Jesus' story in the resurrection was necessary before this could be realized (cf. 16.18). The closing announcement 'Lo, I am with you always, to the close of the age' (28.20) makes clear that now, in the risen Lord, God has drawn near to dwell continuously with the disciples.[1] Nowhere is this authoritative presence of the exalted Son of God and Son of man more felt or more needed than when his followers are fulfilling their mission of teaching the nations. Since it continues to the close of the age, this presence is available throughout the time of the implied readers. By the end of the narrative implied readers can appreciate that, if they too are to carry out their mission as lowly, suffering teachers with authority, they have been told a story about Jesus which, not only with its rehearsal of the content of his teaching but also with its depiction of him as both model and empowerer, makes the fulfilment of this demanding task possible.

Conclusion

This proposal, then, should not be taken as an attempt to obscure the obvious, namely, that Matthew's gospel is a story about Jesus. Rather it is claiming that the best way to appreciate the impact on the reader of this particular story about Jesus is by focusing first on the implied readers and their relationship to Jesus' disciples. In the narrative the major distinctive activity of the disciples in that time between the resurrection and parousia which they cohabit with the implied readers is their teaching, and in the story this activity is emphasized at climactic points designed to have most impact on the implied readers.[2] In fact the implied author tells his story about Jesus in such a way as to prepare his implied readers to be missionary teachers among the nations, carrying on the task of Jesus the teacher. In preparation for this task they have been thor-

---

1   Bauer (*Structure*, pp. 124-27) sees the presentation of Jesus as 'God with us' in the climax as an inclusio. It could also be discussed in terms of Torgovnick's categories of circularity and parallelism (cf. *Closure in the Novel*, p. 13).

2   This is not to deny that the implied reader of Matthew's gospel has other characteristics, but it is to claim that teaching is the distinctive and primary mark of such a reader's identity.

oughly acquainted with Jesus' teaching, mission, and authoritative presence, and have been made aware that their role is set over against the Jewish teachers, the scribes and Pharisees, who are thoroughly lambasted in ch. 23.[1]

This essay has suggested that such a reading of Matthew's gospel, highlighting the implied readers' identification with the disciples, is able to incorporate the main elements of the three major story-lines within the narrative, that about the central character, Jesus himself, that about the movement of God's purposes from Israel to the nations, and that about the disciples. The contemporary reader of Matthew does not therefore have to choose between approaches to Matthew which have emphasized the teaching material and seen it as a teachers' manual[2] and approaches which emphasize the narrative framework but fail to do justice to the large blocks of teaching. Instead Matthew's gospel should be read as a story for would-be teachers. The implied author is in effect saying to the implied reader, 'So, you want to be teacher? Let me tell you a story'.

---

1   This is to arrive by very different means at a conclusion which is similar to the assumption about actual authors and readers with which Minear begins *Matthew: The Teacher's Gospel*, p. 3: 'The author of this Gospel was a *teacher* who designed his work to be of maximum help to *teachers* in Christian congregations'. Cf. also Patte, *Matthew*, p. 205 n. 106: 'Matthew's entire Gospel is aimed at training scribes "for the kingdom"'.
2   E.g. E. von Dobschütz, 'Matthew as Rabbi and Catechist', in *The Interpretation of Matthew*, pp. 25-26; K. Stendahl, *The School of St. Matthew* (Philadelphia: Fortress, 1968), pp. 11-35; Hill, *Matthew*, pp. 43-44; Minear, *Matthew*, pp. 12-23, 107; Wilkins, *Concept*, p. 172.

THE PARABLE OF THE UNJUST STEWARD (LUKE 16.1-13): IRONY *IS* THE KEY

Stanley E. Porter

Irony, one of the most complex concepts to delineate in literary criticism, may be defined as an interpretative situation in which an explainable discrepancy is perceived by the reader between what is said and/or done by the characters in a dramatic story, and what is the established state of affairs in the contextual world. When an interpreter encounters various factors in a text—e.g. factual conflicts, stylistic clashes, but especially conflicts regarding beliefs endorsed and held— there is an obligation to test whether, since the surface meaning is implausible, another meaning can harmonize the context and its attendant picture of the world with apparently inharmonious features. A satisfactory explanation of such a discrepancy often can be secured only by invoking the category of irony.[1] Irony is the key to the parable of the unjust steward (Lk. 16.1-13), a parable which still baffles interpreters, even though a number have drawn attention to its ironic character. This solution was proposed most recently by D.R. Fletcher,[2] but has not been accepted by recent major

---

1 See esp. W.C. Booth, *A Rhetoric of Irony* (Chicago: University of Chicago Press, 1974); D.C. Muecke, *Irony* (Critical Idiom; London: Methuen, 1970); E.M. Good, *Irony in the OT* (Philadelphia: Westminster, 1965), pp. 13-33; P.D. Duke, *Irony in the Fourth Gospel* (Atlanta: John Knox, 1985), esp. pp. 7-42; J.M. Dawsey, *The Lukan Voice: Confusion and Irony in the Gospel of Luke* (Macon, Georgia: Mercer University Press, 1986), esp. pp. 143-56; and H. Clavier, 'L'ironie dans l'enseignement de Jésus', *NovT* 1 (1956), pp. 3-20.

2 D.R. Fletcher, 'The Riddle of the Unjust Steward: Is Irony the Key?', *JBL* 82 (1963), pp. 15-30. See also A.R. Eagar, 'The Parable of the Unjust Steward',

commentaries.[1] And this is not because the parable has been neglected, either recently or in the past.[2]

The major focus of recent research has been on a few specific issues growing out of the parable's major perceived difficulty, that is, how it is that the steward after the accusations against him and his behaviour with the debtors can be commended or held up as an example to the followers of Jesus. Several resolutions have been offered. Some suggest Luke presents a 'new Jesus, one who seems inclined to compromise with evil'.[3] Hence, C.C. Torrey proposes that 'Luke' missed the questions in vv. 8-9 and mistranslated the original Aramaic story by Jesus, giving the story an ironic twist. If resorting to mistranslation of a non-existent document or body of material seems an implausible, to say nothing of unverifiable, solution,

---

Expositor, 5th ser. 2 (1895), p. 473, calling it sarcasm; N. Levinson, *The Parables: Their Background and Local Setting* (Edinburgh: T. and T. Clark, 1926), p. 171; P.G. Bretscher, 'The Parable of the Unjust Steward—A New Approach to Luke 16.1-9', *CTM* 22 (1951), pp. 757-62; G. Paul, 'The Unjust Steward and the Interpretation of Luke 16.9', *Theology* 61 (1958), p. 192, calling it grim sarcasm; G. Schwarz, '"... lobte den betrügerischen Verwalter"? (Lukas 16.8a)', *BZ* 18 (1974), pp. 94-95; cf. E. Trueblood, *The Humour of Christ* (San Francisco: Harper and Row, 1964), pp. 98-110, although his reference to Jesus as 'joking' (p. 101) undermines the seriousness. Contra J. Jónsson, *Humour and Irony in the NT: Illuminated by Parallels in Talmud and Midrash* (Rejkjavík: Menningarsjóds, 1965), pp. 123-25, who, following Clavier, says that the irony is that God as described by Jesus is contrary to the standard conception.

1 E.g. H. Rengstorf, *Das Evangelium nach Lukas* (NTD; Göttingen: Vandenhoeck und Ruprecht, 1965), e.g. p. 189; I.H. Marshall, *Commentary on Luke* (NIGTC; Grand Rapids: Eerdmans, 1978), pp. 613ff.; J.A. Fitzmyer, *The Gospel According to Luke X–XXIV* (AB 28A; Garden City, NY: Doubleday, 1985), pp. 1094ff.

2 See e.g. M. Krämer, *Das Rätsel der Parabel vom ungerechten Verwalter (Lk. 16.1-13): Auslegungsgeschichte–Umfang–Sinn: Eine Diskussion der Probleme und Lösungsvorschläge der Verwalterparabel von den Vätern bis heute* (Zürich: PAS, 1972); W.S. Kissinger, *The Parables of Jesus: A History of Interpretation and Bibliography* (Metuchen, NJ: Scarecrow, 1979), pp. 398-408; updated in Fitzmyer, *Luke X–XXIV*, pp. 1102-4. Most interpretation derives from A. Jülicher, *Die Gleichnisreden Jesu* (2 vols; 2nd edn; Tübingen: Mohr [Siebeck], 1910), 2.495-514.

3 C.C. Torrey, *Our Translated Gospel* (New York: Harper and Row, 1936), p. 59; *idem*, *The Four Gospels: A New Translation* (London: Hodder and Stoughton, n.d.), *loc. cit.* and p. 311; and R. Merkelbach, 'Über das Gleichnis vom ungerechten Haushalter (Lucas 16,1-13)', *VC* 33 (1979), pp. 180-81, without reference to Torrey. Cf. W.O.E. Oesterley, 'The Unjust Steward', *Expositor*, 6th ser. 7 (1903), pp. 273-83; A.H. Baverstock, 'The Unjust Steward', *Theology* 35 (1937), p. 81; R.B.Y. Scott, 'The Parable of the Unjust Steward', *ExpTim* 49 (1937-38), pp. 234-35, for other solutions citing Semitisms.

others simply have blamed Luke for taking Jesus' message to
zealous extremes.[1] Most readings, however, attempt to interpret the parable on the basis of more plausible and accessible
criteria.

J. Jeremias believes that Jesus, the 'lord' of v. 8a, praises the
clever, resolute behaviour of the man threatened by imminent
catastrophe (this is a parable of crisis). Verses 8b-9 are added
to explain Jesus' perplexing endorsement.[2] This interpretation
results in a surgical separation of the text into the parable
proper in vv. 1-7, Jesus' true but trivialized and vague comment in v. 8a, the cryptic and allusive explanation of that
response in vv. 8b and 9, and an almost wanton addition of
only approximately applicable isolated comments in vv. 10-13.
This is beside the fact that it is not entirely clear that the 'lord'
of v. 8a is Jesus (see below).[3]

This position has numerous problems, not least that if it is
not clear how Jesus can be commending the behaviour of the
unjust steward, vv. 8b-9 are no explanation. First, there are
too many phrases begging for clarification, e.g. 'sons of this
age' and 'sons of light', 'mammon of unrighteousness', 'eternal tents'. Second, endorsement of accommodation to the
standards of the world flatly contradicts the message of Jesus
found elsewhere in the Gospels as a whole and in particular in
Luke and this parabolic context (i.e. Lk. 15.11–16.31). The
parable of the prodigal son (Lk. 15.11-32) clearly rejects values associated with monetary standards and attempts to
please those outside the community, and the parable of the
rich man and Lazarus (16.9-31) makes an even stronger
statement regarding the reversal of fortunes for those putting
their trust in this world's riches to ensure eternal reward (see
below). In any case, vv. 8b-9, in their Lukan context, cannot be
a persuasive explanation of the parable, although Jeremias's

---

1 J. Drury, *Luke* (New York: Macmillan, 1973), pp. 158-59.

2 J. Jeremias, *The Parables of Jesus* (3rd edn; London: SCM, 1972), p. 182, cf.
pp. 45-48; earlier suggested by Jülicher, *Gleichnisreden*, 2.512. See Fitzmyer,
Luke X–XXIV, pp. 1096-97, for scholars supporting such analysis; cf. Krämer,
Rätsel, pp. 174-82; B.B. Scott, 'A Master's Praise: Luke 16.1-8a', *Bib* 64 (1983),
pp. 174-77.

3 This view is not significantly altered by variations including some portion of v. 8
or even v. 9 in the parable itself: e.g. Jülicher (*Gleichnisreden*, 2.505-506)
believes that v. 9 was a word of Jesus from a different original context.

straightforward understanding of vv. 1-8a requires such an analysis.

As a result of finding an inherent contradiction among its sections and because of the implausibility of its moral content, Jeremias and others must reject vv. 10-13 from the parable. This excision fails for two further reasons. The first is a difficulty suggested by Jeremias's own method, in which comparison with the other Gospels implies a level of intelligibility he neglects to consider. The other Gospels do not include the parable of the unjust steward, leaving open the possibility that Luke could have excluded it as well. As M. Barth says, 'if Luke wished to counteract or even contradict the naughty story— why then did he not follow or anticipate the way of Mark, Matthew, and John, and omit the parable of the dishonest steward from his gospel? Perhaps he was more faithful to the words and the spirit of Jesus than his moralizing interpreters.'[1] A second, and perhaps more significant failure, one with bearing upon the literary nature of the text, is that Jeremias's understanding not only leaves Jesus' explanatory verses (8b-9) truncated and inadequate, but it neglects the text of the parable as it stands. The textual evidence gives no firm reason for seeing ch. 16 as anything other than a continuous narrative (textual editors alone divide the verses into paragraphs at e.g. vv. 10 and 13). Inclusion of any of the parable implies inclusion of the entire literary unit (vv. 1-13), on the basis of an implied coherence of the narrative.

A second major view of the parable, in some ways the standard view, is based on Jeremias's textual analysis but goes further in explaining the steward's behaviour. This view holds that the steward acted corruptly throughout the story by wasting his master's goods during his stewardship and then by falsifying the accounts of the master's debtors by reducing the amounts owed in order to obtain their goodwill. Jesus' praise of the steward is not for his cheating but for his shrewdness and foresight during his crisis in preparing for the

---

1 M. Barth, 'The Dishonest Steward and his Lord: Reflections on Luke 16.1-13', *From Faith to Faith* (FS D.G. Miller) (ed. D.Y. Hadidian; Pittsburgh: Pickwick, 1979), p. 66.

future.[1] Jesus then commends to the disciples the shrewd use of the goods of this age, possibly in almsgiving, to secure eternal eschatological rewards.[2] As T.W. Manson says, the master is saying, 'I applaud the dishonest steward because he acted cleverly'; not 'I applaud the dishonest steward because he acted dishonestly'.[3] K.E. Bailey goes further and says that the steward was clever enough to appreciate the mercy of his master, who, in the end, does not repudiate him.[4]

This view fails to come to adequate terms with the parable. First, applause of the steward for acting cleverly seems to entail applause of the means evidencing his clever action. The two cannot be separated. Second, the steward is put forward on the basis of his action as an example to the sons of light, and recommendations for their action must include more than simply wise action, but a similar kind of ingratiating action. Third, there is, as P. Gächter argues, an 'inner unreality of the action as ascribed to the steward'.[5] The steward cannot have reasonably expected to expedite his ill-conceived plans of wast-

1 See esp. Marshall, *Luke*, p. 614; P. Gächter, 'The Parable of the Dishonest Steward after Oriental Conceptions', *CBQ* 12 (1950), pp. 122-23; D.E. Seccombe, *Possessions and the Poor in Luke–Acts* (SNTU; Linz: Studien zum Neuen Testament und seiner Umwelt, 1982), pp. 160ff., for summary of this position. Besides many commentaries, see A. Edersheim, *The Life and Times of Jesus the Messiah* (1904; r.p. Grand Rapids: Eerdmans, 1965), 2.266-67, 273-74; C.G. Montefiore, *The Synoptic Gospels* (1927; r.p. New York: Ktav, 1968), 2.528-31; T.W. Manson, *The Sayings of Jesus*, in *The Mission and Message of Jesus* by H.D.A. Major, T.W. Manson, and C.J. Wright (London: Ivor Nicholson and Watson, 1937), p. 583; L.J. Topel, 'On the Injustice of the Unjust Steward: Luke 16.1-13', *CBQ* 37 (1975), pp. 218-20, 223-27; J. Schmid, *Das Evangelium nach Lukas* (4th edn; RNT; Regensburg: Pustet, 1960), p. 257: 'V. 8a spricht den Grundgedanken des Gleichnisses aus: der Verwalter wird wegen der Klugheit, mit der er für seine Zukunft Vorsorge traf, solange er dazu noch Zeit hatte, vom Herrn gelobt. In seiner Klugheit und in nichts anderem liegt die Vorbildlichkeit seiner Handlungsweise.'
2 See esp. F.E. Williams, 'Is Almsgiving the Point of the "Unjust Steward?"', *JBL* 83 (1964), pp. 293-97 (who claims that irony, though a possible reading, is too subtle); F.J. Williams, 'The Parable of the Unjust Steward (Luke 16.1-9)', *ExpTim* 66 (1954-55), pp. 371-72; suggested earlier by Jülicher, *Gleichnisreden*, 2.512; and so most commentators. Parallels often cited (Lk. 12.33-34; cf. Matt. 6.19-21) are quite different, however, in their not appealing to making friends to aid in entry to the kingdom. See Fletcher, 'Riddle', p. 25.
3 Manson, *Sayings*, p. 584.
4 K.E. Bailey, *Poet and Peasant: A Literary-Cultural Approach to the Parables* (Grand Rapids: Eerdmans, 1976), pp. 102-103, 110.
5 Gächter, 'Parable', p. 123.

ing the master's wealth and saving himself; as a matter of fact, he is caught both times. This cannot be a worthy example for the sons of light and can hardly have been commended by Jesus, even in the light of eschatological exigencies.

Facing insuperable difficulties with the prima facie reading of the parable, many interpreters have drawn upon oriental customs regarding the role of a steward and the nature of debt in near Eastern society.[1] J.D.M. Derrett claims that a steward who got into trouble had to secure the good graces of some group, since he would leave his employment with as little as he brought to it. Jewish monetary laws forbade loans at interest, but there were several loopholes whereby a loan with interest could be secured, especially if the person seeking the loan was not under immediate necessity to borrow. Derrett goes further, claiming that this was perverted by the Pharisees so that if a man possessed, for example, a single drop of oil, thereby proving lack of need, he could borrow more at interest. Two common objects of borrowing were oil and grain, which almost anyone would possess. In this parable, Derrett concludes, the steward was actually acting righteously according to God's law as opposed to man's law in releasing debtors from usurious interest he had as yet not collected; this would technically be a payment out of the steward's own pocket since the master would not be held liable for an unlawful deed performed by his steward. The master may well have been ignorant of his steward's activity, although the fact that he was rich indicates that he expected if not actually authorized lending at interest. The steward, in the light of his imminent dismissal, attempts successfully to obtain the support of public opinion by doing what the law of God requires—he does away

1 Apparently this theory was first propounded in English by M.D. Gibson, 'On the Parable of the Unjust Steward', *ExpTim* 14 (1902-3), p. 334; now including C.B. Firth, 'The Parable of the Unrighteous Steward (Luke 16.1-9)', *ExpTim* 63 (1951-52), pp. 93-95; Gächter, 'Parable', pp. 121-31; J.D.M. Derrett, 'Fresh Light on St. Luke 16: I. The Parable of the Unjust Steward', *NTS* 7 (1960-61), pp. 198-219 (r.p. in *Law in the NT* [London: Darton, Longman and Todd, 1970], pp. 48-77); *idem*, '"Take Thy Bond... and Write Fifty" (Luke 16.6): The Nature of the Bond', *JTS* ns 23 (1972), pp. 438-40. See recently e.g. Marshall, *Luke*, pp. 614-17; L. Morris, *The Gospel According to St. Luke* (Tyndale; Grand Rapids: Eerdmans, 1974), pp. 245-48; E.E. Ellis, *The Gospel of Luke* (NCB; London: Nelson, 1966), p. 199; G.B. Caird, *Saint Luke* (Westminster Pelican; Philadelphia: Westminster, 1963), pp. 186-88.

with the usurious interest. The master, rather than appearing an impious man, adopts the steward's actions, forgives the legal debts, and gives the impression of piety, and hence also benefits in reputation with the general public. How then can the master praise his unjust steward? 'Unjust' only refers to his previous actions, which led to his dismissal.[1]

J.A. Fitzmyer tries to soften the impact of Derrett's theory at a crucial point—the implied complicity of the master in usury. 'The master may well have been ignorant of the precise usurious nature of the original transactions',[2] he says, since he could hardly have authorized usury. When the steward does reduce the debts, according to Fitzmyer, the actions can be expected to be ratified by the master, who does not insist on receipt of the usurious gain of the original debts imposed by the steward.

This is not the only difficulty with this view, however. For, first, Derrett assumes much that is not explicitly stated in the parable. He frames his argument using such words as 'assume', 'may', and 'seems' but his conclusions are 'made with confidence' and 'follow'. Second, Bailey has pointed out many of the assumptions Derrett's view works from:[3] the master is dishonest; he is willing to allow his steward's profits of fifty percent to be almost equal with his own; he has no ties to other members of his community; the steward cheats mercilessly on a regular basis; the steward has permission to cheat debtors but is punished only if he cheats the master; and the cheating steward but not the master will be hated mercilessly. Fitzmyer's solution does not help, since the master is simply ignorant or avoids details of running his estate. The praise of such a man can hardly be worth much (if the lord of v. 8 is the master; the words of praise include address of the steward as τὸν οἰκονόμον τῆς ἀδικίας), but such a master would be susceptible to further cheating rather than calling forth repentance. A sudden and strange rationale for transformation is attributed to one inclined to cheating for personal profit, i.e. to respond to God's law rather than man's. The parable is

---

1 Derrett, 'Fresh Light', pp. 198-219.
2 J.A. Fitzmyer, 'The Story of the Dishonest Manager (Luke 16.1-13)', *TS* 25 (1964), p. 38; cf. *Luke X–XXIV*, pp. 1097-99.
3 Bailey, *Poet and Peasant*, pp. 86-94. See also Topel, 'Injustice', pp. 218-19.

really about the sometime dishonest but now honest steward, but honest only for the sake of personal advantage.[1] These assumptions simply do not fit this parable. Third, Bailey cannot accept that only the steward's kickback is involved in the altered debt figures, especially since the debts are obviously known to the master. This argues that the steward is cutting into the master's profit as well (vv. 5 and 7 indicate the money is owed at least in part to the master), and that the steward is still a dishonest steward.

These explanations of the parable of the unjust steward are unconvincing, either because they posit a textual analysis which leaves too many questions unanswered, or because they draw upon unsupported cultural factors. D.O. Via, in his literary-existential reading, claims that the steward's crisis is resolved by the literary genre of the picaresque story. The steward is the rogue who 'makes conventional society look foolish but without establishing any positive alternative. A rogue is one who lives by his wits and partly outside the community's standards of responsibility though not in a really threatening way.'[2] But this reading does not answer the crucial question of the parable—the nature of the commendation of the steward. Via states that this story 'frees the reader for a time from moral demands', whereas the parable demands a moral explanation. Via also has misinterpreted this picaresque hero. The steward is not outside of the community, but very cognizant of communal standards in trying to move from one community to another, when faced with the prospect of bilateral exclusion.

A common flaw of much parable interpretation has been to isolate individual parables and then to analyse them acontextually, as many of the discussions above reveal. The parable of the unjust steward is one of several parables in Luke's central section. There is debate about the exact structure of this section, but most agree that it is highly literary and consciously well-crafted, and probably topically arranged. Thus it is not surprising to discover specific motifs highlighted in it, espe-

1 D.O. Via, Jr, *The Parables: Their Literary and Existential Dimension* (Philadelphia: Fortress, 1967), p. 159.
2 Via, *Parables*, pp. 159-60.

cially in the parables, which are found here in higher concentration than in any other comparable section in the Gospels (including twenty parables unique to Luke).[1] The first major event of the travel narrative is Jesus' sending out of the seventy (10.1-24), establishing the tone for the entire section by highlighting the theme of inclusion and exclusion of Jesus' followers, reception and rejection[2] of the kingdom. Included in Jesus' instructions for his disciples is what to do when a city does not receive them (δέχομαι; cf. 16.8). When the town rejects them and their message of the gospel, they are not only to knock the dust from off their feet but to state explicitly that the rejectors have been excluded from the kingdom which has come near.[3] As Lk. 7.35 says, 'wisdom is justified by her children'. This timeless statement foreshadows the Lukan emphasis on wise choice, that is to say, a decision is defended by the quality and nature of its results, especially as those results are related to the kingdom.[4] Rejection of Jesus' disciples is tantamount to rejection of him, or at least the message he proclaims, and the fate for such rejection is fearful. As Fitzmyer says, 'the day of the arrival of God's complete dominion in human history and its consequent judgment will be more catastrophic for a town that rejects the Christian message than the fate of Sodom, the notorious town of sinners in Jewish history'.[5] Jesus' 'soliloquy'[6] on the cities which reject his ministry—Chorazin, Bethsaida, Capernaum —reiterates the severe judgment which is theirs. Fitzmyer is correct that

1   On the organization of Luke's central section, see C.L. Blomberg, 'Midrash, Chiasmus, and the Outline of Luke's Central Section', *Gospel Perspectives: Studies in Midrash and Historiography* (vol. 3; ed. R.T. France and D. Wenham; Sheffield: JSOT, 1983), pp. 217-61.

2   Marshall (*Luke*, p. 426) notes now much language of reception (Matt. 10.40; 18.5; Mk 9.37; Lk. 9.48; 10.16; Jn 13.20) and rejection (Lk. 10.16) there is in the Gospels.

3   This and v. 9 regarding the acceptance of Jesus' followers are the only places in Luke's Gospel where Jesus refers to the kingdom having come near.

4   See S.E. Porter, *Verbal Aspect in the Greek of the NT, with Reference to Tense and Mood* (Studies in Biblical Greek 1; New York: Peter Lang, 1989), esp. pp. 75-83, 233-37; J.A. Fitzmyer, *The Gospel According to Luke I–IX* (AB 28; Garden City, NY: Doubleday, 1981), p. 681; although seen by R.H. Stein (*The Method and Message of Jesus' Teachings* [Philadelphia: Westminster, 1978], p. 22) as itself ironic.

5   Fitzmyer, *Luke X–XXIV*, p. 849.

6   Marshall, *Luke*, p. 424.

'the woes are hardly pertinent to the work expected of the disciples in the mission-charge',[1] but inclusion of non-Jewish cities which rejected Jesus broadens the scope of the section. The sending of the seventy is not just about the seventy but about any who accept or reject the gospel, and want to be included in or excluded from the kingdom. To be excluded from the kingdom, i.e. to be one of those cities which fails to embrace the gospel, is instead to be brought down to Hades (v. 15; cf. 16.23). This language of inclusion and exclusion is continued in various ways throughout the travel narrative.[2]

Established within this context is another of Luke's major themes, economic issues, as several scholars have recently made clear,[3] but it is economics undeniably tied to eschatology. The thematic and verbal connections between Lk. 16.1-13 and the parable of the rich man and Lazarus (16.19-31) are clear.[4] Throughout ch. 16 strong words are spoken about the dangers of wealth. Luke 16.14 states openly that the Pharisees were lovers of money. Jesus describes them as those who justify themselves in the sight of men, whereas God knows their hearts; in the same way, what they esteem highly is esteemed as detestable by God. In the parable of the rich man and Lazarus, as Marshall says, the theme 'is the reversal of fortunes in the next world for the rich and the poor', a fitting conclusion to ch. 16, as Fitzmyer says.[5] This rich man (cf. 16.1) is painted in striking contrast to the poor man, Lazarus. The rich man is a son of this age, having accumulated all of its much-desired baubles. This is the same man who must beg for some relief, no matter how small, and failing that, for a word of warning to his brothers who remain behind. The request for

---

1 Fitzmyer, *Luke X–XXIV*, p. 852.
2 See just up to Lk. 15: 10.19; 10.25-37; 10.38-42; 11.14-28; 11.37-52; 11.53-54; 12.5; 12.16-21; 12.35-40; 12.41-48; 12.49-53; 13.18ff.; 13.22-30; 14.15-24; 14.25-35.
3 E.g. I.H. Marshall, *Luke: Historian and Theologian* (Grand Rapids: Zondervan, 1970), pp. 206-209; Seccombe, *Possessions*, pp. 160ff.
4 See Blomberg, 'Midrash', p. 245, who labels the parables of Lk. 16 as 'the use and abuse of riches'. Cf. also Marshall, *Luke*, p. 613; C.H. Talbert, *Reading Luke: A Literary and Theological Commentary on the Third Gospel* (New York: Crossroad, 1984), p. 153; A.A. Plummer, *A Critical and Exegetical Commentary on the Gospel According to St. Luke* (ICC; Edinburgh: T. and T. Clark, 1922), p. 379; A. Loisy, *L'Évangile selon Luc* (Paris: Emile Noury, 1924), p. 403.
5 Marshall, *Luke*, p. 632; Fitzmyer, *Luke X–XXIV*, p. 1125.

a miracle is denied, a word of warning having already been given in the parable of the unjust steward.

Although most commentators label the parables of Lk. 15 as related to righteousness, repentance, or the outcast, there is here also an undeniable connection between economics and eschatology, a theme which can be denied only at the risk of skewing interpretation of the parables of Lk. 15 and 16 (cf. 14.15-24).[1] Luke 15 opens as an address to the publicans or tax-collectors and sinners, along with the Pharisees and scribes (cf. 16.14-15), who were grumbling that Jesus received (προσδέχεται)[2] sinners. Jesus then tells three parables, which some might simplistically explain as the application of economic analogies. But in the light of Lk. 16, as well as of treatment of economic and eschatological themes within Luke, more is at stake than simply instructive analogies. In the parable of the lost sheep, the moderately well-off shepherd, perhaps in contrast to the poor woman of the next parable, searches diligently for the one lost sheep and rejoices when he finds it, in the same way as there is great rejoicing in heaven over one repentant sinner as opposed to 99 who are righteous.[3] The persistent concern of the shepherd secures inclusion of the one sheep in the fold, in the same way as one repentant sinner is included in the kingdom.[4] The economic analogy is utilized for the sake of making clear the desired eschatological inclusion.[5] In the parable of the woman and her coins, a similar use of an economic analogy is made. In the same way that

---

1 C.J.A. Hickling ('A Tract on Jesus and the Pharisees? A Conjecture on the Redaction of Luke 15 and 16', *HeyJ* 16 [1975], pp. 253-65) argues from a redactional standpoint for the unity of Lk. 15 and 16 as all originally addressed against the Pharisees. Cf. J. Coutts, 'The Unjust Steward (Luke 16.1-8a)', *Theology* 52 (1949), pp. 55-58.

2 See Bailey, *Poet and Peasant*, p. 143, who indicates that the simple and compound forms of δέχομαι often imply hospitality: Lk. 9.5, 53; 10.8, 11; 16.4, 9; 22.17. Cf. Thucydides 2.12; Aristophanes, *Knights* 735.

3 Fletcher ('Riddle', pp. 27-28) sees the statement as ironically addressed to the Pharisees.

4 Bailey (*Poet and Peasant*, pp. 144-45) organizes the parable with v. 6—focusing on restoration at the return home—lying at the centre of the chiastic structure of the parable.

5 L. Schottroff ('Das Gleichnis vom verlorenen Sohn', *ZTK* 68 [1971], pp. 32-35) argues that v. 7 is ironically referring to the scribes and Pharisees who think of themselves as needing no repentance.

a woman will wisely search for a lost coin until she finds it,[1] the angels rejoice over one sinner who repents and is included in the kingdom.

In the third and final parable, the parable of the prodigal, the crucial economic factors revolve around the prodigal's desire to be well-received by the sons of this age. Correlations between Lk. 15.11-36 and 16.1-13 are striking, as M.R. Austin has recently pointed out.[2] The young man's economic well-being ensures a welcome reception,[3] just as the unjust steward anticipates a welcome reception on the basis of economic manipulation (16.4), but one that lasts only as long as his economic status ensures his contribution to riotous living. The test of the genuineness of his reception comes when his economic resources are exhausted, and then he, like the unjust steward (16.1-2), learns that he is no longer welcome, but is in fact reduced to a lower state than before, the feeding of swine. He is joined to a citizen of that country in a way that he had not anticipated.[4] The situational irony is clear: a Jewish man is reduced to the feeding of swine for a non-Jew and, desirous of food as he may be, is unable to find sufficient. It is then, at the depth of his physical and spiritual condition, that he does his clearest thinking (cf. 16.3), and decides that being a servant for his father back home is better than being a servant for one of the successful citizens of the far country (cf. 16.4).[5] Oesterley indicates that a hired servant, especially a day-labourer, was 'an outsider', not belonging to the estate or having a place

---

1   Bailey (*Poet and Peasant*, p. 156) sees '*joy* in community over restoration' at the heart of the chiastic structure of this parable.
2   On correlations between Lk. 15.11-32 and Lk. 16, especially verbal parallels between the words and actions of the two protagonists, the prodigal and the steward, see M.R. Austin, 'The Hypocritical Son', *EQ* 57 (1985), pp. 307-15; Bailey, *Poet and Peasant*, p. 109.
3   The economic factors at play have been widely disputed. See esp. Bailey, *Poet and Peasant*, pp. 164-69, although his conclusions are debatable.
4   Cf. W.F. Arndt, *The Gospel According to St. Luke* (St. Louis: Concordia, 1956), p. 351, who claims that the young man forces himself on his employer, itself an ironic turn of events.
5   There is some question about the nature of the repentance of the young man. Fitzmyer (*Luke X–XXIV*, pp. 1088-89) and Marshall (*Luke*, p. 609) think that it is genuine, while Bailey (*Poet and Peasant*, pp. 173-77) following J.D.M. Derrett ('Law in the NT: The Parable of the Prodigal Son', *NTS* 14 [1967-68], p. 58) thinks not.

in its affairs.[1] But the father welcomes his son back, putting the best robe on him, with the garment probably an eschatological symbol of the new age.[2] As the father says, not once but twice, there is cause for rejoicing, because the son who was dead is now alive, who was lost is now found.[3] The wise prodigal is reinstated in the community, after having made the tragically wrong decision of thinking that economic status could ingratiate him with those of the far off country.

Although no change of scene from the previous parable is intended, and hence the audience includes from Lk. 15.1-2 tax collectors and sinners, and Pharisees and scribes, as most commentators agree,[4] the parable of the unjust steward focuses specifically on the disciples. The word 'parable' is not actually used at 16.1, but appears in 15.3 as a head-term for the several stories included in chs. 15 and 16. The connection with what precedes is confirmed by καί modifying ἔλεγεν and referring to continued parabolic discourse,[5] with the most pointed irony reserved for Jesus' closest followers.

The first character introduced in the parable is the 'certain rich man'. Some scholars, as has been noted above, argue that the rich man is as dishonest as his steward and is therefore implicated in his entire dishonest affair, endorsement of the steward's actions (v. 8, with the lord taken as the master) being a confirmation of his guilt.[6] In the text itself there is no indication that the master is implicated in any of the wrongdoing, and his response to discovering that his steward is misappropriating funds calls forth immediate and decisive action.

---

1   W.O.E. Oesterley, *The Gospel Parables in the Light of their Jewish Background* (London: SPCK, 1936), p. 186.

2   So Jeremias, *Parables*, pp. 130, 118.

3   Again, the author uses irony, playing on the words for life and death quite clearly with eschatological implications. See Fitzmyer, *Luke X–XXIV*, p. 1090.

4   Cf. E. Kamlah, 'Die Parabel vom ungerechten Verwalter (Luk. 16.1ff.) im Rahmen der Knechtsgleichnisse', *Abraham unser Vater* (ed. O. Betz, *et al.*; Leiden: Brill, 1963), pp. 276-94.

5   A.B. Bruce, 'The Synoptic Gospels', *Expositor's Greek Testament* (5 vols; ed. W.R. Nicoll; Grand Rapids: Eerdmans, n. d.), 1.584; Plummer, *Luke*, p. 381.

6   E.g. Derrett, 'Fresh Light', pp. 201-202; Via, *Parables*, p. 159, referring to the master anachronistically as a 'scheming businessman'; F. Hauck and W. Kasch, πλοῦτος, *TDNT*, 6.328, implying that use of 'rich' in Luke implies more than just the possession of goods (cf. 18.18-27; 16.19-31). In the history of criticism, the master has been equated with a number of entities, including God, the Romans, mammon and Satan (see Plummer, *Luke*, p. 381).

To the contrary, the master of the parable occupies a role similar to that of the father of the prodigal in the equation between inclusion and exclusion regarding economic matters. He is the one who decides whether one is included or excluded. And he has decided to exclude his steward.[1]

The second major character of the parable is the steward (οἰκονόμος), who could have held any one of several positions.[2] Obviously not a civic official or merely a servant, whose punishment for mismanagement would have been more severe than dismissal (v. 2),[3] he is an estate manager with widespread and influential powers. He is charged with wasting his master's goods. The fact that the 'charges were brought to him [the master]' indicates that, contrary to some critics, the master was aware of the condition of his estate. Whereas δια–βάλλω, used only here in the NT, may mean '*bring charges in hostile intent*, either falsely and slanderously... or justly',[4] a hostile intent cannot be determined. That the charges are true seems indubitable,[5] at least in the master's mind. Luke uses the same word, διασκορπίζω, to describe the steward's actions as he uses in 15.13 of the prodigal son's wasting of his inheritance, the only two times that the word is used in the NT figuratively.[6] There may well be an implication that the steward has been spending his master's money on riotous living, because he apparently has no saved resources when called to make account. The master confronts the steward directly: 'What is this that I hear about you?[7] Give up the record of

1 Cf. Dio Chrysostom 2.75: ἐκεῖνον ἐκποδὼν ἐποιήσατο καὶ μετέστησεν; ὡς οὐκ ἄξιον ὄντα βασιλεύειν.
2 H.L. Strack and P. Billerbeck, *Kommentar zum Neuen Testament aus Talmud und Midrasch* (6 vols; Munich: Beck, 1922-61), 3.217: 'Obersklave'; 'Städtischer Beamter'; and 'Haushalter, Gutsverwalter, Rechnungsführer'. See also O. Michel, οἰκονόμος, *TDNT*, 5.149-50.
3 Manson, *Sayings*, p. 583.
4 W. Bauer, *A Greek-English Lexicon of the NT and Other Early Christian Literature* (2nd edn; Chicago: University of Chicago Press, 1979), *s.v.* Cf. W. Foerster, διαβάλλω, *TDNT*, 2.71.
5 So Gächter, 'Parable', p. 127.
6 Austin, 'Son', p. 311. διασκορπίζω may 'imply neglect of duty or misappropriation of funds' (Marshall, *Luke*, p. 617). Marshall opts for the former since no compensation is suggested, but the rest of the parable suggests the latter. See Arndt, *Luke*, p. 355; cf. O. Michel, διασκορπίζω, *TDNT*, 7.421-22.
7 Fitzmyer, *Luke X–XXIV*, p. 1100. This clause can also be interpreted with τί as interrogative meaning 'why' (Arndt, *Luke*, p. 355: 'why have you followed such a

your stewardship,[1] for you are no longer able to act as steward.' The steward expresses no disagreement,[2] but begins to plan for his future (cf. 15.17).

The steward immediately begins a soliloquy, which not only reflects an economy of description[3] but selects the essential factors by which his character may be judged. The steward is beginning to think quickly. Caught unprepared for a future apart from his stewardship, he weighs his alternatives. He immediately dismisses digging and begging. The thought of digging was universally and proverbially abhorred,[4] and begging represented an equivalent degrading non-physical act.[5] In other words, with all other avenues closed to him both physically and emotionally, the steward must find other means of support.

Suddenly the idea comes to him. Luke's asyndetic use of the aorist (ἔγνων) of present reference[6] shows an idea just now entering into the steward's mind, though the plan is exemplified rather than described (cf. 15.18, where the prodigal outlines his plan, even repeating the words he will use when meeting his father). The reader gets a serious inkling of the

course?'); or with a note of surprise ('What! Do I hear this about you?'), but this requires that unwarranted emphasis be put on 'you' (Plummer, *Luke*, p. 382).

1 Cf. Plato, *Phaedo* 63E: ὑμῖν δὴ τοῖς δικασταῖς βούλομαι ἤδη τὸν λόγον ἀποδοῦναι. Is the steward fired immediately? What is he told to do with the books? The steward could be called upon to turn his books over for inspection or to make a final reckoning, but these are unlikely because it would give him time to remedy his situation or perhaps confiscate more property for himself (Bailey, *Poet and Peasant*, p. 96; Bruce, 'Synoptic Gospels', 1.584). The steward's subsequent actions look like those of a man who has no prospect of a second chance. The context, reinforced by the aorist grammaticalizing the action as complete, indicates that the account is given up at this time. On the nature of perfective verbal aspect grammaticalized by the aorist, see Porter, *Verbal Aspect*, chs. 2 and 4. Whereas λόγος may refer to a general accounting (see Strack–Billerbeck, *Kommentar*, 3.218; Gächter, 'Parable', p. 127 n. 32), it more likely is the account books entrusted to the steward by the master (see Bailey, *Poet and Peasant*, p. 97).

2 Contra Bailey, *Poet and Peasant*, p. 96, who goes much too far in interpreting the steward's lack of disagreement.

3 See e.g. Lk. 12.17, 45; 15.17-18; 16.3-4; 18.4-5; 20.13. Cf. R. Bultmann, *The History of the Synoptic Tradition* (tr. J. Marsh; Oxford: Blackwell, 1972), pp. 189-90.

4 Aristophanes, *Birds* 1432: τί γὰρ πάθω; σκάπτειν γὰρ οὐκ ἐπίσταμαι.

5 Cf. Lk. 18.35; Sophocles, *Oedipus at Colonus* 1364: ἐπαιτῶ τὸν καθ' ἡμέραν βίον. Bauer (*Lexicon*, p. 282) says begging is reserved for mendicants, which is what the steward fears he will become.

6 See Porter, *Verbal Aspect*, esp. pp. 225-30, for recent discussion of non-past use of the aorist; and Plummer, *Luke*, p. 383.

steward's motives, however, when he states that his reason is so that (ἵνα) he may be received into 'their' houses when (ὅταν) he is removed from his stewardship. The ὅταν clause modifies the verb for reception, rather than implying that the stewardship is still in question, although the steward has yet to turn the books over to his former master. This means that the steward has a short period in which to act before his removal becomes fully known. The impersonal third person plural (δέξωνται)[1] refers most likely to the debtors of v. 5,[2] although the reference need not be specific. The impersonal sense well illustrates the desperate situation of the steward. There is situational irony in that the steward who has just been excluded from his employment on the basis of untrustworthy behaviour now uses the same means he was caught exploiting. He does this in order to secure a place where he can be received by others who can guarantee a life similar to the one he is used to enjoying.[3]

The panic of unemployment and the thought of being discovered in his plan account for the steward's haste in dealing with the debtors. He summons them individually because of the need for secrecy,[4] and carries out his transactions, with no recorded formal greetings or chit-chat to draw focus away from the action. The two incidents in which he acts as representative for all of his master's debtors conform to a pattern. First he asks how much each owes. Since it is unlikely that the steward is completely unaware of the status of the debtor's account, this information forecasts for the listener the potential scope of the steward's activity.[5] Then the steward tells the

---

1   The standard opinion, that the impersonal third person plural is Semitic (see M. Black, *An Aramaic Approach to the Gospels and Acts* [3rd edn; Oxford: Clarendon, 1967], pp. 126-28; followed by most commentators), has been refuted by L. Rydbeck, *Fachprosa, vermeintliche Volkssprache und Neues Testament: Zur Beurteilung der sprachlichen Niveauunterschiede im nachklassischen Griechisch* (Acta Universitatis Upsaliensis; Uppsala: Uppsala University Press, 1967), pp. 27-45.

2   So Plummer, *Luke*, p. 383; Loisy, *L'Évangile*, p. 405; M.-J. Lagrange, *Évangile selon Saint Luc* (ÉBib; Paris: Gabalda, 1948), p. 432; J.M. Creed, *The Gospel According to St. Luke* (London: Macmillan, 1965), p. 203; Marshall, *Luke*, p. 618.

3   Eagar, 'Parable', p. 461.

4   Morris, *Luke*, p. 247.

5   Creed, *Luke*, p. 204; contra Bailey, *Poet and Peasant*, p. 101 n. 58, who presses the details.

debtor to sit down quickly and change the debt form, no doubt written in each debtor's own hand. The steward's insistence maintains dramatic tension. The steward is working against two clocks, hence his reminder that what is done must be done quickly, because he is trying to complete his actions before his master gets suspicious and before the debtors learn that he is no longer functioning in an official capacity. Much is made by commentators of what kind of debt is at issue, how large the owed sums are, how large the reductions are, and why the debtors write them in their own hands. These details are secondary. The important factor is that the amounts are sufficiently large and reduced to a large enough extent[1] that the steward has a claim to being received out of gratitude by the debtors. The reader is not to be concerned with the role which the debtors play in reducing their debts,[2] although there should be some concern with the fact that they have complicity in the deed. Either they believe in good faith that the steward is still empowered to act,[3] although they should be a little suspicious of such a radical and hastily-conceived reduction. Or else, even if they suspect something is amiss, they are also sufficiently dishonest to take advantage of the situation.[4] But this is to be expected from sons of this age.

Verse 8 is the recognized crux of the parable.[5] Confirmation that the steward has acted dishonestly is presented by the address of the lord as τὸν οἰκονόμον τῆς ἀδικίας linked with a causal statement (the first ὅτι) referring to his immediately preceding actions. Whereas most interpreters see the genitive as adjectival or as a genitive of quality, possibly Semitic in background,[6] there is good reason for seeing it as causal or

---

1 Jeremias (*Parables*, p. 181) details how heavy the obligation is, although he suggests that the figures reveal the oriental story-teller's love for exaggeration and large numbers.
2 Bruce, 'Synoptic Gospels', 1.584-85.
3 Bailey, *Poet and Peasant*, p. 100.
4 Bruce, 'Synoptic Gospels', 1.585.
5 So Krämer, *Rätsel*, p. 139.
6 E.g. H. Kosmala, 'The Parable of the Unjust Steward in the Light of Qumran', *ASTI* 3 (1964), pp. 114-15, and many others. F. Blass and A. Debrunner (*A Grammar of NT Greek and Other Early Christian Literature* [tr. R.W. Funk; Chicago: University of Chicago Press, 1962], § 176 [1]) label it the 'genitive with verbs of emotion', but the genitive noun goes with οἰκονόμον because of proximity rather than with the verb, ἐπήνεσεν, at the beginning of the clause.

objective.[1] In this case the steward is the one who does unrighteousness, with the genitive following a verbal noun which is cognate to the verb form used in v. 2 (the noun form and other cognates are used in vv. 1, 2, 3, 4).

But who is the lord who praises the steward in v. 8?[2] Krämer has summarized the arguments for taking it as referring to the lord of the parable or to the lord, Jesus.[3] They may be evaluated several ways. Linguistically,[4] putting aside for the moment the question of the content of the lord's statements in v. 8, the arguments clearly lie with the lord being the master of the parable. First is reference to the master in vv. 1-7, including ἄνθρωπός τις, ὅς, and αὐτῷ in v. 1, ὁ κύριος in v. 3, and τοῦ κυρίου ἑαυτοῦ and τῷ κυρίῳ in v. 5, establishing a clear presumption that the κύριος in v. 8 must still be the master of the parable. There is no linguistic indication, apart from the difficulty with v. 8b, that a shift has occurred. Second, as Bailey indicates, absolute use of κύριος in the parables of Luke does not clearly refer to Jesus, as some have posited, but is fairly equally divided between reference to Jesus and to the lord of the parables.[5] Third is use of direct speech in v. 9 after indirect speech in v. 8, a phenomenon known to biblical and extra-biblical Greek.[6] In the parallels from the NT often cited, the transition occurs without warning in the midst of the reported speech (except for Acts 25.5, with φησί),[7] but Lk. 16.9

1   Cf. C.F.D. Moule, *Idiom Book of NT Greek* (2nd edn; Cambridge: Cambridge University Press, 1959), pp. 39-41.
2   Schmid (*Lukas*, p. 259) argues that it really makes no difference to the parable whether Jesus or the master is referred to by 'lord' in v. 8. The literary reading given in this paper shows the importance of this question.
3   Krämer, *Rätsel*, pp. 139-43.
4   This argument does not consider form-critical reasons noted above.
5   Bailey, *Poet and Peasant*, p. 103, who cites Lk. 12.37, 42b; 14.23 with reference to the master of the story and 12.42; 18.6 with reference to Jesus.
6   See Blass–Debrunner, *Grammar*, § 470 (2); R. Kühner and B. Gerth, *Ausführliche Grammatik der griechischen Sprache: Satzlehre* (2 vols; 4th edn; Leverkusen: Gottschalksche, 1955), 2.556-57. Cf. Mk 5.23; 6.8-9; Longinus, *Sublime* 27; Homer, *Il.* 4.301; 14.346.
7   The examples which Marshall cites—Lk. 5.14; Acts 1.4; 17.3; 23.22; 25.4-5; and possibly 14.22—are not true parallels (*Luke*, pp. 619-20; cf. *idem*, 'Luke 16.8— Who commended the unjust steward?', *JTS* ns 19 [1968], pp. 618-19), as Fitzmyer (*Luke X–XXIV*, p. 1108) indicates. For example, Lk. 18.6 has the word 'judge' in the quoted words, indicating by contrast that the 'lord' is probably Jesus. Marshall is correct in introducing a more probable parallel: Lk. 14.23f.

has clear words of introduction spoken by Jesus:[1] 'and I say to you', with 'to you' (ὑμῖν) emphatically placed, thus highlighting a contrast between the speaker and the listeners.

On the basis of content, the reasons are likewise unconvincing for supposing that the lord is Jesus. First, there would be an unsuitable, abrupt ending to the parable, with the master of the parable introduced but dropped without reappearing to finish his instigated act of dismissal.[2] Second, there is widespread agreement that neither the master of the parable nor Jesus could praise the behaviour of the steward. This has led to several solutions mentioned above, regarding either praise of the steward's foresight although not his actual behaviour, or reconstruction of the background so that commendation is because the unjust steward has suddenly become the just steward. Neither approach is plausible on the basis of the internal content of the parable or its surrounding context. And third, in the light of the interpretation offered below, the first words of evaluation are better made by the master in terms of the earthly situation, before Jesus makes an application of the economic metaphor to a wider humanity regarding its eschatological fortunes.

The context of this parable as outlined above posits in clear terms that financial advancement in the world outside the community is not to be endorsed or commended, i.e. wisdom's justification is not found in deeds which curry favour with the sons of this age if one expects a place in the kingdom. If that is not entirely clear in Lk. 15, it is without a doubt in the parable of Lazarus and the rich man in 16.19-31, the parable virtually always linked with the parable of the unjust steward. In other words, the normative values established by the surrounding parabolic context are that one is called upon to make wise choices about one's relation to the world outside of the kingdom community. The ideal is one of harmony with the kingdom community, shunning the values which degrade and bring ruin. If the statements of v. 8 are taken simply at their surface value, they are at odds with this context. More importantly still, if the statements of v. 8 are taken simply at their

---

1 Fitzmyer, 'Story', p. 27; Lagrange, *Évangile*, p. 433.
2 See Manson, *Sayings*, p. 584; Fitzmyer, 'Story', pp. 27-28.

surface value, they are at odds with the parable itself. For first, the master is commending a villain, as numerous commentators have aptly noted, but, what is worse, the master is commending one who is in fact a failure. The steward has been caught out twice, and, even utilizing his dishonest practices before being caught for the first time, he was unable to accumulate enough wealth to support himself or to secure a place with others.[1] As Good says, 'Is not a source of irony's attraction and repellance alike that it may plausibly be taken literally, invites us to take it literally, makes certain sense when taken literally? Yet a nagging doubt hints at a meaning hidden behind the mask.'[2] The master of the parable has discovered that his steward had already been associating with the sons of this age in his dishonest and probably wasteful behaviour (he is 'praised' as τὸν οἰκονόμον τῆς ἀδικίας). The steward is then faced with a choice when he is dismissed from his position. He may choose to make the hard choice of doing honest work, or he may choose to sell out completely by ingratiating himself with the sons of this age so that they will receive him. He chooses the latter. It is this behaviour which the observant and insightful master ironically comments upon, in pointing out that the steward has not made a wise choice but a wrong choice. He is heading towards becoming a prodigal son, by setting as his goal becoming friends with the sons of this age. The commendatory statements of vv. 8ff. are clearly ironic.[3] The steward, becoming like the prodigal son, is by his behaviour attempting to make himself popular with the sons of this age, so that he may join their community. But he does not realize how fleeting are the values of this age. He is attempting to get inside the gates of the rich man's house, but he too will suffer the fate of Lazarus's rich man, if he is not reduced to the prodigal's condition sooner. This ironic understanding does not need to posit a special sense of ἐπήνεσεν as a

---

1 Eagar, 'Parable', p. 460.
2 Good, *Irony*, p. 22. Contra H. Martin, *The Parables of the Gospels and their Meaning for To-Day* (London: SCM, 1937), pp. 176-77, who blames the difficulty on allegorizing. Cf. F.W. Danker, *Jesus and the New Age: According to St. Luke* (St. Louis: Clayton, 1972), p. 173.
3 See Booth, *Rhetoric*, pp. 5-6, who defines stable, covert, fixed and finite irony, the characteristics of the irony found here.

word of condemnation or an uncharacteristic sense of
φρονίμως.[1] In fact, the usual senses of the words to describe one
who grasps the eschatological condition[2] are well suited to this
ironic context: the steward has taken a short-sighted view of
his circumstances and neglected the larger and eternal picture. As Fletcher says, 'Surely the steward of the parable is not
a man who has grasped the eschatological situation of the
kingdom of God: his own "eschatological situation" is simply
that he is losing the livelihood he has been enjoying, and
presumably enjoying intemperately at his master's expense.'[3]
Irony 'clarifies with extreme sharpness the incongruity
involved in a matter of great moment',[4] and the steward has
proven himself to be unwise.[5]

Fletcher has perceived the irony but he does so in terms of a
contrast with the prodigal son as endorsing a faithful and wise
use of money. But the irony extends much further: these
parables are about money, but they are about money as analogies for values which address the question of wise choice
regarding inclusion in or exclusion from the kingdom.[6] This is
confirmed by reference in v. 8 to ἀδικία as the corrupt nature
of the world, of which the steward is fully a member, but even
more so by reference to the sons of this age and the sons of
light.[7] The opposition of 'sons of this world' and 'sons of light' is
generally conceded to contrast inhabitants of this worldly age
and those who are either spiritually or in reality inhabitants of
the kingdom.[8] The sons of this age are unfavourably con-

1 So Schwarz, ' "... lobte den betrügerischen Verwalter"?', pp. 94-95, who posits
   mistranslation of Aramaic equivalents.
2 Matt. 7.24; 24.25; 25.2, 4, 8, 9; Lk. 12.42. Jeremias, *Parables*, p. 46 n. 83; contra H.
   Preisker, 'Lukas 16.1-7', *TL* 74 (1974), p. 89. By taking the traditional view A.J.
   Mattill, Jr (*Luke and the Last Things: A Perspective for the Understanding of
   Lukan Thought* [Dillsboro, NC: Western North Carolina Press, 1979], pp. 37-39)
   misses these points of connection.
3 Fletcher, 'Riddle', p. 18.
4 Good, *Irony*, p. 24.
5 Bretscher, 'Parable', p. 759.
6 Seccombe (*Possessions*, pp. 160ff.) grasps the eschatological dimension, but
   misses the irony.
7 The second ὅτι appears to be causal. When the irony of the passage is appreciated
   in the light of a single speaker, this proves to be unproblematic. See Plummer,
   Luke, p. 384; Loisy, *L'Évangile*, p. 408.
8 See H.K. Luce, *The Gospel According to S. Luke* (Cambridge: Cambridge University Press, 1933), p. 261.

trasted with the sons destined for God's kingdom of light.[1] And the irony is equally pronounced: the sons of this age believe that by their 'wise' behaviour in this generation they are able to effect an influence on the age to come, but, as the parable of the prodigal son shows with reference to this world and the parable of the rich man and Lazarus confirms for the age to come, nothing could be further from the truth.

In v. 9, Jesus enters in his own words (καὶ ἐγὼ ὑμῖν λέγω) and applies the parable directly to his hearers (emphatic use of ὑμῖν), with an emphatically placed reflexive pronoun (ἑαυτοῖς) preceding the imperative.[2] It becomes clear that ethical irony is being utilized, i.e. 'verbal incompatibilities set up and provoke a deeper interrogation of self-consciousness'.[3] The hearers, certainly in the first instance the disciples but others as well, are commanded in no uncertain terms to make (cf. use of ποιέω in v. 8) for themselves friends 'by (ἐκ[4]) the mammon of unrighteousness', which serves as God's rival (see 16.13).[5] Much has been written on the μαμωνᾶς τῆς ἀδικίας. Hauck, although encountering opposition from some interpreters, posits that every reference in the NT to the mammon as something one puts trust in has negative connotations.[6] This is confirmed here by the genitival modification, designed to make a linkage with the description of the steward. The irony is clear: Jesus is commending his followers for using worldly wealth in its most negative sense to secure

1 Marshall, *Luke*, p. 621.
2 See Plummer, *Luke*, p. 385, on the balance of the introductory words, as well as the emphatic pronoun. On the unity of vv. 8 and 9 see R.H. Hiers, 'Friends by Unrighteous Mammon: The Eschatological Proletariat (Luke 16.9)', *JAAR* 38 (1970), pp. 32-33.
3 G.J. Handwerk, *Irony and Ethics in Narrative: From Schlegel to Lacan* (New Haven: Yale University Press, 1985), p. 2.
4 This is probably an instrumental use of the preposition (so Marshall, *Luke*, p. 621; Fitzmyer, *Luke X–XXIV*, p. 1109). Cf. Fitzmyer for a list of various interpretations, which he evaluates as follows: 'But all these are desperate attempts to get around a sense of "mammon of dishonesty"'. These are unnecessary when irony is appreciated.
5 Manson, *Sayings*, p. 585.
6 F. Hauck, μαμωνᾶς, *TDNT*, 4.389-90; Fitzmyer, *Luke X–XXIV*, p. 1109; Seccombe, *Possessions*, pp. 163-67 (surveying the several positions); Danker, *Jesus*, p. 174; contra Marshall, *Luke*, p. 621; Strack–Billerbeck, *Kommentar*, 3.220; C.H. Dodd, *The Parables of the Kingdom* (New York: Scribners, 1961), p. 17; Jeremias, *Parables*, p. 47.

reward, a clear impossibility for this world, as the prodigal learned, and for the world beyond, as the rich man regretted. The 'friends' have been variously interpreted as those in need who are aided by benevolence in the use of wealth, especially almsgiving, as well as heavenly or divine beings, including God.[1] But the context indicates that the friends are any with whom one wants to be inappropriately ingratiated,[2] especially the sons of this age. This may be sarcasm on Jesus' part,[3] but on the basis of the obvious exaggeration, perhaps emphatic ethical verbal irony is more to the point. The irony is found on two planes: dishonest wealth cannot be expected to produce earthly friendship, as the prodigal realizes, but more than that, this means of ingratiation cannot be used to buy eternal friends, as the rich man so painfully learns. Whenever worldly wealth might give out (ὅταν ἐκλίπῃ; cf. v. 4),[4] as both the prodigal and rich man discover, reception into eternal habitations is impossible, both for the sons of this age and for any of their followers.[5] 'The eternal tents' (τὰς αἰωνίους σκηνάς), occurring only here in the NT, refers not to the abode of the unrighteous, but to the desired abode of the righteous, i.e. the kingdom,[6] represented in its earthly sense as the banquet to which the prodigal is invited on his return and in its

---

1 Hiers, 'Friends', pp. 33-34; Jeremias, *Parables*, p. 46; Creed, *Luke*, p. 205; R.D. Middleton, 'St. Luke 16.9', *Theology* 29 (1934), p. 41; Williams, 'Almsgiving', p. 296; Bruce, 'Synoptic Gospels', 1.586; Ellis, *Luke*, pp. 201-202; N. Perrin, *Rediscovering the Teaching of Jesus* (New York: Harper and Row, 1967), p. 115.

2 See Fitzmyer, *Luke X–XXIV*, p. 108.

3 Paul, 'Steward', p. 192. It does not seem to have the derogatory, wounding sense required of sarcasm, however.

4 See Kosmala, 'Parable', p. 118, who notes the eschatological implications of this clause.

5 On use of the impersonal third person verb see above. The impersonal verb reinforces the irony, because it leaves unexpressed those doing the receiving, since no receiving is to be done. The poorly attested variant ἐκλίπητε (W 33 69 131 pm lat; Majority), translated 'you might die', would make this point even more forcefully.

6 Hiers, 'Friends', p. 31; Marshall, *Luke: Historian and Theologian*, p. 136. Cf. Plummer, *Luke*, p. 386: 'The combination of "eternal" with "tabernacles" is remarkable, because σκηναί is commonly used of dwellings which are very temporary'; and Eagar, 'Parable', p. 462. This ironic juxtaposition of the eternal and the temporal presents a striking image. See most recently M.G. Steinhauser, 'Noah in his Generation: An Allusion in Luke 16.8b, "εἰς τὴν γενεὰν τὴν ἑαυτῶν"', *ZNW* 79 (1988), pp. 152-57, for an interesting but unconvincing hypothesis.

eschatological sense as the bosom of Abraham where Lazarus goes after his death. The use of σκηνή is thus contrasted with οἶκος in v. 4. The ironic application of the parable puts the consequences of human deeds in eschatological perspective, as well as heightening the irony by drawing attention to the seriousness of the consequences. For the prodigal the habitation is the pig trough and for the rich man it is the unrelieved torment of Hades; for the unjust steward it is not the eternal abode of the righteous.[1]

In vv. 10-13 the irony is developed further, driving home the point with clear and unmitigated force through Jesus' continued ironic commentary.[2] In v. 10 a piece of secular wisdom is held up to ironic ridicule by the steward's actions. The received tradition is that one who is faithful in little is faithful in much, and one who is unrighteous in little is unrighteous in much. All of the parables of Lk. 15 and 16 have exemplified consistent characters. But focusing upon the prodigal, the unjust steward and the rich man well illustrates that they are especially consistent in their failed judgment about the use of the material of this world, the nature of this world itself, and their relation via it to the kingdom. They have been consistently bad in their judgment, both in little things and, in consequence, in big things. The irony reaches further, however, since those whom the main characters have come into contact with, such as the residents of the far country and the steward's compatriots, are not able to execute faithfully even such a simple thing as hospitality, much less provide eternal habitation. This principle is further applied in vv. 11-12, through two inverted questions.[3] The first question is whether, if one is not faithful with the unrighteous mammon, one will be given

---

1   See Bretscher, 'Parable', p. 759.
2   Most do not consider this part of the original parable, but once the irony is explicated, objections to unity disappear. Many see these verses as unified around a financial theme (Paul, 'Steward', p. 192); or the idea of 'worldliness' (Kosmala, 'Parable', pp. 118-20). On the unity of vv. 10-13 see e.g. J. Pirot, *Paraboles et allégories évangeliques: La pensée de Jésus, Les commentaires patristiques* (Paris: P. Lethielleux, 1949), p. 318, on the basis of antithesis; Bailey, *Poet and Peasant*, pp. 110-18; Bultmann, *History*, p. 90; cf. A. Descamps, 'La composition littéraire de Luc 16.9-13', *NovT* 1 (1956), pp. 47-53, who argues for unity of vv. 10-13 as Lukan composition on the basis of vv. 1-8.
3   Contra Marshall, *Luke*, p. 623, who believes that v. 12 is 'too obscure to be regarded as an explanation of anything'. He also does not see the irony of vv. 8ff.

that which is true, 'or that which pertains to the Kingdom'.[1] Certainly, if one were unfaithful, one would not be trusted with something of more value, as the truism of v. 10 so clearly states. But more importantly, the fact that one has anything to do with the unrighteous mammon excludes one from that which is eternally true, as the case of the unjust steward illustrates. The same applies to v. 12. If one is not faithful with others' property, no one will trust that person with his own possessions, as the unjust steward again rightly proves.[2] Shunning the 'unrighteous mammon' is the way to be entrusted by God with that which is true wealth,[3] and not making use of the unrighteous mammon which belongs to those outside the kingdom[4] is the way to have a fine robe put on one's back, a ring put on one's finger, sandals put on one's feet and a place reserved in Abraham's bosom.[5] To expect to buy eternal reward by dishonest manipulation is to expect the impossible, and justly draws ironic comment on such foolish behaviour.

The parable concludes in v. 13 with Jesus' final ironic comment upon the actions of the steward. The steward, like the prodigal and the rich man, tries to serve two masters. In other words, they all hope to use the things of this world to secure a place for themselves in the kingdom. But all three parables reveal that this is impossible. Only by the graciousness of the forgiving father is the prodigal allowed a second chance, a chance denied the rich man. The unjust steward attempts to maintain his position within the good graces of his master, while at the same time using the goods of this world to his own advantage. When a time of crisis and choice comes, he forsakes the former and attempts by means of the latter to secure

---

1 See Seccombe, *Possessions*, pp. 170-71, who notes that this is the only use of ἀληθι-νός in Luke–Acts.

2 There is possibly further irony in the juxtaposition in v. 11 of 'mammon' as something one puts trust in and reference to 'faithful/entrust' (πιστοί/πιστεύσει). See R. Caemmerer, 'Investment for Eternity: A Study of Luke 16.1-13', *CTM* 34 (1963), pp. 69-76.

3 See Fitzmyer, *Luke X–XXIV*, p. 1110.

4 See Marshall, *Luke*, p. 623.

5 As Marshall (*Luke*, p. 624) says, even though he does not recognize the irony, 'The passage demands a contrast between what does not belong to the disciples and what will really belong to them. The treasure of heaven will be their own inalienable possession.'

a new place of eternal habitation. Jesus implies, ironically, that the choice should be a clear one to anyone who has ears to hear (including his audience), but in all three instances, and certainly in the case of the unjust steward, the wrong choice is made. They set out to serve two masters. At one point each loves both the goods of this world and the 'heavenly' place it seems to secure, but each learns to hate both. If wisdom is justified by her children, then the steward has proved himself eternally unwise.

The final recorded remark of Jesus puts the entire parable in appropriate context by asking a question which can only be answered ironically: οὐ δύνασθε θεῷ δουλεύειν καὶ μαμωνᾷ; The syntax allows for reading this either as a statement or as a question implying an affirmative answer. Understanding it as a statement is plausible and accepted by virtually all commentators,[1] resulting in a straightforward statement which puts the above irony in its proper perspective. This certainly is the final message of the parable,[2] that one cannot serve two masters. But the heavily ironic context does not support this abrupt transition to a sombre and confrontative tone.[3] Repunctuation as a question solves this problem and retains the author's ironic tone. In his final remarks, which draw the parable to a close, Jesus asks his listeners, using the second person plural, 'Are you able to serve God and mammon?'—i.e. after all you have heard about and seen in the parable of the prodigal son and especially the parable of the unjust steward, are you going to try to be first to be able to do the impossible? The use of οὐ implies a positive answer, and it is here that the irony is at its strongest, as if it read, 'Of course, you will be the first to do what cannot be done, won't you?' It is in the light of this that the reader is to understand reference to the strongly indignant response in v. 14 of the money-loving Pharisees, who are attempting to

1 E.g. Marshall, *Luke*, p. 624, who stumbles over the apparent exclusivity of the contrast. Cf. parallels in Plato, *Republic* 555C; Philo, frag. II 649; Poimandres 4.6 (cited in Manson, *Sayings*, p. 425).
2 Scholars are virtually agreed that v. 13 is authentic to the Jesus tradition on the basis of parallels in Matt. 6.24. See Marshall, *Luke*, pp. 622-23.
3 Fitzmyer (*Luke X–XXIV*, pp. 1110-11) recognizes the 'starkness of the summary', although he believes it does not warrant comment!

embody the impossible dichotomy, and to view the following parable of the rich man and Lazarus.

Is this ironic interpretation of the parable of the unjust steward (Lk. 16.1-13) convincing? It must, to be sure, fight the weight of years of influential interpreters who have argued for the apparent meaning of the words of vv. 8-9, although the survey of such interpretations shows that they lack explanatory power. But this ironic interpretation has force for several reasons.[1] First, it is internally consistent, unifying vv. 8-9 with 10-13, and vv. 8-13 with the rest of the parable, vv. 1-7, in a way unknown to most interpretations, including Fletcher's. Second, it is contextually consistent with the parables of Lk. 15, especially the parable of the prodigal, and the advocacy of wise economic choice for promoting the values of the kingdom, and with the parable of Lk. 16.19-31 and the advocacy of wise economic choice for acquiring eschatological membership in the kingdom. Third, this analysis makes Jesus' words in Lk. 16.14-18 regarding the Pharisees consistent with Lk. 15–16 and the larger context.[2] The Pharisees, and any potential followers of Jesus including the disciples, are condemned for failing to make the necessary hard choices to ensure eternal reward. The implication is that they too easily find it possible to act like the prodigal, the rich man, and especially the unjust steward, by attempting to utilize the possessions of the world to secure eternal rewards.

---

1 See Bretscher, 'Parable', pp. 759-61.
2 Eagar, 'Parable', pp. 464-65.

Part 2

STUDIES IN THE SOCIAL WORLD
OF ISRAEL AND EARLY CHRISTIANITY

THE FIGURATIVE ASPECT AND THE CONTEXTUAL METHOD IN THE EVALUATION OF THE SOLOMONIC EMPIRE (1 KINGS 1-11)

K. Lawson Younger, Jr.

As biblical historians continue to formulate and to debate their methodology for writing histories of Israel,[1] it is becoming more and more apparent that one of the greatest needs in establishing a method is the realization that a literary reading of the biblical text must precede any historical reconstruction.[2] It is also clear that such a reading is advantaged by anchoring the reading in the literary environment from which the text is derived.[3]

Yet there are two items in the development of a method of reading which seem to have been overlooked in most of these recent discussions: the figurative and ideological aspects of the biblical narrative. This is especially true in political contexts.

---

1 See the numerous important articles in recent *JSOT* issues, especially 39 (Oct., 1987).

2 This is true whether one is attempting a study of biblical or ancient Near Eastern history writing. See M. Liverani, 'Memorandum on the Approach to Historiographic Texts', *Orientalia* 42 (1973), pp. 178-94; M. Waldman, *Toward a Theory of Historical Narrative: A Case Study in Perso-Islamicate Historiography* (Colombus: Ohio State University Press, 1980); and K.L. Younger, 'Near Eastern and Biblical Conquest Accounts: Joshua 9–12' (Ph.D. Dissertation, Sheffield University, 1987), pp. 4-58.

3 W.W. Hallo spells this out clearly in 'Biblical History in its Near Eastern Setting: The Contextual Approach', in *Scripture in Context: Essays on the Comparative Method*, ed. C.D. Evans, W.W. Hallo, and G.B. White (Pittsburgh: Pickwick, 1980), pp. 1-12. See also M. Liverani, 'Storiografia politica Hittita—I. Šunaššura, ovvero: della reciprocità', *Oriens Antiquus* 12 (1973), pp. 267-97. Such an approach serves as a control on the literary reading, and makes the analysis not simply a 'New Critical' enterprise.

In order to illustrate this, I would like to examine the description of the Solomonic monarchy in the book of 1 Kings and thereby to demonstrate the need for the full recognition of the figurative and ideological aspects of the biblical narrative in their ancient Near Eastern context.

One thing is evident from an initial reading of the biblical text: particular kinds of statements in the narrative seem historically more reliable than others when viewed through the lens of *certain* modern critical qualifications. This has led some biblical historians to treat certain items as 'more authentic' (usually because of their degree of detail and lack of editorial hyperbole). This has certainly been the case in the Solomonic materials.[1] Texts like the lists of officials (1 Kgs 4.1-6, 7-19), the list of cities (9.15-19), the reports of international involvements (9.26-28; 10.11-12, 22), the sources and the costs of horses (excluding, however, the size of the chariot force) (10.28-29), and the conflicts with Hadad and Rezon (11.14-25) have received favourable treatments at the hands of most biblical historians.[2]

On the other hand, passages where 'editorial hyperbole' seem to be present have not fared so well. These have been judged as secondary embellishments which must be rejected. The process works, for example, something like this. 1 Kings 10.23-25, 27 state:

---

1   One recent example is J. Maxwell Miller and John H. Hayes, *A History of Ancient Israel and Judah* (London: SCM Press, 1986), pp. 189-217. Doubtless, this opinion is partially reinforced by the perception that the material in 1 Kgs 1–11 does not comprise a literary unity because of its apparent awkward editorial insertions and amplifications. However, this perception may be inaccurate. See the discussion on structure below.

2   Miller and Hayes, *A History of Ancient Israel and Judah*, pp. 187-217. Unfortunately, this attitude towards these texts has eliminated any deeper analysis of them. Obviously, the fact that certain information is conveyed in the form of a list does not guarantee its reliability. Concerning these lists, see B. Long, 'On Finding the Hidden Premises', *JSOT* 39 (1987), pp. 12-13. In some instances, biblical scholars have seen the account of the building of the temple and palace as historical, but the bulk of the remainder as legendary, as Gray demonstrates: 'In the section 3.1–10.29, the great difficulty is to distinguish objective fact from legend in the sources, apart from the account of the Temple and its furniture (chs. 6 and 7), which is in the former category, and its dedication (ch. 8) which, like its sequel (9.1-9), is largely and obviously Deuteronomistic, though doubtless based on actual fact' (John Gray, *1 & 2 Kings* [Old Testament Library; Philadelphia: Westminster, 2nd edn, 1970], p. 115).

King Solomon excelled in riches and wisdom more than all
the other kings of the earth. The whole world sought audience with Solomon to hear the wisdom God had put in his
heart. Year after year, everyone who came brought a gift—
articles of silver and gold, robes, weapons and spices, and
horses and mules... And the king made silver as common
in Jerusalem as stones and cedar as plentiful as sycamore-
fig trees in the Shephelah.

One could not possibly accept this as literally true. Therefore,
this must be deemed 'editorial hyperbole' and rejected as part
of any authentic history. Indeed, J.B. Pritchard argues that
the narrative's references to gold, pure gold and silver and its
allusions to the respect which Solomon's peers showed to him
are 'popular—even folkloristic' elements of the history of
Solomon's age.[1]

The problem, however, may not lie so much with the veracity of the narratives where hyperbole occurs, but with the
interpretative method of the modern critic. Beside the obvious
problem of whether accounts which contain a high degree of
detail and lack of figurative language are really more authentic,[2] there is also the question of whether biblical scholars have
been judging the historicity of biblical texts which contain
hyperbole on the basis of similar literal (and consequently
wrong) interpretative standards. Do detail and literality signal
historicity? And the lack thereof the reverse?

While it is important in the reading of any text, it is especially important in the reading of a political text to discover the
codes that may be underlying the communication of the text's
message. It is also important to realize that such codes will
have ideological overtones. It is at this point that the ancient
Near Eastern literary context is most helpful in the interpretation of the biblical text.

---

1   J.B. Pritchard, 'The Age of Solomon', in *Solomon and Sheba* (London: Thames
 Hudson, 1974), pp. 32-34. To him 'the exaggeration that appears in 1 Kgs 3–11' is
 simply the 'tributary fabrication of a later writer' (p. 34). He is especially dis-
 gruntled over the 666 talents figure for Solomon's income (p. 32). Yet, there are
 contextually-based explanations (cf., for example, H.W.F. Saggs, *The Greatness
 That Was Babylon* [New York: Mentor, 1962], pp. 249-52).
2   Along these lines of discussion, see M. Sternberg's recent arguments: *The
 Poetics of Biblical Narrative* (Bloomington: Indiana University Press, 1985),
 pp. 23-34.

Hyperbole as Ideological Indicator

The usage of hyperbole in the encoding of ideological messages is very common. For example, one will hear American political leaders and historians say from time to time that 'the United States is the greatest economic force in the world'. Yet when one considers the trade balance, the national deficit, the plight of the poor in America, and other economic indicators, the United States has severe economic problems which must certainly cause the interpreter of this message to understand it as ideological hyperbole.

On the other hand, such statements are not totally devoid of truth; otherwise, they lose all possible effectiveness as rhetorical figures.[1] Foremost in importance here is the realization that ideology manipulates the figure in order to communicate. A figure thus utilized is not necessarily a mask to truth (though it may be);[2] but it functions primarily as an effective communicative code.

This is the situation in the biblical description of the Solomonic era. The hyperbolic statements concerning Solomon's economic and political might must be understood in their ancient Near Eastern and biblical ideological framework. For example, 1 Kgs 10.20 reads:

> Twelve lions stood on the six steps, one at either end of each step. Nothing like it had ever been made for any other kingdom.

The reader is faced with the choice of either taking the text literally (and then questioning or defending its veracity), or recognizing that it is hyperbole loaded with political ideology. The first choice leads either to scepticism[3] about or apology for the

---

1 See U. Eco, *Semiotics and Philosophy of Language* (Bloomington: Indiana University Press, 1984), pp. 88-100. Eco correctly stresses that seeing the metaphor as a cognitive tool does not mean studying it in terms of truth value (p. 89).
2 See in this regard the discussion of Clifford Geertz, 'Ideology as a Cultural System', in *Ideology and Discontent*, ed. David E. Apter (New York: Free Press, 1964), pp. 47-76 (esp. p. 57).
3 Such scepticism can hinder the reconstructive effort. For example, the attitude of Miller and Hayes toward Ezion-geber and Ophir is one of total scepticism. However, if one compares the account of Ezion-geber and Ophir to that of the mysterious Punt of the inscriptions of Hatshepsut, there is no reason for such scepticism. For the most recent discussion, see A. Malamat, 'A Political Look at the Kingdom of David and Solomon and its Relations with Egypt', in *Studies in the*

narrative as a whole. The latter leads to a closer analysis and understanding of the text.

When one realizes, however, that such a phrase as 'nothing like it had ever been made for any other kingdom' is a kind of stereotyped phrase common in ancient Near Eastern royal inscriptions to describe some activity of the monarch, the choice of a literal reading is even less likely an option.[1] For example, Amenhotep III stated:

> It pleased his majesty's heart to make very great monuments, the likes of which *had not existed since the beginning of the Two Lands* [italics mine].[2]

Period of David and Solomon and Other Essays (ed. T. Ishida; Tokyo: Yamakawa-Shuppansha, 1982; henceforth, *SPDSOE*), pp. 201-203. For Hatshepsut's text, see É. Naville, *The Temple of Deir el Bahari* (London: Paul, Trench, Trübner, 1929), esp. pp. 11-20; and also the discussion of K.A. Kitchen, 'Punt and How to Get There', *Orientalia* 40 (1971), pp. 184-207; and S. Ratié, *La reine Hatchepsout. Sources et problèmes* (Leiden: Brill, 1981), pp. 141-61. Another example of Miller/Hayes' scepticism can be seen in the following quote: 'No ancient texts, biblical or otherwise, suggest that Solomon had mines. This is pure speculation of recent vintage' (p. 214). But the kings of Egypt had mines in the Sinai from a very early period (Middle Kingdom at the latest). So why such doubt? A main reason is the general absence of 'archaeological evidence' to support the literal reading. This is altogther a different problem (for which see R. de Vaux, 'On Right and Wrong Uses of Archaeology', in *Near Eastern Archaeology in the Twentieth Century. Essays in Honor of Nelson Glueck* (ed. J.A. Sanders; New York: Doubleday, 1970), pp. 132-63). Here, my concern is with the literality = historicity equation. For a recent review of the archaeological data, see W.G. Dever, 'Monumental Architecture in Ancient Israel in the Period of the United Monarchy', *SPDSOE*, pp. 269-306.

1 Liverani identifies this type of phrase as 'heroic priority', and comments: 'The king is the first to execute something which no one of his predecessors (not to speak of common people) had done or attempted (*ša ina šarrāni ālikūt maḫrîya mamma lā epušu* or the like). The theme is applied to any situation or action: the knowledge of a place, or the opening of a road, a victory or conquest, a new technique or an artistic achievement, *the construction of a building* [italics mine] or the cultivation of an area, the introduction of a festival or of a norm' (M. Liverani, 'The Ideology of the Assyrian Empire', in *Power and Propaganda: A Symposium on Ancient Empires* [ed. M.T. Larsen; Mesopotamia. Copenhagen Studies in Assyriology, no. 7; Copenhagen: Akademisk Forlag, 1979], pp. 308-309). One example can be seen in the Annals of Sargon II: 'He brought to me as his present 12 big horses of Egypt, their like not to be found in my land' (see H. Tadmor, 'The Campaigns of Sargon of Assur', *Journal of Cuneiform Studies* 12 [1958], p. 78).

2 *Urk.* IV 1646-57; M. Lichtheim, *Ancient Egyptian Literature* (Berkeley: University of California Press, 1976), II, p. 44.

When it came to describing the splendour of their kingdoms, most kings of varying political and economic power of
many different nations in the ancient Near East utilized a
great amount of hyperbole since this most effectively communicated their royal ideology.[1] Merenptah, for example,
describes the splendour of his kingdom thus:

> How beloved is he, the victorious ruler!
> How exalted is he, the king among the gods!
> How splendid is he, the lord of command!
> O how sweet it is to sit and babble!
> One walks free-striding on the road,
> For there's no fear in people's hearts;[2]
> Fortresses are left to themselves,
> Wells are open for the messengers' use.
> Bastioned ramparts are becalmed,
> Sunlight only wakes the watchmen;
> Medjai are stretched out asleep,
> Nau and Tekten are in the fields they love.
> The cattle of the field are left to roam,
> No herdsmen cross the river's flood;
> There's no calling out at night:
> 'Wait, I come', in a stranger's voice.
> Going and coming are with song,
> People don't lament and mourn;
> Towns are settled once again,
> He who tends his crop will eat.[3]

Sounds like utopia! But no more than the utopian ideological
language employed in the description of the Solomonic splen-

---

1   In this connection, Liverani's insight into Assyrian royal ideology is very inter-
    esting: 'The Assyrian kingship is the only one to legitimately exercise universal
    dominion, the Assyrian king "has no equal" (*maḫīru, šāninu, gabarû*), he is the
    only one endowed with those qualities which render legitimate the exercise of
    power, and for this reason he has been explicitly and carefully chosen by the gods
    (cf. *migir ilāni*, etc.). Other so-called kings, who emerge from time to time
    among the foreigners, reveal themselves as totally inadequate to such a
    demanding task. The correct link with the divine, besides yielding legitimacy,
    yields a highly emblematic element, "trust" (*tukultu*; cf. also *nērāru*)' ('The
    Ideology of the Assyrian Empire', pp. 310-11). The implications for the biblical
    narrative are tantalizing!
2   Compare the inscription of Azitawadda A ii 4-6.
3   K.A. Kitchen, *Ramesside Inscriptions, Historical and Biographical* (Oxford:
    Blackwell, 1969–), IV, pp. 12-19.

dour.[1] One must fully consider the figurative aspect[2] of these texts as the vehicle of their ideologies.[3]

Even statements which are often accepted as 'historical', such as the sources and costs of horses, may be found in hyperbolic ideological contexts. Ikeda has correctly pointed out that

> The account of Solomon's import of chariots and horses is given in a literary context whose main theme is to display his glory and great wealth (1 Kgs 10.23; cf. also 3.13)—not just in 'quantity' but, more important, in 'quality'.[4]

---

1 Compare 1 Kgs 10.27: 'the king made silver as common in Jerusalem as stones and cedar as plentiful as sycamore-fig trees in the Shephelah' with the statement of Sargon II: 'I accumulated in Dur-Sarrukin treasures without number, which my forefathers had not received. They valued the purchase price of copper like (that of) silver in Assyria' (A.G. Lie, *Sargon* [Paris: Geuthner, 1929], lines 232-34 [pp. 38-39]).

2 For a recent discussion of the figurative aspect (or metaphor) in historical texts (particularly the use of depictive metaphor in sequential history), see Phillip Stambovsky, 'Metaphor and Historical Understanding', *History and Theory* 27 (1988), pp. 125-34, esp. pp. 128-31.

3 This may also be true of geographical boundary descriptions. Often in the ancient Near East, the empire was described as encompassing broad territories for which only great natural obstacles such as oceans, rivers and mountains served as boundaries (M. Weinfeld, 'Zion and Jerusalem as Religious and Political Capital: Ideology and Utopia', in *The Poet and the Historian: Essays in Literary and Historical Biblical Criticism* [ed. R.E. Friedman; Harvard Semitic Studies, 26; Chico, CA: Scholars Press, 1983], pp. 97ff.). Hence, the description of Solomon's boundaries in 1 Kgs 4.21, 'from the River to the land of the Philistines, as far as the border of Egypt', should be considered to be a broad imperial description which is not based on concrete boundaries but seeks to articulate an absolute dominion in the whole region. This is a good example of the blend of the figurative and ideological aspects. In this instance—besides numerous ancient Near Eastern examples—one could compare the American ideological notion of 'manifest destiny' as reflected in the figurative border description: 'from Sea to shining Sea'. Thus Malamat argues: 'Allerdings haben die Vertreter dieser minimalistischen These keine überzeugende Erklärung für die Entstehung der vermeintlichen Legende von der weiten Erstreckung des davidisch-salomonischen Reiches anzubieten' (*Das davidische und salomonische Königreich und seine Beziehungen zu Ägypten und Syrien: Zur Entstehung eines Grossreichs* [Vienna: Österreichische Akademie der Wissenschaften, 1983], pp. 9-10).

4 Y. Ikeda, 'Solomon's Trade in Horses and Chariots in its International Setting', *SPDSOE*, p. 219. He also points out that it is 'most plausible that "600 shekels" was the "highest price" ever put to an Egytian chariot in the time of Solomon—another effort of the biblical writer to display Solomon's extravagance as distinctly as possible' (p. 225; cf. also his very useful chart on the prices of chariots and horses, p. 226).

Thus this material is also part of the ideological code underlying the Solomonic text.

Another example (especially with reference again to the hyperbole of 1 Kgs 10.23-25, 27) is the inscription of Bar-Rakib:

> And the house of my father profited more than all others.
> And I ran at the wheel of my lord, the king of Assyria,
> in the midst of powerful kings, lords of silver and lords of
>   gold.
> And I took control of the house of my father.
> *And I made it better than the house of any powerful king.*
> *And my brother kings were desirous for all that is the good*
>   *of my house* [italics mine].[1]

Hyperbole is only really effective when there is an element of truth to its claim relative to its basis of comparison. Otherwise, it is self-falsifying, and falls dead upon its audience. Thus, in figurative language there is, of course, a stratification of meaning, in which an incongruity of sense on one level produces an influx of significance on another. As W. Percy has pointed out, the feature of metaphor that has most troubled philosophers (and he might have added, scientists) is that it is 'wrong':

> It asserts of one thing that it is something else. And, worse
> yet, it tends to be most effective when most 'wrong'.[2]

The power of a metaphor derives precisely from the interplay between the discordant meanings it symbolically coerces into a unitary conceptual framework and from the degree to which that coercion is successful in overcoming the psychic resistance such semantic tension inevitably generates in anyone in a position to perceive it.

Hence, while Solomon's opulence may have been great, spending exceeded income. Solomon created an impressive monarchy, but did not proportionately increase his conquests (or other revenues to match this increase in expenditure). Although he increased trade, Solomon apparently imported more goods than he exported so that the balance of trade pro-

---

1 For this inscription, see my article 'Panammuwa and Bar-Rakib: Two
   Structural Analyses', *JANES* 18 (1986), pp. 91-103.
2 W. Percy, 'Metaphor as Mistake', *The Sewanee Review* 66 (1958), 79-99.

duced a soaring national deficit. Even the raising of taxes, the use of slave labour, the implementation of the *corvée* for his own Israelite subjects, and the selling off of certain cities and territory could not remedy the economic problems of Solomon's fiscal policy.[1] Solomon was attempting to finance an imperialistic economy without military conquests with their subsequent tributes and *corvées* to fuel the fires of an empire's economic growth (see the section below on economic wealth).

Thus the biblical account's use of hyperbole must be interpreted through the matrix of its royal ideology, just as is the case with other contemporary ancient Near Eastern monarchies' descriptions of their kingdoms' wealth and might. The inscription of Azitawadda vividly illustrates this:

> Ba'al made me a father and a mother to the Danunians.
> I quickened the Danunians.
> I enlarged the land of the plain of Adana from East (lit. 'the rising of the sun') to West (lit. 'its setting'), and in my days the Danunians had all good and abundance and luxury.
>
> And I built fortifications in those places in order that the Danunians might dwell in the ease of their hearts.
> And I humbled strong lands in the West (lit. 'the going of the sun') which no king who was before me ever humbled.
> Now I, Azitawadda, have humbled them.
>
> Now there was in all my days abundance and luxury and good living and ease of heart for the Danunians and for all the Plain of Adana.
>
> As in my days there was for the land of the Plain of Adana abundance and luxury.
> And there was never any night for the Danunians in my days.[2]

Claims such as these by a minor vassal king like Azitawadda go a long way in demonstrating the fact that Solomon's success, wealth, and reputation are the stuff of ancient Near

---

1 While J. Bright recognized this, his treatment of the Solomonic material is less than satisfactory (*A History of Israel* [Philadelphia: Westminster, 3rd edn, 1981], p. 221). On the *corvée* in ancient Israel, see now J.A. Soggin, 'Compulsory Labor under David and Solomon', *SPDSOE*, pp. 259-67.

2 Text: I.3-6; I.17-20; II.7-9; II.15-17. Note the word play in this last line between the terms *ll* ('night') and *bymty* ('in my days').

Eastern royal inscriptions.[1] They are an integral part of the very code through which the texts communicate.

Finally, it is important also to recognize the ideological use of hyperbole in the negative assessment of Solomon. For example, the biblical writer relates that after Solomon's apostasy, Yahweh raised up Hadad and Rezon who harassed the monarch 'all the days of Solomon' (1 Kgs 11.26). Again as with the positive assessment which utilized the hyperbole, it would be a serious interpretative mistake to understand this statement literally.

Structure as Figurative Indicator

A number of writers have demonstrated that the narrative of 1 Kgs 1–11 is built on a sophisticated structure.[2] Such a narrative structure, which is artificial or figurative,[3] is utilized in order to communicate and reinforce the narrative's message.[4] There is a remarkable symmetry that undergirds the message. In fact, the narrative seems to be built around the account of the building and dedication of the Temple[5] with the

---

1 A.R. Millard, 'King Solomon's Gold: Biblical Records in the Light of Antiquity', *The Society for Mesopotamian Studies Bulletin* 15 (1988), pp. 5-11. He states: 'The amounts of gold ascribed to King Solomon are not utterly incredible when set beside the figures reported for other kings before and after his time'. Thus 'it is no longer possible to dismiss the [biblical] records as fantastic and impossible. When they are investigated in the context of the ancient world, they have to be adjudged as entirely plausible' (pp. 10-11).

2 Bezalel Porten, 'The Structure and Theme of the Solomon Narrative (1 Kgs 3–11)', *HUCA* 38 (1967), pp. 93-128; B. Halpern, *The First Historians: The Hebrew Bible and History* (San Francisco: Harper and Row, 1988), pp. 144-80; C. Meyers, 'The Israelite Empire: In Defense of King Solomon', in *The Bible and its Traditions* (ed. M.P. O'Connor and D.N. Freedman [= *Michigan Quarterly Review* 22 (1983)]), pp. 421-28; and K.I. Parker, 'Repetition as a Structuring Device in 1 Kgs 1–11' *JSOT* 42 (1988), pp. 19-27. For the detailed structure of 1 Kgs 1–2, see K.K. Sacon, 'The Study of the Literary Structure of "The Succession Narrative"', *SPDSOE*, pp. 27-54.

3 See H. White, 'The Question of Narrative in Contemporary Historical Theory', *History and Theory* 23 (1984), pp. 24-25, and 'Historicism, History, and the Figurative Imagination', *History and Theory*, Beiheft 14 (1975), p. 60. He argues that historians use the same techniques as any literary artist to arrange or fashion their materials.

4 Geertz, 'Ideology as a Cultural System', pp. 47-76.

5 Halpern, *The First Historians*, p. 148; Meyers, 'The Israelite Empire: In Defense of King Solomon', p. 422.

description of the construction of the Solomonic palace being its very pivot point.

Meyers feels that this Solomonic section constitutes a self-contained and highly-structured work. In her opinion, these chapters, with their unifying themes of Solomonic wealth, honour, and wisdom, 'stand out as unique in biblical historiography even though they are carefully integrated into the narrative of the Book of Kings'.[1] Along similar lines, Parker assumes that the apparent repetitions and contradictions are 'deliberate and part of a sophisticated narrative strategy'. He argues that the text manifests 'an internal logic and coherence within the narrative' which justifies its unity.[2] On the other hand, Halpern argues that the writer of the section 'appears to have incorporated or tolerated sources occasioning tension in his treatment', which nevertheless still achieves a type of unity.[3]

Which of these understandings is correct is not important to the point that I am arguing; each is a possible explanation. My point is that the text does have a structural unity—on this there is agreement—and that this structure manifests the text's figurative nature. Recognition of this important point allows one to take the interpretative endeavour one step further.

---

1 Meyers argues that 'the source upon which the Solomonic section is based can be deemed an independent work, different from the annals which supplied materials for the rest of the monarchic history'. She attributes these chapters to the Book of the Acts of Solomon (1 Kgs 11.41), which obviously may not be correct ('The Israelite Empire', p. 423).

2 Parker, 'Repetition as a Structuring Device', pp. 21-22.

3 Halpern, *The First Historians*, p. 148. The use of any earlier sources is not excluded. In fact, Halpern feels that the passage is a composite of numerous units (e.g. 1 Kgs 1–2) that has been 'skillfully resculpted to fit with the rest of the reign' (pp. 145-46). On the possible apologetic character of 1 Kgs 1–2, see now J.S. Rogers, 'Narrative Stock and Deuteronomistic Elaboration in 1 Kings 2', *CBQ* 50 (1988), pp. 398-413; T. Ishida, 'Adonijah, the Son of Haggith and his Supporters: An Inquiry into Problems of History and Historiography in 1 Kings 1–2', in *The Future of Biblical Studies* (ed. R.E. Friedman and H.G.M. Williamson; Semeia Supplements; Decatur: Scholars Press, 1987), pp. 165-87; *idem*, 'Solomon's Succession to the Throne of David—A Political Analysis', *SPDSOE*, pp. 175-88; P.K. McCarter, 'Plots, True or False: The Succession Narrative as Court Apologetic', *Interp* 35 (1981), pp. 355-67; and K.K. Sacon, 'Study of the Literary Structure', pp. 27-54.

Ancient Near Eastern Royal Ideology
and the Solomonic Splendour

There are certain points at which the royal ideologies of the ancient Near East illuminate the biblical narrative. I will investigate a number of these features by category.[1]

Concept of Capital / Temple

The foundation of a new capital is the apex among the actions of the king as creator. The construction of a monumental capital at the centre of an empire can be compared, for its symbolic value, only to the works of basic creation, owed to gods. While David was the one who founded Jerusalem as the capital of the Israelite empire, Solomon established it even more firmly. This is clearly seen in words put into Yahweh's mouth in Solomon's first address to the people at the dedication of the temple: 'Nevertheless, you [David] are not the one to build the temple, but your son [Solomon], who is your own flesh and blood—he is the one who will build the temple for my Name' (1 Kgs 8.19).

The description of Solomonic trade is related to this symbolic role of the capital as centre. As a microcosm, the centre should contain all the elements of the world. Therefore, it must bring into itself the various elements from the periphery of the empire. The variety of imported materials mentioned in the different Solomonic constructions and the accumulation of his wealth served as symbols of the centre's domination of that periphery. As Meyers comments:

> It was not simply a demonstration of exotica and wealth that Solomon effected; it was a message of Jerusalem's cosmic centrality and therefore of its right to dominate. If imported monkeys and rare ivories, among other precious commodities, were part of the Jerusalem scene, according to the information in 1 Kings 10, the whole creation was thus contained within the center of creation.[2]

---

1 The following categories are taken from M. Weinfeld, 'Zion and Jerusalem as Religious and Political Capital: Ideology and Utopia', pp. 93-115; and Liverani, 'The Ideology of the Assyrian Empire', pp. 297-317.
2 Meyers, 'The Israelite Empire', p. 422.

Thus the centrality of Jerusalem held together the concept of empire, which included both the politically dependent states as well as those with more mutual commercial ties.

In conjunction with this concept of capital, a very common element of ancient Near Eastern royal ideology is the concept of the temple. The temple is pictured as the universal centre to which nations stream from all the ends of the earth, bringing with them offerings and gifts to the great god in the sanctuary.[1]

The place that the temple-building project occupies within the structure of 1 Kings seems to indicate that the temple structure was intended as much to impress foreigners as to serve a domestic function.[2] Moreover, the vast assembly gathered at the dedication ceremony was made up of 'people from Lebo Hamath to the Wadi of Egypt' (8.65; cf. also Solomon's words in his dedicatory prayer in 8.41-43).

Assyrian royal ideology vividly illustrates this concept of capital/temple as cosmic centre, siphoning in from the remotest corners of the periphery those contributions that were owed to it. This was expressed in numerous ways: the building of gardens (*kirimḫu*) with exotic trees and plants from all regions; the construction of parks and buildings in the style of foreign lands; the accumulation in the royal treasury of rare items; and the extraordinary variety of materials in the construction of palaces and/or temples by foreign workers. In this way, the capital city with its temple 'contained everything, all that is known, all that is possessed—so that creation is complete'.[3] This is especially seen in the zoological and botanical interests of the Assyrian monarch. A few quotations will exemplify:

a. Tiglath-Pileser I (1115-1077 BCE) (note also his stress on chariots, horses, peace and prosperity):

> I formed herds of horses, oxen (and) asses... also, I got control of (and) formed herds of *nayālu*-deer, *ayālu*-deer,

---

1 See Weinfeld, 'Zion and Jerusalem...', pp. 104-15.

2 Weinfeld, 'Zion and Jerusalem...', p. 423.

3 Liverani, 'The Ideology of the Assyrian Empire', p. 314. For a good recent survey, see L.D. Levine, 'Cities as Ideology: The Neo-Assyrian Centres of Ashur, Nimrud, and Nineveh', *The Society for Mesopotamian Studies Bulletin* 12 (1986), pp. 1-7.

gazelles, and ibex... I took cedar, box-tree, Kanish oak from
the lands over which I had gained dominion—such trees
which none among previous kings, my forefathers, had ever
planted[1]—and I planted (them) in the orchards of my land. I
took rare orchard fruit which is not found in my land (and
therewith) I filled the orchards of Assyria. I had in harness
for the forces of my land more chariots and teams of horses
than ever before. To Assyria I added land, and to its people,
people. I brought contentment to my people. I provided them
with a secure abode.[2]

b. Aššur-nasir-pal II (883-859 BCE):

I took away 50 lion cubs. I herded them into Kalach and the
palaces of my land into cages. I bred their cubs in great
numbers. I captured live tigers (*mindinaš*). I formed herds
of wild bulls, elephants, lions, ostriches, male apes, female
apes, wild asses, deer, *ayālu*-deer, female bears, leopards,
senkurru, *tušēnu*, beasts of mountain (and) plain, all of
them in my city Kalach. I displayed (them) to all the people
of my land.[3]

I dug out a canal from the Upper Zab, cutting through a
mountain at its peak, (and) called it Patti-hegalli. I irrigated
the meadows of the Tigris (and) planted orchards with all
(kinds of) fruit trees. I pressed wine and gave the best to
Aššur my lord and the temples of my land. I dedicated that
city to the god Aššur my lord. In the lands through which I
marched and the mountains which I crossed, the trees (and)
seeds which I saw [I planted]: cedars, cypress ... [37 other
types named]... The canal crashes from above into the gardens. Fragrance pervades the walkways. Streams of water
(as numerous) as the stars of heaven flow in the pleasure
garden. Pomegranates like grapes on the vine... in the
pleasure garden... [... I], Aššur-nasir-pal, in the delight-
ful garden pick fruit like a mouse [...].[4]

---

1 Compare 1 Kgs 10.1-12: '... from Ophir... from there they brought great cargoes
   of almug-wood... So much almug-wood has never been imported or seen since
   that day'.
2 Cols. VI.105–VII.10 and 17-35 (*AKA*, pp. 89-92). Also see 'The Broken Obelisk of
   Ashur-bel-kala (Col. IV.6-34. *AKA*, pp. 128-49) and Borger, *EAK*, I, pp. 140-41;
   ARI II, § 248.
3 Y. Le Gac, *Les Inscriptions d'Aššur-nasir-aplu III* (Paris: Paul Geuthner, 1907),
   pp. 175-75 (lines 15b-20a [IV.27-50]); *ARI* II, § 598.
4 D.J. Wiseman, 'A New Stela of Aššur-nasir-pal II', *Iraq* 14 (1952), pp. 24-44,
   Plates 2-6; *ARI* II, § 678; on the last lines of the text, see G.N. Postgate, *Governor's
   Palace Archive* (London: British School of Archaeology in Iraq, 1973), p. 239.

In the light of all these flamboyant descriptions of 'cosmic centres', Solomon's description is very simple and straightforward; and yet its function in the narrative is very similar. The Solomonic narrative contains descriptions of: gardens with various exotic trees and plants, the accumulation of rare items in the royal treasury, and the extraordinary variety of materials that foreign workers utilized in the construction of palaces and/or temples.

Economic Wealth

Here one might profitably compare the imperialistic economies of other ancient Near Eastern empires with that of Solomon's. Study of the Assyrian imperial economy, in particular, is very instructive because it was so heavily dependent on the influx of goods through military conquests as the means of achieving economic growth and prosperity. Solomon's policy was in contrast to that of his father, David, who apparently supported his more modest kingdom from his personal income and from tribute gained through the conquests of foreign peoples.

The economic structure of any empire will consist of the imposition of an administrative pattern upon underlying and largely unchanging economic realities. In the case of the Assyrian monarchs, they did not have much interest in manipulating the economy of either the central or annexed regions of their empire, except in the crude sense of extracting wealth. Here the Solomonic empire seems to be parallel. From the descriptions of its administrative policies, Solomon's government also seems to have been primarily interested in the extracting of wealth.[1] The influx of tax and tribute enabled the administration to initiate the numerous building enterprises of Solomon, just as the influx of tribute, tax and slaves enabled

---

1 In its relations with other peoples of the ancient Near East, the Solomonic empire seems primarily interested in acquiring wealth *through* diplomatic manoeuvres: marriage alliances, treaties (such as with Hiram I of Tyre), and trade policies with Que and Sheba. On these, see now H. Donner, 'The Interdependence of Internal Affairs and Foreign Policy during the Davidic-Solomonic Period', *SPDSOE*, pp. 205-14; A. Malamat, *Das davidische und salomonische Königreich*, pp. 20-30; and Alan R. Schulman, 'The Curious Case of Hadad the Edomite', in *Egyptological Studies in Honor of Richard A. Parker* (ed. L.H. Lesko; Hanover and London, 1986), pp. 122-35.

the Assyrian emperors to build material wealth and initiate many of their building endeavours. The gaining of access to Syria was important to both the Assyrian and Israelite empires. There were resources in Syria that the two lacked and could exploit as long as they were able to maintain possession there. Direct access to the materials of this region had a radical effect on the empires' economies, in particular, on their currency systems. Equally, the disruption and/or loss of direct control of this area meant the reverse.[1] Moreover, as with all great empires, the political centre must have become economically dependent on supplies from outside. Postgate's recent evaluation of the Assyrian evidence shows that this dependence may be attributed to the existence of two, doubtless largely interlocking groups: (a) large numbers of state servants who did not participate in productive activities of any kind: the army and the administration; (b) most of the population of the large cities had to derive their food supply from beyond the city's immediate vicinity.[2]

In the case of the Solomonic empire, the former was very probably a contributing factor to the empire's demise, whereas concerning the latter it is uncertain.

Concept of Dynasty
The king has the role of founder-hero. The king's function is not only to found new things, but also to prevent their ageing, to renew them and to revive them periodically. In so far as he is the one who completes the work of creation, the king stands in the line of the founder heroes and ultimately in the line of the creating gods. (This helps to explain the interesting use of numerous 'creation' motifs in the Solomonic narrative, and

---

1   J.N. Postgate, 'The Economic Structure of the Assyrian Empire', in *Power and Propaganda*, pp. 199-200, 218. See also C. Hauer's discussion of Solomon's economic and military policies: 'The Economics of National Security in Solomonic Israel', *JSOT* 18 (1980), pp. 63-73.

2   J.N. Postgate, *Taxation and Conscription in the Assyrian Empire* (Rome: Pontificium Institutum Biblicum, 1974), p. 201: 'The existence in the heart of Assyria of so large an "artificial element" naturally made the empire's stability dependent on the flow of produce back from the provinces to the centre, and any interruption of this flow could cause the most difficulty and distress in the least time. Further, the "top heaviness" of the empire was probably accentuated by the relative poverty of the provinces outside their central area.' The Solomonic empire seems to have manifested a similar type of situation.

has obvious links to the concept of 'the capital' discussed above.)

Concepts of Wisdom / Righteousness / Justice / Peace
The idea that the kingship should be founded on the basis of wisdom, justice and righteousness was a widespread notion in the cultures of Mesopotamia, Egypt, and Israel.[1] Corresponding to the acquisition and centralization of raw materials in the economic sphere was the spreading of ideological goods (order, justice, peace, etc.) which only the king was able to provide. Through this ideological exchange, the imperial state became more palatable. These motifs can be seen in numerous ancient Near Eastern royal inscriptions,[2] as well as in Solomon's case: 'in wisdom and wealth you have far exceeded ... because of the LORD's eternal love for Israel, he has made you king, to maintain justice and righteousness (*m špṭ wṣdqh*)'.[3]

Thus in these various ways, the biblical description of Solomon follows that of the ideal ancient Near Eastern monarch. Solomon's reign, however, saw both the peak and the decline of the Israelite empire. Hence, in many ways, the Solomonic empire was a whited sepulchre. On the outside it was very glorious and impressive. But on the inside, it con-

1 Weinfeld, 'Zion and Jerusalem...', p. 100.
2 For example, Samsuiluna (king of Babylon) stated: 'At that time Marduk... the god who creates *wisdom*, gave me, Samsuiluna, the king of his desire, the entire land for shepherding. He greatly instructed me to cause his land to lie down in pastures and to guide his broad people in *well-being* forever. I... with my own *power and wisdom*... moulded bricks for the fortress Dimat-Ellil...I built greatly... [italics mine]' (R. Borger, *Babylonisch-assyrische Lesestücke* [Analecta Orientalia 54; Rome: Pontificium Institutum Biblicum, 1979], I, pp. 51-52). Also Nebuchadnezzar I: 'When Nebuchadnezzar, the exalted and noble prince ... who makes his people to prosper,... the king of justice who pronounces a righteous judgment... (L.W. King, *Babylonian Boundary Stones* [London: British Museum, 1912], p. 31). See M. Weinfeld's discussion, '"Justice and Righteousness" in Ancient Israel against the Background of "Social Reforms" in the Ancient Near East', in *Assyrien und seine Nachbarn*, ed. H.G. Nissen and G. Renger (Berliner Beiträge zum Vorderen Orient, 1; Berlin: Dietrich Reimer, 1987), pp. 491-511.
3 Weinfeld argues that this pair is semantically equivalent with the Akk. pair *kittum u mīšarum*, and connotes the idea of 'maintaining equality achieved by freeing the enslaved, indebted, captive, prisoned [sic], etc.' through the issuing of royal edicts ('"Justice and Righteousness" in Ancient Israel', pp. 510-11).

tained many macabre features. The language which describes the kingdom in its splendour is the language of patriotic political ideology and must be interpreted as such. Otherwise, an inaccurate picture will emerge, filled with distortions.

In many respects one's evaluation of the Solomonic empire should follow the same principles by which one might evaluate any ancient Near Eastern empire. For instance, while economically the empire of Aššurbanipal was generally very prosperous, it had its financial problems too. Aššurbanipal regularly claims in his inscriptions that he maintained great prosperity, giving details concerning the cheapness of corn, wine, oil and wool during his reign (cf. the inscription of Azitawadda above). Moreover, Aššurbanipal describes how through various conquests the market was flooded with certain commodities (e.g., camels and slaves after the Arabian campaign).[1] But, as a prayer to Šamaš illustrates (in which Aššurbanipal prays for the reduction of inflation), not all of his reign was as prosperous as he would have us think.[2] Thus, as Aššurbanipal's empire, in many respects, was very mighty (though having a plethora of problems which eventually led to its dissolution), so too the Solomonic empire was splendorous for a Levantine kingdom (though it also was raked by difficulties). The writer of 1 Kings obviously had access to sources which not only described the Solomonic empire in glowing terms as most royal inscriptions would, but also depicted the darker side of that kingdom. He has given to us exactly what we should expect from the ancient Near Eastern literary context.

Conclusion

This study has emphasized the importance of integrating a literary reading with a contextual method as a preliminary to the reconstructive task. It has stressed the need for recognizing and correctly dealing with the figurative aspect of the biblical narrative so that the interpretative endeavour is not frustrated by literality. This is especially true since hyperbole

---

1 A.C. Piepkorn, *Historical Prism Inscriptions of Ashurbanipal* (Assyriological Studies, 5; Chicago: University of Chicago Press, 1933), pp. 12-22, 27-38, 83.
2 E. Weidner, *Archiv für Orientforschung* 13 (1939-41), pp. 210-13 (with 324-25).

was effectively utilized in the communicative process of ancient Near Eastern royal ideology. Thus the study has also shown the importance of the cognizance of biblical royal ideology in its ancient literary context. And finally it has attempted to demonstrate—though admittedly in an indirect manner— that detail and literality are illegitimate grounds for maintaining a minimalist or sceptical view of Israelite history-writing.[1]

The point is this. It is insufficient to present an image of the Solomonic empire along the lines of the Miller/Hayes reconstructive description. Solomonic splendour was relative. It was not as fantastic as many other ancient Near Eastern monarchies, but it was undoubtedly the greatest of the ancient Israelite kingdoms. Consideration, therefore, of the figurative aspect of Israelite royal ideology in its ancient Near Eastern context proves to be essential in the interpretation of the splendour of Solomon's empire.

---

1 One must certainly question Hayes's disclaimer: 'we are not prone to be overly skeptical' ('On Reconstructing Israelite History', *JSOT* 39 [1987], p. 7). Long concludes: 'what finally appears to Miller and Hayes as a believable reconstruction is a list-like, minimalist plot summary' ('On Finding the Hidden Premises', p. 13). But even more so must one question Garbini's overt scepticism (*History and Ideology in Ancient Israel* [New York: Crossroad Publishing, 1988], pp. 25-32).

DEVIANCE AND LEGITIMATE ACTION IN THE BOOK OF JUDGES

David J. Chalcraft

Introduction

In a recent study, Ericson, Baranek and Chan (1987) have focused on the part journalists play in the construction of public images of deviance.[1] Drawing on a number of traditions in the sociology of deviance, the authors seek to establish that journalists have a major role in actually defining what constitutes deviance and that such activity serves to create and maintain a certain level of consensus on questions of public order, appropriate behaviour and the nature of social control.

Their analysis draws on two essential insights of the sociology of deviance. First, in agreement with the Labelling Approach to deviance[2] the authors work from the assumption that deviance is not a quality of any particular action, but that actions become deviant when they are so defined by a social group who are in a position to put forward definitions of deviance and who, moreover, have the authority to give their defi-

---

1 Deviance 'consists of those actions which do not follow the norms and expectations of a particular social group' (Haralambos 1985: 406). In this paper, 'legitimate action' is simply the opposite to deviance. For a critical history of the sociology of deviance see Downes and Rock (1988).

2 The classic statement of the Labelling Approach to deviance is by Becker (1973). For introduction, see Abercrombie, Hill and Turner (1984: 116); Haralambos (1985: 29-38); Thio (1978: 55-62). Fuller accounts can be found in Taylor, Walton and Young (1973: 39-71), Schur (1971). The approach emphasizes the role of societal reaction in the identification of deviants and concentrates on the possible effects such deviant labels may have on the promotion and amplification of deviant actions. That is, labels encourage, and even force, offenders to embark on a 'deviant career' (Haralambos 1985: 431; Becker 1973: 24-25, 101-102).

nitions some moral and political force (Ericson *et al.* 1987: 5; cf. Becker 1973: 9). Journalists, through the media, have access to a wide audience and this gives them a position of great influence. To be sure, they may well draw on certain commonly held assumptions in identifying deviance, and thus reinforce those value positions, but this is not necessarily always the case and they also have a creative role.

Secondly, their study pays attention to the possible functions of journalistic concentration on issues of deviance (Ericson *et al.* 1987: 6; cf. Durkheim 1938; 1970; 1984; Downes and Rock 1982: 77-114). On one level deviance is 'newsworthy' and entertaining, and focusing on 'deviant items' serves to sell newspapers and attract viewers. On a deeper level, the concentration on deviance and the defining of it serves to identify and maintain group boundaries through the isolation of 'outsiders' and, through the media, actions and beliefs considered to be admirable and worthy of social approval and emulation are communicated (Ericson *et al.* 1987: 59).

This essay seeks to demonstrate that the narrator[1] of the book of Judges had a similar interest in the issue of deviance and legitimate action and that he, through entertaining storytelling, sought to create and maintain the boundaries of his own social group.[2] The discussion seeks to establish that there is a theme of social deviance in the book and that the narrator was at pains to identify and label deviant actions and appropriate action patterns in an attempt to secure the stability of

---

1 I use 'the narrator' as a short-hand expression for the author(s) responsible for the final form of the text; that is, in so far as that final form relates to the theme of social deviance discussed in this essay. The narrator is to be distinguished, therefore, from the hand(s) responsible for the theological introduction(s) and the Deuteronomic framework(s). Treatments of the redactional history can be found in: Mayes (1977: 286-93; 1983: 53-80; 1985: 9-36), Soggin (1980: 175-83), Fohrer (1968: 206-15), Kaiser (1975: 142-51).

2 The analogy with modern day journalists should not, of course, be taken too literally. It is merely a way of introducing the reader to the discussion by way of the more familiar. The comparison is only meant to suggest that written texts which discuss deviance often have the intention, and the effect, of promoting particular definitions of normative behaviour. Indeed, from a sociological point of view 'deviance' does not 'exist' until it is labelled and these labels must be communicated.

his own social group. In the process the out-group[1] is correspondingly delimited.

The following discussion is divided into sections which broadly correspond to the contexts treated by the narrator in his attempts to provide a more or less complete guide to deviant action in a variety of situations. First, the discussion focuses on Judges 19–21 where the in-group/out-group distinction can be most clearly seen and where the narrator's intentions appear most clearly. This section acts as a point of departure for the reconstruction of the narrator's attitude to deviance in the rest of the book. In the second section, the essay focuses on the treatment of the theme of deviance in the Jael, Ehud and Samson narratives and maintains that the narrator is here concerned with emphasizing which actions are deviant in dealings with the out-group. In the third section, the discussion elaborates which action patterns are considered deviant and legitimate in the context of inner-group relationships as they are treated by the narrator in the Gideon, Abimelech and Jephthah cycles. This essay, therefore, seeks to make some contribution to the understanding of Israelite social worlds and to the reconstruction of some of the possible processes whereby social group identity was articulated.

1. *Judges 19-21*:
The Identification of Deviance and the Creation of Consensus

That the narrator of the book of Judges is concerned with questions of deviance and with its labelling for purposes of group creation and maintenance can be readily seen in the so-called appendix to the book (chs. 19–21). It is generally agreed

---

1 'In-Group' (cf. Coser 1956: 87-110) refers to those social groups—individuals, families, clans, tribes, cities—considered by the narrator to be actual members, relapsed past members and potentially future members of Israel. The concept is not static but capable of expansion and retraction in the processes of social life. The listing of various social groups in the narratives (e.g. chs. 5, 19–21) need not be taken as an exclusive listing. The narrative provides examples of groups moving over to Israel and of Israelite groups becoming, in effect, out-groups. For further discussions of the role of deviance in social group maintenance, see Erikson (1967) and Ben-Yehuda (1985).

that these chapters portray a period of social breakdown
(Niditch 1982; Mayes 1983: 61; Lasine 1984), and present
unambiguous acts of deviance. The notice, 'In those days there
was no king in Israel and every man did that which was right
in his own eyes' (17.6; 21.25; cf. 18.1; 19.1), supports this reading (Boling 1974; cf. Dumbrell 1983). At the same time, however, the narrator documents a collective punitive action
against the perpetrators of crime, which appears to suggest
that social breakdown is not as deep-rooted as would first
appear, in that all social group members are agreed that it
should be punished. This may seem to present a paradoxical
situation. However, it is possible to suggest that the narrator's
purposes are served by presenting the situation in this way.

First, the request of the men of Gibeah to abuse the Levite
and their action in raping and bringing about the death of his
concubine are presented in no uncertain terms as deviant
actions.[1] What is noteworthy here is that the labelling of their
actions as deviant is communicated through the narrator's
own voice and through the speeches of most of the actors in
the episode.[2] The narrator thus supports his identification of
these actions as deviant by presenting all the actors in the
story as being in agreement. The labelling of the action is
shared by all, and this fact provides the background for the
collection punitive action against the men of Gibeah and the
tribe of Benjamin who have given the criminals refuge.

For the narrator the deviance of the men of Gibeah relates
to their breaking of the code of hospitality (cf. 19.3-10) and
their acts of rape and murder. But more fundamentally their
deviance is constituted by the fact that they have committed

1 At the same time the Levite's treatment of the concubine is presented as somewhat
   objectionable (19.26ff.) and the fact that he does not mention his own role in the
   events suggests that he himself is aware of some 'crime' on his part (Trible 1984:
   65-91).
2 The host (19.23-24), the Levite (20.4ff.), the people of Israel (20.3, 12-13) and the
   narrator (20.10) all label the action as deviant, i.e. as, 'a vile thing', as 'wanton-
   ness' and as a 'wanton crime' (נבלה); as 'wickedness' and 'evil' (רע); as an
   'abomination' (זמה) and as 'murder' (רצח). Also the men of Gibeah are described
   as 'base fellows' (אנשי/בני־בליעל 19.22; 20.13); similar designations denote
   deviance in other contexts: 18.25 (אנשים מרי־נפש); and 9.4 (אנשים ריקים); 11.3 (אנשים
   ריקים). In the Abimelech narrative deviance is labelled through the designations
   'treachery' (בגד), 'violence' (חמס), 'wickedness' and 'crime' (רע).

these actions within Israel.[1] That is, these actions were deviant primarily because they were committed within the social group. Equally, the narrator portrays the collective punitive action as being generally unsuccessful because the use of violence, even in the necessary punishment of crime, is almost as destabilizing to the group as the crime they are attempting to outlaw. In this way the narrator indicates how punishment should be regulated.[2] Throughout this episode the narrator is at pains to highlight how deviance and punishment can threaten the stability of the social group.

The narrator also discusses deviance in chs. 17–19, as is apparent from the way in which he connects these chapters with those which follow.[3] The main action which the narrator wishes to highlight is that of the Danites, whose deviance is constituted by the fact that, like the men of Gibeah, they fail to discriminate between the social group and the out-group. Both Micah and the men of Laish dwell in isolation and both have their possessions taken from them by the Danites, who make use of violence and intimidation.

Hence, the major social theme of these chapters is the identification of deviance as a failure to distinguish correctly between in-group and out-group. It is this distinction which underlies the identification of deviance in the rest of the book and it will be seen that deviance is often constituted by the perpetration of certain actions appropriate in one context to another inappropriate context, such as treating group members as 'outsiders' and out-group members as 'insiders'. The appropriate way for in-group members to treat out-group members is presented by the narrator in the Jael and Ehud

1 The Levite is aware that such treatment of guests is to be expected at the hands of the out-group (19.12). Notice also the stress on 'Israel' (19.30; 20.6, 10, 13) and the emphasizing of the fact that the punitive action is against 'brethren' (20.13, 23, 28).

2 This is shown by the facts that it takes three attempts to defeat the Benjamites (20.19-28) and that the punitive action brings about acts of deviance ironically similar to those they are seeking to outlaw (ch. 21).

3 The deviance is identified here by reference to chs. 19–21 and to other deviant features throughout the book. The Levite's actions are not above suspicion: he is persuaded to serve at Micah's shrine—which has been financed by dubious means (17.1-6; cf. 8.24ff.) and the construction of which is labelled as deviant (17.6)—by offer of financial reward (17.10; cf. 16.5), and he agrees to serve the Danites for reasons of increased prestige (18.19; cf. 9.2). The Danites have 'deviant elements' among them (18.25; cf. 19.22; 20.13; 9.4; 11.3).

stories, whereas the Samson cycle provides an example of how
not to treat out-group members. It is to these narratives that
the discussion now turns.

2. *Deviance and the In-group/Out-group Distinction*

Jael

The legitimate ways of dealing with the out-group are communicated by the narrator in the Jael (4.11ff.; 5.24-31) and
Ehud (3.12-30) episodes. However, the narrator takes care to
indicate that such actions would be considered deviant if performed within the social group. He achieves this by presenting
the actions of Jael and Ehud as potentially deviant. In the process the narrator highlights the in- and the out-groups and
seeks to persuade others to emulate the actions of Ehud and
Jael. That Jael's actions are considered legitimate and worthy
of emulation and social approval is communicated in the Song
of Deborah and is confirmed by the contrasting reaction to the
tribes who failed to participate in the war against Sisera. In
the Song, Jael is 'blessed among woman', her praises are sung
and she is accorded heroic status (5.24). In direct contrast to
this, the tribes which failed to muster do not receive praise but
ridicule and curses (5.15-17, 23).

At the same time, Jael's actions are potentially deviant. As a
woman in a patriarchal society she is an unlikely candidate
for heroic treatment and her actions subvert the social conventions of her gender (Klein 1988: 42). Moreover, she breaks
the code of the host;[1] indeed, she uses the trust of her guest to
betray him and to carry out the murder.

Further, in murdering Sisera she breaks the social obligation she has to her husband and the social obligation owed to
Sisera on the basis of the pact between the Kenites and the
Canaanites. She does not defer to the authority or the honour-
claims of her husband or of Sisera (4.11). All these actions
would be considered deviant if performed within Israel, but it
is precisely in her deviance that Jael qualifies not only as a

---

1 This is shown by comparison with 19.3-10. Also, there are parallels with the interaction of Achsah and Caleb. She asks for water from her father and she receives
water in plenty (1.12-15). Sisera asks for water and gets more, both a better substance and a fatal headache (5.25ff.); cf. Klein (1988: 42).

member of the narrator's social group but as an heroic member of that social group. Jael is praised for breaking social conventions on behalf of Israel. The tribes which failed to muster, on the other hand, are criticized for not fulfilling their social obligations. Jael's deviance is legitimate, and therefore not deviant, because it is performed within the out-group against the out-group. It is the context of the action that determines for the narrator which actions are to be considered and labelled as deviant.

Ehud

Commentators have often seen Ehud's actions and character as deviant in some way (Klein 1988: 37-47; Sternberg 1985: 331ff.; Polzin 1980: 60; Webb 1987: 128-32). However, in similar fashion to the Jael story, these features are presented by the narrator as only potentially deviant; such actions would not be legitimate if performed within the narrator's social group. Like Jael, Ehud is an unlikely candidate for heroic treatment since he is physically abnormal (Soggin 1981: 50; Webb 1988: 131). He appears to misuse the divine name to gain access to the king and to gain his trust (Klein 1988: 38; McKenzie 1966: 123). His method of murdering the king is calculated to disgust. And Ehud does not respect the trust that Eglon has extended to him: in the privacy of the king's chamber he commits the fatal deed (3.12-30).

While these elements portray Ehud in potentially deviant ways, and arouse the caution of the audience, all these deviant features take on an heroic dimension in the story. Ehud's deformity is what enables him to gain access to the king without suspicion. Ehud veils the origin of his word/thing (דבר) from God (3.20) but the veiling serves to portray Eglon as presumptuous and does not indict Ehud. On the contrary, Ehud's cleverness is emphasized. While the killing of Eglon is described in all of its gory and scatological details (3.21-23) much as Jael's violent slaying of Sisera is celebrated 'frame by frame', the descriptions do not cast any reflection on the characters of either Ehud or Jael. Rather, the depiction serves to indicate the sub-human level of the enemy, and that evaluation, in turn, maintains the in-group/out-group distinction and justifies Ehud's actions (cf. Speier 1969: 224). Similarly,

Ehud's betrayal of trust and his lack of respect for the privacy of the king serve to highlight the stupidity of the enemy. The servants, deferring to Eglon's royalty and honour, do not want to undermine his privacy and this enables Ehud to escape to safety and to summon the Israelite tribes for a collective military action (3.24-27). As in the Jael episode, Ehud's potential deviance is legitimate for the narrator because of its context. Ehud moves over to the out-group, behaves deviantly and in the process qualifies for heroic status within the in-group. The narrator seeks to maintain the boundary of the social group in this way and the out-group is isolated as a deserving victim of maltreatment. The narrator also seeks to encourage similar attitudes and actions towards the out-group, holding up the promise of social approval and heroic reward for those who behave in like manner.

The action patterns considered by the narrator to be legitimate in these episodes are illustrated in the following figure:

Legitimate Action	*Goal*
1. Use of Violence	Social Group
2. Use of Trickery/Treachery	Maintenance in
3. Breakage of Kinship Obligations[1]	the Face of
4. Non-deference[2]	External Threat
5. Disregard of Social Obligation[3]	
6. Pursuance of Societal Ends	
7. Non-normal Interactions with Out-group	
8. Choosing for Israel	

FIGURE ONE
Context: Social Interactions with the Out-Group

---

1 Kinship obligations are legitimately broken in this case because the obligations were owed to members of the out-group. This rule does not relate to breaking one's kinship obligations within the social group. This suggests that there were members of the social group who owed allegiance to kin in the out-group and were being encouraged to abandon those ties. The issue of kinship claims within the social group in the face of higher societal norms is discussed below.

2 'Deference' is a short-hand expression for showing respect to those in positions of authority and to those who have a certain amount of social prestige. For a sociological history of deference, see Collins (1975: 161-24).

3 Jael disregards social obligations—i.e. obligations not included in kinship/family obligations—in that she undermines the previous alliance with Jabin. However, as the man of Luz (1.22-26) and Rahab (Jos. 2; 6.25) episodes make clear, if members of the out-group have chosen for Israel the alliance with them is to be respected.

It must be remembered that these legitimate patterns of action relate only to interactions with the out-group. As such they do not provide a complete guide to social action. More precisely, deviant action patterns in dealings with the out-group and, more importantly, legitimate action within the social group, are not covered. Nevertheless, some indications of how deviance might be identified in those contexts can be given on the basis of the above table.

First, it is possible that deviance within the social group would be constituted by implementing those actions within the social group which were considered legitimate in dealings with the out-group. This would represent a confusing of action contexts on the part of social actors. In reality, this has already been shown by the fact that Jael's and Ehud's actions were described as potentially deviant and also by the fact that the tribes which failed to muster in the Song of Deborah were castigated. However, the issue of legitimate actions within the social group is more complex, not least because of the fact that not all of the prescriptions can carry equal force simultaneously within the social group. For example, a possible situation could arise where an actor must break kinship ties in order to fulfil societal ends. Because of this complexity the narrator deals with this action context in the Gideon, Abimelech and Gideon stories. I return to discuss these stories later in the paper.

Secondly, deviant action with respect to interactions with the out-group would appear to be constituted by the perpetration of the opposite of the tabulated prescriptions above in dealings with the out-group,[1] for example, having *normal* relationships with the out-group in contradistinction to prescription 7. That this is in fact the case is confirmed in the Samson cycle, which provides an example of deviant action in interactions with the out-group, and to which the discussion now turns.

---

1 This is certainly a possibility in that stress on the means of violence, trickery and so on for the achievement of social goals may have the unintended consequence of promoting such actions irrespective of goal or context. Unless there is an equal stress on legitimate goals and on legitimate means, an anomic situation may arise (cf. Merton 1957: 121-94). This is one major reason why the narrator must proceed to focus on legitimate action within the social group.

Samson

The first indication of Samson's deviance is given by the narrator in his portrayal of Samson's demand that his parents secure his marriage to the woman of Timnah (14.1-3). His parents are aware of the dangerous and deviant nature of this request and seek to persuade him to choose a wife from his own social group. From this point on, Samson embarks on a 'deviant career' which estranges him from his own social group until he is restored to it after his death when his brethren fetch him back for burial (16.31).

The theme of Samson's 'not-telling'[1] of his exploits and his secrets is used by the narrator to connect a number of episodes and to indicate that Samson is unwilling to extend his trust, or fulfil his obligations, to either his wife, his lover or his parents. The woman of Timnah and Delilah are presented as not being so wide of the mark when they suggest that Samson does not love them (14.16; 16.15).

The motif of Samson's secrets also serves to portray the social deviance of the Philistines. Social relationships among the Philistines are characterized by mistrust and by the threat and use of violence. Both the Timnite woman and Delilah are persuaded to comply with the wishes of their countryman, not on the basis of kinship loyalties but through the threat of violence and the promise of financial reward respectively (14.15; 16.15). In this way the narrator relates Samson's deviance to the deviance of the Philistines. From the perspective of the narrator, the actions of the Philistines are deviant by definition. This in turn highlights Samson's deviance since he seeks to have normal relationships with them in his search for emotional and sexual gratification.

The equation of the actions of the Philistines with those of Samson is most pronounced in the depiction of the cycle of violence which follows the Philistines' solving of the riddle (14.19ff.) and only ends with the death of the chief protago-

---

1 Samson does not tell his parents that he has killed a lion (14.6), or that he retrieved honey from its carcass (14.9). He does not tell his parents or the Timnite woman the meaning of the riddle (14.16) and withholds the secret of his strength from Delilah (16.4-17). To be sure, the Timnite woman and Delilah are seeking this information to protect themselves. Both sets of actors, therefore, take illegitimate positions with relation to the secrets.

nists. The cycle of violence is motivated by retribution. Both Samson and the Philistines explain to the men of Judah that they are only seeking justifiable revenge against the actions of the other (15.11, 12). The intercession of the men of Judah (15.9-14) provides a momentary respite and their restraint from the use of violence is emphasized by contrast. They are still willing to observe their social obligations to Samson even though his deviance has threatened their existence. Samson is persuaded to agree to their binding of him in order to turn him over to the Philistines, so long as they promise not to kill him. Keeping their side of the contract they lead him to the waiting Philistines, but Samson, as soon as they are within shouting distance, breaks free and the violence begins once more. At this point, Samson is both estranged from his own social group and is an outsider (as he really was all along) in the Philistine society. This is illustrated by the narrator through Samson's visit to the harlot, another social outcast (16.1-3).

The occasion for the final conflict is provided when the Philistines, while celebrating their great victory in capturing Samson and reducing him to a blind working animal, call for him to be brought forward to provide them with sport. The narrator brings the violence to an end with Samson's destruction of the temple, killing himself and all those inside (16.23-30).

By reference back to Figure One, the precise nature of Samson's deviance, from the perspective of the narrator, can be shown. In his replacement of an individual goal for a societal one, Samson seeks to have normal relationships with the Philistines, and this breaks prescriptions 6, 7 and 8. In order to do this he does not show deference to his own kin or to the men of Judah and does not fulfil his social obligations (he inverts prescriptions 3 and 4, applying them in the wrong context). Once within Philistine society, he resorts to violence and trickery and shows disrespect for his kinship ties to the Timnite woman. While this attitude to the out-group is similar to those of Ehud and Jael (and fulfils prescriptions 1, 2 and 3), they, unlike Samson, were not pursuing individual goals and they had not previously acted deviantly within Israel.

In fact, prescription 3 is both broken and fulfilled by Samson—which shows the ambiguity of personal relationships when they span two cultures. Nevertheless, the fact that Samson begins by treating his own parents with disrespect casts doubt on the legitimacy of his treatment of kinship relationships while in Philistine society. This seems especially to be the case when it is noted that this is precisely how the Philistines, who, as outsiders, are deviant by definition, regard their own kinship obligations. While this definitely confirms the deviance of the Philistines it also dramatically establishes Samson's foolishness in seeking to have normal relationships with them. Although Samson's victories against the Philistines agree with the narrator's attitude toward the way the out-group should be treated, these exploits are not enough to legitimate Samson's actions considered as a whole. For the narrator, Samson's deviant status has become the controlling one; his deviant status has become his 'master status' (Becker 1973: 32; Haralambos 1985: 430).

Summary
On the basis of the foregoing analysis of the Ehud, Jael and Samson stories, it appears that deviance is determined by reference to the context of the social actions. This accords with the labelling perspective which holds that 'Whether or not the [deviant] label is applied will depend on *how* the act is interpreted by the audience. This in turn will depend on *who* commits the act, *when* and *where* it is committed, *who* observes the act, and the negotiations between the various actors involved in the interaction situation' (Haralambos 1985: 430, my italics). In the present instance the 'audience' is the narrator and the negotiation takes place on paper. Deviance also relates to whether the actors are pursuing individual or societal goals—which is closely related to the decision to choose for or against Israel. Deviance, therefore, relates to the inversion of one set of legitimate action patterns and their transference to a context where they are not appropriate. What actually constitutes legitimate social action within the social group is discussed in more detail by the narrator in the Gideon, Abimelech and Jephthah episodes, to which the following discussion is devoted.

3. Claims of Honour and Claims of Kinship:
Deviance and Legitimate Action within the Social Group

Gideon

As with Ehud and Jael, Gideon is introduced by the narrator as an unlikely candidate for heroic treatment and his first action—of destroying the altar of his own social group—is potentially deviant. However, from the narrator's point of view, there is no doubt that this action qualifies Gideon for heroic status. By acting deviantly within his own social group, he has chosen for Israel.[1] The destruction of the altar is Gideon's first action in the proposed defeat of the Midianites. His next action is to summon the tribes to arms. This fighting force is subsequently reduced to only three hundred (7.1-7). While this may have been a realistic strategy, the import of this reduction is clearly stated in the narrative: in the event of victory no man will be able to say, 'my own hand has delivered me' (7.2). Attributing victory to Yahweh serves to maintain the equality of the fighting force in keeping claims of honour within bounds (Soggin 1981: 139). For the narrator social stability is ensured by the regulation of the claims of honour and, as will be seen, deviance relates to certain infractions of this social code. In this narrative, the narrator attempts to convey precisely how far the claims of honour should extend. In the treatment of social honour it can be supposed that the narrator is both drawing on some established precedents at the same time as creating some new normative orientations.[2]

The theme of the claims of honour is continued in the report of the interaction of Gideon with the men of Ephraim (8.1-3).

---

1 He is an unlikely hero in that he is the least in his family, which is the weakest clan in Manasseh (6.15). Gideon is aware of the deviancy of his action since he undertakes the action under cover of darkness (6.27). Also, the enquiry of the men of the town, 'Who has done this thing?' (6.29), has echoes with the questions of other groups when a deviant action has been committed (cf. 8.1; 5.6; 20.12). The action is legitimate, even though it breaks the code of his family and social group, because, as with Jael's and Ehud's actions, the action is committed within the out-group, in this instance an 'out-group enclave' within Israel. Gideon chooses for Israel by this action, a choice which his family and the men of the town have not yet made.

2 For a dicussion of the themes of honour and shame in early Israel, see Pedersen (1964: 213-44). For a sociological perspective on such issues, see Weber (1948); Gouldner (1965); Collins (1975).

Their complaint against Gideon is that he has failed to acknowledge the social obligations of the social group in that he calls for their assistance only after the main event. In their view, Gideon's actions are an affront to their own honour, for not only will they fail to receive social praise and prestige, but Gideon's honour will begin to out-strip their own. Gideon recognizes the force of their complaint and points out that any honour or material reward he has attained is minimal compared with the honour the men of Ephraim already have. The Ephraimites are convinced by this explanation and the conflict is avoided. In a similar interaction in the Jephthah narrative (12.1-6), which ends in violent conflict, the Ephraimites' complaint is unfounded. They fail to respond to the call to arms and hence do not act in accordance with social obligations. In the eyes of the narrator the use of violence within the social group in this case is legitimate.

The issue of social prestige and wealth is explored further in the record of the offer of kingship to Gideon.[1] Gideon is aware that acceptance of the kingship will create disparity in Israel. Such an elevation of a hero would be destabilizing. Rather, Yahweh must rule (8.22-24). However, Gideon does request the richest part of the spoil and the Israelites willingly give their acquired wealth to him (8.24-27). That Gideon may well have overstepped the boundaries of honour is communicated by the fact that the ephod he constructs at Ophrah is a source of deviance within the social group (8.27). The description of this deviance—'and all Israel played the harlot after it there, and it became a snare to Gideon and his family'—echoes other Deuteronomic descriptions of cultic deviance and may reflect a later development. Nevertheless, the ephod is detrimental to Gideon's honour since, as a monument to Gideon's social prestige (Driver 1903: 725), it implies that he sees his social obligations as fulfilled. They have become static, whereas his honour should be the source for further social action. His honour gives him social prestige but that prestige is accompanied by responsibility. At the same time, those without such prestige are portrayed as failing to respect Gideon (8.35). For the nar-

---

1 On Gideon's reply to the offer of kingship, cf. Soggin (1981: 160); Lindars (1965); Henton Davies (1963); Buber (1967: 59-65).

rator, the obligations that honour creates apply to holders and non-holders alike.

Of equal importance to the stability of the social group is the restrained use of violence. In the Jephthah narrative the use of violence against the men of Ephraim is legitimate; in contrast, Gideon refrains from violence and this shows how, for the narrator, its use is connected with honour. The use of violence against the men of Penuel and of Succoth (8.5-17) is legitimate because they have insulted Gideon's honour in doubting his ability, and have failed to offer him and his men hospitality. This, in turn, constitutes a failure to choose for Israel.[1] The kings, Zebah and Zalmunna, however, do acknowledge Gideon's honour and appeal to it in their plea for mercy (8.18-21). But Gideon cannot accede to their request because the claim of honour placed upon him by his having to exact retribution for the death of his brothers takes precedence.

The Gideon cycle, then, begins to explore the issues of honour and indicates that the narrator is aware of some of the possible functional and dysfunctional effects of this social commodity for the stability of the social group. The possible range of these functions and dysfunctions can be illustrated by reference to sociological insights based on the study of various societies.

Socially, honour 'works' in a number of ways. First, by offering social prestige—which brings, in turn, wealth, influence and power—honour motivates individuals to achieve social norms. However, the possible dysfunctions of this are to emphasize the goal of achieving honour and to derogate the legitimate means by which such honour should be attained (cf. Merton 1967: 121-94).

Secondly, the offering of social prestige functions to select individuals worthy of positions of authority, at least in theory. However, those in such positions must fully appreciate the responsibilities that their position places upon them. They

---

1 From the perspective of the narrator, the deviance of these groups does not depend on whether or not they were already part of Israel; they had the chance to choose for Israel, but by giving no respect to Gideon's honour and by refusing to offer hospitality, they fail to do so.

must be encouraged to use that position in a legitimate way and for the continued pursuit of legitimate societal ends.

Thirdly, honour places obligations on those without social prestige to defer to, respect and recognize the claims of those who possess it and to discriminate between those who have it and those who aspire to it. Since honour is awarded to those who have achieved social goals, emphasizing the respect that is due to them serves to reinforce social norms. The deferring to honour is especially pronounced among those having such prestige: the status group. Honour is a zero-sum commodity: if one claims too much honour or receives too much honour, the result is the taking away of honour from others, with resultant conflicts.

If the status group does not respect the honour of its other 'members' it cannot expect those without such prestige to do so. Social conflict is also caused in the wider society by barring access to social status and failing to accord prestige to those deserving recognition (cf. Weber 1948; Collins 1975; Davis and Moore 1967; Tumin 1967; Haralambos 1985: 30-38; Bottomore 1987: 176-91; Hamilton and Hirszowicz 1987).

The narrator of the book of Judges is aware of some of the potential stabilizing and destabilizing qualities of the social commodity of honour, and he discusses, in the Gideon, Abimelech and Jephthah episodes, how it might be used as a potential resource of social maintenance. At the same time, the narrator is aware that the illegitimate pursuit and illegitimate attribution of honour must be outlawed. Honour is therefore the source of legitimate action but also a possible source of deviant behaviour. In the Abimelech narrative the illegitimate pursuit of honour is illustrated.

Abimelech

The Abimelech narrative (Judges 9) continues with the theme of honour, its claims and obligations. It also discusses the relationship between claims of honour and claims of kinship. From the perspective of the narrator, Abimelech's deviance is that he does not show deference to the honour of his family and father. His attitude is doubly deviant because he shows disrespect to the claims of kinship. Abimelech replaces this set of kinship obligations with another. He appeals to the

men of Shechem on the basis of his kinship relations to them
(9.2). They agree to appoint Abimelech as their leader on this
basis (9.3, 19) and in the process they also do not defer to the
claims of Gideon's family, their present overlords. Abimelech
resorts to violence in his individual pursuit of social prestige
and murders his brothers, with only Jotham escaping.[1]

Abimelech's failure to defer to claims of honour is brought
out in Jotham's fable (8.7-15);[2] it is only because Abimelech is
without any social honour to speak of that he seeks to gain it
by illegitimate means. Abimelech's deviance is also shown up
by the narrator by his labelling of the actions of the men of
Shechem as 'violent' and 'treacherous' (8.22-24). They have
acted deviantly in relation to Gideon's family in appointing
Abimelech and in assisting him in the murder of his brothers,
and they have not deferred to Gideon's honour. They are now
about to act treacherously with Abimelech, respecting neither
the leadership they have given him nor the claims of kinship
they previously honoured. Interestingly, the root of this second
treachery is the revolt of Gaal, who is also supported by his
own kinsmen (8.26, 31).

Kinship, then, is the source of deviance in this narrative
when its claims are adhered to over above claims of honour in
the pursuit of social prestige. Thus, kinship relations are an
unstable resource for legitimate action and social stability. The
claims of kinship, in the view of the narrator, should be sub-
jected to the higher authority of honour and the good of the
social whole, in determining social actions.

Jotham is able to keep claims of honour and claims of kinship in the correct balance in that his own family is the social
grouping deserving respect. And yet, in the process, he comes
close to claiming total honour for his father and almost over-
steps the boundaries laid down in the Gideon narrative (9.17-
19). That is, Jotham bases much of his complaint on the basis

---

1 Abimelech achieves this through the hiring of 'worthless and reckless fellows'
(9.4); such individuals are deviant in other episodes also.

2 On Jotham's fable generally, see Lindars (1973). That the matter of honour is at
issue here is conveyed by the similarity in the description of the vine that has honour and the honour of the men of Ephraim (9.11; cf. 8.2). Furthermore, the theme of
honour is reiterated by the stress on fidelity (חסד, 8.35; אמת, 9.15, 16, 19) and the
stress on the need to acknowledge Gideon's efforts (8.35; 9.16).

of kinship rather than on claims of honour.[1] For the narrator, claims of honour and claims of kinship have to be kept in the correct balance but he is aware that achieving this balance is fraught with difficulties.

The deviance of the men of Shechem and of Gaal meets with its just deserts and they are punished through the legitimate use of violence. But the wielder of this violence is also a deviant character and he too will meet with a violent end. Abimelech begins the episodes without honour and in his deviant pursuit of social prestige he brings about the dishonourable death that befalls him at the hand of his armour-bearer after an unnamed woman has broken his skull (9.53-55).

Jephthah

The Jephthah cycle (10.17–12.7) also contributes to the narrator's working out of the relationship between kinship and honour. A narrow interpretation[2] of kinship (11.2) results in Jephthah being expelled by his brothers from the family and from the inheritance and social prestige that membership provides. Jephthah thereupon embarks on a 'deviant career', surrounding himself with 'hired worthless fellows' (11.3). In this process he acquires military skills which the Gileadites require for the defeat of their enemies. They fail to distinguish between valour gained through deviant means and legitimate honour, and offer him the leadership of their tribe. Jephthah, realizing that this offers him a further opportunity for achieving his own individual ends, agrees to their suggestion (Webb 1988: 75).

In the face of the ensuing battle Jephthah swears on oath to Yahweh that 'who' or 'whatever' should meet him after the battle shall be sacrificed, if victory is his. Jephthah is in the

---

1 The battle cry of the 300 is 'for the Lord and Gideon' (7.18, 20), and Gideon defers to Yahweh's honour (8.23); the error of the men of Israel is in not honouring Yahweh or Gideon (8.33-35). Jotham only mentions the efforts of his father: 'for my father fought for you, and risked his life; and rescued you from the hand of Midian' (9.17).

2 This is narrow because the rest of the book seems to indicate that concubines and lesser sons (chs. 9, 19) are members of the social group. While such liaisons are seen as potentially destabilizing and possibly to be avoided, members of the in-group who have such a background are to be treated equitably.

event successful, and when he returns home his daughter rushes out to greet him to give him the praise he now deserves as a valiant victor. However, this means that she must now be sacrificed and Jephthah complains of the trouble *she* has now caused him (11.35). He does not hold back from sacrificing her, and the social prestige he has achieved is shown to be shallow and ill-founded. It is the daughter, and not he, who will be remembered in Israel (11.40).

The daughter is the victim in this account (Trible 1984: 93-116), and yet her deference to her father's honour and her fidelity to his wishes evidences the destabilization and violence that accompanies failure to discriminate between legitimate and illegitimate honour, and the error of respecting kinship claims over and above the demands and obligations of honour. Jephthah's deviance may well have been precipitated by the actions of others but his pursuit of individual ends does not qualify him for heroic status. The narrator welcomes Jephthah's defeat of the enemy, but, as with Samson, his victory does not legitimate his actions considered as a whole. In this cycle, the narrator introduces a character who is almost forced to pursue honour in a deviant way because of the dishonourable behaviour of his own kin; their deviance causes Jephthah's deviance, Jephthah's deviant pursuit of honour in turn disrupts the social order and ends with the death of a member of his own immediate family. In this narrative, therefore, it can be said that extending honour to those undeserving, withholding prestige from those deserving, failing to discriminate between legitimate and illegitimate honour, and failing to discriminate between claims of kin and claims of honour all disrupt social life and threaten the stability of the social group.

On the basis of the Gideon, Abimelech and Jephthah episodes the action patterns considered by the narrator to be legitimate within the social group can be summarized in the following way:

Legitimate Action	*Goal*
1. Restraint in the Use of Violence	Social Group
2. Honesty in Dealings with Group Members	Maintenance in
3. Acknowledgment of Kinship Ties	the Face of
4. Deference to Honour	Internal and
5. Fidelity to Social Obligations/Alliances	External Threats
6. Pursuance of Societal Ends	
7. Non-Normal Interactions with Out-Group	
8. Choosing for Israel	

FIGURE TWO
Context: Social Interactions in the Social Group

It was suggested earlier, on the basis of Figure One, that deviance within the social group is constituted by the perpetration within the social group of actions considered legitimate in interactions with the out-group. The table above indicates similarly that deviance is constituted by the inversion and transference of one set of action patterns to an inappropriate context. At the same time, it can be seen that the pursuit of individual ends and failure to choose for Israel are deviant irrespective of the action context. In other words, with the exception of prescriptions 6, 7 and 8, the legitimate action patterns appropriate to in-group interactions are either the opposite of, or a qualified form of, those action patterns considered legitimate in dealings with the out-group.

The Gideon, Abimelech and Jephthah narratives also show how much more complex is the prescribing of action patterns with relation to the in-group. This is particularly the case with respect to honour and kinship. Honour has a 'double-bind', so to speak, and places obligations on its recipients as well as on those who attribute honour. Equally, kinship, while it is to be acknowledged, often must take a secondary place to honour, but more specifically it is to be accorded a secondary status—as are all social norms—in the face of emphasis on the well-being of the social whole. Similarly, the use of violence is not illegitimate in all circumstances but rather may be used for the punishment of normative infractions. The emphasis is on restraint in its use to ensure the stability of the social group.

Conclusion

In the view of the narrator of the book of Judges, deviance is constituted by transferring certain action patterns legitimate in dealings with the out-group to dealings with the social group. This most often occurs when societal goals are replaced by individual ends. Social stability within the group is reliant on the regulation of the claims of honour, on the regulation of the use of violence and on the fostering of a discriminatory attitude to claims of kinship when they conflict with societal goals. Honour and kinship appear to provide the main resources for stability but both of these, and this is particularly the case with respect to kinship, have the potential to become destabilizing. The determination of what a social goal might be in any particular instance cannot of course be normatively prescribed with any certainty. Rather, conformity to social norms is encouraged by the offer of social prestige, social honour, material and social reward. Deviant action, on the other hand, is discouraged by reference to the sanctions of disapproval, torture and death. Thus the narrator encourages social actions of an heroic nature, such as those of Ehud, Jael and Gideon, but also indicates that these heroic individuals do not thereby achieve a moral licence.

On the contrary, they acquire further responsibilities which they will ignore at their peril. Through the narratives in the book of Judges, the narrator provides examples of heroic and deviant individuals in an effort to provide some indication of appropriate action patterns and to encourage emulation. In this way the narrator seeks to maintain and constantly reaffirm the boundaries of the social group in an attempt to secure social stability and group cohesion.[1]

---

1 A number of issues naturally remain, which for reasons of space cannot be discussed here. Chief among these is the role of religion in the identification of deviance. This is especially important since, in its final form, the book of Judges is apparently interested only in cultic deviance. Since this problem is closely related to the complex redactional history of the book I must restrict myself to a few comments. In my view, the theological introduction (2.1–3.6; cf. 6.7-10; 10.6-16) and the 'framework' actually attract attention away from the theme of social deviance in their concentration on cultic deviance. The framework passages provide the introduction for most of the stories and in the process the legitimacy or deviance of the characters and their actions is not discussed. Indeed, these characters are all implicitly approved in that they all bring about the defeat of the

BIBLIOGRAPHY

Abercrombie, N., Hill, S., and Turner, B.S.
1984   *The Penguin Dictionary of Sociology*. Har-
            mondsworth: Penguin Books.
Becker, H.
1973   *Outsiders: Studies in the Sociology of Deviance*.
            Glencoe: The Free Press.
Ben-Yehuda, N.
1985   *Deviance and Moral Boundaries: Witchcraft, the
            Occult, Science Fiction, Deviant Sciences and Sci-
            entists*. Chicago: University of Chicago.
Boling, R.G.
1974   'In Those Days there was no King in Israel.' In *A
            Light Unto My Path: Old Testament Studies in
            Honor of J.M. Myers*, pp. 33-48. Philadelphia:
            Temple University Press.
Bottomore, T.
1987   *Sociology: A Guide to Problems and Literature*.
            3rd edn. London: Allen and Unwin.
Buber, M.
1967   *Kingship of God*. New York: Harper and Row.
Collins, R.
1975   *Conflict Sociology: Toward an Explanatory Scie-
            nce*. New York: Academic Press.
Coser, L.
1965   *The Function of Social Conflict*. London: Routledge
            and Kegan Paul.

foreign nations. (In distinction to Klein [1988], I do not think that the elements of the framework, by their absence or presence, provide a reliable guide for the identification of deviance.) While there is agreement between the theme of cultic deviance and social deviance with respect to the attitude to the foreign oppressors, the full significance of social deviance is undermined. In the search for theological consistency these editors have lost sight of social reality (cf. Weber 1952: 61-75). This is not to say that our narrator was unconcerned with theology. (Legitimate and deviant action is identified with the aid of divine intervention and comment in 9.56-57, and Gideon's actions, and the punitive action of ch. 21, are worked out in relation to Yahweh's character and will.) But, generally speaking, deviance is identified by reference to action contexts and by reference to social institutions. Naturally, the development of this growing theological labelling of deviance is worthy of sociological analysis on its own account and it cannot be reconstructed without paying close attention to the redactional history of the book.

Davies, K., and Moore, W.E.
  1967   'Some Principles of Stratification.' In *Class, Status and Power*, pp. 47-53. Ed. R. Bendix and S.M. Lipset. London: Routledge and Kegan Paul.

Downes, D., and Rock, P.
  1982   *Understanding Deviance: A Guide to the Sociology of Crime and Rule Breaking*. Oxford: Oxford University Press.

Driver, S.R.
  1903   'Ephod'. In *A Dictionary of the Bible*. Vol. 1, pp. 725-27. Ed. James Hastings. Edinburgh: T. and T. Clark.

Dumbrell, W.J.
  1983   ' "In those days there was no king in Israel; every man did what was right in his own eyes." The Purpose of the Book of Judges Reconsidered.' *Journal for the Study of the Old Testament* 25: 23-33.

Durkheim, E.
  1938   *The Rules of Sociological Method*. Trans. George Catlin. Glencoe: The Free Press.
  1970   *Suicide*. Ed. G. Simpson. London: Routledge and Kegan Paul.
  1984   *The Division of Labour in Society*. Trans. W.D. Halls. London: Macmillan.

Ericson, R.V., Baranek, P.M., and Chan, J.B.L.
  1987   *Visualising Deviance: A Study of News Organisation*. Milton Keynes: Open University Press.

Erikson, K.
  1965   *Wayward Puritans: A Study in the Sociology of Deviance*. New York: Wiley.

Fohrer, G.
  1968   *Introduction to the Old Testament*. Trans. David Green. London: SPCK.

Gouldner, A.W.
  1965   *Enter Plato*. New York: Collins.

Hamilton, M., and Hirszowicz, M.
  1987   *Class and Inequality in Pre-Industrial, Capitalist and Communist Societies*. Sussex: Wheatsheaf Books.

Haralambos, M.
  1985   *Sociology: Themes and Perspectives*. London: Bell and Hyman.

Henton Davies, G.
1963   'Judges VIII 22-23.' *Vetus Testamentum* 13: 151-57.

Kaiser, O.
1975   *Introduction to the Old Testament: A Presentation of Its Results and Problems.* Trans. J. Sturdy. Oxford: Basil Blackwell.

Klein, L.R.
1988   *The Triumph of Irony in the Book of Judges.* Bible and Literature Series, 14. Sheffield: Almond Press.

Lasine, S.
1984   'Guest and Host in Judges 19: Lot's Hospitality in an Inverted World.' *Journal for the Study of the Old Testament* 29: 37-59.

Lindars, B.
1965   'Gideon and Kingship.' *Journal of Theological Studies* ns 16: 315-26.
1973   'Jotham's Fable—A New Form Critical Analysis.' *Journal of Theological Studies* ns 24: 355-66.

Niditch, S.N.
1982   'The "Sodomite" Theme in Judges 19-20: Family, Community and Social Disorganization.' *Catholic Biblical Quarterly* 44: 365-78.

Mayes, A.D.H.
1977   'The Period of the Judges and Rise of the Monarchy'. In *Israelite and Judaean History*, pp. 285-331. Ed. J.H. Hayes and J. Maxwell Miller. London: SCM Press.
1983   *The Story of Israel between Settlement and Exile: A Redactional Study of the Deuteronomistic History.* London: SCM Press.
1985   *Judges.* Old Testament Guides. Sheffield: JSOT Press.

McKenzie, J.L.
1966   *The World of the Judges.* Englewood Cliffs: Prentice-Hall.

Merton, R.K.
1967   *Social Theory and Social Structure.* Glencoe: The Free Press.

Pedersen, J.P.
1964   *Israel: Its Life and Culture, I-II.* London: Oxford University Press.

Polzin, R.
1981   *Moses and the Deuteronomist. A Literary Study of the Deuteronomistic History.* New York: The Seabury Press.

Schur, E.M.
1971   *Labelling Deviant Behavior: Its Sociological Implications.* New York: Harper and Row.

Soggin, J.A.
1980   *Introduction to the Old Testament.* 2nd edn. Trans. J. Bowden. London: SCM Press.
1983   *Judges: A Commentary.* Trans. J. Bowden. London. SCM Press.

Speier, H.
1969   *Social Order and the Risks of War: Papers in Political Sociology.* Cambridge: MIT Press.

Sternberg, M.
1985   *The Poetics of Biblical Narrative: Ideological Literature and the Drama of Reading.* Bloomington: Indiana University Press.

Taylor, I., Walton, P., and Young, J.
1973   *The New Criminology: For a Social Theory of Deviance.* London: Routledge and Kegan Paul.

Thio, A.
1978   *Deviant Behavior.* Boston: Houghton Mifflin Co.

Trible, P.
1984   *Texts of Terror: Literary-Feminist Readings of Biblical Narratives.* Philadelphia: Fortress Press.

Tumin, M.M.
1967   *Social Stratification: The Forms and Functions of Social Inequality.* Englewood Cliffs: Prentice-Hall.

Webb, B.G.
1987   *The Book of Judges: An Integrated Reading.* JSOT Supplement Series, 46. Sheffield: JSOT Press.

Weber, M.
1948   'Class, Status and Party.' In *From Max Weber*, pp. 180-95. Ed. H.H. Gerth and C.W. Mills. London: Routledge and Kegan Paul.
1952   *Ancient Judaism.* Trans. H.H. Gerth and D. Martindale. Glencoe: The Free Press.

THE PROPHET AND HIS EDITORS

R.E. Clements

The study of the prophetic literature of the Old Testament has undergone many substantial shifts of emphasis since the work of J.G. Herder and J.G. Eichhorn heralded in a new era at the beginning of the nineteenth century.[1] In fact, such a shift had already begun to emerge with the work of J.C. Doederlein and Robert Lowth in the second half of the eighteenth century, since the newer literary insights of these earlier scholars had inevitably carried implications regarding the authorship and context of the prophetic writings. Doederlein rightly receives recognition for having argued for the full separation of Isa. 40–66 as the work of a different prophet from that who gave us Isa. 1–39.[2] It is true that even this was not a wholly new conclusion, having already been anticipated in mediaeval times by Ibn Ezra, but it undoubtedly marked a strikingly new recognition that our extant prophetic books cannot be assumed to represent the work of single authors. Rather we must be prepared, from a critical perspective, to find evidence of a more varied range of authors, compilers and editors at work in the formation of the preserved biblical collections. In Doederlein's view 'Second Isaiah' could be regarded as a

---

1 Cf. especially E. Sehmsdorf, *Die Prophetenauslegung bei J.G. Eichhorn* (Göttingen: Vandenhoeck & Ruprecht, 1971). The development of the study of the prophetic literature since H. Ewald is outlined in P.H.A. Neumann, *Das Prophetenverständnis in der deutschsprächigen Forschung seit Heinrich Ewald* (Wege der Forschung, 307; Darmstadt: Wissenschaftliche Buchgesellschaft).

2 For the work of Doederlein cf. especially J.M. Vincent, *Studien zur literarischen Eigenart und zur geistigen Heimat von Jesaja. Kap. 40–55* (Beiträge zur biblischen Exegese und Theologie 5; Frankfurt-am-Main, Bern, Las Vegas: Peter Lang, 1977).

wholly independent prophet from 'First Isaiah', but by the time of the publication of commentaries by Bernhard Duhm on Isaiah (1892) and Jeremiah (1901), the literary complexity of these two prophetic writings had become even more fully evident. A very significant amount of material in each of these books had come to be ascribed to 'secondary' authors.

In turn, and perhaps understandably, a conservative reaction to such critical dissection of the prophetic writings emerged during the nineteenth century. This reaction sought to defend their traditional literary unity under the names of the authors to which they had traditionally been ascribed. The assumption concerning unity of authorship appeared to be a major factor in defending their inspiration and authenticity as prophetic writings. As a consequence a very wide range of convictions about the nature of the prophetic literature came to be adopted by both critical and conservative scholars regarding the nature and contents of the prophetic writings. At one time the classification of 'authentic' and 'inauthentic' sayings attributed to individual prophets rose to become a primary goal of serious criticism. It is also noteworthy that recent trends of scholarship have witnessed in some circles a strong reaction against the conclusions and methodology of such critical analysis. In this there is an *a priori* assumption that, until proven otherwise, the sayings contained within a particular prophetic writing should be assumed to emanate from the period of activity of the prophet to which the book as a whole is ascribed. Yet this is to impose upon the interpretation of such writings a very far reaching assessment about their nature prior to an evaluation of the actual nature of their contents.

Admittedly there is no doubt that any attempt to analyse and locate the historical setting of a particular prophetic saying must be fraught with some measure of uncertainty. Over against this, however, to make the *a priori* assumption that the prophetic writings were composed as books in the modern manner, with the strict intention of preserving only those sayings which were known, or believed, to have been delivered by a single identifiable prophet, is to impose upon these complex ancient writings a purpose and literary intention which is itself a very questionable and doubtful assumption. The first requirement is therefore that some adequate critical evaluation should be made of the nature of such documents.

Consistently throughout the study of the prophetic literature both ancient and modern, there has existed an awareness that prophets were primarily spokesmen and preachers. Written collections of prophecies therefore represent a secondary phase of development within prophecy which has resulted in the collection, preservation and editing of messages that prophets originally gave orally.[1] The phenomenon of prophecy that was written from the outset marks a late development of Old Testament prophetic activity and appears to have had only a relatively minor impact upon the production of the major prophetic writings of the Old Testament. This is not to deny that such a prophet as Isaiah wrote down certain sayings, but to note that, as in the case of Jeremiah (Jer. 36), these were messages that had first been given orally. Fundamentally, we encounter prophetic literature as a written record based on messages that prophets originally spoke to their contemporaries.

The question of orality and literacy has a significant bearing upon the present issue under investigation, which is that of the nature of the relationship which existed between the prophet and his editors. This itself then breaks down into further questions concerning the identity of such editors, their relationship to the prophet and to other religious groups, and their purpose in recording his prophecies for a larger posterity to study. Answers to these questions, if they can be found, will then raise further questions regarding the extent to which such editors themselves added material in order to form a coherent written document. They may, in certain cases, have drawn material from other prophets or they may themselves have fashioned material as a kind of primitive commentary in order to clarify what they understood to be the essential meaning of the prophet's message.

In a sense the conservative attempts to resolve such issues have inevitably tended to classify the contents of the prophetic

---

1 Cf. my essay 'Prophecy as Literature. A Re-appraisal', in *The Hermeneutical Quest. Essays in Honor of J.L. Mays for his 65th Birthday*, ed. D.G. Miller (Princeton Theological Monographs, 4; Allison Park: Pickwick Publications, 1986), pp. 56-76.

books as predominantly of only one kind and either to regard the prophet as his own literary executor or at most to treat the prophet's editors as self-effacing literary traditionists who left little material of their own in the books they compiled. For the sake of simplicity and clarity we shall restrict the examples we are concerned with to the Book of Jeremiah, where a relatively definable situation appears. At the same time we shall need to recognize that there are no grounds for assuming that all four of the major collections which constitute the Latter Prophets were formed in precisely the same way.

1. Prophetic Editors as Preservationists

By the beginning of the twentieth century it had become clear that the primary mode of spoken prophetic address in ancient Israel was poetic in its nature and rhythmic in its structure. This further suggested that many prophetic sayings were originally quite short in their form as originally delivered. Hence B. Duhm's important commentary on Jeremiah published in 1901[1] made a sharp distinction between the primary prophetic sayings of Jeremiah which were in rhythmic poetry, the prose narratives in which Jeremiah's actions and experiences were recorded, and addresses in an elevated prose form which were markedly unlike the prophet's original poetic utterances. Duhm ascribed these 'prose sermons' to a late (fourth–third centuries BCE) nomistic editing of the book. These sermons were significantly distinct from the historical Jeremiah tradition and displayed a proto-Pharisaic concern with ideas of covenant and *torah*.

In many ways Duhm's insights into the different classes of literary material to be found in the Book of Jeremiah took on a much deeper significance in the light of S. Mowinckel's reaction to them. There can be little doubt that Duhm's work was the primary target that Mowinckel had in mind when he published his own assessment of the literary 'sources' of the Book of Jeremiah in 1914.[2] This lay greatest emphasis upon the different literary types of material that are evident and

---

1   B. Duhm, *Das Buch Jeremia* (KHAT; Göttingen: Vandenhoeck & Ruprecht, 1901).

2   S. Mowinckel, *Zur Komposition des Buches Jeremia* (Kristiania: Dybwad, 1914).

the different channels of preservation to which these bear testimony. So important has Mowinckel's classification of the sources A, B, C and D in the Book of Jeremiah become that any detailed summary of it would be superfluous here.[1] In particular Mowinckel's identification of a source C, consisting largely of the prose sermons that Duhm had characterized as marking the late nomistic editing of the book, has become a central feature of subsequent investigation. Mowinckel argued, against Duhm, that these marked a distinct stream of prophetic material deriving from Jeremiah which had been handed down separately from the rhythmic poetic sayings.[2]

The point that is of primary concern here is the way in which Mowinckel framed the basic questions. In line with the aims of scholarship that had emerged at the period, these focused attention almost exclusively upon the closeness of the relationship between the original prophet and the written record of his prophesying. For Mowinckel, as for Duhm, this was a question about 'authenticity', or 'closeness', of the preserved written material attributed to the prophet and the prophet himself. An element of 'distance' could be perceived which was evident in the fact that the different types of material in the book revealed the varied lines through which the message had been handed down until fixed in writing.

Mowinckel himself was later (1946) to define this relationship between the prophet's own activity and the book recording his prophecies and actions as one of 'Prophecy and Tradition'.[3] It remains essentially the problem with which we are concerned here, but scarcely still in the terms that Mowinckel envisaged it. For him the issue remained that of the authenticity of the preserved form of the prophet's sayings. More recent study has recognized that this does not exhaust the

---

1   Cf. the essays by W.L. Holladay, 'A Fresh Look at "Source B" and "Source C" in Jeremiah', *VT* 25 (1975), pp. 394-412, reprinted in *A Prophet to the Nations. Essays in Jeremiah Studies,* ed. L.G. Perdue and B.W. Kovacs (Winona Lake: Eisenbrauns, 1984), pp. 213-88).

2   A very positivist evaluation along these lines is presented by J. Bright, 'The Date of the Prose Sermons of Jeremiah', *JBL* 70 (1951), pp. 15-35 (= *A Prophet to the Nations,* pp. 193-212).

3   S. Mowinckel, *Prophecy and Tradition. The Prophetic Books in the Light of the Study of the Growth and History of the Tradition* (ANVAO; Oslo, 1946).

possibilities concerning the relationship between a prophet and his editors.

Following Mowinckel's original publication on the sources of the Book of Jeremiah two features came increasingly to dominate the scholarly discussion of this question, especially in Scandinavia. The first of these was a concern to posit the existence of a small community of 'disciples' who could be regarded as the preservers and transmitters of the original prophet's sayings.[1] Indeed Mowinckel's study of 1914 already pointed in this direction without saying as much. The very existence of the prophetic books could be regarded as proof that such circles of prophetic followers had been active in transmitting their master's sayings. How else could the prophetic writings have been produced?

The second feature of the study of the prophetic writings came to be inseparably linked to this, since it was to explore the possibilities inherent in the idea of oral transmission.[2] In this, not only was it recognized that the prophet had originally proclaimed his messages orally, but it appeared probable that the first stages in their preservation were also undertaken orally. Prophecy had originally been an oral literature which assumed a written form only after some interval of time had elapsed since its initial delivery. Differences in form and style in the material could then be explained as occurring during this stage of oral transmission, which the modern scholar could hardly be expected to retrace in detail.

It should certainly be noted that, although Mowinckel was staunch in his advocacy of such groups of 'disciples' having acted as the transmitters of the original prophet's sayings, he was noticeably more cautious than other Scandinavian scholars in pressing the claims of oral, over against written, transmission. His study of 1946 paid special attention to the Jeremiah tradition and was particularly concerned to argue

1 Cf. the study by A.S. Kapelrud, 'The Traditio-historical Study of the Prophets', in *The Productions of Time: Tradition History in Old Testament Scholarship* (ed. K. Jeppesen and B. Otzen; Sheffield: Almond, 1984), pp. 53-66.
2 Cf. especially E. Nielsen, *Oral Tradition* (SBT 1/11; London: SCM, 1951). A strong statement of the contention that prophecy was given and preserved orally through groups of disciples is presented by I. Engnell, 'Prophets and Prophetism in the Old Testament', *Critical Essays on the Old Testament* (tr. J.T. Willis; London: SPCK, 1970), pp. 123-79.

that oral and written transmission took place side by side.[1] Certainly no single consistent pattern of transmission and preservation should be presumed to have taken place. This contrasted with the quite dogmatic insistence that other scholars placed on the central role played by a relatively long period of oral transmission in giving rise to the extant prophetic books. Overall, however, in spite of many variations in emphasis and detail, the point that primarily concerns us in the present context is that the relationship between a prophet and his editors could be defined almost exclusively in terms of the accuracy and faithfulness with which the transmission had preserved the prophet's own words. The idea that the editors might have had some more creative and formative role to play in shaping the literary form and interpretation of the prophet's message was scarcely entertained at all. Rather, the contrary was assumed to be the case: the further the prophet's editors strayed from reporting his actual words the less satisfactory was their work assumed to be. In this both the more critical and the more conservative approaches to the prophetic literature shared many common assumptions, even where they differed considerably over their conclusions. Knowing only the prophet's actual words was taken to be all that really mattered in the study of a prophetic book.

Certainly it may be claimed that the study of the prophetic literature in the first half of the twentieth century, even where it brought many new insights, found itself largely dominated by assumptions and aims that had been formulated in the early part of the nineteenth century. The editors of the prophetic writings were simply regarded as the necessary mediators between the inspired preaching of the prophet and the preservation of this preaching within the biblical record. This accorded fully with the belief that the task of the scholar was essentially to recover a clear portrayal of the prophet's life and times. So the literary side of this task was conceived in terms of identifying, and where necessary eliminating, the distortions left by the prophet's editors.

---

1 Cf. also C.R. North, 'The Place of Oral Tradition in the Growth of the Old Testament', *ExpTim* 61 (1949-50), pp. 292-96.

2. *The Prophetic Editors as Creative Originators of Tradition*

It is not unfair to claim that, after half a century of studies of
the Book of Jeremiah in the wake of the work of Duhm and
Mowinckel, scholarship found itself faced with as much of an
impasse at the end of it as it had at the beginning. It appeared
to be equally possible to arrive either at a very positive estimate
of the degree to which Jeremiah's editors had preserved his
actual words and pronouncements or at a rather negative
one. The nature of the divergent types of material which was
in question was what such divergencies implied. New approaches were certainly called for and we may single out certain of
them as indicating a significant shift in the line of scholarly
questioning.

The first of these, by E.W. Nicholson,[1] was concerned primarily with the material which Mowinckel had identified as
'source C', and which took the form of prose sermons scattered throughout Jer. 1–25. The very title of Nicholson's book,
Preaching to the Exiles, indicates much of the argument
regarding the content. The prose sermons were seen not to be
from Jeremiah himself but rather to represent fresh creative
addresses delivered to the small community of Judaean exiles
in Babylon.[2] They used the name of Jeremiah because they
addressed the situation of exile which his prophecies had
served to interpret and foretell, but they bore little other effective relationship to Jeremiah himself. Their importance was
to be found in the way in which they brought new messages to
bear upon the situation which formed the aftermath of the
events which had formed the background to Jeremiah's
prophetic activity. In particular, the loss of confidence that had
survived in Judah after 587 BCE became a dominant feature
of their message.

What was important regarding this fresh line of questioning was that, in spite of some attention still to the question of
whether or not they represent part of the preserved Jeremiah
tradition, these prose sermons were viewed as creative
attempts to address a situation subsequent to that of

---

1   E.W. Nicholson, *Preaching to the Exiles. A Study of the Prose Tradition in the
    Book of Jeremiah* (Oxford: B.H. Blackwell, 1970).
2   Nicholson, *Preaching to the Exiles,* pp. 116ff.

Jeremiah's prophetic activity. They expanded further upon the meaning of the Babylonian exile which Jeremiah's own prophecies had addressed in an earlier, and still emergent, phase. In other words it was the situation which had arisen subsequent to Jeremiah's own preaching that had elicited the concern to elaborate and expand upon his own pronouncements. The prophet's editors had done more than simply strive to preserve his own words. They had added words of their own to make the prophet's sayings more meaningful! It is true that a living connection could still be traced between Jeremiah and the work of these exilic preachers, but it was far too oblique for it to be classed simply as that of the transmission of a body of sayings.

Nicholson's work explored the connections and overlap between the style and content of the Jeremianic 'prose sermons' and the vocabulary and theological interests of the Deuteronomistic literature. This connection formed the central focus of attention for the two volumes from W. Thiel[1] which sought to demonstrate the point that Jeremiah's literary editors can be seen, on the basis of literary and theological evidence, to have belonged to the circle of the Deuteronomistic 'School'. The importance of this observation, which had become part of the investigation into the literary make-up of the Book of Jeremiah since the work of Duhm and Mowinckel, was only now beginning to be fully appreciated. What was abundantly clear was that Jeremiah's editors had assimilated his prophetic message into the framework of the aims and theological ideals of a dominant scribal group of the sixth century BCE.[2] Accordingly, it was not the relationship of the preserved literary tradition to Jeremiah the prophet that mattered, but rather the ideological circle into which the prophet's message had been incorporated.

---

1 W. Thiel, *Die deuteronomistische Redaktion von Jeremia 1–25* (WMANT 41; Neukirchen-Vluyn: Neukirchener Verlag, 1973); *idem*, *Die deuteronomistische Redaktion von Jeremia 26–45* (WMANT 52; Neukirchen-Vluyn: Neukirchener Verlag, 1981).

2 Cf. also J.P. Hyatt, 'The Deuteronomic Edition of Jeremiah', *Vanderbilt Studies in the Humanities L* (ed. R.C. Beaty, J.P. Hyatt and M.K. Spears; Nashville: Vanderbilt University Press, 1951), pp. 71-95 (= *A Prophet to the Nations*, pp. 247-67).

212 *The Bible in Three Dimensions*

With Thiel's work, combined with that of other scholars, the relationship between a prophet and his editors could be set in a fresh light which made the assumption of a group of prophetic 'disciples' an increasingly irrelevant one. The tradition of Jeremiah's preaching had evidently been 'adopted' into a major scribal and reforming circle of Judaean leaders at the time that Judah collapsed in its attempts to resist Babylonian imperial control. The same basic assumption, that the editors of Jeremiah's prophecies belonged, in significant measure, to the same scribal circle that had produced the law-book of Deuteronomy and the Deuteronomistic History, was fundamental also to P. Diepold's study of the concept of 'The Land'[1] during this vitally important period of the collapse of the Judaean state. He could build upon the recognition that the editing of the prophecies of Jeremiah represented the third of the major literary productions of this Deuteronomistic 'School'.

A further major attempt to re-evaluate the aims and methods of the editors who had been responsible for producing a book, or more accurately, a scroll of Jeremiah's prophecies has been forthcoming from Robert Carroll.[2] We should note however, that even before the appearance of Carroll's studies, P.R. Ackroyd had addressed very directly the question of how we should understand the nature of the preserved Jeremiah tradition.[3] In particular he focused attention upon the recognition that written prophecy, based upon a preserved collection of a prophet's spoken words, could be used to legitimate changes in cultic and political institutions. Such a written prophetic testimony could appeal to the prophet's words as divine authorization for political changes which had been made inevitable by events, or to bolster the claims of particular religious groups over against those of rival groups. Written prophecy could become a literature of legitimization affecting the political and religious shape of a community in a very dif-

1 P. Diepold, *Israels Land* (BWANT V.15; Stuttgart: W. Kohlhammer, 1972).
2 R.P. Carroll, *When Prophecy Failed. Reactions and Responses to Failure in the Old Testament Prophetic Traditions* (London: SCM, 1979).
3 P.R. Ackroyd, 'Historians and Prophets', *SEÅ* 33 (1968), pp. 18-34 (= his *Studies in the Religious Tradition of the Old Testament* [London: SCM Press, 1987, pp. 121-51]).

ferent way from that in which the original spoken words of the prophet had done.

In a number of respects Carroll's work has developed very extensively the contention that written prophecy, in his judgment often only very tenuously related to the work of the prophet to which it was ascribed, served to legitimate developments within a community.[1] By claiming divine foreknowledge in advance of events, the prophetic tradition sought to affirm that a divine purpose had shaped those events. The starting-point of Carroll's study *When Prophecy Failed* is to be found in Leo Festinger's analysis of the responses shown by millennial prophetic movements to the experience of disappointed hopes.[2] Hence rather extreme forms of disappointed hope provide a norm of comparison for community responses to prophecy more generally. At the same time a psychological concern with the phenomenon of cognitive dissonance, where reality stands at some distance from prior expectations, occupies the central field of attention. Written prophecy is then seen by Carroll as one way by which the ancient Israelite community learned to cope with the frustration and disappointment of its expectations.

It is not surprising that, in the light of this broad social setting for prophetic activity, Carroll adopts a rather dogmatic scepticism over many aspects of the Jeremiah tradition in his study entitled *From Chaos to Covenant*. He remains doubtful whether we may at all know if the material ascribed to Jeremiah derived in any recognizable sense from his actual sayings. Rather all attention is devoted to the question of how a community responded to the catastrophic events which took place during Jeremiah's lifetime and how they used the figure of Jeremiah as a prophet to interpret their own confusion and despair. To this extent, with Carroll's work, the question of whether or not Jeremiah's editors had faithfully preserved and recorded the tradition of his sayings has largely become an irrelevance. Their concern is assumed to have been throughout one of understanding and interpreting the disas-

---

1 Carroll, *From Chaos to Covenant*, pp. 249ff.
2 L. Festinger, H.W. Riecker and S. Schachter, *When Prophecy Fails* (Minneapolis, 1956).

ters and despair which followed the prophet's period of activity. Prior hopeful expectation and painful historical reality had given rise to a situation of cognitive dissonance which only a prophetic hermeneutic could dispel.

We can certainly recognize that Carroll's studies provide an important corrective to the earlier work which took it for granted that all that mattered in examining the relationship between a prophet and his editors was whether or not they had painted his theological and spiritual portrait faithfully. This was never their intention, and in most respects the very nature of prophecy indicates that its concerns were far too urgent and existential for such a careful literary proceeding to have been their aim. Nevertheless to explain the origin of a major part of the Book of Jeremiah on the basis of a need for a hermeneutic arising out of the experience of cognitive dissonance is to lose sight of the uniqueness and inspired charisma which lent a very distinctive divine authority to the prophet's words in the first place. Carroll's picture of Jeremiah is one of a figure so lacking in definition that he appears virtually lost altogether behind the tradition that has made use of his name.

Clearly there is a need for recognizing that the relationship which existed between the prophet and his editors, and which led to determined efforts to record a prophet's actual words, was a more genuinely reciprocal one than this. The prophet did stand apart from other men, and he was believed to possess an inspiration accorded to only a very few individuals which made his actual words memorable and vital. At the same time there was evidently a need, as the complex literary structure of all the biblical prophetic collections reveals, to edit, record and interpret those words with the help of some additional material and supplementation. If an emphasis upon the prophetic editors as preservationists erred in one direction, the attempt to present them as freelance writers who used the prophet's name simply for their own convenience erred in another.

3. The Prophetic Editors as Interpreters

If we are to look for some guidance as to the overall role which the editors of the prophetic literature adopted for themselves then we find some helpful guidelines in Max Weber's basic studies of prophetic tradition.[1] In this he placed strong emphasis upon the role of the prophet as an inspired individual. The prophet's charisma was personal to himself and lent him a unique divine authority, not transferable to others. Yet against this his messages, often brief and some times cryptic, needed to be interpreted to make them more effective and meaningful for the life of the ongoing religious community to which he belonged. Accordingly, what the prophet's words meant for the future of established religious leaders and institutions needed to be spelled out. Weber described this process as one of 'routinization' in which the implications of what the prophet had said were adapted and interpreted in more precise and concrete terms and in relation to organized religious life. The prophet's message was perceived to lend direction and support to some groups, while he brought reproof, and sometimes outright rejection, to others.

So far as the theory of cognitive dissonance is concerned, it is noteworthy that Weber discerned an element of tension between the religious meaning of what a prophet declared and the empirical experience of what actually happened to the groups the prophet addressed. However this is peripheral to the more substantive feature that the 'routinization' of prophecy marked its integration into the life of a community. Its meaning was spelled out in terms of priestly administration, pastoral care and the spiritual development of the individual's life. Revealed truth became embodied in the institutional life of a larger group and spelled out in ethical rules and support for specific forms of administrative authority.

Our argument is that this process of 'routinization' is the most appropriate one to describe the nature of the relationship

---

1   M. Weber, *The Sociology of Religion* (tr. Ephraim Fischoff; Boston: Beacon Press, 1963), pp. 60-79; cf. especially pp. 60-61: 'Primarily, a religious community arises in connection with a prophetic movement as a result of routinization (Ger. *Veralltaglichung*), i.e. as a result of the process whereby either the prophet himself or his disciples secure the permanence of his preaching and the congregation's distribution of grace, hence insuring the economic existence of the enterprise and those who man it, and thereby monopolizing as well the privileges reserved for those charged with religious functions'. Cf. also 'The Sociology of Charismatic Authority, in *From Max Weber. Essays in Sociology* (ed. H.H. Gerth & C. Wright Mills; London: Routledge and Kegan Paul, 1947), pp. 245-52.

between a prophet and his editors. Especially does it highlight the difference in status and perceived authority between the individual *persona* of the prophet and that of the editors and interpreters who transmitted his sayings. It explains the aims and characteristics of the editorial supplementation which shaped and adapted the prophet's words in order to give them a more permanent and practical meaning. Most especially such a process serves to show why it was important to retain some recognizable portrait of the prophet himself, together with a record of his actual words so far as this was possible. and to relate these words to the events which formed the sequel of the situation to which the prophet had originally spoken. In such a context the uniqueness and individuality of the prophet was of the very essence of his charismatic authority to which his editors need to appeal. At the same time it was clear to these editors that the actual import of the prophet's words would be lost if their implications were not spelled out with great clarity to those who held the prophet in high regard as the spokesman of God.

We may contend therefore that this process of 'routinization' best describes the relationship between the prophet and his editors. Certainly this is so in the case of both Jeremiah and Ezekiel where the connections between the editorial word and more central circles of Jewish life have long been recognized.[1] In regard to the complex literary histories of the books of Isaiah and of the Twelve Prophets the situation is not so obviously clear, although in these also many facets of the routinization process are evident. In the case of Jeremiah this routinization has taken place in very direct application to central concerns of what we have broadly come to identify as as a Deuteronomistic party, or group. These concerns show themselves in regard to three major features of Judah's national life: temple, kingship and national sovereignty.

So we find that the meaning of Jeremiah's prophecies has been spelled out very forcefully in respect of the temple as the primary religious institution of the nation, the Davidic king-

---

1 Some initial observations along these lines were presented in my essay, 'The Ezekiel Tradition, Prophecy in a Time of Crisis', *Israel's Prophetic Tradition* (ed. R. Coggins, A.C.J. Phillips and M. Knibb; Cambridge: Cambridge University Press, 1982), pp. 119-36.

ship as its foremost political pillar, and the future of the remnants of the nation, in Judah and in Babylon, under a prolonged period of Babylonian political control.

It is not difficult to see how the fact of the destruction of the temple in Jerusalem has exercised a formative effect upon the literary shaping of the Jeremiah tradition. A conditional warning of the destruction of the building is set out in Jer. 7.1-15 in a unit which has long been recognized as showing traces of editorial reworking. It heads a substantial section dealing with false worship extending down to Jer. 10.25. Furthermore a repetition of this warning of the temple's destruction commences the narrative section in Jer. 26.1-15, where it is highlighted as a major cause of conflict between Jeremiah and the Jerusalem authorities. It is then noteworthy that this threat of the destruction of the temple is coupled with threats concerning the fall of the city of Jerusalem (cf. Jer. 7.34; 8.1-3; 9.12; 25.29; 38.3, 23). This is given such emphasis as to suggest that the presence of the temple there had provided the basis for the belief that the city as a whole would be spared for the temple's sake.

Since the book of Jeremiah, unlike the comparable books of Isaiah, Ezekiel and the Twelve, contains no explicit promise regarding the temple's restoration, the way in which the prophet himself envisaged the future of the cultus is never made wholly clear. It is often assumed that he advocated a very inward and spiritual form of worship which needed no formal cultus.[1] Nevertheless it has to be kept in mind that this is not made formally explicit. Rather the staunch advocacy, undoubtedly by the scroll's editors, of a necessary role for the levitical priests in the future (Jer. 33.18, 21-24) suggests that a restored temple was certainly not precluded.

Significantly too the ambiguity of this situation is left even more marked by the inclusion of an assurance that the loss of the ark would not inhibit the divine blessing of all Jerusalem in future years (Jer. 3.15-17). This loss, and the fact that it would not be replaced, appear at a point where we should readily have expected the temple itself to have been mentioned. Nor

---

1 Cf. the classic exposition in J. Skinner, *Prophecy and Religion* (Cambridge: Cambridge University Press, 1922), pp. 165-84.

can we leave out of reckoning the very surprising fact that the return of the temple vessels to Jerusalem, with the implication that they embodied much of the holiness of the temple itself, is introduced in Jer. 27.16-22, once again by the prophet's editors, as a major point.[1] Obviously such a concern for the temple vessels could only have meaning on the assumption that the temple itself would eventually be restored.

Overall the question of what Jeremiah's prophecies implied about the future of the temple was evidently a major point of concern for his editors. The end result is more than a little ambiguous as to what it discloses both about the attitude of Jeremiah to the matter and about the role a restored temple might have for a renewed and re-united Israel. Clearly a strong concern was felt to show why the temple had to be destroyed, and how Jeremiah had declared as much. At the same time this had to be set out in such a way as not to preclude the expectation that, in future, Jerusalem would once again become the spiritual centre of Israel's life. The absence of any prophecy concerning the rebuilding of the temple suggests that this had still not been raised as a major issue by the time the editing of the prophetic scroll was completed. At the same time such a rebuilding is clearly not ruled out.

The future of the kingship also becomes an issue where a significant level of tension exists between what appears to have been Jeremiah's own attitude and the expectations that were nursed by his editors. The finality with which Jeremiah ruled out any possible return to the throne of Jehoiachin, or his descendants (Jer. 22.24-27, 28-30) contrasts strikingly with the forthright assurance about the future of the Davidic dynasty set out in Jer. 33.14-26. The latter must certainly be the work of the editors, and this must also be true of the even more enigmatic prophecy of Jer. 23.5-6, with its play on the name of Zedekiah. Uncertainty about Jeremiah's hope for Zedekiah is shown up by 38.17-23, with its muted words of hope which events evidently refuted. Because the kingship was the central political institution of Israel's life, and because

1 Cf. P.R. Ackroyd, 'The Temple Vessels: A Continuity Theme', *Studies in the Religion of Ancient Israel*, VTSup 23 (1972), pp. 166-81 (= his *Studies in the Religious Tradition of the Old Testament*, pp. 46-60).

the return to the throne of Jerusalem of an heir of David's line became so important an aspect of the exilic hope (cf. Isa. 11.1-5; Ezek. 37.24-28), editorial work on Jeremiah's prophecies has endeavoured to give room to it.

It seems unlikely that Jeremiah personally attached much importance to the issue of restoring the Davidic monarchy after Zedekiah's removal from his throne. Since such a restoration in any case did not eventually take place, in spite of evident hopes that the survival of Jehoiachin's family in Babylonian exile would make it possible (as is suggested by 2 Kgs 25.27-30), it is striking that it is the editorial work which has generated an element of dissonance. It is Jeremiah's editors who, in upholding Jeremiah's condemnation of Judah's last kings, have nevertheless sought to show that the Davidic monarchy would play an important role in the future of a renewed Israel, even though actual events turned out contrary to this.

The third point that has deeply affected the editorial shaping of the Jeremiah scroll was evidently that of Judah's national sovereignty under the suzerainty of Babylon. This comes most startlingly into the forefront in the narratives of Jer. 40–43 which contain so much valuable and detailed information about the events in Judah under Gedaliah's brief governorship. What stands out is the repeated emphasis upon the necessity for continued submission to Babylon for the time being (Jer. 40.5, 7; 41.2, 18). This is spelled out so affirmatively as to insist that there was nothing to fear under such Babylonian jurisdiction:

> Gedaliah the son of Ahikam, son of Shaphan, swore to them and their men saying, 'Do not be afraid to serve the Chaldeans, Dwell in the land and serve the king of Babylon, and it shall be well with you' (Jer. 40.9).

Similarly Jeremiah could be presented as affirming as God's word:

> Do not fear the king of Babylon, of whom you are afraid; do not fear him, says the Lord, for I am with you, to save you and deliver you from his hand. I will grant you mercy, that he may have mercy on you and let you remain in your own land (42.11-12).

Clearly the Jeremiah scroll has been the subject of an editorial shaping which has made a very major issue of the necessity for the remnant in Judah to remain subservient, for an indefinite period, to the rule of the king of Babylon (cf. Jer. 25.11-14, 17, 26; 27.1-7; 29.10; 38.2). This has been felt to stand wholly in line with Jeremiah's personal advocacy of surrender to the Babylonian forces at the time of the siege of Jerusalem in 587 BCE (Jer. 38.2, 17-23). It clearly also had much to do with the condemnation of those prophets who declared the fall of Babylon and the return of the exiles to be imminent.

K.F. Pohlmann's tracing of this 'pro-Babylonian' editing in Jeremiah places it very late,[1] whereas all the indications are that it arose as an urgent issue affecting the survival of Judaean exiles very much closer to the time consequent upon Gedaliah's murder.[2] There seems little reason for dating it much later than the middle of the sixth century BCE. However our primary concern is to note how it was the emergence of such a basic political issue, and its evident relationship to a position which Jeremiah himself had adopted, which has elicited extensive treatment by Jeremiah's editors. It falls fully within the process which we can identify as that of the routinization of prophecy. This necessitated the elaboration and clarification of an inspired prophet's message in relation to concrete political and religious issues. The message itself was sensed to lack the specificity which was needed if its import was to be fully heeded by the community which looked back with genuine trust and confidence to the prophet who was the interpreter of their times. Hence we can claim that a genuine and positive relationship existed between the prophet and his editors. In no way were these latter trying to compensate for the limitations, or even errors, of the prophet whose heirs they felt themselves to be. Rather their profound respect for him made them eager and anxious interpreters of his words, spelling out in detail how they could be applied to the situation which his warnings and reproof had forewarned them of.

---

1 K.F. Pohlmann, *Studien zum Jeremiabuch. Ein Beitrag zur Frage nach der Entstehung des Jeremiabuches* (FRLANT 118; Göttingen: Vandenhoeck & Ruprecht, 1978).

2 Cf. C.R. Seitz, 'The Crisis of Interpretation over the Meaning and Purpose of the Exile: A Redactional Study of Jer. xxi–xliii', *VT* 35 (1985), pp. 78–97.

THE LIVING VOICE:
Scepticism towards the Written Word in Early Christian and in Graeco-Roman Texts*

Loveday Alexander

In a 1959 article on 'Teaching and Writing in the first Chapter of the *Stromateis* of Clement of Alexandria', E.F. Osborn wrote:

> The prejudice against writing was strong in the church of the second century. The living voice was the best medium for the communication of Christian truth. Writings were public and it was wrong to cast pearls before swine... If one must write, it were better that one should write badly (1959: 335).

The first chapter of Clement's *Stromateis* begins with an elaborate justification for the use of writing, and apparently feels the need to apologize for producing a book at all:

> Ἤδη δὲ οὐ γραφὴ εἰς ἐπίδειξιν τετεχνασμένην ἥδε ἡ πραγ-
> ματεία, ἀλλά μοι ὑπομνήματα εἰς γῆρας θησαυρίζεται,
> λήθης φάρμακον, εἴδωλον ἀτεχνῶς καὶ σκιαγρα'α τῶν
> ἐναργῶν καὶ ἐμψύχων ἐκείνων, ὧν κατηξιώθην ἐπακοῦσαι
> λόγων τε καὶ ἀνδρῶν μακαρίων καὶ τῷ ὄντι ἀξιολόγων.

> Now this treatise is not a carefully-wrought piece of writing for display, but just my notes stored up for old age, a 'remedy for forgetfulness', nothing but a rough image, a shadow of

* A version of this paper was first given at the Ehrhardt Seminar, University of Manchester, in February 1981, and subsequently (in abbreviated form) at the 1986 meeting of the *Symposium de Traditione Evangelica*, held in Salvan under the chairmanship of the late Bo Reicke, at Salvan. I am grateful to colleagues there and elsewhere for discussion and encouragement.

those clear and living words which I was thought worthy to hear, and of those blessed and truly worthy men.

Probably the most famous expression of this prejudice in favour of the 'living voice' is found in Papias' preface to his *Collection of Dominical Sayings*, preserved by Eusebius (*Hist. Eccl.* III 39.1):

οὐ γὰρ τὰ ἐκ τῶν βιβλίων τοσοῦτόν με ὠφελεῖν ὑπελάμ– βανον, ὅσον τὰ παρὰ ζώσης φωνῆς καὶ μενούσης.

For I did not imagine that things out of books would help me as much as the utterances of a living and abiding voice.

Yet, for all their familiarity, Papias's words demand a context: not so much the irrecoverable literary context from which Eusebius has excerpted the fragments, as the social and cultural context in which these (and Clement's) assumptions made sense. Was this a view peculiar to Christians in the second century? Are there other areas of Graeco-Roman culture where such a view would have found acceptance, or were the Christians alone in espousing this prejudice against the written word?

Birger Gerhardsson, in his major 1961 study, *Memory and Manuscript*, suggested that a close parallel to this attitude could be found in the rabbinic academies and their reluctance to commit the Oral Law to writing. It is no part of our purpose here to provide a new assessment of the rabbinic evidence;[1] but it is rapidly becoming apparent that the rabbinic academies cannot be studied in isolation. As Gerhardsson realized, the work of Saul Liebermann[2] had already demonstrated that

---

1 *Memory and Manuscript* sparked off a lively debate on rabbinic attitudes in the first century: cf. especially Morton Smith, 'A Comparison of Early Christian and Early Rabbinic Tradition', *JBL* 82 (1963), pp. 169-76; J. Neusner, 'Rabbinic traditions about the Pharisees before 70', *JJS* 22 (1971), pp. 1-18; *idem*, *Early Rabbinic Judaism* (Leiden: Brill, 1975). E. Urbach, *The Sages* (Jerusalem: Magnes Press, The Hebrew University, 1975), pp. 286-314, contains a more general discussion of the Oral Law, and there is a full account with survey of all recent literature in Peter Schäfer, *Studien zur Geschichte und Theologie des rabbinischen Judentums* (Leiden: Brill, 1978), pp. 153-97. For Gerhardsson's own more recent thinking on the Gospel tradition, see Gerhardsson, *The Origins of the Gospel Traditions* (London: SCM, 1979); *The Gospel Tradition* (Coniectanea Biblica, NT Series 15; Lund: C.W.K. Gleerup, 1986).

2 Especially in 'The publication of the Mishnah', in *Hellenism in Jewish Palestine* (New York: Jewish Theological Society of America, 2nd edn, 1962), pp. 83-99.

these academies need to be seen in relation to the schools of the hellenistic world; far from being an isolated phenomenon, the rabbinic schools form part of a cultural continuum covering the whole of the eastern Mediterranean. Gerhardsson himself throws out the challenge that hellenistic attitudes towards oral and written communication would repay a more detailed examination (1961: 197); he speaks in general terms of 'the opposition to letters and writing which manifested itself in many cultures at the time when the art of writing was introduced and which lives on, in various ways and in various forms, long afterwards' (1961: 157), and makes it clear that we are dealing not with a 'rabbinic' speciality but with 'a commonplace which we recognise from elsewhere in Antiquity, an attitude of scepticism towards the written word'. In similar vein, Anthony Harvey in 1976 described the first-century milieu of the Gospels as 'a culture which tended to frown upon the writing of books as such' (1976: 189). It is this wider Graeco-Roman context which we intend to investigate in this paper.

On the face of it, these confident assertions are rather surprising. Seen in the context of 'Antiquity' as a whole, the Graeco-Roman world from the fourth century BCE onwards is surely one of the world's more bookish cultures: 'When we pass on another stage, from the generation of Plato to that of Aristotle, a very distinct change is marked. Whereas in the early period, while books must have been produced in considerable numbers, a reading public could hardly be said to exist, we have now reached a period of readers and libraries… It is not too much to say that with Aristotle the Greek world passed from oral instruction to the habit of reading' (Kenyon 1951: 25). By the second century CE there is evidence for widespread literacy and an explosion of commercial book-production, aimed at a new broadly-based middle-class reading public (Perry 1967: 63). This has always been the stumbling-block for any attempt to flesh out an 'oral stage' of tradition behind our written gospels: in Talbert's words, 'Christianity emerged in a Mediterranean culture that was not illiterate. Education was widespread. Books were produced on a scale theretofore unknown. A large reading public consumed prose written with a rhetorical cast...'[1] And even within the Christian church, the prejudices of Papias and Clement cannot be taken as normative; compare these statements about the situation in fourth-century Antioch: 'The Christians seem to have followed Civil Service practice in their methods of propaganda, and to have appealed to a wider audience than that for which the traditional oral method of the Sophist catered... While the Christians made some attempt at mass production of texts, the pagan practice was actually to restrict the output of new works, in accordance with the orator's loyalty to the oral tradition and his upper-class clientele' (Norman 1960: 123, 127).

A full-scale investigation of attitudes towards the written word in antiquity is clearly beyond the scope of this paper. Such a study would have to take into account not only a vast amount of ancient literature, but also the concrete evidence of the papyri (Roberts 1979). Here we are attempting no more than to cut a trench (to borrow a metaphor from archaeology) across the 'tell', in the hope that this will give us at least a better idea of the complexity of the socio-cultural milieu in which the first Christian literature was produced; and to do this we shall focus narrowly on Papias's phrase 'the living voice'.

1. *The proverb*

Papias's phrase finds a close echo in a passage written by his near-contemporary Galen, in the opening words of *De compositione medicamentorum secundum locos* VI (Kühn XII 894):

Ἀληθὴς μὲν ἀμέλει καὶ ὁ λεγόμενος ὑπὸ τῶν πλείστων τεχνιτῶν ἐστι λόγος, ὡς οὐκ ἴσον οὐδ' ὅμοιον εἴη παρὰ ζώσης φωνῆς μαθεῖν ἢ ἐκ συγγράμματος ἀναλέξασθαι.

---

1 Talbert makes this point (pp. 101-102) in his discussion of Albert Lord's paper in the 1978 *Relationships among the Gospels* seminar (William O. Walker, ed., *The Relationships among the Gospels: an Interdisciplinary Dialogue* (San Antonio: Trinity University Press, 1978). Lord had put up a persuasive case for assessing the similarities and differences between our written Gospel texts against the background of oral folk literature successfully used to throw light on the Homeric epics (pp. 33-91). But, as Talbert pointed out in reply to Lord, the world of Homer and the world of the Yugoslavian epics surely differed from the milieu of the Gospels at precisely this point.

> There may well be truth in the saying current among most craftsmen, that reading out of a book is not the same thing as, or even comparable to, learning from the living voice.

This passage is notable in several ways. first, Galen is apparently expressing essentially the same sentiment as Papias—and this is no illiterate speaking, but a man whose surviving works fill twenty closely-printed volumes in the Kühn edition, and who was notorious even in antiquity for his prolixity as a writer (Athenaeus, *Deipnosophistae* I.1.e-f). We shall return later to assess the significance of the sentiment for a man like Galen. More immediate to our purpose at this stage is the second point, the common phraseology shared by the two writers in the striking phrase παρὰ ζώσης φωνῆς: Papias's rather odd word-order can be explained neatly by supposing that this was a 'given' phrase, to which Papias himself has tacked on καὶ μενούσης, perhaps in echo of 1 Pet. 1.23 (or some similar phrase current in the Christian rhetoric of second-century Asia Minor). Thirdly, Galen himself points to the 'given' nature of the phrase, which he describes as a 'saying' or 'proverb'; and, finally, Galen gives it a social context among 'craftsmen'.

Given the clue that Papias is quoting a proverb, it is no great task to discover further examples. Otto's *Sprichwörter* (Otto 1890) cites some twenty allusions to the greater efficacy of the 'living voice' over the written word. Most of these are Latin, and in view of the alliteration of the Latin tag *viva vox* it is tempting to assume that the saying was originally a Roman one. But in fact the earliest instance cited in the lexica is Greek: Cicero, *Letters to Atticus* II 12.2, comparing a verbal report of some titbit of news to a letter he has just received, exclaims,

> *Ubi sunt qui aiunt* ζώσης φωνῆς?

> Where are those who talk about the 'living voice'? I got an infinitely better idea from your letter than from his talk about what was going on...

Cicero's Greek words and phrases are generally a good guide to the idiomatic *Koine* of his day (Rose 1921), and since the phrase has not (to my knowledge) been found in Greek literature before Cicero we may take it that it was in the first cen-

tury BCE a current phrase in common speech. The question
we need to ask now is: exactly where (among whom) was it
current? Cicero, unlike Galen, gives the saying no particular
social context: the point made is quite general, as it is in many
of the other passages cited by Otto. However I believe it is possible, with the help of Galen and other ancient writers, to isolate a number of specific contexts in which the superiority of
the spoken over the written word remained a commonplace
long after the time of Aristotle when, in Kenyon's words, 'the
Greek world passed from oral instruction to the habit of reading' (Kenyon 1951: 25). We shall focus on the three areas
where the 'living voice' catchphrase is found (rhetoric; the
crafts; and the schools), and shall then look briefly at philosophical esotericism before turning to reconsider the position
of the Christian attitudes against the broader canvas.

2. *Rhetoric*

Rhetoric is the first and most obvious area of Greek culture
where 'loyalty to the oral tradition' (Norman 1960: 127) per-
sisted long after the wide dissemination of written texts.
Ancient rhetoric was first and foremost the art of *speaking*
effectively in public: it was a 'performance art', and as such
fought long and hard to maintain the superiority of the truly
'live' performance over the exercise of verbal skill in writing.
Isocrates is credited with being the first to compose 'written
speeches', and sending (rather than reciting) them to his chosen target: cf. *Ad Philippum* 25-27. He had to defend this
practice against spirited attacks, and rhetoric continued to
preserve not only the conventions of oral discourse ('speaking'
and 'hearing' as against 'writing' and 'reading'), but also the
conviction that a speech should be delivered in person, and
should at least give the impression of *ex tempore* composition.
Despite the loss of political independence (with the attendant
loss of opportunity for political speechmaking lamented by
Isocrates), public appetite for 'live' rhetorical performance
continued undiminished right through to the most famous
flowering of later Greek rhetoric in the Second Sophistic. Particularly popular was the so-called *ex tempore* show-piece, in
which a travelling sophist undertook to declaim at a few

moments' notice on any subject proposed by the audience. Philostratus recounts how such a sophist could be exposed when, having launched into a speech in answer to a planted request, he was discomfited to find the audience reading back to him his own supposedly *ex tempore* speech from a copy taken down in his last port of call (*Vit. Soph.* II.8). In this context it is easy to see why, as late as the fourth century CE, rhetors discouraged the use of shorthand note-taking, 'in keeping with their tradition of memorisation, public exhibition, and limited distribution' (Norman 1960: 123, 126).

Two allusions to the importance of the 'living voice' belong in this sphere:

> Quintilian *Inst.* II 2.8 *viva illa, ut dicitur, vox alit plenius...*
>
> that 'living voice', as the saying goes, provides more nourishment.
>
> Pliny *Ep.* II 3 *multo magis, ut vulgo dicitur, viva vox adficit*.
>
> the 'living voice', as the common saying has it, is much more effective.

In the first, the setting is a rhetorical school, and the contrast is one between giving pupils show declamations to read, and giving them a live performance from the teacher. In the second, Pliny is urging a friend to come and hear a great orator in the flesh rather than reading at home out of books. Note that in both cases the phrase is treated as proverbial (*ut dicitur*); and also that there is no wholesale prohibition against writing in the rhetorical schools. Written texts of speeches do exist, even if their use is deprecated; and the rhetorical schools also produced handbooks on rhetoric, like those of Quintilian or Hermogenes (see next section). But the stress on the primacy of the live performance of a show declamation, and the discouragement of note-taking, did have one practical effect: as von Arnim demonstrated in his work on Dio of Prusa (1898: introduction), it is not easy to establish a reliable text for such show pieces, precisely because we cannot be sure that there was ever a single author's autograph.

3. *The crafts*

Galen's quotation of the proverb provides us with a second cultural location, and affords us a rare glimpse into the mind of a numerically important but normally inarticulate section of ancient society. It is indeed something of a testimony to the extent to which medicine always remained 'craft' as much as 'science' (Temkin 1953) that Galen should quote such a source with approval. The literary establishment of Galen's time is more typically represented in Plutarch's snobbish dismissal of manual workers, even the great artists of the classical past, in *Life of Pericles* 2.[1]

A disdain for 'booklearning' among skilled craftsmen in the Graeco-Roman world should occasion no surprise. It is an attitude which can be paralleled in many times and cultures,[2] and it will probably always remain true that manual skills are not easily learned from books alone. In the nature of the case, however, it is rather difficult to find *written* expression of this sentiment. The nearest we can come to it, perhaps, is in the technical manuals of the more practical professions of antiquity. Galen himself quotes more than once another proverbial saying of similar bent:

> I blame the earliest writers on the forms of plants, holding it better to be an eyewitness (αὐτόπτης) by the side of the master himself and not to be like those who navigate out of books (*Temp. med.* VI Pref., Kühn XI 796-97).

> The people who ask this sort of question [i.e. theoretical questions] are those who are not learning from a teacher, but are like those who—according to the proverb—try to navigate out of a book (*De libr. propr.* 5, Kühn XIX 33/Scripta Minora II 110.25-27).

Here Galen is concerned with the difficulty of learning a particular skill from books alone. The obverse of this concern may be seen in the doubts expressed by a number of writers on practical subjects as to the feasibility of expressing their meaning fully in writing. Thus Hippocrates and Apollonius of

---

1   Cf. also *Life of Marcellus* 14f.; Valerius Maximus VIII.14.6.
2   Cf. Caleb Garth's remarks in George Eliot's *Middlemarch*, p. 599: 'A good deal of what I know can only come from experience: you can't learn it off as you learn things out of a book'.

Citium both express such a doubt about surgical practices (Hippocrates, *De articulis* 33; Apollonius of Citium, *Comm. in Hipp. de Art.* II pref.). Vitruvius similarly expands on this problem in his description of hydraulic machinery (*De architectura* X.8.6; cf. also IV.8.7, X.8.1, X.11.9), and Athenaeus Mechanicus, a contemporary writer on siege-engines, resorts to illustrations to make clear what is 'difficult to express verbally' (pref. 9).

The production of an illustrated textbook in antiquity can never have been cheap, and with the best will in the world could never totally solve the problem of 'booklearning' for the practising doctor.[1] For Galen, the solution was not illustration but 'live' teaching and practical demonstration:

> The herbs which form the ingredients of these drugs must be identified not once or twice or three times but very many times, even if you are learning them from someone who can demonstrate examples at the same time as expounding the subject—which is the ideal method of learning. If on the other hand you are approaching the question of identification without anyone to show you, but are relying on the reading of some book, such as Heracleides'... or Crateuas' or Dioscorides'..., you will need a lot more personal experience (*autopsia*) for the exact identification of each drug and its virtues and vices (*De antidotis* I Pref., Kühn XIV 6).

Even today, anyone who has tried to learn to identify wild flowers this way will appreciate the problem; and how many of us would entrust ourselves to a doctor who had obtained his or her medical training solely 'out of a book'?

---

1 It is natural to assume that Apollonius of Citium's illustrated commentary on the Hippocratic *De Articulis* (first century BCE) was a de luxe production for its royal dedicatee, rather than a mass-produced manual for the average surgeon. On the other hand, Riddle (1985: 176-217) argues that Dioscorides' *Herbal*, like the mathematical texts, carried illustrative diagrams from its first appearance (c. 70 CE). Pliny (*N.H.* XXV.4.8) speaks of illustrated herbals, though he disparages their effectiveness in proportion to the effort involved in their production. If Riddle is right, the original papyrus text would have contained stylized line drawings rather than the more natural illustrations found in the later vellum codices (1985: 215-16). Yet even when the technology existed for the production of high quality paintings, the tendency of copyists was to copy the illustrations from the text rather than from nature, with the result that divergences from nature grow more pronounced as the text is recopied.

4. *The schools*

The attitude of the 'craftsmen' to books may thus be seen primarily as a matter of common sense and realism. Galen's own attitude, however, is more ambivalent. On the one hand, as we have seen, he clearly has every sympathy with the anti-book lobby when it comes to the practical problems entailed in learning to identify medicinal herbs. But he uses the 'living voice' proverb as the opening gambit to Book Six of a large compilation, so we may expect that his apparent rejection of written communication will be qualified in some way. In fact the next sentence reads:

> But at least those who are diligent and naturally intelligent often gain no common advantage from reading books which are clearly written. Therefore I too realized that this work would be of no small profit, first of all to my friends who already know from practical demonstrations the force of the logical method in the preparation of drugs; and [secondly] I also wished to help the others, those who do not shrink from toil in the pursuit of the best ends. This is why I set about the exposition of the subject. I have not hastened or abbreviated the teaching here, but have presented it in long and extended form, just as I always used to in my unwritten discourses [διὰ τῶν ἄνευ γραφῆς λόγων] before my friends (Galen, *De comp. med. sec. loc.* VI Pref., Kühn XII 894).

The proverb is thus quoted only in order that it may be rejected. But the passage's interest does not end there. Galen here shows an awareness of a boundary between oral teaching and written teaching which is not crossed automatically or without thought. Moreover it is not only in the practical side of the subject that a doubt arises as to the propriety of 'learning out of a book':

> I ordered that these notes should be shared only with those who would read the book with a teacher (*De libr. propr.* 11, Kühn XIX 42/Scripta Minora II 118.22-24).

Here there is a definite prohibition, not on writing but on circulating the text outside a teaching situation; and the subject-matter is not medical practice but Aristotelian philosophy. A similar limitation governed the reading of Hippocrates (Smith 1979: 72).

Galen thus reflects a cultural background whose assumptions on the writing of books are not quite what we might have expected in the very literate world of the second century CE. For Galen the production of a book was not an inevitable, or even necessarily a desirable end in itself: books are secondary to oral teaching, and the ideal method of learning is to use the book under the guidance of a teacher. Many of Galen's books are in fact extended (or in some cases summarized) versions of lectures and demonstrations he had already given, sometimes circulated simply among his 'friends' (*hetairoi*) as a 'reminder' of teaching already given orally; cf. especially *De methodo medendi* VII pref. (Kühn X 456-58) and *De anatomicis adminstrationibus* VIII pref. (Kühn II 651); the circumstances behind the latter case are described more fully in *De libris propriis* II (Kühn XIX 20-22/*Scripta Minora* 100-102).[1] But in these cases, as in the passage quoted above, it is clear that Galen envisages that the written version of his lectures will also reach a wider audience, especially among the *philiatroi* whose interest in medicine was theoretical rather than practical;[2] and there is no sign that this wider dissemination is in any way unwelcome. Thus while books may be secondary in Galen's ideal teaching situation, it would be an exaggeration to see in Galen a prejudice against writing as such.

But what is the cultural world to which Galen here belongs? He is in many ways an ambiguous figure, a practising doctor with literary pretensions, his public lectures rivalling in popularity the rhetorical displays of the Second Sophistic (Bowersock 1969, ch. 5). But his attitudes to written and oral communication belong not so much to the world of display rhetoric as to the established wisdom of the hellenistic schools, which in different fields (medicine, philosophy, rhetoric, engineering, mathematics, astronomy, architecture) had been training its pupils since the fifth century BCE by a combination

---

1 Despite the element of conventional modesty in Galen's description of this work ('just a few notes I threw together...'), there is no reason to doubt the basic accuracy of his picture of the genesis of *De anat. admin.*
2 See further on this, Alexander, forthcoming, chs. 4 and 9. On non-professional interest in medicine, cf. G.E.R. Lloyd, *Hippocratic Writings* (Harmondsworth: Penguin Classics, 1978), pp. 37-39.

of written and oral methods. We have two other 'living voice' sayings from this world, both from Seneca and both relating to the philosophical schools of the first century CE.

> Seneca, *Epist.* VI 5: *plus tamen tibi et viva vox et convictus quam oratio proderit.*
>
> However, you will gain more from the living voice and from sharing someone's daily life than from any treatise.[1]

This is really another form of the commonplace that the philosophic way of life can only be learned from daily intimacy with a philosopher.[2] In another passage, however, Seneca shows some impatience with the high value traditionally assigned to the 'living voice':

> Seneca, *Epist.* XXXIII 9: *Quid est enim quare audiam quod legere possum? 'Multum', inquit, 'viva vox facit'. Non quidem haec quae alienis verbis commodatur at actuari vice fungitur.*
>
> Why, after all, should I listen to what I can read for myself? 'The living voice', it may be answered, 'counts for a great deal.' Not when it is just acting in a kind of secretarial capacity, making itself an instrument for what others have to say (trans. Campbell).

Here Seneca is arguing for a more mature attitude to philosophy, moving on from the ideal of memorizing Zeno or Cleanthes towards being able to think and teach for oneself. If the 'living voice' is simply an instrument for the passing on of tradition, then a book can do the job just as well: the true philosopher should be producing his own memorable sayings, not just passing on the sayings of others: 'Let's have some difference between you and the books!' (*ibid.*, trans. Campbell).

There is an air of deliberate paradox in this reversal of the proverbial superiority of the 'living voice'; here it is not Seneca

---

1 The contrast is with the philosophical books which Lucilius has requested; Seneca promises to send them, but protests that their usefulness is limited. *Oratio* must therefore mean here a *written* treatise.

2 Seneca's sentiment is essentially the same as that expressed in *Letter of Aristeas* 127: 'for [he said] good living consists in living a life according to the law. But this is much more to be achieved through listening (διὰ τῆς ἀκροάσεως, i.e. through oral instruction) than through reading (διὰ τῆς ἀναγνώσεως).' Despite Pelletier's comment (p. 56), this reflects not 'pharisaic leanings' but the standard wisdom of the Greek school tradition.

but the position he ridicules (and which he endorsed in Letter VI), that represents the standard wisdom of the schools. What is interesting here is that the value of the 'living voice' is no longer simply the value of 'live' performance or teacher-contact over 'dead' discourse in a book. The phrase is also linked with the accurate *memorization* of a master's teachings and their *transmission* to later generations via a chain of tradents. Galen was in no doubt that this 'live' transmission of a school tradition carried a guarantee of authenticity which could never be matched by outsiders:

> As for me, even if none of Erasistratus' books had been preserved, but they were all now lost as has happened with Chrysippus', I would rather trust what his disciples say about their teacher than [I would trust] people who have never seen Erasistratus himself or even one of his disciples (Galen, *De venae sect.* 5, Kühn XI 221).

Again, we find that books are of secondary importance in the passing on of a school tradition. The position is well described by Dillon in his account of the philosophical schools in the second century CE:

> In all this identification of sources we must bear in mind the obvious fact, all too often overlooked, that the chief vehicle for the transmission of Platonic doctrine during all this time is not so much a series of written and published treatises as the oral tradition of the schools, embodied, perhaps, in notes written up by either teacher or pupil (such as, for instance, Albinus' records of Gaius' lectures), but only rarely taking a public form even theoretically observable to us. To talk of the 'influence', then, of Antiochus, Posidonius or Arius Didymus on the scholasticism of the mid-second century AD is grossly to oversimplify the situation. They are indeed there, as remote influences, but the chief influence upon a philosopher is that of his own teacher, and the works of Plato and Aristotle as seen through his eyes, and his chief influence in turn was his teacher, and so on ... (Dillon 1977: 338).

Second-century Platonism is often associated with a full-blooded 'esotericism' in the restricted sense of deliberate secrecy (which will be discussed below); but it is important to stress that the state of affairs described by Dillon here is not a peculiarly 'Platonist' phenomenon but simply a pattern of behaviour and expectation which was common in all the hellenistic schools. The importance of contact with the living tradition may be assessed from the frequency with which it is claimed in the prefaces of writers on subjects as diverse as surgery, architecture, mechanical engineering, and rhetoric; see the extended study of these prefaces in Alexander, 1977 and forthcoming.

With these writers, as with Galen, the precise relationship between the surviving written text and the oral instruction which is presumed to lie behind it is a matter for further investigation. In many cases it seems clear that the written text was regarded simply as a more permanent form of the teaching already given orally, and distributed by a teacher to people who had already heard this oral teaching, as in an anonymous geographical epitome dating probably from the third century CE:

ὡς ἂν ἐπὶ μνήμης ἔχῃς, ὦ Φίλων ἄριστε, ὅσα καὶ διὰ ζώ–
σης φωνῆς παρ' ἡμῶν ἀκήκοας.

so that you may possess, my dear Philon, a [written] reminder of the things you have heard from us 'through the living voice' (Anon. Geog. Epit. I, Müller, GGM II 488).

A similar statement is made at the beginning of Hermogenes, *De inventione* III (second century CE):

Τὸ τρίτον μοι σύνταγμα τουτὶ γέγονεν, ὦ κράτιστε 'Ιούλιε
Μᾶρκε, περὶ ὧν ἤδη σοι φθάνω καὶ δι' ἐμαυτοῦ πολλάκις
τεχνολογήσας ...

This is now my third compilation, most excellent Julius Marcus, about the subject on which I have often already given you systematic instruction myself...

In other cases it was the pupils who made their own notes, either for personal use or for circulation among fellow-students, as in the famous instance cited by Quintilian as a reason for producing his own written version of his teaching:[1]

---

1   For further examples, cf. Cicero, *De Orat.* I.5; *Ad Att.* XIII.21a1 (21.4) with Suda III.661, p. 281; Arrian, *Discourses of Epictetus* I pref.; Iamblichus, *De Vita Pythagorica* 28.158 (115); Galen, *De libris propriis* I.8.1–11.13 (Kuhn XIX/*Scripta Minora* II).

I have been all the more desirous of doing so because two books on the art of rhetoric are at present circulating under my name, although never published by me or composed for such a purpose. One is a two days' lecture which was taken down by the boys who were my audience. The other consists of such notes as my good pupils succeeded in taking down from a course of lectures on a somewhat more extensive scale: I appreciate their kindness, but they showed an excess of enthusiasm and a certain lack of discretion in doing my utterances the honour of publication... (Quintilian, *Inst. Or.* I pref. 7, trans. Butler).

Other texts appear to stand at a greater distance from the school situation (e.g. the works of Vitruvius and Apollonius of Citium, which are presented for the attention of an elevated patron); yet they still choose to present themselves as a record of received teaching.

One final point. It is natural to assume that this reverence for the passing on of an oral teaching tradition would be accompanied by a concern for exact preservation, perhaps with a stress on memorization. In fact the opposite is the case. Thus Seneca makes the rather acid comment that the tradition of 'the master's words' in the Epicurean school actually contains many sayings originated by Epicurus' disciples:

Seneca, *Epist.* XXXIII 4: Among Epicureans whatever Hermarchus or Metrodorus says is credited to one man alone; everything ever said by any member of that fraternity was uttered under the authority and auspices of one person.

This is not an isolated phenomenon; the received tradition is treated not as an inviolate, fixed body of doctrine but as a developing, organic system open to constant improvement. The effects of this attitude can be seen clearly in the written texts, where alongside the insistence on received tradition is the assurance of continual addition, selection and correction in line with the author's own experience of 'what is useful':

Vitruvius X 13.8: as I have received it from my teachers and as it seems useful to me.

Hero, *Pneum.* pref. I p. 2.5-7: what has been handed down by the ancients... with the additional discoveries made by ourselves.

Anon. Geog. Epit. I pref. (Müller, GGM II 488): verifying...
correcting...

An 'improved' text of this type was discovered in a second-
century papyrus herbal described by Riddle (1985: 177-78):
'Probably, then, the herbal was composed by an author who
used Dioscorides, who perhaps added his own experiences, and
who seemed to be more interested in medicine than botany.
The differences in the text [sc. from Dioscorides] are not sloppy
copying errors nor are they mere condensations. What we
seem to have is the first evidence of a pattern that repeated
itself many times in the centuries afterward. Future users of
Dioscorides' text contributed their experiences with plant,
animal and mineral drugs by adding to and subtracting from
the text as they made their own copies.' This phenomenon is
found throughout the hellenistic school tradition and is well
known to the editors of the major school *corpora*.[1] The only
point of contention was whether it was fairer to attribute the
improved tradition to the ultimate master, as the Epicureans
did, or to attach later versions to the names of their real
authors in the Stoic manner: Iamblichus, writing on the
Pythagorean school in the fourth century CE, clearly regards
the Epicurean practice as praiseworthy (*De Vita Pythagorica*
28.158, 31.198), where Galen two centuries earlier found it
infuriating.[2]

From this brief survey some important points emerge:

(a) A preference for orally-transmitted teaching is not con-
    fined to the rabbinic academies, but is also found in the
    hellenistic schools.
(b) This oral teaching tradition is recognized to have a high
    authenticity-value over against written texts; but
(c) This tradition is not concerned to transmit a particular
    body of teaching inviolate through the centuries, but is
    constantly updated and emended in the light of
    improvements in practice or changing circumstances.

---

1 Cf. e.g. Jaeger (1912) (Aristotle), and on the Hippocratic Corpus Lorentz, art.
   'Hippokrates XVI (von Kos)', *Pauly-Wissowa* Suppl. VI (*Nachträge*), 1935: 1333-
   34.
2 Galen, *De libris propriis* I.9.4-8 (Kühn XIX/*Scripta Minora* II). Cf. Pliny's complaint that scientific writers never cite their sources: *N.H.* pref. 22.

(d) There is however no *prohibition* against writing in the schools, as may be seen from the multitude of school texts we possess. What the prefatory phrases do show, however, is a scale of values in which written texts are of secondary importance over against a living oral tradition.

(e) The dissemination of written texts may be hedged about with caution (as in Galen's concern about his notes on Aristotle), but it is not actually *forbidden*.

(f) Since the written text often represents essentially the same teaching as that which has already been given orally, there can be no hard and fast distinction *in content* between an 'esoteric' oral teaching and a written text which may be made public.

(g) As in the case of Dio, the secondary status of the written text over against the developing oral tradition often results in grave difficulties for the editor: in many cases it is virtually impossible to establish a firm manuscript stemma or to postulate a single autograph in the manner of classic textual criticism.

5. *Philosophical esotericism*

In the foregoing we have tried to draw a distinction between the attitude of caution and suspicion towards writing associated with the 'living voice' proverb and a full-blooded esotericism. The distinction can be usefully illustrated by a brief examination of attitudes to writing in the Platonic corpus.

The most famous expression of hostility to writing in Greek literature is also one of the oldest: Plato's lament in the *Phaedrus*. In an extended passage from 274c Socrates recounts the myth of the invention of writing by the Egyptian god Thoth, on which Ammon is said to have commented, 'this invention will produce forgetfulness in the minds of those who learn to use it, because they will not practise their memory' (275a2-4, trans. Fowler). Thus, Socrates goes on to argue, the true *logos* is 'written with intelligence in the mind of the learner',

λόγον ... ζῶντα καὶ ἔμψυχον, οὗ ὁ γεγράμμενος εἴδωλον ἄν τι λέγοιτο δικαίως.

> the living and breathing word of him who knows, of which
> the written word may justly be called the image (276a6-10,
> trans. Fowler).

It is undoubtedly significant that this protest comes not at a
time when writing was an unusual accomplishment reserved
for a scribal élite, but at the beginning of the explosion of literacy and book-production which marked the fourth century
BCE. Plato's attack may be seen as a rearguard action, a mark
of nostalgia, of awareness and apprehension of the new world
of written literature that was beginning to break out of the
confines of the city-state and spread over the whole Mediterranean basin.

The *Phaedrus* discussion is set in the context of a debate
about 'written speeches', and thus on the surface takes us
back to rhetoric (section 2 above); but as the dialogue develops
it becomes clear that Plato's real concern is with the
difference between oral and written *teaching* rather than
with rhetoric or with books in general. The dialogue in fact
reflects a more intense crisis within Platonic philosophy itself,
triggered by the appearance of a new fourth-century phenomenon, the technical handbooks to rhetoric like Anaximenes'
Rhetorica ad Alexandrum, a *techne* in written form. Plato
also knows of medical handbooks (268a-b) and of handbooks
which claim to impart the rules for composing speeches in
tragedy, and argues that the sort of knowledge gained in this
way is totally insufficient for the acquisition of the whole
techne (269a). What Plato is rejecting is the belief that a
handbook can be a passport to a kind of 'instant' skill. He
himself chose deliberately to write not systematic treatises
but—faithful to the spirit of Socrates as he saw it—dialogues
which would preserve the Socratic tradition of 'enquiry'
(Friedländer 1958: 157-70). Among Plato's successors,
Aristotle too wrote dialogues (now lost) for public consump-
tion: the treatises which survive, misleadingly known as
'esoteric' in contradistinction from the 'exoteric' treatises
designed for a wider public (cf. e.g. EN 1102a26), are probably
based on lecture-notes circulating within the school (Jaeger
1912) and, though not in any sense secret, were not originally
intended for universal publication. As Jaeger points out, such
treatises might not even be comprehensible to outsiders:

> The prose of the πραγματεῖαι is a scholastic deformation, a skeleton, joined together from the bare bones of terminologically fossilized school concepts. It cannot hold the attention of anyone who has not learnt to handle such concepts in the school (Jaeger 1912: 132-33).

The praxis of the Aristotelian school thus effectively supports the point made in the *Phaedrus*, where books are considered deficient as teachers, unable to 'defend themselves' (i.e. to indulge in dialogue) against their interlocutors (275d-e), and fit only to be used as 'reminders' of something already known:

> He who thinks, then, that he has left behind him any art in writing, and he who receives it in the belief that anything in writing will be clear and certain, would be an utterly simple person, and in truth ignorant of the prophecy of Ammon, if he thinks written words are of any use except to remind him who knows the matter about which they are written (275c-d, trans. Fowler).

The *Phaedrus*, then, disparages the writing of manuals and their use as a substitute for 'live' teaching. It does not, however, forbid their writing: as Edelstein points out, the philosopher clearly does write and takes a legitimate pleasure in so doing (Edelstein 1966: 83). The situation is significantly different in the Platonic *Seventh Letter*. Here we read first that Plato himself has never written anything and will not write anything on the true centre of his philosophy (341c):

> There is no writing of mine on these matters, nor will there ever be one. For this knowledge is not something that can be put into words like other sciences (μαθήματα); but after long-continued intercourse between teacher and pupil, in joint pursuit of the subject, suddenly, like light flashing forth when a fire is kindled, it is born in the soul and straightway nourishes itself (341c-d, trans. Morrow).

Only the few are capable of reaching this state of illumination, and writing would simply expose the subject to the potential ridicule of 'the multitude' without benefitting the few who could 'with a little guidance discover the truth by themselves' (341d-e). The fixed nature of a written text makes it unsuitable for expressing the deepest perceptions of reality (342e-343a), and

> For this reason anyone who is seriously studying high mat-
> ters will be the last to write about them and thus expose his
> thought to the envy and criticism of men. What I have said
> comes, in short, to this: whenever we see a book, whether the
> laws of a legislator or a composition on any other subject, we
> can be sure that if the author is really serious, this book does
> not contain his best thoughts; they are stored away with the
> fairest of his possessions. And if he has committed these
> serious thoughts to writing, it is because men, not the gods,
> 'have taken his wits away' (344c-d, trans. Morrow).

Edelstein (1966: 83) is surely right to see this as differing
significantly from the *Phaedrus*. The *Seventh Letter* moves
from a general disparagement of writing as a deficient substitute for teaching to a total rejection of writing as a medium of
expression for serious philosophy. It sets up a firm divide
between the 'few' and the 'multitude' which transcends the
intellectual exclusivism found elsewhere in Plato (Edelstein
1966: 81-82, 107). More importantly, for our purposes, it sets
up an equally firm divide between the mass of Plato's
thoughts, which are (and were well known to be) set out publicly in the dialogues, and his 'deepest thoughts' which are
never written down: in other words there is a shift here
towards the full-blooded esotericism of a body of 'unwritten
doctrine' which is distinct not only from the rest of Plato's
teaching but also from 'all other sciences' (341c). As we have
seen, this is not the normal state of affairs in the schools, nor
does the writer of the letter expect it to be seen as such: this is a
new development arising at a particular date and for particular reasons within the Platonist tradition.[1]

A further step is taken in the *Second Letter* (Edelstein 1966:
134-38), where the multitude are not only despised but deliberately deceived:

> According to his report, you say that the nature of 'the first'
> (περὶ τῆς τοῦ πρώτου φύσεως) has not been sufficiently
> explained. I must speak of this matter to you in enigmas (δι'
> αἰνιγμῶν), in order that if anything should happen to these
> tablets 'in the recesses of the sea or land', whoever reads

---

1 Edelstein (1966: 85). Fuller reasons for this development (which Edelstein dates
not long after Plato's death) are suggested by Edelstein (pp. 56-69). For a rather
different assessment of Plato's 'unwritten doctrines', see Cherniss, *The Riddle of
the Early Academy* (Berkeley: University of California Press, 1945).

them may not understand our meaning (312d, trans. Morrow).[1]

> Only take care that these letters do not fall into the hands of uninstructed men...The best precaution is not to write them down, but to commit them to memory; for it is impossible that things written should not become known to others. This is why I have never written on these subjects. There is no writing of Plato's, nor will there ever be; those that are now called so come from an idealized and youthful Socrates. Farewell and heed my warning; read this letter again, and burn it (314a-c, trans. Morrow).

Note, behind the melodramatic atmosphere, that once again it is a certain portion of Plato's teaching that is to be treated in this way: the prohibition on public discourse on 'the nature of the first' is strongly reminiscent of the prohibitions on public discussion of *Ma'aseh bereshith* in rabbinic literature.[2] But here the writer has a clear agenda not only of distinguishing this material from Plato's written teaching (Edelstein 1966: 85) but of disowning the latter. Note too the new role of memorization as an aid to secrecy and as a substitute for writing: this is not the normal practice of the schools, where written texts are seen, on the contrary, as an aid to memory.

We are now in a position to draw further conclusions about the variety of attitudes towards the written word in the hellenistic school tradition.

(a) A distinction must be drawn between the general preference for the 'living voice' in the schools and the esotericism of the Platonists.

(b) The latter presupposes a distinct body of oral teaching which is never written down, and cannot be written down, and which therefore constitutes a body of secret lore *different in content* from anything which appears

---

1 The parallel with Mk 4.11-12 is striking. V.C. Robbins, *Jesus the Teacher* (Philadelphia: Fortress Press, 1984), makes an interesting comparison with Socratic teaching methods, but does not cite the *Second Epistle*. He treats Mk 4.11-12 as ironical (p. 138), but I am not as sure as he is that a first-century reader would inevitably understand the passage that way.

2 Mishnah, *Hagigah* 2.1. See further P.S. Alexander, 'The Rabbinic Lists of Forbidden Targumim', *JJS* 27 (1976), pp. 177-91; David J. Halperin, *The Merkabah in Rabbinic Literature* (New Haven, Connecticut: American Oriental Society, 1980).

in the written works of Plato. This is not the case in the broader school tradition, where written texts are frequently stated to be the same in content as the oral teaching on which they are based.

(c) The relationship between oral tradition and written text is therefore quite different in the two cases. For the author of the *Second Letter*, the true adept has nothing to gain from a study of Plato's written works. Within the schools generally, on the other hand, written texts came to play an increasingly important role (see below).

6. *Papias and Clement*

It has not been possible within the scope of this paper to explore further pathways along the networks which link first- and second-century Christians to their cultural surroundings—such as the empiricist rejection of *logos* as theory or dogma, or the broader and more widespread rejection of *logos* as rhetoric or 'empty words'.[1] However even this brief exploration of the networks associated with the 'living voice' saying has demonstrated, I think, the richness and complexity of that cultural mesh. We have seen that the 'living voice' had a wide currency as a proverb of general import, but also that it is possible to identify three cultural worlds in which it has a more specific application. In rhetoric, it reinforces the centrality of live performance. Among craftsmen, it expresses the widely-felt difficulty of learning practical skills without live demonstration. And in the schools generally it serves as a reminder of the primacy of person-to-person oral instruction over the study (or the production) of manuals and handbooks. It remains to consider how Papias and Clement can best be linked into this complex.

Clement can conveniently be dealt with first. He is a philosopher, known to have links with contemporary Platonism; he quotes not only the *Phaedrus* but also the *Second Letter* at length, both in *Strom.* I.1 and again at *Strom.* V.10.65.1. There would be no difficulty, then, in attributing to Clement a deep-rooted, genuine esotericism drawn from his Platonism.

---

1   Further material on these themes in Alexander, forthcoming, ch. 5.

But even here the evidence falls short of a wholesale rejection of writing. The writing of Clement's other works had needed no justification (Osborn 1959: 343); it was the particular exercise of forming and committing to writing the 'Christian philosophy' of the *Stromateis* that caused Clement's Platonist heartsearchings, and even so his scruples were quickly overcome. In fact the passage with which we began contains little that could not be paralleled from Galen (who also alludes to the *Phaedrus* in the preface to *De methodo medendi* VII, Kuhn X 456). Clement's chief concern, as Osborn describes it, is above all 'the justification of *teaching* through writing' (Osborn 1959: 342, my italics); the *Stromateis* are 'a record of teaching', aimed at the preservation of 'true tradition' (Osborn 1959: 343). None of this is exclusively Platonist: it belongs squarely within the broader hellenistic school tradition.

Papias, a couple of generations earlier, was no intellectual and has no links with Platonism. He may simply be quoting the proverb known to Galen as a piece of wisdom current among 'craftsmen', a social group which we know to have been a significant component among early congregations. But again it should be noted that Papias' concern in his preface is with *teaching* and with the passing on and preservation of authentic tradition, not with instruction in manual skills—so that once again the school tradition seems to provide the most helpful cultural background.[1]

We can thus confirm the correctness of Gerhardsson's assertion that there remain, in the highly literate Greco-Roman world of the first and second centuries CE, certain cultural contexts in which the written word is treated with a marked degree of scepticism. Indeed it may well be felt that *prima facie* the hellenistic schools could provide a more direct cultural link with the churches of the second century than the rabbinic academies, of which Gentile Christians can have had little direct experience. More importantly, the hellenistic schools provide evidence for a view of the importance of the 'living voice' which is in many ways distinct from the classic

---

1   It is worth noting also that Eusebius is quoting from Papias's preface. See above p. 233 and further Alexander, forthcoming, ch. 5, on the importance of allusions to tradition in the prefaces of school texts.

rabbinic doctrine of Oral Torah (which seems on the face of it closer to Platonism). On a broader canvas, however, we would wish to concur with Gerhardsson's contention that the schools of the Mediterranean world, both rabbinic and hellenistic, can perform a vital role in filling out our understanding of many aspects of the teaching and literary activities of the early churches.

In particular, the schools provide a social framework, close in time and in culture to the New Testament, in which it is possible to observe a diversity of relationships between oral instruction and written text. Two aspects of this relationship may be noted here in conclusion. On the one hand, as we have seen, there is in the schools a strong tendency to see written texts as secondary to and subordinate to oral instruction. It is the 'living voice' of the teacher that has priority: the text both follows that voice (as a record of teaching already given) and stands in a subordinate position to it (in that it may only be studied with the aid of a teacher and stands ready at any time to be corrected, updated or revised). This would mean that, in this context at least, few ancient readers would have picked up a text to read *de novo* as we would a new novel; writers, conversely, could rely on the nurturing matrix of the teaching situation to expand and explain what was gnomic or technical in the text. (Galen's 'amateur' readership may count as a partial exception here, but even they had frequently heard the lecture and seen the demonstration before reading the text.) Even where instruction was supposedly based on the teachings of an ancient master, the role of the living teacher was crucial; compare Wesley Smith's description of Galen's understanding of 'studying Hippocrates under a teacher':

> Galen remarks that Julian and Thessalos... could not have gone so wrong if they had read Hippocrates under a teacher (K10.8; cf. CMG 5.10.3, p. 36). It was not enough to read Hippocratic works as medical textbooks. Hippocrates needed interpretation, like a proverb or a religious text, whereon, from a brief, pregnant statement, one can construct lengthy sermons and whole philosophies of life or of medicine... Like people who 'know the Lord's will' in the most ambiguous situations, Galen knew to a certainty what Hippocrates would have thought about any subject, indeed did think, whether or not he had said so explicitly (Smith 1979: 72-73).

If this was the kind of social context which produced the gospels (and I have argued elsewhere that the literature of the schools provides a convincing literary context for Luke at least: Alexander 1986), then we might need to reassess some assumptions about the expectations of gospel writers and readers, and indeed about the relationships in general between written texts and oral instruction in the churches of the first century.

On the other hand, the production of written texts itself can in time generate a new kind of teaching in which the written text is primary and oral instruction becomes exegesis of a fixed, canonical body of literature. The first lists of 'canonical' texts were those of the literary classics (Marrou 1956: 225 with 524 n. 2) studied under the grammarians (Clarke 1971: 18-25) and rhetors (Clarke 1971: 38-39); but the medical and philosophical schools exhibited an equally strong tendency to become text-based. The process is well described by Marrou (1956: 285) and Clarke (1971: 87-88, 112), and was not unnoticed in antiquity: cf. Seneca's lament that 'philosophy has become philology' (*Epist.* CVIII 23) and Epictetus' warning on the danger that he might 'become a grammarian instead of a philosopher, except that I exegete Chrysippus instead of Homer' (*Ench.* 49).[1] Both Papias and Clement may reflect tensions within a Christianity which was about to enter its own 'scholastic' phase. The second century sees the church in the process of defining its own canon of 'prescribed texts' from which all future Christian teaching would be derived, and simultaneously in the process of suppressing the 'living voice' of developing tradition, whether exhibited in Montanist prophecy or in Gnostic gospels. The sociology of this process may well be illuminated not only from a study of the contemporary codification of Oral Torah which was taking place in the rabbinic academies, but also from the parallel processes which can be observed over the centuries in the hellenistic schools.

---

1 Clarke quotes also *Discourses* II.21.10-11 and III.21.7. On medicine, cf. Pliny, *NH* XXVI.11; Galen II.280-81.

BIBLIOGRAPHY

Alexander

1977   *Luke–Acts in its contemporary setting, with special reference to the prefaces.* D.Phil. thesis, Oxford.

1986   'Luke's preface in the pattern of Greek preface-writing', *Novum Testamentum* 28, pp. 48-74.

forthcoming   *Luke to Theophilus: the Lucan Preface in Context* (SNTSMS; Cambridge University Press).

von Arnim

1898   Hans von Arnim, *Leben und Werke des Dio von Prusa* (Berlin: Wiedmann).

Bowersock

1969   G.W. Bowersock, *Greek Sophists in the Roman Empire* (Oxford: Clarendon Press).

Clarke

1971   M.L. Clarke, *Higher Education in the Ancient World* (London: Routledge).

Dillon

1977   John Dillon, *The Middle Platonists* (London: Duckworth).

Edelstein

1966   Ludwig Edelstein, *Plato's Seventh Letter* (Leiden: Brill).

Gerhardsson

1961   Birger Gerhardsson, *Memory and Manuscript: Oral Tradition and Written Transmission in Rabbinic Judaism and Early Christianity*, trans. E.J. Sharpe (Acta Seminarii Neotestamentici Upsaliensis XXII; Lund: Gleerup).

Harvey

1976   Anthony Harvey, review of M.D. Goulder, *Midrash and Lection in Matthew*, *JTS* ns 27, pp. 188-95.

Jaeger

1912   W.W. Jaeger, *Studien zur Entstehungsgeschichte der Metaphysik des Aristoteles* (Berlin: Wiedmann).

Kenyon

1951   F.G. Kenyon, *Books and Readers in Ancient Greece and Rome* (2nd edn; Oxford: Clarendon Press).

Marrou
1956

H.-I. Marrou, *A History of Education in Antiquity*, trans. George Lamb from the 3rd French edition (New York: Sheed and Ward/New American Library).

Norman
1960

A.F. Norman, 'The book-trade in fourth-century Antioch', *JHS* 80, pp. 122-26.

Osborn
1959

E.F. Osborn, 'Teaching and writing in the first chapter of the *Stromateis* of Clement of Alexandria', *JTS* ns 10, pp. 335-43.

Otto
1890

A. Otto, *Die Sprichwörter und sprichwörterlicher Redensarte der Römer* (Leipzig: Teubner). Cf. also R. Häussler (ed.), *Nachträge zu A. Otto Sprichwörter* (Hildesheim: Georg Olms, 1968).

Pelletier
1962

A. Pelletier, *Lettre d'Aristée à Philocrate* (Paris: Éditions du Cerf).

Perry
1967

B.E. Perry, *The Ancient Romances* (Sather Classical Lectures; Berkeley: University of California Press).

Riddle
1985

John M. Riddle, *Dioscorides on Pharmacy and Medicine* (Austin: University of Texas Press).

Roberts
1979

C.H. Roberts, *Manuscript, Society and Belief in Early Christian Egypt* (Schweich Lectures, 1977; London: Oxford University Press for the British Academy).

Rose
1921

H.J. Rose, 'The Greek of Cicero', *JHS* 41, pp. 91-116.

Smith
1979

Wesley D. Smith, *The Hippocratic Tradition* (Cornell Publications in the History of Science; Ithaca and London: Cornell University Press).

Temkin
1953

O. Temkin, 'Greek medicine as science and craft', *Isis* 44, pp. 213-25.

BAPTISM IN THE FIRST-CENTURY CHURCHES: A CASE FOR CAUTION

C.J.A. Hickling

What counted, during the first decades of the Christian movement, as identifying a man or a woman as an adherent? By the middle of the following century there was no doubt about the answer. 'None is allowed to partake of [the Eucharist] but he that believeth that our teachings are true, and has been washed with the washing for the remission of sins and unto regeneration' (Justin Martyr, *Apology*, 66).[1] A similar answer is given by the *Didache*: 'Let no one eat or drink of this eucharistic thanksgiving but they that have been baptized into the name of the Lord' (*Didache* 9.5).[2] In Rome, then, and presumably elsewhere, by 150, and possibly earlier than that in whatever area of early Christianity is represented by the *Didache*,[3] we can say with certainty that baptism had become the generally recognized mark of membership of the Christian community. It was the rite of admission, of initiation in the fullest sense; it was the *conditio sine qua non* for participation in the characteristic Christian act of worship. Baptism had become a rite of what might be called juridical significance.

---

1 Translation in H. Bettenson (ed.), *Documents of the Christian Church* (Oxford: Oxford University Press, 1943), p. 94.
2 Translation in J.B. Lightfoot, *The Apostolic Fathers* (London: Macmillan, 1907), p. 232.
3 Syria, and specifically Antioch, have often been suggested; see, e.g., W. Rordorf, in W. Rordorf and others, *The Eucharist of the Early Christians* (New York: Pueblo, 1976), pp. 1f. Rordorf thinks of a date 'at the end of the first century or the beginning of the second'; cf. similarly A. Tuilier, art. 'Didache', in *TRE* 8 (1981), pp. 731ff.

We find nothing like this in the New Testament. The nearest approach is in the longer ending of Mark's gospel, which may itself be second-century. Yet even here, the omission of baptism from the second half of Mk 16.16, creating an asymmetry which no reader can fail to note, suggests something a little short of the unambiguous confidence of Justin and the *Didache* that baptism was the necessary and indispensable qualification for admission—in their case—to the Eucharist.[1] This evidence is, however, too late to count as modifying the observation that the New Testament—admittedly, a collection of texts whose survival is in varying degrees somewhat adventitious—nowhere regards baptism as having the function ascribed to it in the writings just quoted. Almost certainly,[2] Paul takes it for granted that all those to whom he writes have been baptized. But, first, Paul and his churches represent only one strand in the very diverse development of the Christian movement in the first vital decades. In other circles, especially those of strongly Jewish-Christian cast, the possibility that some adherents had not been baptized may well have been one that would arouse no sense of scandal. Secondly, no one can doubt the supreme importance of baptism in Paul's thought. But its importance is never precisely that of a unique and universally required qualification for admission. 1 Cor. 12.13 comes very near to saying that it is, but does not quite do so.[3]

There is room, therefore, for some hesitation about the claims sometimes made[4] for baptism as having been from the

---

1 Naturally, one who did not believe would be condemned whether baptized or not. But the form of the saying is symmetrical, and this highlights the omission of reference to baptism in the second clause.

2 The qualification is justified, for both at Rom. 6.3 and at Gal. 3.27 Paul uses the pronoun ὅσοι which in strict classical usage allows exceptions; see Liddell and Scott, *s.v.* It is true that in the koine ὅσοι means 'all those who . . .' (so Bauer–Arndt–Ginrich, *s.v.* But Paul could have chosen to express himself absolutely unambiguously, and instead uses a word which would, strictly, allow that some of those he addresses had not been baptized.

3 The emphasis in vv. 12f. falls on the contrast between the many members and the one Body, not on the way in which the former entered the latter. Paul takes for granted the experience of his correspondents, which would not necessarily have been the same as that of Christian groups in (say) Alexandria.

4 So, e.g. J.D.G. Dunn, *Unity and Diversity in the New Testament* (London: SCM, 1977), p. 155: 'Acts is most probably right—*baptism was an integral part of Christianity from the first*' (author's italics). Dunn alludes to the proposals once argued with some vigour to regard water baptism as originating in the mission of Hel-

first the rite of initiation for all members of the Christian communities. In, for example, the statement of H.C. Kee that 'almost certainly, baptism was the initiatory rite for the Christian movement from the outset',[1] the qualifying phrase must be taken seriously. It will, then, be the purpose of this essay to enter a note of caution about the extent to which baptism came to be regarded in this sense during the first century. We shall consider first some evidence suggesting that, however exceptionally, persons (presumably Jewish-Christians) who had not been baptized might have been regarded as admissible to the local Christian assembly. We shall then consider some texts which leave it a matter for legitimate doubt whether their authors shared the view that baptism was the invariable requirement for membership.

The evidence for the acceptability in some Christian circles of those who had not undergone baptism 'in the name of the Lord'[2] is principally in the *Didache*, but the cases of Apollos (Acts 18.24-28) and, more tentatively, of Paul himself must also be considered. Before turning to the passages in question, however, it is appropriate to give some attention to the striking fact that Jesus himself either did not baptize at all or, if the evidence of Jn 3.22 is to be admitted in conjunction with the Fourth Gospel as a whole and the Synoptics, did so only for a short time.[3] Several passages in the synoptic material render

lenistic Christianity. Perhaps this possibility has been too easily lost sight of. In any case, Dunn's qualification ('most probably') is significant.

1 *Christian Origins in Sociological Perspective* (London: SCM, 1980), p. 112.
2 The formula appears in different forms in Acts, with εἰς and ἐν twice each, and 'Jesus Christ' and 'the Lord Jesus' also twice each.
3 Jn 3.22, 26 and 4.2 illustrate more than one of the problems arising in the interpretation of ostensibly factual information in this gospel. Interaction between Christians and followers of the Baptist is almost certainly to be detected in the narrative introduction to 3.27-36 as well as in John's testimony itself. On the other hand, there are good reasons for thinking that the evangelist has used a tradition with sound historical value; so C.H. Dodd, *Historical Tradition in the Fourth Gospel* (Cambridge: Cambridge University Press, 1963), p. 286; see also E. Haenchen, *John I. A Commentary on the Gospel of John Chapters 1-6* (Philadelphia: Fortress, 1984), *ad loc.* The question that concerns us is whether Jn 3.22, if historically trustworthy, might be the sole surviving evidence that Jesus continued to baptize—or to authorize baptism—throughout his ministry, despite the silence of the synoptic gospels. This is unlikely. The context of this verse in John strongly suggests that the practice of Jesus in this respect belonged to the time of the 'overlap' in the Johannine account between the activity of the Baptist and that of

it almost incredible that the communities in which they first took shape attached major significance to their own baptismal practice. The baptism of Jesus himself is narrated by all three synoptic evangelists in such a way as to leave no doubt of the immense importance of the event, both for themselves and for the tradition they were using. But this importance is very largely christological.[1] There is no hint to suggest that the narrators and hearers of the story had themselves experienced a baptism having some features in common with that of their Lord.[2] The mission discourses, where it would have been easy to think that the command to baptize could have been included (the tradition has accepted an anachronism elsewhere, Mk 8.35, where it is hard to give εὐαγγέλιον a sense applicable during Jesus' earthly activity, and 13.14) do not, of course, do so. If baptism, whether for Jesus himself or for the first Palestinian communities which were probably the first tradents of the mission discourses,[3] had the importance that John ascribed to his baptism, and still more if it had the significance attached to it by the later church, this omission would be inexplicable. At Mt. 10.13 the household which is proved by its acceptance of the disciples' preaching to be 'worthy' is to receive simply the latter's 'peace'. No 'initiation' seems to be thought necessary. Rather tentatively, we might add at this point Mk 10.38f. and Lk. 12.50. For, at the level of oral transmission in the early communities, the regular practice of baptism as the universal requirement of admission might have led us, in these contexts (especially the former), to expect some

Jesus, and specifically to a period when Jesus was in Judaea. See the cautious discussion by G.R. Beasley-Murray (*Baptism in the New Testament* [London: Macmillan, 1963], pp. 67–72).

1 See the overall findings of F. Lentzen-Deis, *Die Taufe Jesu nach den Synoptikern* (Frankfurter Theologische Studien, 4; Frankfurt: Josef Knecht, 1970).

2 Bultmann indeed thought that the inclusion of the descent of the Spirit in the Markan account of Jesus' baptism indicated the influence of Christian baptismal practice (*History of the Synoptic Tradition* [Oxford: Blackwell, 1963], p. 250). But this is a comment on the introduction of a motif, not on the possible shaping of the way the narrative was transmitted, and in any case Mark associates very closely the two things Jesus *saw*—the heavens 'split open' and the Spirit descending (Mk 1.10).

3 If G. Theissen is right (*The First Followers of Jesus* [London: SCM, 1978], pp. 3f.), it was not so much the communities as the itinerant charismatics who were involved. If anything, this would perhaps strengthen the case here being argued.

allusion to that practice. But little weight, perhaps, should be attached to this.

When, therefore, Lohfink speaks of the 'remarkable, enigmatic phenomenon: Jesus himself did not baptize, yet the early community practised baptism as something ecclesiastically and theologically to be taken for granted',[1] we may reasonably ask whether it really was, in the first decades, so completely taken for granted. If the disciples of Jesus had not been baptized by him during his ministry (Andrew and an unnamed companion are indeed said to have been disciples of John, Jn 1.35, and had therefore presumably been baptized by him; but this will hardly have been true of all, perhaps any, of the rest) when, and by whom, were they baptized? The brothers of Jesus were at an early stage accorded status as privileged members of the Christian community (1 Cor. 9.5). Are we to think that they, too, received baptism at some unspecified moment? The Acts narrative, indeed, places them with the disciples in the upper room just after the Ascension (Acts 1.14). The author—with whatever historical basis or lack of it—clearly regarded them as included in the nascent Christian community from the first. The question how they had entered it does not seem to have come into his mind.

The point may be made more broadly. At the time of Jesus' death there must have been a substantial number of adherents of his movement who were not in contact with the nuclear group of disciples in Jerusalem. It has even been thought that there were established communities of such people in Galilee.[2] In Jerusalem, Joseph of Arimathea is described by Matthew as a disciple (27.57).[3] These, like the Jerusalem disciples themselves and the brothers of Jesus, would not naturally have seen themselves as in need of initiation into some new state or into a community other than that of Israel, to which they already belonged. Indeed, the baptism of John was hardly an initiation: it was, according to the

---

1 G. Lohfink, 'Der Ursprung der christlichen Taufe', *TQ* 156 (1976), pp. 35–54 (35).

2 This was the claim of L.E. Elliott-Binns, *Galilean Christianity* (Studies in Biblical Theology, 16; London: SCM, 1956), esp. pp. 43–52.

3 So Matthew interprets Mark's less clear statement that he was προσδεχόμενος τὴν βασιλείαν τοῦ θεοῦ. But Joseph's action, with the risks it must have involved, speaks of a regard for Jesus which makes Matthew's deduction at least plausible.

gospels, an expression of repentance[1] undergone in preparation for the coming eschaton. In the absence of any, or at least
of any extended, practice of baptism by Jesus, and of any
teaching by him about a baptism other than John's (Mt. 28.19
can confidently be ascribed to the evangelist), there was no
motive for followers of Jesus during his lifetime to seek for any
kind of initiation, and it is hard to see why they should have
done so later. When, therefore, in a recent publication M.
Quesnel has revived the view that baptism began to become a
general requirement only some fifteen years or so, at best,
after the death of Jesus, we must surely see good reasons for
agreeing with him.[2] In the fifties, and even later, it might be
known (or, hardly less significantly, suspected) that some
Jewish Christians had never received baptism, even though
they were regarded without hesitation as in the fullest sense
members of the Christian community.

Such, on one reading, seems to have been the case in the
community (at Antioch?)[3] of which the *Didache* gives us some
information. The *Didache*'s exclusion from the Eucharist of
all those not baptized 'into the name of the Lord' has already
been quoted. Such an exclusion, in a document of church order
which is in general detailed and specific, will not have been
made gratuitously. There were those who thought
themselves, or were thought by others, to be entitled to
participate in the Eucharist, but who had not received
Christian baptism.[4] Their presence in the Christian assembly
suggests a stage of development at which it could be thought
that some—presumably Jewish-Christians—could be members of the community on a basis other than that of admission
by baptism as a rite of initiation.

It may be, however, that we can reconstruct the development more precisely. J.P. Audet, in a detailed study of *Didache*
9 and 10,[5] detects two stages in the composition of these chap-

1   So Mk 1.4, followed by Lk. 3.3. Matthew has excluded baptism from the subject-
matter of John's evangelism.
2   See M. Quesnel, *Baptisés dans l'Esprit* (LD, 120; Paris: Cerf, 1985), p. 203.
3   See p. 249 note 3.
4   It is of course possible, if we date the *Didache* early enough, that these were men
who had received the baptism of John (from himself or from his followers).
5   *La Didache. Instructions des Apôtres* (ÉBib; Paris: Gabalda, 1958), pp. 375ff.

ters. The author, he thinks, has incorporated into his work a eucharistic text of earlier origin. In editing this, he has included on his own account the sentence restricting participation to the baptized (thereby indicating the presence under previous arrangements, as has just been suggested, of some unbaptized persons). By doing this, Audet points out, he has created a discrepancy with 10.6 ('if any be holy, let him come'). On this basis Audet offers a reconstruction of a change in liturgical procedure to which the literary work of the redactor bears witness. The original practice, he thinks, was dictated by the rules of hospitality. Those not baptized, provided they were 'holy', were at first admitted to the Eucharist. At a later stage a change had taken place. Now we find a Eucharist in two parts. The first element was the Breaking of Bread, from which the unbaptized were now excluded. The company then moved into another room for the remainder of the liturgy. The invitation at 10.6, now presumably understood in a new sense, in the light of 9.5, as identifying the 'holy' as the baptized, had a new function as the invitation to move to the second stage of the liturgy.

It is not clear why Audet feels obliged to read into the text this dual location of the eucharistic rite. But his account of the secondary nature of 9.5 in relation to 10.6 may bear some weight. Stressing that in all probability we are dealing with a community largely composed of Jewish-Christians, he claims that, in the earlier of the two situations he envisages, there would be 'nothing strange' in the participation of the unbaptized. Thereby he gives some support for the conjecture just offered about the position of Jewish-Christians of the earliest generation of all.

Mention of *Didache* 10.6 naturally leads us to consider 1 Cor. 16.22, so tantalizingly close in its phrasing. The verse deserves some consideration in the context of the present enquiry, if only because Conzelmann concludes his comment on the 'anathema' pronouncement by asking the question, 'Does the formula mark, in the liturgy, the separation of the baptized from the unbaptized before the Eucharist?'[1] To this

---

1 *Der erste Brief an die Korinther* (MeyerK, 11th edn; Göttingen: Vandenhoeck & Ruprecht, 1969), *ad loc.*

the answer must surely be in the negative. It is something inward, affective, an attitude of the most basic kind towards 'the Lord', that is desiderated, not the quasi-juridical status of having received baptism. The criterion for applying the anathema is of a very different order from the lack of ecclesiastical qualification for admission. Bornkamm's interpretation is more convincing: this verse 'does not draw boundaries between the baptized and unbaptized', and he goes on to generalize in a manner which gives some support to the view being put forward in the present contribution: 'the Pauline letters in no way give reason to see baptism from the first as a *conditio sine qua non* for participation in the Lord's Supper'.[1]

This verse is indeed difficult to assess. The linguistic grounds for attributing it to pre-Pauline tradition seem, granted its extreme brevity, to be sound.[2] What is not so clear is its proposed Sitz in the liturgy.[3] But this does not affect the considerable interest of the verse for our present purposes. 'Loving the Lord' sounds, indeed, a somewhat bland qualification. It appears to be a less rigorous test than the confession of faith, 'Jesus is Lord' (1 Cor. 12.3). Yet this is not necessarily so. It is true that only in one place in the synoptic tradition (Mt. 10.37) is φιλέω used of the relationship between Jesus and his disciples. It is nevertheless an appropriate way, indeed the most appropriate way of all, by which to identify that relationship. The implication of 1 Cor. 16.22 is that the anathema is pronounced on everyone (presumably, though not necessarily, everyone who might take it on himself to participate in the church's worship) who is not a known disciple or follower of Jesus. If this is indeed early tradition, it might attest a period in the life of the church when it had become necessary to be able

---

1   *Early Christian Experience* (New Testament Library; London: SCM, 1969), p. 171.

2   Bornkamm (see previous note) points out (as do many others) that φιλεῖ is non-Pauline; J.A.T. Robinson (*Twelve New Testament Studies* [Studies in Biblical Theology, 34; London: SCM, 1962], p. 154) adds that ἤτω is not otherwise found in Paul, who prefers the form ἔστω.

3   See C.F.D. Moule, 'A Reconsideration of the Context of *Maranatha*', now in his *Essays in New Testament Interpretation* (Cambridge: Cambridge University Press, 1982), pp. 222–26. The view that the context is liturgical is, however, maintained by a recent commentator on this epistle; see H.-J. Klauck, *Erster Korintherbrief* (EB, 7; Würzburg: Echter, 1987), *ad loc.*

to exclude individuals from the church's common life on the grounds of their not in fact being adherents of the Christian movement; but when it had not yet become possible to judge this to be the case on the basis of being unbaptized. There being, at that early date, no formal or juridical criterion for exclusion to hand, the more imprecise one was used of the relationship which constituted discipleship.

We turn now to the two prominent figures in the Christian community whose baptism can be held to be in some doubt. Paradoxically enough, it is Paul himself who is the first of these. We owe to Paul the overwhelming majority of what we know about the beliefs of (at least some of) the first Christians about baptism. Yet it has recently been possible for R.H. Fuller to raise again[1] the question, 'Was Paul baptized?'[2]

Fuller gives no clear answer to the question in terms of water baptism 'into the Name'. He proposes to 'draw a distinction between "foundation baptism" (direct experience of the Christ event) and "subseqent believers' baptism"'.[3] In this way, he can count as baptized—in the one sense or the other—the whole cohort of those listed at 1 Cor. 15.5f. as witnesses of the risen Christ, even though we have no record of the water baptism of any of them. With appropriate qualifications drawing attention to the peculiarly ambiguous status of Paul, Fuller places him in the same category. Whether 'by direct immersion in the Christ event' or by 'subsequent believers' baptism... Paul was most certainly baptized'.[4] But Fuller clearly thinks that there are fairly strong grounds for doubting that Paul received baptism in water. Paul

> never explicitly refers to his own baptism as the decisive moment of his past which constitutes him a believer, but rather to his apostolic call. This call, he states most emphatically, came through no human agency (Gal. 1.1, 11-12). It pleased God to reveal his Son to (in) him (Gal. 1.16). He

---

1 Like the larger question whether baptism was an innovation on the part of Hellenistic Christianity, that of Paul himself having received baptism was controverted by the *religionsgeschichtliche Schule* (Fuller, 'Was Paul baptized?', in J. Kremer (ed.), *Les Actes des Apôtres* (BETL, 48; Leuven: University Press, 1979), p. 505.

2 Fuller, 'Was Paul baptized?', pp. 505-508.

3 Fuller, 'Was Paul baptized?', p. 506.

4 Fuller, 'Was Paul baptized?', p. 508.

appeared to him (1 Cor. 15.8). He saw the Lord (9.1). How is it possible to reconcile such a claim with Paul's implicit recognition that he like all other Christians was baptized?'[1]

Closer scrutiny of the autobiographical narrative at Gal. 1.15-17 strengthens Fuller's insistence that this narrative stresses the call vision as being sufficient, so that a second or supplementary enlistment of Paul as a servant of Jesus—i.e. baptism—would have been unnecessary. Paul's anxiety throughout this passage is to make it absolutely incontrovertible that at no point, from the call onwards, had he accepted the authority of any of the apostles or indeed of any other human being. It is therefore in principle to be assumed that the narrative leaves no gaps, either chronological or geographical.[2] When, therefore, Paul asserts uncompromisingly at Gal. 1.16b that 'immediately' (εὐθέως) after receiving his call he went away to Arabia without having taken counsel with anyone, it is difficult to resist the conclusion that he has excluded from his narrative any opportunity to receive baptism. It is true that the simple act of baptism might not be included in the disclaimer οὐ προσανεθέμην σαρκὶ καὶ αἵ-ματι. προσανατίθεσθαι implies exchange of information or opinions, but the eliciting and affirming of the baptismal confession of faith (if this is what was involved) would hardly count. However, the whole thrust of Paul's narrative is his total independence, as a Christian, from any Christian predecessor or contemporary. Receiving baptism is, after all, *receiving* something. Paul claims to be speaking on oath (v. 20). It is difficult to think that he deliberately suppressed his recollection of having received baptism—and no less difficult to think that he regarded it as too unimportant to include in the story. The balance of probability weighs, perhaps, a little more heavily against Paul (at this very early date)[3] having been baptized by some member of (presumably) the church in Damascus

---

1   Fuller, 'Was Paul baptized?', p. 506.

2   U. Borse stresses the continuity of the 'geographisch-chronologische Kette' constituted by this passage (*Der Brief an die Galater* [RNT; Regensburg: Pustet, 1984], *ad loc.*).

3   AD 34 or 31 according to R. Jewett, *Dating Paul's Life* (London: SCM, 1979), pp. 29f.; G. Lüdemann proposes 30 or 33 (*Paul: Apostle to the Gentiles* [London: SCM, 1984], p. 262).

than Fuller will allow himself to concede—Acts 9.10-19 and 22.6-16 notwithstanding.[1]

What, then, of the baptismal status of Apollos? We have to rely for the answer on Acts 18.24-28. As one of the narratives incorporated into the 'travel document', this account has a reasonably good claim to impart sound historical information. The difficulty, from our point of view, lies in knowing how best to interpret the silence of the text on the question of Apollos' receiving Christian baptism. The end of 18.26 is the point at which we strain to know what the writer implies. In the previous verse Apollos is said to have been accustomed to teach 'the things concerning Jesus' ἀκριβῶς. This 'accuracy' is then a little bewilderingly qualified: Apollos was aware only of John's baptism.[2] Somewhat pointedly, then, the narrator informs us at v. 26b that Priscilla and Aquila 'explained the way of God to him' ἀκριβέστερον. Does this improved accuracy imply, not only the supplying of information about a baptism better than John's, but also the actual conferral of this baptism? Or should we take the silence of the narrator (and this, we must note, is a relatively full and detailed account) as implying the opposite—Apollos' two instructors refrained from baptizing him?

---

1 It is easy to see reasons why friends as well as critics of Paul should have wished to make it clear that Paul was baptized. See G. Linton's influential article, 'The Third Aspect', *ST* 3 (1949), pp. 79-95, and especially p. 83, where a relationship is proposed between the account underlying Acts 9 and the report circulating in the Galatian churches. Linton does not deal with the claim in Acts that Paul received baptism, but this coheres well with his reconstruction. Paul's dependence on the existing church from the moment of his conversion onwards was, Linton believes, the main contention of the alternative account of Paul's career circulating in the Galatian churches; and the same dependence is clearly asserted in Acts.

2 Käsemann's attribution of the clause ἐπιστάμενος μόνον τὸ βάπτισμα ' Ἰωάννου to the redactor seems arbitrary, and does not deal with one question it poses: if τὰ περὶ τοῦ Ἰησοῦ means, as this and similar phrases about Jesus in Luke–Acts seem to do, the events of Jesus' life rather than his teaching or the religion that emerged from his life and resurrection, then what baptism other than John's *could* Apollos have understood? The context, in fact, makes it necessary to take τὰ περὶ τοῦ Ἰησοῦ here in some such sense as is contained in 'way of God' (v. 26), i.e. the common life of Jesus' followers in all its aspects.

260   *The Bible in Three Dimensions*

B.T.D. Smith is among those who think that the former 'may safely be inferred from the narrative'.[1] F.F. Bruce is cautious: 'Apollos is not said to have received Christian baptism'. He adds, however, that 'for him... John's baptism *plus* the receiving of the Spirit [as implied by ζέων τῷ πνεύματι, v. 25] conveyed all that Christian baptism could have conveyed';[2] Bruce seems, therefore, to assume that Apollos was not baptized in Ephesus.

On what basis can we make a sound decision? The effect on the attentive reader of the juxtaposition of the two narratives of 18.24-28 and 19.1-7 must be given due weight. The two stories are both similar to and different from one another, not least in the prominence given to John's baptism, to which a whole verse is devoted at 19.4. The second story gives a very clear impression of the supreme importance of the gift of the Spirit, and of Christian baptism as both superior to John's and as conveying this vital gift. Alerted to the value thus attached to baptism, and noting that Paul had, in the case of the twelve at Ephesus, supplemented the baptism of John by baptizing them afresh 'into the name of the Lord Jesus', the reader has his attention drawn back to the Apollos episode. He might reasonably expect that, had Apollos been similarly treated, this would have been made clear in his case as well as in that of the twelve. The sequence of events involving Apollos, Priscilla and Aquila is traced rather fully. Then, from the information about Apollos' more accurate instruction at the hands of his teachers we move straight into an account of his travel plans and their implementation, with every suggestion that he goes to Achaia as a Christian in the fullest sense. Surely, such a reader might think, it is because of the gifts of oratory and exegesis that made him so Paul-like in his mission to the Jews that Apollos was accorded the status of Christian without being baptized. That he *was* baptized and that such a major event was passed over in silence must seem, to one reading the first narrative in the light of the second, the less likely option.

'Apollos and the Twelve Disciples at Ephesus', *JTS* 16 (1914-15), pp. 241-46, cited by F.F. Bruce, *The Book of the Acts* (NICNT; revised edn; Grand Rapids: Eerdmans, 1988).
2 Bruce, *Acts*, p. 360 n. 74.

Before leaving these two passages, we should note a further significant feature. Apollos, introduced into the story as simply a Jew, is then said to be κατηχημένος τὴν ὁδὸν τοῦ κυρίου. Probably (not, perhaps, quite unambiguously) this means that we are to understand that he was at that point already a Christian, even though without knowledge of any baptism other than John's. Bruce's comment is apt, and gives some support to the claim of the present essay: 'It may seem strange, no doubt, that one who was indwelt and empowered by the Spirit'—and, we might add, 'instructed in the way of the Lord'—'should nevertheless know nothing of Christian baptism; but primitive Christianity was made up of many strands, and of some of these strands we have little or no knowledge'.[1] The same comment applies to the fact that the twelve at Ephesus are described as μαθηταί (19.1), a term used in Acts exclusively for Christians. Two factors are involved here. The indications are that there were 'strands' in the Christianity of the first few decades for which a baptism other than that of John was not yet a universally required rite of admission to the Christian community. But, further, at the time of the composition of Luke–Acts—i.e. the last decades of the first century, by fairly wide agreement—no embarrassment was felt in reproducing material which betrayed this attitude.

Throughout the material so far considered, we have been moving in the area of exegesis varying between the possible and the probable. No one would deny outright the reception of Christian baptism by either Paul or Apollos; and some would find ways of reading the *Didache* with conclusions other than those advanced here. But our concern has been to show that, equally, it is impossible to show that Gal. 1 or Acts 18 implies that Paul and Apollos respectively *were* baptized, or that the community behind the *Didache* had never received 'unbaptized Christians' into its midst. A verdict of *non liquet* serves almost as well as one setting the balance of probability against the reception of Christian baptism by Paul and Apollos to support our main contention: we cannot without major qualifications assert that baptism was the *conditio sine qua non* for the

---

1 Bruce, *Acts*, p. 360 n. 74.

membership of the Christian community until a very late period.

We turn now to material which in varying degrees gives further support to this contention. First, let us consider the Matthean commission to baptize (Mt. 28.19) in the context of Matthew's understanding of the Christian mission as a whole. Who were to be the recipients of the evangelistic activity enjoined on the eleven disciples by the risen Christ? Were they to 'make disciples of' all mankind, or all Gentiles? D.R.A. Hare and D.J. Harrington have argued that the latter interpretation is the correct one.[1] Having examined other contexts in which Matthew uses the word ἔθνος (singular and plural), they argue that in the majority of cases the meaning is 'Gentile'.[2] In particular, 'for the eight uses of ἔθνος in material peculiar to Matthew the obvious meaning in six is "Gentiles"'.[3] It is in this sense, then, that the term is to be understood in 28.19. Israel is excluded from the scope of the disciples' mission. For 'Matthew does not envision the conversion of Israel as a nation; the time for that has passed'.[4] 'The twofold mission agreed on by Paul and the pillar apostles at Jerusalem has now'—for Matthew—'been replaced by a single one. Henceforth, the mission is to Gentiles.'[5] It would naturally follow (though the authors do not draw this conclusion) that the command of the risen Christ to baptize applies only to Gentiles.

The article by Hare and Harrington was answered by J.P. Meier, who reviewed the evidence for Matthew's understanding of the meaning of ἔθνος and came to the opposite conclusion.[6] The debate at least highlights the inconsistency of Matthew's employment of this word. Some evidence supports each of the possible meanings, and in a surprisingly large number of instances it is very difficult to make a confident decision. Hence—yet again—discussion of 28.19 must be somewhat tentative, especially in view of the fact that in the

1 ' "Make disciples of all nations" (Mt 28.19)', *CBQ* 37 (1975), pp. 359-69.
2 Hare and Harrington, "Make disciples", pp. 362f.
3 Hare and Harrington, "Make disciples", p. 363.
4 Hare and Harrington, "Make disciples", p. 363.
5 Hare and Harrington, "Make disciples", p. 363.
6 'Nations or Gentiles in Matthew 28.19?', *CBQ* 39 (1977), pp. 94-102.

other three uses in Matthew of the complete phrase πάντα τὰ ἔθνη[1] the meaning, as Meier points out, almost certainly includes Israel. Yet three considerations may be put forward in favour of the view that the reader of this gospel could be expected to identify the ἔθνη here as the Gentiles. First, the reference to Galilee might well evoke the quotation of Isa. 8.23 at 4.15: here ἔθνη clearly means '[of the] Gentiles'. Secondly, the missionary command follows as a logical consequence (οὖν) on the statement by the risen Christ that to him has been given all authority, both celestial and terrestrial. Now the last occasion on which Matthew had used the term ἐξουσία was at 21.23-27. In this pericope the word occurs no fewer than four times. It is an exchange between Jesus and the 'high priests and elders of the people' in which it can fairly be said that the latter have rejected Jesus' authority, or at least have failed to recognize its source. So the attentive reader of the gospel's closing words, responding to them in the light of the gospel as a whole, could well reflect that, for the time being, there was one area—namely Israel—in which authority had indeed been given to Christ but not acknowledged. Thirdly, the participle πορευθέντες suggests a journey to be undertaken before the missionary activity can be begun. It is true, of course, that the journey might simply be from Galilee back to Jerusalem. But it is surely more natural to take it as conjuring up a picture of centrifugal travel away from Israel, as the centre, towards the Gentiles as a more distant periphery.

It is, however, more to the point to refer back, as Hare and Harrington do,[2] to some of what is said about the mission to Israel in Matthew 10. As is well known, Matthew envisages the disciples' mission during Jesus' lifetime as being exclusively limited to Israel (10.5f., 23). May we agree with the two writers just mentioned that Matthew believes that this mission has failed? Mt. 10.23, indeed, seems to tell in the opposite

---

1   In Mt. 24.9 and 14 the phrase seems equivalent to 'all men', though, despite Meier, it is not absolutely clear that Israel is included. The interpretation of 24.14 naturally depends largely on the view taken of Matthew's understanding of the mission to Israel. 25.32 introduces other problems, principally the identity of the 'brothers'. Again, 'Gentiles' is not ruled out. Matthaean usage as a whole seems to leave it a reasonable possibility that 'Gentiles' is the sense at 28.19.

2   ' "Make Disciples" ', p. 366.

sense. It suggests that some, at least, of the eleven are to continue to preach to Israel 'until the Son of Man comes'. But two passages support the view of Hare and Harrington. At 21.43 the rejection of Israel is unqualified. At 23.37-39 there is a promise of hope for a change of heart in an undefined future. But for the present, 'your house is left to you desolate'. Above all, the Matthaean passion narrative is calculated to reinforce the suggestion that there is no hope left for Israel in the present age.

There are reasonably good grounds, then, for thinking that Mt. 28.19 has the Gentile world in view. Israel has already been evangelized, and here there has never been any question of baptism. Now the possibility of being made disciples is to be opened to the Gentiles, and to them baptism is to be offered. This would be a natural way to read the implications of the commands of the Risen One, and to that extent is a further indication that baptism—even as late as the probable date of the final redaction of this gospel—had not yet become a universal requirement.

Secondly, Heb. 6.2 requires a brief mention. The whole passage is full of difficulties, and it is a serious possibility that there is no reference to baptism at all.[1] If, however, baptism is the subject of the 'teaching', there are two problems. First, why does the author use the general term βαπτισμός when, from the first, this rite was known by the neuter noun βάπτισμα? Secondly, how could he use the word in the plural? P.E. Hughes deals with both problems together when he takes the word to embrace all kinds of Jewish ritual ablutions along with Johannine baptism and Christian baptism.[2] If this is what the author meant, his view of the last-named rite cannot have been very high. One could hardly think that he would subsume the act constituting the sole and universal means of entry into the covenant community within a general bracket including matters such as the washing of vessels. But it is surely the case that the very diversity of interpretations of this verse found among commentators establishes the same point.

---

1   So F.F. Bruce, *Commentary on the Epistle to the Hebrews* (NLC, London: Marshall, Morgan & Scott, 1964), *ad loc.*

2   See *A Commentary on the Epistle to the Hebrews* (Grand Rapids: Eerdmans, 1977), *ad loc.*

If baptism were for the author all that is claimed for it elsewhere, then in any listing of components in a 'foundation' for
Christian practice baptism must have been named, and
named unambiguously. (Is it perhaps also significant that at
6.4 and 10.32 entry into Christian status is referred to by the
purely metaphorical use of the participle φωτισθέντες? Further, although there would seem to be a reference to baptism
at 10.22, it is, like 6.3, far from unambiguous.)[1]

Finally, much has been written about the 'sacramentalism'
of the Fourth Gospel. 3.5 is one of the texts discussed. A recent
study of the background of this and other passages suggests
that 'the Evangelist is addressing a situation in which sacramental abuse may have been close at hand. This situation may
have stemmed from the increasing institutionalizing of the
church and the rigidity of sacramental use, from the changing climate brought on by the mystery cults, or even from the
despair engendered by the delay of the parousia.'[2] May it not
have been a factor in the situation behind the Fourth Gospel
that there were some within the community from which it
sprang who had not received baptism? This might be particularly likely if, following a fairly widely accepted proposal, the
'Johannine community' had its origin as a group of adherents
of Jesus who, as Jews, remained members of their synagogue
and worshipped there. Their position would be very similar to
the one thought of by R.H. Fuller for the disciples and for the
other witnesses of the risen Christ listed by Paul at 1 Cor. 15.5-
7. Indeed, taken as it stands, Jn 3.5 itself might suggest an
insistence by some of the Johannine Christians that others
who had not received Christian baptism should make good
this deficiency.

As was said at the outset, the material considered does not
amount to proof. It would be impossible to argue that Jewish-
Christian (let alone other) groups existed in which new believers in Jesus were admitted without baptism. But it is also inappropriate to assert or assume the converse. Our picture of the
diversity of the Christian movement in its early years should

---

1 A reference to baptism here is strongly denied by Beasley-Murray (*Baptism in the New Testament*, p. 249).
2 G.M. Burge, *The Anointed Community* (Grand Rapids: Eerdmans, 1987), p. 170.

be elastic enough to admit, as a plausible conjecture, that baptism, at least in some places, only slowly came to be seen as defining the boundary between membership and non-membership. A recent writer has spoken of the followers of Jesus 'making baptism into a ritual of initiation', and has rightly said that when this took place they had taken 'a major step towards sectarian identity'.[1] But when it is claimed that we are to think of a time 'very soon after the death of Jesus', we are entitled to hesitate. Did this crucial development occur, as it were, overnight? Was it applied (and if so, on whose authority?) for all followers of Jesus at once? And can we really situate the transformation of baptism into a rite of admission within months, or at most a year or two, of Jesus' death? The suggestion put forward in the present essay has been that negative replies are permissible in each case.

'Sectarian identity' is indeed a phrase which sharply defines a major shift in self-awareness within a group which began, and for a time remained, in a fully open relationship to the Judaism which gave it birth.[2] It was indeed the openness of Jesus' table-fellowship which gave scandal;[3] and the incident of the 'strange exorcist' (Mk 9.38-41)—and, more particularly, the fact of its conservation in the tradition—strongly attests an attitude which is the reverse of sectarian. The only Christian community of the first century of which we have detailed knowledge was also open in its attitude towards non-members—surprisingly so, perhaps, to contemporary observ-

---

1   W.A. Meeks, *The Moral World of the First Christians* (London: SPCK, 1986), p. 99.

2   Of course the seeds of the ultimate separation of the nascent Christian movement from all forms of Judaism were there from the first, as the persecution of Christians attested in Acts and in the Pauline letters makes clear. But the separation itself, the point at which 'sectarian identity' was fully achieved, was slow to become complete. The story of James the brother of the Lord as narrated by Hegesippus (Eusebius, *The History of the Church*, 23.4ff. [tr. G.A. Williamson; Harmondsworth: Penguin, 1965, pp. 99ff.]) is instructive. Even allowing for some legendary accretion, the high regard in which James was held among many Jewish contemporaries suggests that his belief in the Messiahship of Jesus had not—until the final attack on him by the Sadducees and Pharisees—made him unacceptable to his Jewish contemporaries.

3   Lk. 15.1f. Many have stressed the central place of table-fellowship in the ministry of Jesus. Acceptance, on these occasions, of those excluded by the Pharisees was of the essence of their nature.

ers.[1] The presence in the Christian assembly of persons either neutral (if this is what ἰδιῶται implies)[2] or consciously negative (ἄπιστοι) towards the community's Christian convictions is taken for granted as entirely predictable. If the occasion of 1 Cor. 11 and 14 was identical, as it may well have been,[3] these outsiders were presumably participants in the Lord's Supper. If so, this would represent a state of affairs distant indeed from the practice attested by Justin Martyr. The need to erect a firm boundary between those 'inside' and those outside was, at the earlier stage, only beginning to be felt. Some imprecision over the requirement of baptism as the universal condition for acceptance as a Christian would cohere well with such a gradualist view of the emergence of distinctively Christian self-identification.

---

1 S.C. Barton and G.H.R. Williamson have drawn attention to features which distinguish the early Christian house-churches from an otherwise fairly closely comparable group which met regularly for worship under the tutelage of a number of cult divinities. Among these features they note that 'the elitist tenor of the Philadelphian cult's entrance requirements and of its secretive practices must be contrasted with both the Christians' openness to the outsider and the basic continuities between their practice in church and in the world at large' ('A Hellenistic Cult Group and the New Testament Churches', *Jahrbuch für Antike und Christentum* 24 [1981], pp. 7-41 [39]).

2 Bauer–Arndt–Gingrich *s.v.* see the ἰδιῶται as 'a kind of proselytes or catechumens'. C.K. Barrett (*A Commentary on the First Epistle to the Corinthians* [London: Black, 1968; 2nd edn: London: SPCK, 1978], *ad loc.*) is surely right in preferring 'outsider' as the appropriate translation.

3 H.J. Klauck (*Herrenmahl und hellenistischer Kult* [NTAbh, N.F. 15; Münster: Aschendorf, 1982], pp. 346ff.) has an extended discussion of the issues. He regards the parallels in vocabulary between the two chapters as the strongest argument for thinking that chs. 11 and 14 describe the same occasion. However, even if ch. 14 is judged to refer to a meeting other than the one when the Supper was celebrated, it was still an occasion of intensive worship, from which it would be natural to think that those not members of the church would be excluded.

A COIN OF THREE REALMS
(Matthew 17.24-27)

B.D. Chilton

The stater which Peter is instructed to find by opening the mouth of the first fish he angles for, is good money in three systems of currency. It discharges a responsibility which impinges upon the Matthaean community, upon Judaism as faithful to worship in the Temple, and upon Jesus and Peter. Those three realms of responsibility are delineated within the passage by means of its literary setting, its association with contemporary developments, and the speculation it invites. Ordinarily, common sense would dictate that we proceed from the social matrix best known to that least known; in this instance, we would move from the community addressed by the Gospel (Matthew's ἐκκλησία), though the community referred to within the passage (Judaism, as true to the cult in Jerusalem), and on to the group which generated the vignette (Jesus' movement). But in the case to hand common sense has been overtaken by the history of discussion; we must adjust our itinerary, and understand why we do so.

Two recent contributions represent a significant change in scholarly attitudes towards the passage, each of them arguing—in one way or another—that it substantively reflects the teaching and miraculous action of Jesus. William Horbury has argued that Jesus insisted that paying tax for the upkeep of the Temple was not required by the Torah, but was prudent in order not to cause offence.[1] He also concludes, albeit cautiously (and during the course of his discussion, rather than at its close), that v. 27 accords well with the teaching in vv. 25-26, and is distinct from similar motifs in folklore;[2] 'despite the strong *prima facie* case for suspecting the narrative, it is more likely to have originated in an incident than in pious imagination alone'.[3] Horbury's article is a model of logical restraint and historical acumen; recourse to his work on the part of Richard Bauckham is a credit to both authors.[4] Bauckham, however, focuses upon 17.27, and is primarily concerned with the origin and significance of Peter's miraculous find. He argues that the miracle 'is a way of paying the tax which strongly reinforces the argument of vv. 25-26',[5] when they are understood on Horbury's terms. Both Horbury and Bauckham offer a welcome correction to the discipline of exegesis, by refusing to posit fragments of tradition divorced from the sense of the passage. They discipline their speculations regarding the ultimate source of the passage by means of an insistent recourse to the probable meaning of the entire complex of material.

Their orientation is representative of an invigorated concern for history among those who attend to Matthew as scripture. *Gospel Perspectives,* in which Bauckham's piece appears, is programmatically geared to the issue of historicity,[6] and Horbury refers to Jesus as 'the Lord' throughout his article. But neither scholar finds it necessary or appropriate to invoke the historicist presupposition of an earlier day, which had it that the Gospels should be assumed to be accurate, unless proven otherwise. They come to the conclusion they do because, on balance, the textual phenomena to be accounted

---

1	W. Horbury, 'The Temple Tax', in *Jesus and the Politics of His Day* (ed. E. Bammel and C.F.D. Moule; Cambridge: Cambridge University Press, 1984), pp. 265-86 (282-85).

2	Horbury, pp. 273-76.

3	Horbury, pp. 275-76.

4	R. Bauckham, 'The Coin in the Fish's Mouth', in *Gospel Perspectives VI. Miracles in the Gospels* (ed. D. Wenham and C. Blomberg; Sheffield: JSOT, 1986), pp. 219-52.

5	Bauckham, p. 224; cf. pp. 233-37, and the comparison with similar stories, pp. 237-44.

6	Cf. Bauckham, pp. 5-7.

for are explicable of the strength of their hypotheses. History is now what emerges heuristically, in the course of exegesis, not a status quo to be defended.

The force of the contributions of Horbury and Bauckham is such that our itinerary needs to be changed. They emphatically focus upon the stater as a tax imposed for the upkeep of the Temple. The coin has long been understood in that manner, but Horbury and Bauckham accept the Temple as the horizon of the passage in its present form, and in its origin within Jesus' movement. In other words, one realm, that of Judaic relations with the Temple, is held to determine the sense of the passage within the Matthaean community and within the circle of Jesus' disciples. The purpose of the present essay is (1) to suggest that the three realms are spheres of distinct meanings, conveyed within and through Matthew, and (2) to argue that, in this instance, a concern with what actually happened only subverts an appreciation of the text.

The First Realm: the Temple

In Nehemiah 10.33-34, Nehemiah, the nobility, the priests, the Levites, assorted functionaries of the Temple, and 'all who have separated themselves from the peoples of the lands to the law of God' undertake to pay for the service of the Temple and its sacrifices by means of an annual obligation of one third of a shekel. Exod. 30.11-16 specifies the payment of one half-shekel, which became the standard amount of cultic tax, although 30.11-14 makes the occasion of payment a census, not an annual tax. Nonetheless, Josephus takes a tax of a half-shekel a year as the norm (*AJ* 18.9.1; *BJ* 7.6.6), and the impression he gives is confirmed emphatically from the perspective of the Diaspora by Philo (*Spec. Leg.* 1.14).[1] In the tractate *Sheqalim*, Mishnah—from a later, and theoretical, perspective—prescribes the collection of the half-shekel in Adar, and specifies its appropriate use (1.1–4.6). Schürer remarks, and in so doing represents a consensus, that the tax reflects an accommodation to the reality that the monarchy

---

1 Cf. 2 Kgs 12.4, 5 and 2 Chr. 24.6-14. It seems clear that Josephus and Philo confirm the existence of a settlement which was reached by the period of the Chronicler.

could no longer defray such expenses as the tax was designed to meet (cf. Ezek. 45.17).[1] But that socio-economic reality which makes the collection of the half-shekel seem an obvious necessity should not be confused with the ideological programme of Mishnah, which stresses the regular and universal nature of the tax, as part of its programme of portraying the Temple as the centre of Israel's sanctification. Even the new edition of Schürer's opus, which puts itself forward as a conceptual advance, mixes the apples of Josephus with the oranges of Mishnah.

Although Mishnah may well suggest that the collection of the half-shekel was more universal than it was, reference to the tax as the δίδραχμα in Matthew (17.24) corresponds to Josephus' understanding that the shekel was valued at four drachmas or denarii (AJ 3.8.2). In that a stater equalled four drachmas, it would do as payment for two people.[2] The form δίδραχμα is most easily taken as a plural, although it has been argued that it represents an Aramaic spelling.[3] Matthew refers to the collectors as if they constituted a familiar group, as conforms to the general picture of Mishnah, and—more significantly—to that of Josephus and Philo. Both the latter authors refer to the tax as routine,[4] and—perhaps more tellingly—mention special envoys who bring the tax in from the Diaspora.[5] To some extent the impression they give is supported by Cicero[6] and Dio Cassius.[7] Smallwood dates the earliest reference in Josephus (AJ 14.7.2) to 88 BCE,[8] and the verisimilitude of the reference may be supported by Cicero's

---

1   E. Schürer, *A History of the Jewish People in the Time of Jesus Christ*, vol. 2 (ed. G. Vermes, F. Millar, M. Black; Edinburgh: T. and T. Clark, 1979), p. 271.

2   A. Plummer, *An Exegetical Commentary on the Gospel according to S. Matthew* (New York: Scribner, 1910), pp. 244-47; E.M. Smallwood, *The Jews under Roman Rule* (Studies in Judaism in Late Antiquity, 20; Leiden: Brill, 1976), pp. 124-25.

3   Cf. M. Black, 'ΕΦΦΑΘΑ (Mk 7.34), [TA] ΠΑΣΧΑ (Mt 26.18 W), [TA] ΔΙΔΡΑΧΜΑ (Mt 17.24 [bis])', in *Mélanges bibliques en hommage au R.P. Béda Rigaux* (ed. A. Descamps and A. de Halleux; Gembloux: Duculot, 1970), and Bauckham, p. 245 n. 4.

4   *AJ* 3.8.2; 14.7.2; 18.9.1; *BJ* 7.6.6; *Quis Rerum Divinarum Heres* 186; *Spec. Leg.* 1.14.

5   *AJ* 18.9.1; cf. 16.2.2-7; *Spec. Leg.* 1.14; *Sheqalim* 3.4; Smallwood, p. 125 n. 18.

6   *Pro Flacco* 28.

7   *Historia* 65.7.

8   Smallwood, p. 126.

remarks on practices which are to be dated in 62 BCE (*Pro Flacco* 66-69).[1] Smallwood also richly documents her conclusion that the theft of moneys collected for 'the Temple tax and the repeated Roman reassertion of the Jews' rights in the matter' constituted 'the chief bone of contention between them and the Greek city authorities in the East'.[2]

Comparatively speaking, the collection of the half-shekel may be regarded as a recent innovation, and such is Horbury's point of departure. He observes that Exod. 30.13f. does not itself refer to annual payment, notes the discrepancy in the fraction of the shekel involved in Neh. 10.33 and *Sheqalim*, and points out that the tax is not mentioned in certain texts which do mention offerings in the Temple (Tob. 1.6-8, the Letter of Aristeas, Jubilees).[3] But the strongest evidence he cites is from Qumran: 4Q159 explicitly limits the payment of Exod. 30.13 to a single event in a person's life.[4] Horbury also cites passages from later, rabbinic literature, which he claims 'further illuminates this opposition'.[5] The texts themselves, however, refer to non-payment, not to opposition in principle.[6] Horbury's own conclusion is that 'Palestinian Jews were not paying the tax in a manner beyond reproach'.[7] The opposition at Qumran appears *sui generis*. Insofar as the customs of early Judaism may be inferred, then, the issue posed by Peter's interlocutors in v. 24 focuses on whether Jesus followed the normal custom.[8]

---

1 Smallwood, p. 126.

2 Smallwood, p. 143.

3 Horbury, pp. 277-78.

4 Horbury, p. 279. For an earlier version of such an approach, cf. the analysis of W.F. Albright and C.S. Mann, *Matthew* (Anchor Bible; Garden City: Doubleday, 1971), pp. 212-14.

5 Horbury, p. 279.

6 Cf. *Sheqalim* 1.4; *Mekhilta Bahodesh* 1 (Exod. 19.1). Horbury goes on (pp. 280-81) to speak of other passages (related to *Nedarim* 2.4), but he is justifiably reluctant to agree wholeheartedly with S. Freyne (*Galilee from Alexander the Great to Hadrian* [Wilmington: Glazier, 1980], pp. 277-81) that one may infer from an alleged Galilaean refusal to acknowledge vows of undefined heave-offering that they were unwilling to pay the tax from which the heave-offering was purchased.

7 Horbury, pp. 281-82.

8 Horbury offers the translation, 'Does your master pay the half-shekel?' (p. 282). He suggests that 'the question was linked with the Pharisaic testing of Jesus', and we shall have reason, in the next section, to agree with that exegesis of the *Matthaean* sense of the text. The alternative view, that the issue is whether Jesus

Peter's unqualified 'yes' (v. 25a) would seem to put paid to the question, as well as to the tax. But Jesus' reaction (vv. 25b-27) makes his overall position appear ambivalent. As we explore that ambivalence, however, it is crucial that we do not confuse our purpose within the present section. The issue now is not Jesus' position *per se*, but how vv. 25b-27, which happen to be attributed to Jesus, are to be read within the realm of that Judaism which expected the tax to be paid as a matter of course. Verses 25b-26 appear to constitute an emphatically negative response: since kings tax their subjects for the benefit of their sons, the sons themselves are exempt. God does not tax his own people.[1] A somewhat comparable parable is given in *Sukkah* 30a,[2] where a king pays customs while on a journey, as an example to travellers, although he is rightly understood as not obliged to pay. In both cases, an exemption in principle is maintained, even as the tax is compiled with in practice.

The sting in the tale of the parable in Matthew, of course, is that its attitude is developed in respect of the Temple, not Rome. Moreover, the 'payment' is made in practice only in the sense that v. 27 refers to an action. Within the Matthaean realm of meaning, as we are about to see, a miraculous event is evidently at issue, but—within its own terms of reference and its contemporary, Judaic context—the command Jesus gives Peter may well be taken as parabolic. The apparent action is an insistence of the *topos* of a valuable item found in a fish (cf. *Shabbath* 119a);[3] what meets the requirement of the half-shekel, within the purview of v. 27, is an extraordinary coincidence. As Bauckham remarks,[4] God himself provides the payment in order to avoid giving offence. Even on the supposition that v. 27 refers to the *topos* as an actual event, the tax is not paid by Peter or Jesus. What may at first sight appear an

is supported by a patron, cannot be commended. Fundamentally, the verb τελεῖ establishes the issue as whether the tax is observed, not as the agency of payment.
1   As Bauckham shows (pp. 221-23), the parable is best understood in that sense within a Judaic context. He convincingly demonstrates the difficulty of taking the parable to refer to foreigners or to members of the king's household in general.
2   Cf. S.T. Lachs, *A Rabbinic Commentary on the New Testament* (Hoboken: Ktav, 1986), pp. 265. In the present case, however, the king is understood as God, to whom all may rightly be given.
3   Lachs, p. 265.
4   Bauckham, p. 224.

ambivalent response is in fact negative: the stater is a sop, not a solution. That a negative response is involved is not surprising *per se*: there was a considerable body of opinion that the half-shekel was not owed after the Temple was destroyed, a view which is reflected in *Sheqalim* 8.8. But once the passage is read on the supposition that the Temple still stands, which is implicit within the first realm of meaning to which Matthew refers, an ordinary practice is invoked, only to be rejected.

The Second Realm: the Matthaean Community

The sense of the pericope within its Judaic context appears to be plain: in narrative terms, Peter believes Jesus complies with the tax, and Jesus contradicts that belief. A blanket is thrown over the inevitable scandal by the advice to fish for a stater, although the pericope itself gives no indication whether the advice was understood literally, or followed, or whether—if followed literally—the coin was in fact discovered. That narrative sense of the pericope to some extent resonates positively with motifs in Matthew, but it also poses a problem.

Matthew's position in regard to Judaism might fairly be characterized as anti-Semitic. 'Jews' spread the false report of the theft of Jesus's corpse (28.15). Although Jesus' own activity leads to the God of Israel being praised (15.31), the marvels involved are greater than those of Israel (9.33), and the faith they awaken is qualitatively superior (8.10; cf. Lk. 7.9). In Matthew uniquely among the Gospels, even ethnic guilt for Jesus' death is imputed to, and accepted by, the Jews (27.25), and in that sense the charge of anti-Semitism appears tenable.

The willingness of 'all the people' in 27.25 to accept responsibility for Jesus' death, even on behalf of their children, is the result of the incitement of high priests and elders in v. 20. The Matthaean community is painfully at odds with the hierarchy of the synagogue, as ch. 23 makes unmistakably plain. Moreover, Jesus in Matthew alone makes 'I desire mercy, not sacrifice' (Hos. 6.6) into a slogan against observing a discipline of fellowship at table (Mt. 9.10-13) and against observing regulations of the Sabbath (12.1-8). Further, in the latter passage (again, in Matthew alone), Jesus declares himself

greater than the Temple (12.6); the polemic against leaders of
the synagogue also involves attacks on more strictly cultic
observance. The Matthaean movement of Jesus is obviously
from 'the lost sheep of the house of Israel' (10.6; 15.24) to 'all
nations' (28.19), with a clear understanding that the Jews,
their practices, and their Temple have been left behind.

The pericope concerning the tax fails easily and evidently
within the progression from Israel to all the world as Peter,
who has particularly been designated as empowered in
halakhic matters (Mt. 16.17-19), is taught that he is free from
such obligations in principle. But precisely that freedom poses
a severe problem within the social context of Matthew. The
imposition of the half-shekel, subsequent to the firing of the
Temple, was directed, at Vespasian's order, to the temple of
Jupiter Capitolinus.[1] Smallwood demonstrates convincingly
that the tax for the Capitoline temple was initiated shortly
after the Temple in Jerusalem was burned, and she observes
that it was collectable from both sexes beyond the age of three,[2]
while the half-shekel had been payable by males above the age
of twenty (cf. Exod. 30.14). There was a rough justice in the
punishment, in that half-shekels had been minted at the time
of the outbreak of the revolt[3] as part of an attempt to revive
cultic nationalism. She observes also that the tax was officially
known as the *didrachmon*,[4] which would make the coherence
with Mt. 17.24 striking.

Commentators have been historically reluctant to concede
that any imperial aspect is at issue in the pericope.[5] But their
reluctance should be more than overcome by considerations of
the content and style of Matthew. In the famous signature
(9.9), the Gospel is associated with a publican, and therefore
with the complex system of taxation which prevailed outside

1 *BJ* 7.6.6; Dio, *Historia* 65.7; Suetonius, *Domitianus* 12; R.H. Gundry, *Matthew. A Commentary on his Literary and Theological Art* (Grand Rapids: Eerdmans, 1982), p. 357; E. Schürer, *A History of the Jewish People in the Time of Jesus Christ*, vol. 3 (ed. G. Vermes, F. Millar, M. Goodman; Edinburgh: T. and T. Clark, 1986), p. 111; Smallwood, p. 371.
2 Smallwood, pp. 372, 373.
3 Smallwood, pp. 300, 301.
4 Smallwood, p. 372.
5 Cf. Gundry, p. 357.

Judaea as well as within.[1] The Gospel also betrays cognizance
of the common feeling that the taxes involved were unjust
(21.31).[2] Notably, in the saying just cited (which is also uniquely Matthaean), publicans and harlots are said to precede high
priests and elders into the kingdom (cf. v. 23), and so a consistent theme of the Gospel, realized in the person of Matthew, is
brought to articulation. Stylistically, it is striking that Jesus is
referred to as 'teacher' in 17.24, which is what he is called in
22.16, concerning the payment of tribute to Caesar (22.17).
The question τί σοι δοκεῖ... features in both passages (17.25;
22.17),[3] and 17.25 itself generalizes the case to include tax and
tribute (κῆνσος), and so is well coordinated with 22.17.[4]

On the basis of the relationship between Ignatius and
uniquely Matthaean material, Bauckham argues for the specific association of Matthew with Antioch.[5] That viewpoint has
been conventional since the time of Streeter (although it is
nothing more than an inference);[6] our reading of the pericope
would suit the consensus well. The aftermath of the revolt saw
troubled times for Jews in Antioch,[7] and friction with non-
Jewish Christians was at least as old as the events reflected in
Acts 11 and Galatians 2. Since even rabbis concluded the half-
shekel was not an obligation in the absence of the Temple
(*Sheqalim* 8.8),[8] it is not surprising that Jesus corrects Peter
within the Judaic realm of meaning. But that correction is
problematic within the imperial realm of Matthaean Antioch,

---

1   Cf. Schürer, vol. 1, pp. 374-76; Lk. 19.1, 2, 8; *BJ* 2.14.4; *Baba Kamma* 10.1, 2;
    Nedarim 3.4.

2   Tacitus, *Annales* 2.42.5 and H. Furneaux, *P. Cornelii Taciti Annalium...*
    vol. 1 (Oxford: Clarendon, 1896), p. 335 (cf. F.R.D. Goodyear, *The Annals of
    Tacitus* [Cambridge: Cambridge University Press, 1981], p. 322); Schürer, vol. 1,
    p. 373; cf. Lk. 3.13.

3   Cf. Bauckham, p. 229 and Mt. 18.12; 21.28; 22.42.

4   Cf. A.H. M'Neile, *The Gospel according to St Matthew* (London: Macmillan,
    1957), p. 258, who notes the generality of v. 25 and even relates it to Rom. 13.7.

5   Bauckham pp. 229, 230, 248 nn. 44-46. Cf. J.P. Meier, 'Part One: Antioch', in
    Antioch and Rome. New Testament Cradles of Catholic Christianity (with
    R. Brown; New York: Paulist, 1983).

6   Cf. B.H. Streeter, *The Four Gospels* (London: Macmillan, 1924), p. 504.

7   *BJ* 7.5.2-4; *AJ* 12.3.1. Cf. W.A. Meeks and R.L. Wilken, *Jews and Christians in
    Antioch in the first Four Centuries of the Common Era* (SBL Sources for Biblical
    Study, 13; Ann Arbor: Scholars Press, 1978), pp. 4-13.

8   Cf. Schürer, vol. 2, p. 273 n. 59.

where recognition of duly constituted authority is essential to survival.[1]

Once it is appreciated that the tax is no longer paid for the Temple, but to its Roman analogue, the pericope discovers its Matthaean sense. The intended hearers or readers of 17.24-27 are not 'Jews', but 'sons' (17.25, 26); they may, as Gentiles (or as Jews whose Christianity separates them from Judaism), be exempt from the *fiscus iudaicus*. The implicit tension between 'the Son of God and his followers' and the Matthaean Jews led M'Neile to doubt the 'genuineness' of the passage on the grounds of 'so strong an anti-Jewish feeling'.[2] But that exemption (again in principle alone) can only imply *laesa maiestas,* as applied to the indubitably Jewish Jesus and Peter: what works for the Matthaean community cannot, by identity, work for Jesus and his immediate circle.

Peter immediately assumes, within the narrative world of the pericope, that Jesus complies with the tax. It is only Jesus' parables, of king's sons and a stater discovered in a fish, which cause problems. Once v. 27 is understood as referring to a miracle, however, Jesus complies with the tax (along with Peter), and the Matthaean community is free, all without offending Rome. The transformation of v. 27, from a parable into a miracle, is achieved by the specifically Matthaean context of the story. In addition to references to Jesus' ministry of healing and to events such as the feedings of thousands, we have encountered by this point in Matthew the unique story of Peter's excursion on the water (14.28-33), as well as the scene of his special authorization (16.17-19), which is expressed in supernatural terms. In addition, he has (as in Mark and Luke) been up the mount of the transfiguration and has received (as in Mark) special instruction (17.1-13). Even though 17.27 is formally parabolic, only a rationalistic reader of Matthew could fail to conclude that a miracle is the intended reference. The intended hearer or reader, however, knows that Peter was too anxious to fulfil a requirement which is not truly binding on Christians (cf. Gal. 2), that Jesus fulfilled a Jewish tax by directing Peter to a heavenly provision

1 Cf. Meeks and Wilken, pp. 4-9.
2 M'Neile, p. 258.

of a stater, and that the 'sons' of the community are not bound
by the rules imposed upon the defeated Jewish nation.

The Third Realm: Jesus and his Movement

Any Jewish teacher could claim (and some did claim) that, in
principle, the chosen people are of royal stock, and that they
are exempt from some tax or another. Any Jewish teacher
could refer (and some did refer) to the image of a coin in a
fish's gullet or gut.[1] The startling factor in the Matthaean
attribution of such teaching to Jesus (in its Judaic context) is
that he is portrayed as resisting payment for the upkeep of the
Temple. We have already found, *pace* Horbury, that such a
stance was radical. On the other hand, the Matthaean sense of
the pericope (in its imperial context), with its supposition of
distance from Judaism, must not be imputed to Jesus and his
immediate followers.

The radicalism of Jesus may be recovered only by understanding the pericope within its Judaic sense and therefore (by
definition) within its Matthaean sense, but also by permitting
those senses to be corrected by legitimate inferences regarding
Jesus himself. The Matthaean sense transforms v. 27. As
Dodd observed:

> In all probability the saying is a true *Bildwort*. The *pericopé*
> is not a miracle story, nor a story of action of any kind; it is a
> 'pronouncement story'.

But at the next stage of development it might have been
accepted as the record of an incident—as it is probably
accepted unthinkingly by many readers.[2] Within our analysis,
Matthew is understood as that next stage, although signs of an
earlier (literary or oral) context are evident in the association
of the passage with parables.[3] The discourse of the pericope is

---

1   The coin of 17.27 is not in the mouth of the fish, as Bauckham maintains; rather, it
    is discovered by opening its mouth. Presumably, the point is that the coin has only
    recently been swallowed.
2   C.H. Dodd, *Historical Tradition in the Fourth Gospel* (Cambridge: Cambridge
    University Press, 1965), p. 227; cf. also V. Taylor, *The Formation of the Gospel
    Tradition* (London: Macmillan, 1945), p. 74.
3   Cf. T.W. Manson, *The Teaching of Jesus* (Cambridge: Cambridge University
    Press, 1955), p. 68, where 17.25 is listed with the parables of 'M'.

certainly of a parabolic nature, as the sense within the Judaic realm makes plain.

Both Horbury and Bauckham proceed in their analyses to construe the pericope as representing an incident. Our analysis has rather focused upon the issue of the pericope's sense within specifiable realms of meaning. Within the Judaic realm, a set of parables releases Jews from the necessity of paying the half-shekel; within the Matthaean realm, a miracle assures that the imperial tax is paid by Peter within his status as a Jew, not as a Christian. It is obvious that the third realm, defined by Jesus and his immediate followers, is only accessible inferentially, as a *tertium quid* one must posit to understand how the meanings of the other two realms emerged. The third realm is not to be assumed to be a specific event or action, nor need we presuppose that it is conveyed directly by the pericope as we might read it. Rather, the sense of the third realm is a figment of literary history (not to be confused with literal history);[1] the meaning implied within the meanings that may be read.

Such a literarily historical Jesus is but a shadow cast by the primary realms of meaning within which the pericope operates. Primarily, Mt. 17.24-27 speaks of a tax which need no longer be paid, whether it be understood as half-shekel or *fiscus iudaicus,* because the 'sons' of the Matthaean community are released from such constraints by Jesus himself. Insofar as anything is paid, the payment is parabolic (in the Judaic realm of meaning) or miraculous (in the Matthaean realm of meaning). Within the context of the dominical realm of meaning, however, the sense which emerges clearly is Jesus' resistance to ordinary provisions concerning the cult, which is most obviously attested in his occupation of the Temple.[2] Mishnah places the collection of the half-shekel in Adar, just before Passover; it has long been observed that the placement in Matthew would suggest an earlier time of year was

---

1 That distinction is developed in B.D. Chilton, *Profiles of a Rabbi. Synoptic Opportunities in Reading about Jesus* (Brown Judaic Studies; Atlanta: Scholars Press, 1989).

2 Cf. Mt. 21.12-17; Mk 11.15-17; Lk. 19.45, 46; Jn 2.13-16; B.D. Chilton, *A Galilean Rabbi and his Bible* (London: SPCK, and Wilmington: Glazier, 1984), pp. 17, 18; *idem*, 'Caiaphas', forthcoming in the *Abingdon Dictionary of the Bible.*

involved.[1] Matthew associates the pericope with a cycle of Petrine material which assures the passage will be taken as reflecting a miraculous event. But within a paschal cycle, the passage reflects Jesus' refusal to pay what the Petrine opinion declared he would pay. If *Sheqalim* is any guide, Jesus may be operating on the supposition that the priestly exemption from payment applied to his circle (*Sheqalim* 1.3).[2]

Conclusion

The third realm of meaning is obviously the most indeterminate and problematic. Nonetheless, we have inferred a meaning, within the literary history of the text which lies to hand, whose function is to explain how Jesus could be held both to resist an ordinary tax within Judaism (the first realm) and to avoid setting his Matthaean followers on a course of collision with Rome (the second realm). This *tertium quid,* the Jesus of literary history, is a sense (not a historical figure) generated within the interstices of meaning defined by the social worlds of Judaism and Christianity. It is not a secondary inference, but a tertiary one. It emerges from a consideration of what the Matthaean text conveys (the second realm) and the inferential grounds of its conveyance (the first realm). On that basis, a further movement of abstract inference gives us a sense, not a person who said such and so, but a sense which is congruent with behaviour along definable lines. That behaviour may in turn be attributed to the person held responsible for teaching both the payment and the non-payment of tax: abstraction and speculation is occasioned and justified by that apparently contradictory attribution.

At no point in our analysis of traceable meanings has it proved possible, useful, or even imaginable, to assert anything of Jesus in overtly historical terms. The Jesus of literary history, that inferential *tertium quid,* emerges as an object of our cognition as we engage meanings, never as a datum to which

---

1 Cf. J. Lightfoot, *A Commentary on the New Testament from Talmud and Hebraica* (r.p. Grand Rapids: Baker, 1979), p. 251.

2 *Sheqalim* 1.4 would appear to contradict that principle, in the name of Yohanan ben Zakkai; have we in the tension between 1.3 and 1.4 a ghost of the dispute in which Jesus was involved?

the text simply refers. Jesus, within the pericope, speaks the language of miracle, the language of parable, and the language of rebellion, and the more clearly it is Jesus who speaks, the less evident is the meaning involved. But the meanings themselves are at their most lucid as senses within realms of concern. They are only obscured by premature judgments of 'authenticity' because every meaning authentically pays in the currency of the realm which generates it.

Part 3

QUESTIONS OF METHOD

'WHAT DOES IT MEAN TO BE HUMAN?'
The Central Question of Old Testament Theology?*

J.W. Rogerson

At the International Old Testament Congress in Salamanca in 1983, Erhard Gerstenberger put some straight and disturbing questions to the discipline as we know it in the West in his lecture, 'The Relation of Old Testament Interpretation to Reality'.[1] Having taught for six years in the south of Brazil, Gerstenberger interpreted his invitation to address the Congress as a request to confront Western scholarship with the insights and imperatives of Old Testament scholars working in Latin America.[2] Beginning from the observation that

> Every exegete has his setting in life; the burning question is simply how the reality of life which has shaped him and of which he himself is a living part determines his outlook and way of thinking,

he posed the question,

> to what extent are the exegetical results of interpreters constrained by their time-conditioned circumstances and in what direction in the pursuit of our cooperative work as exegetes should we correct, extrapolate from or further develop these circumstances?[3]

* A Lecture given as the Presidential Address to the Society for Old Testament Study, 4 January 1989.

1 E. Gerstenberger, 'Der Realitätsbezug alttestamentlicher Exegese', in J.A. Emerton (ed.), *Congress Volume Salamanca 1983* (VTSup, 36; Leiden: E.J. Brill, 1985), pp. 132-44.
2 Gerstenberger, p. 132.
3 Gerstenberger, p. 132 (translations by J.W. Rogerson).

In answering these questions, Gerstenberger left no doubt as to where his sympathies lay. He argued in some detail that both the content of Western Old Testament interpretation and the organization of its teaching and research were based on ideas of power that were alien to the Old Testament itself. He did not deny, of course, that the Old Testament concerns itself a good deal with kings, priests and other forms of authority. But he threw down an uncompromising challenge in the following sentences:

> Are the Old Testament structures of power useful for us in any kind of form? After everything that we can learn from Jewish and Christian ethical tradition in the light of the whole of scripture, and after everything that we possess as information about the present-day world, we can only, in my view, describe the world situation in the following way. The traditional power and economic structures have already brought about the final catastrophe—in the form of mass poverty, destruction of the environment, sexism, racism, the arms race, wars and genocide. They have thus shown themselves to be in opposition to both God and humanity, and thus can no longer be considered as parameters for interpretation.[1]

Old Testament scholarship, in Gerstenberger's view, needed to take into account the fact that the reality of God in the Old Testament was a liberating reality, and that the world of the interpreter was one in which a majority of people lived in poverty so that a minority could enjoy affluence. Each interpreter needed to be aware of the understanding of reality that both informed his or her work and was implied in the text of the Old Testament.

The majority of people who hear or read a paper such as that of Gerstenberger react in one of two ways. Either they are hostile (and this was a noticeable reaction in the questions that followed the lecture in Salamanca), or they feel guilty, and ask themselves whether they should not, in fact, adopt liberation hermeneutics and abandon what they have up to now understood as the critical approach. Both reactions are understandable; but both seem to me to be inappropriate. On the one hand, any method that claims to be critical must be self-critical, and

1 Gerstenberger, p. 142.

ought to welcome questions that probe the pre-understanding that we bring to texts.

On the other hand, it is not clear to me that the world of Old Testament interpretation is in fact one world, in which we are obliged to discover a hermeneutical method which must be applied to every situation in which the Old Testament is studied and taught. That there is a hermeneutic that is appropriate for Basic Communities in the churches of Latin America I do not doubt. Whether that hermeneutic is appropriate for non-confessional academic situations in the industrial West is a matter that needs to be considered carefully before any decision is reached.

Careful consideration is especially important in view of the fundamental changes that are taking place in western society, and which are calling into question the place of the humanities within our society.[1] Whereas the voices from Latin America are urging us to disassociate ourselves from the power and economic structures of the industrial world if we wish to interpret the Old Testament authentically, the realities of our industrial society demand, at least from those of us in secular universities and secular polytechnics and colleges, that we justify our academic work in terms of its ability to attract private funding and to produce graduates who will have the skills to participate in the creation of material wealth.

It seems to me that if we are to come to terms with these seemingly diametrically opposed points of view—and to ignore them would be unwise, both academically and practically—we must look for analytical tools that will enable us to see more clearly the issues at stake, and will open up a dialogue that will hopefully resolve some of the tensions.

As a starting point, I want to suggest that underlying the three positions that I have been talking about, that is, traditional critical academic Old Testament study, liberation hermeneutics and commercially-orientated enterprise culture, is a view of what it means to be human; an answer,

---

1 See the analysis by J. Habermas in 'Die Krise des Wohlfahrtsstaates und die Erschöpfung utopischer Energien', in *Die neue Unübersichlichkeit* (Kleine Politischen Schriften, 5; Frankfurt am Main: Suhrkamp, 1985), pp. 141-66, esp. 154-55.

implicitly or explicitly to the question, What does it mean to be human?

Underlying traditional critical academic studies is what Eckhard Meinberg has described in his recent book, *Das Menschenbild der modernen Erziehungswissenschaft*, as 'der Verstandesmensch', a term that I shall use in German because I do not like its suggested English translation of 'rational man'.[1] According to this view, what distinguishes the human race from other creatures is its ability to discover, by means of reason, the 'laws' which lie behind the regularities of the natural world, and the ability to harness the potentialities of the natural world to the benefit of humanity. The *Verstandesmensch* must expose everything that is false or illusory and must oppose anything that threatens the unfettered use of reason in the search for truth. The unfettered search for truth is an essential safeguard for human freedom; that is to say, the *Verstandesmensch* cannot truly be itself if limits are placed upon the use of reason.

A quite different view of what it is to be human underlies liberation hermeneutics.[2] One must not, of course, overlook the theological basis of liberation theology, including its belief in God's identification with the poor and the oppressed. But, apart from its theological basis, liberation theology accepts the Marxist critique of the notion of the *Verstandesmensch*. It rejects the idea of a human reason which is exercised in isolation from economic and social conditions, and which is entirely interest-free. Liberation theologians insist time and again that exegesis is fundamentally shaped by the social conditions in which it is practised, and that for them, the human race is a species in which a powerful minority enslaves the majority, thus calling forth the need to see God as the liberator of that majority from economic and social degradation. This sort of view clearly underlies what is expressed in the paper by Gerstenberger.

It is more difficult to articulate the view of humanity underlying what I have called commercially-orientated enterprise

1 E. Meinberg, *Das Menschenbild der modernen Erziehungswissenschaft* (Darmstadt: Wissenschaftliche Buchgesellschaft, 1988), pp. 27-38.
2 See the influential *Pedagogy of the Oppressed* by Paulo Freire (Harmondsworth: Penguin, 1972).

culture. On the one hand, it shares with the *Verstandes-mensch* view a stress on individual freedom and achievement; but it also has a strong anti-intellectual strain at two levels.[1] First, it blames intellectuals for the economic crisis of capitalism in the 1970s and 1980s, and prefers practice to theory, against the background of the regulating effects of market forces. Secondly, it desires social integration to be achieved by, among other things, conventional religion, and is thus hostile to anyone who calls into question, by the use of reason or research, the traditional fundamentals of religion. In Britain this last point is well illustrated by the provision, in the recent Education Reform Act, that religious instruction in schools should be 'broadly Christian', implicitly rejecting a non-traditional pluralist approach.

Now if what I am saying is correct, that Old Testament study as most of us know it depends on a view of what it is to be human that is being challenged by two other views, what is to be done? An obvious answer is that there needs to be a dialogue between the views, assuming that a forum can be found. Another question that arises is that of the place of the Old Testament itself in all of this. Is our interpretation of it entirely shaped by the circumstances in which we work and by the pre-understanding that we bring to it? Does the Old Testament affect its readers in any way, so that, on the one hand, western critical scholars might find that they have much in common with interpreters in Latin America, and on the other hand, western critical scholarship might be able to articulate a prophetic critique of their industrial society that will hope to make political opinion appreciative of Old Testament study?

These are obvious and important questions; but I do not propose to follow them up here. Instead I want to suggest that the recent work of the German political philosopher Jürgen Habermas can provide insights of value to Old Testament scholarship at many levels, which may well enable us to cope with the dilemmas that I have been outlining.

In what follows, I am not going to attempt to expound Habermas's system. His most important work, *Theorie des kommunikativen Handelns* (1981) runs to almost 1,200 pages

---

1 See Habermas, 'Die Krise des Wohlfahrtsstaates', p. 154.

of philosophical and analytical German, to which must be
added works such as *Der philosophische Diskurs der
Moderne* (1985) and *Die neue Unübersichtlichkeit* (1985)
which alone add another 700 pages to the task of anyone who
tries to become familiar with the basic sources of Habermas's
thought.[1] There are commentaries in English, of which the
most recent, David Ingram's *Habermas and the Dialectic of
Reason* (1987), is in many ways more difficult than Habermas
himself.[2] For our purposes, the heart of what he has to say lies
in the second 'Zwischenbetrachtung' of *Theorie des kommunikativen Handelns* entitled *System und Lebenswelt* (vol. 2,
pp. 173-293); but before I comment on this section I want to
indicate how I think that Habermas can help us.

In his *Zur Rekonstruktion des historischen Materialismus*
(1976), Habermas considerably modified Marx's theory of the
various levels of social reality—infra-structure, structure and
superstructure—in which the economic factors which belong
to the infrastructure affect the other levels, with religious
beliefs belonging to the superstructure.[3] (Marx's view is used
by Norman Gottwald in his reconstruction of the origins of
Israel, and is partly responsible for his conclusion that Israelite
belief in its God was the *result* not the *cause* of the formation of
a liberated, egalitarian tribal community in late Bronze Age
Canaan.[4])

Habermas stresses the importance of two factors in social
and economic change, first, the accumulation of technical
knowledge and second, the development of new types of political organization which permit the more effective use of
labour, but which must be given a rational justification if they
are to succeed.

If we apply these ideas to the rise and fall of the united
monarchy in ancient Israel, we can say that the military suc-

---

1 J. Habermas, *Theorie des kommunikativen Handelns*, 2 vols (Frankfurt am
   Main: Suhrkamp, 1981); *Der philosophische Diskurs der Moderne* (Frankfurt am
   Main: Suhrkamp, 1985).
2 D. Ingram, *Habermas and the Dialectic of Reason* (New Haven: Yale University
   Press, 1987).
3 J. Habermas, *Zur Rekonstruktion des historischen Materialismus* (Frankfurt
   am Main: Suhrkamp, 3rd edn, 1982).
4 N.K. Gottwald, *The Tribes of Yahweh. A Sociology of the Religion of Liberated
   Israel 1250–1050 BCE* (Maryknoll, N.Y.: Orbis Books, 1979), pp. 631ff.

cess and religio-political ambition of David enabled accumulated technical knowledge to be used to transform Israel. This technical knowledge extended into the areas of warfare, building and fortification, irrigation, agriculture and viticulture. The united monarchy also enabled labour to be made available on a larger scale than hitherto. This involved weakening the tribal system, by creating new agencies for coordinating the production of foodstuff agencies that replaced the traditional function of kin-based groups.

However, such a radical reordering of social life required a rational justification. This was sought by way of the theological legitimation of the Davidic dynasty; but this legitimation was not powerful enough to become part of the accepted agenda of the people as a whole. While the revolt of the northern tribes had as its immediate ground a protest against the social injustices of Solomon's reign, a deeper reason for the revolt was that the northern tribes possessed a rationalized view of their corporate identity that prevented acceptance of the Davidic legitimation. In the terms of Habermas's theory, this meant that a rationalization of the system of political integration did not succeed in becoming part of the communicative life-world of the northern tribes.

This introduction of some of Habermas's key technical terms makes it appropriate at this point to set out some of his leading ideas. In answer to the question, What does it mean to be human?, Habermas would maintain that what distinguishes human beings from other life forms is an interdependence based upon the ability to communicate with each other. Of course other species, for example bees and ants, are inter-dependent, and also apparently communicate with each other. Human communication, however, contains the potential to form abstract concepts, and, with the invention of writing, to pass on cultural and other knowledge in an objective form from one generation to the next. To be born as a human being means to take one's place within a network of shared meanings based upon a transmitted cultural heritage.

Habermas in fact rejects the idea of the *Verstandesmensch* as he rejects the philosophy of consciousness, that is, that predominant western philosophical tradition that goes back through Heidegger, to Hegel and Kant and on to Descartes, and which defines philosophical activity as reflection upon human subjective awareness of the world.[1] Habermas substitutes for philosophy of consciousness what he calls a philosophy of communicative inter-action, that is to say, reflection upon the means by which humans articulate their interdependence, together with an examination of the way in which economic and other factors affect these communication processes.

To achieve his aim, Habermas uses the two notions of 'communicative life-world (*Lebenswelt*)' and 'system'.[2] To the communicative life-world belongs everything that is necessary for humans to communicate with each other in all the manifold circumstances of life. Habermas gives a trivial example of what he means, in order to show the complexity of the communicative life-world. The example is that of a senior member of a group of builders' labourers telling a young and newly-arrived worker to run and get some beer for the rest of the group so that they can all have their breakfast. This situation implies the acceptance, by all concerned, of the right of the most senior to give these orders and the duty of the newest worker to comply, the existence in that part of Germany of the so-called second breakfast, and the fact that there is a place that sells beer that is open and is close enough for the junior worker to run there and back in a relatively short period of time. The negative of any one of these preconditions, e.g. the information that the beer shop is closed that day, would vitiate the communicative action. Thus, the communicative life-world is in this case not just speech, but social authority, local custom, commercial practice and physical ability. It is not difficult to see how complex this theoretical notion of communicative life-world would be in practice if we could work out all its ramifications.

By system, Habermas means systems of social integration: marriage exchange, the exercise of power, the development of law, monetary exchange. It is his contention that social development is the result of uncoupling of the system from the

---

1 See Habermas, *Der philosophische Diskurs der Moderne*, for discussions of these thinkers.
2 *Theorie des kommunikativen Handelns*, vol. 2, pp. 171ff. For an exposition, see Ingram, pp. 115ff.

communicative life-world, after which there is an increasingly complex dialectical relationship between the two.

In the simplest types of society, where the kinship group is
the basic self-supporting economic unit, the system and the
communicative life-world are united. If that group expands,
or needs to cooperate with other groups, the system of social
integration begins to be uncoupled from the communicative
life-world. However, if social integration is achieved by marriage exchange, fictitious genealogies can restore the bond
between system and communicative life-world. The system
will be justified by the inclusion of the fictitious genealogies into
the communicative life-world. The exercise of power does not
lead to an uncoupling of system and communicative life-
world so long as power is exercised within dominant lineages.
Uncoupling takes place when the exercise of power is
detached from the kinship system, and administration and
law are formalized independently of kinship. Curiously
enough, formalized law is a product of the communicative
life-world in that it requires the formulation of abstract principles; but according to Habermas the uncoupling of system
and communicative life-world is complete under a regime of
formal law. This is presumably because the need for formal
law is occasioned by the development within the communicative life-world of groups with divergent interests which
cannot be reconciled by communicative interaction, and
which thus have to have recourse to law. All must accept this
law. The development of monetary exchange indicates a
further uncoupling of system and communicative life-world,
especially where the control of monetary exchange is left to
market forces. At this point, the system of social integration is
almost independent from the communicative life-world, but
can invade the domain of the communicative life-world by
imposing financial restrictions upon some of its subsystems.

Within the communicative life-world, the effect of uncoupling from the system is to allow an ever-increasing diversity of
communicative activity to develop. Culture is differentiated
from society, and this allows important institutions to be freed
from religious world views. In our own history, we can think
of the secularization of schools and universities in the past
century. Individuals gain greater freedom to be able to criti-

cize and revise accepted traditions. Specialized disciplines develop in order to solve particular problems or to deal with complex pieces of cultural information—such as the Old Testament, I would add.

All this is an unfolding of the potential that is within the human ability to engage in communicative interaction; yet there is no doubt that the uncoupling of system from communicative life-world which makes possible this unfolding of human potential exacts its price. There arise conflicts of interest, a lack of common purpose and identity, the restriction of communicative activity by the invasion of system, especially the system of monetary exchange, and interference with communicative interaction by means of propaganda and misinformation.

The solution of this paradox lies in a proper analysis of the tensions between system and communicative life-world, to enable humanity to become more effectively what it is, namely, a community of interdependent beings sharing the potential for communicative interaction.

In the hope that this very inadequate outline has given some inkling of what Habermas is trying to do, I shall try to address it to the Old Testament and to some of the problems from which I began.

The Old Testament, taken as a whole, is arguably very concerned with the question of communicative interaction, what hinders it and what can restore it. The foundation stories, set in beginning time, picture a scene of perfect intercommunication between the man and the woman without rivalry, between the humans and the other living creatures, and between the humans and God. This is shattered by the human desire to become like God. Communicative harmony breaks down as Adam and Eve accuse each other of disobeying God, Cain murders and denies responsibility for his brother Abel, and Lamech boasts about the scale of retribution that he has exacted. The story of the tower of Babel marks a further breakdown in the human ability to communicate, to be followed by God's intention, in calling Abraham, to bring blessing to *all* the families of the earth.

The freeing of the Hebrews from slavery in Egypt is a story with strong communicative potential: those whom God has freed may not enslave each other or turn their brothers aside in time of need—a powerful principle even if it is not wholly extended to non-Israelites. The covenant—whenever it was established (I am speaking essentially synchronically)—is an elaborate communicative apparatus designed to integrate Israel's life into the worship and service of a God who demands exclusive loyalty so that human interdependence will not be compromised by the misuse of power. The sacrificial and penitential systems are means of restoring broken communication.

The conflicts between prophetic groups and power-exploiting kings can be read as the attempt of the prophets to counteract a disregard of human interdependence; and it is interesting that prophetic visions of a recreated world seem to stress communicative inter-action. The nations that flow to Zion in Isa. 2.2-4 wish to be taught God's ways. The law and word of God will go forth out of Zion, and implements of war will be turned into tools of agricultural cooperation. When God establishes the New Covenant described in Jeremiah 31 there will be no need for people to teach each other to 'Know the Lord'. All will know him.

What exactly am I doing here? As far as I can work it out, it is something as follows. I have outlined Habermas's theory of communicative interaction because it seems to throw much light upon the development of human society and the problems that we face currently in the world. At the heart of Habermas's position is a premise that is essentially speculative. We cannot prove that what makes us human is our ability to live in interdependence based upon communicative interaction; nor can we prove that it is our obligation as humans to work for a world in which our intercommunication is as perfect as we can make it. None of this can be proved; but it is also the case that the Old Testament can be read, without distortion, in such a way as to support this basic assumption, except with the difference that it looks to God as the only agency that can accomplish the goal of an ideal communicative world. Why it is possible to read the Old Testament in this way is not something that I have time to discuss here. But if there is truth in my contention, then I suggest that the time is right for an interpretation of the Old Testament to be worked out along those lines, not just for the sake of the specialized study of the Old Testament, but also as a contribution to the wider discussion of the question, What does it mean to be human?, which is taking place in philosophical and political circles. No notice may be taken in these circles of Old Testament specialists; yet the Old Testament is a collection of texts that still commands attention and excites interest outside of scholarship and the churches, and it would do no harm to show that, while there are legitimate specialisms within Old Testament study that can only be the preserve of experts, there is also a way in which a scholarly and non-politicized reading of it can play an important role in contemporary discussions about the goals and priorities of our society.

The other point that I want to make concerns the way we think about the discipline of Old Testament study. Reading Habermas has made me aware that my own work on the history of scholarship has been largely inspired by the *Verstandesmensch* model, and that I have overlooked factors which are suggested by a philosophy of communicative inter-action.[1] In my work on de Wette, about whom I am writing a critical biography, I have concentrated principally on the intellectual background to de Wette's early critical work, and believe that I can demonstrate that his epoch-making *Beiträge zur Einleitung in das Alte Testament* of 1806-1807 can be perfectly understood in terms of the work on mythology that was being undertaken in literary and philosophical circles by Karl Philipp Moritz and F.W.J. Schelling.

None of this is wrong; yet it is all at the level of intellectual influences, and what I have overlooked is the communicative inter-action aspect. De Wette was able to write as he did in 1804-1807 because critical scholarship had developed as a specialist discipline, free, at any rate in Jena, from ecclesiastical constraints that could prevent the criticism of traditional opinions. At the same time, poetry and literature were so much a part of the intellectual scene that it was not surprising that they played such a large part in shaping de Wette's pre-

---

1 See my *Old Testament Criticism in the Nineteenth Century: England and Germany* (London: SPCK, 1984).

understanding.[1] For most of his time in Berlin, from 1810 to
1819, de Wette had little contact with organized religion and
continued to produce radical writings; however in Basel,
where he went unwillingly because no other jobs were offered
to him (he had been sacked from Berlin in 1819 on political
grounds and the Prussian government had done its best to
frustrate his further employment in Germany) he was expected to play an important part in church life, and was in fact
later ordained. De Wette did indeed become less certain about
some of his younger radical views during his time in Basel; but
he accepted many of the radical arguments of Strauss's *Life of
Jesus* in 1835 and appears to have become more conservative
in Basel only because of the need to adapt some of his works
for use by the church and schools of Basel. In other words, we
see him in Basel participating in more ecclesiastical
communicative sub-groups than he had done before, with a
consequent effect upon some of his writings.

Turning to the modern situation, the persistence of fundamentalism is almost certainly due to the fact that it is an
essential part of the communicative system of certain religious sub-cultures. When students from these sub-cultures
come to study the Bible at a university, they can adapt, to some
extent, to the conventions of the communicative system in
whose context they have to do their studies; but this system is
only a small part of their communicative life-world compared
with what is provided by their religious affiliation. It should
come as no surprise that their contact with academic study
either makes them give up religion, or returns them to their
religious group only marginally affected by their studies.

It is easy for some scholars to dismiss fundamentalists as
misfits on whom academic study is wasted. Their existence,
however, challenges academics to think more deeply about
the communicative life-world in which academic study is
located. This life-world has become a highly-specialized sub-
culture whose relationship to the outside world is not only
questioned by fundamentalism, but by liberation hermeneu-

1 See the comprehensive account in F. Strich, *Die Mythologie in der deutschen Lit-
eratur von Klopstock bis Wagner*, 2 vols (Bern and Munich: Francke Verlag,
1970, reprint of original 1910 edition).

tics and the enterprise culture. Yet, if what is being
maintained in this lecture is correct, the Old Testament has
something vitally important to say to the question that is basic
to liberation hermeneutics and enterprise culture: what is
humanity?

It may not be an exaggeration to say that the future existence of Old Testament study depends upon how it reacts to the
questions that are being put to it by liberation hermeneutics
and the enterprise culture. Yet what is really at stake is not
the existence of Old Testament study as an academic sub-
culture; the real issue is whether Old Testament scholars,
without sacrificing any of their intellectual integrity, can
make the Old Testament speak to the fundamental question of
today: what does it mean to be human? In the past, theology
has never ignored the help offered by philosophy in the work-
ing-out of its proclamation. Neo-Platonism, Aristotelianism,
Kantianism, speculative idealism and existentialism have all
been help-mates in the task. In my view, the political philosophy articulated by Habermas can not only help us today to
understand better what we are about. It can help us to
expound the Old Testament as a set of documents that address
fundamental contemporary questions about the nature and
destiny of the human race.

READING 'THE TEXT'
AND READING 'BEHIND THE TEXT'
The 'Cain and Abel' Story in a Context of Liberation

Gerald West

Introduction

'The time has come. The moment of truth has arrived. South Africa has been plunged into a crisis that is shaking the foundations and there is every indication that the crisis has only just begun and that it will deepen and become even more threatening in the months to come. It is the KAIROS or moment of truth not only for apartheid but also for the Church' (*The Kairos Document* [1987], p. 4). Thus begins *The Kairos Document*'s challenge to the church in South Africa, a challenge which, the Kairos theologians go on to argue, 'impels us *to return to the Bible* and to search the Word of God for a message that is relevant to what we are experiencing in South Africa today' (p. 17). South Africa is in a crisis, perhaps even *the* crisis of its history. This crisis is evident in the uncertainty, the tension, and the violence which are never far from the surface. This crisis is also evident in the interpretation of the Bible, a book which has played such a significant role in South Africa's history. And as David Tracy points out, 'A crisis of interpretation within any tradition eventually becomes a demand to interpret this very process of interpretation' (Tracy, 1987: 8). But this crisis is also a *kairos*, an opportunity, to explore crucial hermeneutic questions in a context where they matter.

This essay considers two modes of reading the 'Cain and Abel' story in the South African context. One mode of reading has its focus on the text while the other has its focus behind the text. It is not my concern to ask which method is 'right', but rather to analyse what is going on methodologically in a particular mode of reading and how this relates to the struggle for liberation in South Africa. In the South African situation these are not merely 'interesting' questions, they are questions that matter.

This essay is concerned specifically with those who are committed to reading the Bible within and for the community of struggle, the community of those who are victims of and who are opposed by the apartheid system.[1] The essay will focus on the work of two black South African writers, Allan A. Boesak and Itumeleng J. Mosala, particularly on their readings of the 'Cain and Abel' story. I will include a detailed outline of their respective readings of the 'Cain and Abel' story and an analysis of their particular modes of reading. This discussion will lead into a analysis of the relationship between a particular mode of reading and the liberation situation. Finally I will sketch why it is that such analysis matters, particularly in the South African context, but also within Biblical Studies generally.

Reading the Text

Boesak's reading of the story itself begins with a brief discussion of the possible significance of the names 'Abel' (perhaps derived from the Hebrew *hebel*) and 'Cain' (Hebrew *qayin*), suggesting that 'In this story, then, there is a younger brother, a smaller and weaker brother; and a stronger brother, the ruler, the creator' (Boesak, 1984: 149).

He then draws attention to what he sees to be the narrative emphasis on 'brother': 'The author time after time underlines the fact that Cain and Abel were brothers. We are not to forget that they were brothers' (p. 149). Boesak then elaborates what it means to be a brother:

> This responsibility involves being human in community with one another in God's world. It means to seek together

1   For further details on 'the struggle' see Albert Nolan's recent work *God in South Africa* (1988).

for true humanity; to attempt together to make something of God's objectives visibly operative in the world; to let something of God's own heart become visible in fraternal relationships; and, in corporate relationship to history, to humanize the world and keep it humanized. This is what it means to be a brother (p. 149).

But 'Cain rejects this human responsibility in the most abominable manner: he murders his brother'. 'The story does not focus merely on a crime, but on the most heinous crime. Cain did not kill some anonymous person; he murdered his own brother.' In other words, 'this story concerns the core of humanity' (p. 149).

Boesak detects sarcasm and humour in Cain's response to God's question, 'Where is you brother Abel?' 'Cain asks God, "Am I the herdsmen of the herdsmen?" But God does not share Cain's humour, for the matter at hand is very serious. It involves life and death' (pp. 149-50).

God's punishment of Cain is then discussed in some detail. Boesak underlines Cain's fear, even though Cain is not punished with death. 'Why do you do this to me? My punishment is too heavy to bear.' Boesak argues that 'Cain knows, however, what it means that he no longer fits in with the land'. As a farmer the 'whole of his life and all his hope is bound up with the land'. 'Now Cain must leave all this. He no longer possesses the land. He must go and live in the land of Nod.' And, Boesak continues, 'Nod is "east of Eden"—that is, away from the land that God designated as the place where Cain and Abel were to live human lives, where they were to be men, brothers, real people. Eden was the place, the garden, where true humanity was born; where God brought people together; where God said, "Here, together, in community, we begin human history"' (p. 150). Boesak concludes his discussion of the first curse by developing the image of 'the earth'. 'The earth can no longer be fruitful for him. It is after all the same earth that opened its mouth and drank the blood of Abel, his brother. Therefore, the earth can no longer bear the fruit for him. The earth mourns. The earth chokes in blood, and cannot respond to Cain. The earth can no longer converse with him. The earth can no longer return anything to him. Cain's relationship to the land is ruptured' (pp. 150-51).

Cain also comes under a second curse. 'He must be a wanderer, a vagabond, in the world. Nod is a "state of the mind" in which one wanders forever. Cain must live as someone who has no goal. Never again will he be at rest. Never again will there be fixed ground, a known place, beneath his feet. Never again will there be a place where he belongs, where he is at home' (p. 151).

Having followed the contours of the text Boesak then relates his reading to 'us', and more specifically to the South African situation.

> What does this mean for us? I think the story meant to tell us that oppressors shall have no place on God's earth. Oppressors have no home. Oppressors do not belong, are not at home in God's objectives for this world. They have gone out of bounds. They have removed themselves from the world. Cain did not only break his relationship to the land, but also his relationship to God. Because Abel is no longer there, there is no longer a relationship to God. This is what the story says. When Abel no longer lives and Cain is 'brotherless,' then Cain immediately is 'Godless'. 'Look', he says, 'you hide your face from me. You send me from your presence.' Oppressors have no place, no rest for their souls (p. 151).

Later he adds, 'those who take another's life can never again be certain about their own life. They continue to wonder when the hour of vengeance will toll for them.' The 'violent and oppressive are very anxious, uncertain, frightened people. They live in anxiety and fear because they are the constant cause of anxiety and fear in others. They must live with their own conscience. They do not sleep well. It may appear that they do, but that appearance is deceptive. They do not have rest for their souls' (p. 152).

Boesak goes on to say that he could 'give countless illustrations of this from South Africa' (p. 152).[1] After a number of illustrations he sums up:

> And so whites remain anxious and fearful. They live in anxiety because they never know what might happen next. The really frightened ones who are eaten up with anxiety, are

1 Although he mentions South Africa for the first time here, his reading is pregnant with allusions to the South African context.

those who think that peace lies in the insecurity and oppression of the other; those who think that peace lies in the ability to destroy the other; to take the life of the other; those who think that to intimidate the other and to threaten the death of the other constitutes their own security and certainty (p. 153).

Boesak then continues with his reading of the story. 'Cain continues to live. He continues to live, I suspect, to make it clear that his type of life—a life of restlessness, uneasiness, uncertainty, violence, ceaseless wandering, a life in which there is no peace with God and one's fellows—is not what is intended for those who earnestly seek God.' 'There is a second reason', he continues, 'why Cain remains alive: God gives Cain an opportunity to ask forgiveness' (p. 154). Boesak does not offer any support for the latter contention from the story; instead he goes to the New Testament and the example of Jesus who forgives the murderer on the cross.

Boesak then returns to the story and follows its final form through the 'Lamech story'. 'History moves on. Does Cain's generation learn anything? Does it improve? Or do we learn rather, that Cain's generation cannot change, cannot improve? It seems that things cannot change' (p. 154). However, once again he draws on the New Testament. 'Here again, we can see what a difference Jesus of Nazareth makes in human history: the words of Lamech are reversed by Jesus. Lamech says that he will be avenged seventy-seven times over. But Jesus tells his followers to forgive others not seventy-seven times, but seventy times seven times' (p. 155).

Once again the South African is addressed. 'Is it possible to transcend our present situation in South Africa? Can it still happen? I do not know. I do not know how to tell the Blacks in South Africa to forgive seventy times seven times—those who have seen their own children shot and killed in the streets. I do not know how to tell them this' (p. 155). Boesak goes on to catalogue other examples of black suffering and oppression. In the face of such oppression, he argues, 'We ought not to speak too hastily about forgiveness and similar matters'. 'And yet', he continues, 'we read these words of the Lord, words that we cannot avoid. Ought we to believe that what is impossible for us is possible for God? With God all things are possible, including forgiveness welling up out of the hearts of suffering and oppressed Black South Africans. That too. Precisely that' (pp. 155-56).

Boesak concludes his reading of the Cain and Abel story by following the final form of the text through to its end in the birth of Seth.

> The story of Cain ends with the report of a joyful event. Adam and Eve have another son. His name is Seth. Eve says, 'God has given me another son in the place of Abel whom Cain killed'. She does not repudiate history. She does not bypass this tragic event as if it had not happened. She does not ignore reality. She knows this, only this: with this child God wishes her to begin all over again with her—and therefore also with other people. The story ends not in tragedy but in words of hope: 'At that time men began to call upon the name of the Lord' (Gen. 5.26). After murder, after death, after annihilation and inhumanity, God begins again (p. 156).

'That, brothers and sisters, is, I think, the most hopeful word in the gospel of Jesus Christ. After oppression: murder, terror, inhumanity, apartheid, and the gobbling up of the profits of apartheid, and finally death—after all this, God still wishes to begin all over again with us' (p. 157).

In his reading of the 'Cain and Abel' story Boesak does not advocate an explicit methodology underlying his mode of reading. Although he refers to the author he shows no interest in the author's intentions except as these are manifest in the text. Also, he gives no evidence here of any interest in the usual historical-critical concerns.[1] Throughout his reading of the Cain and Abel story he follows the final form of the text with careful attention to literary detail.

However, attention to the way in which Boesak describes his mode of reading another text, *Revelation* (Boesak, 1987), may be useful here to clarify his reading methodology. He rejects a number of interpretative approaches for two reasons: either they are too historical and so lack relevance for today or they are too symbolic and so show little concern for the historical context of the text. He advocates, rather, a

---

1 Boesak uses the phrase 'text behind the text', but by it he means the presuppositions and interests behind *theologies* (Boesak, 1977: 84-85).

contemporary-historical understanding of this text. Such an approach argues that this text cannot be understood outside of the historical and political context of its time. But this approach also argues that the book has relevance in more than one historical moment; in other words, 'we see with some astonishment how truly, how authentically, that John, in describing his own time, is describing the times in which we live' (pp. 28-29). In sum, Boesak is interested in the broad historical and political context to which *the text* refers and so draws on historical-critical research. However, he always reads the text in its final form and always has his focus on the text itself rather than on the historical (and sociological) particularities behind the text. Although he is here dealing with a rather different genre of text, I would argue that what he calls a 'contemporary-historical understanding' sums up his approach to the 'Cain and Abel' story as well.

There are three interpretative strategies which consistently underlie Boesak's mode of reading.

A crucial interpretative strategy in Boesak's mode of reading is to read this text from within a particular community of struggle, the oppressed black South African community. This interpretative strategy is quite explicit in his reading of the 'Cain and Abel' story.[1]

A related interpretative strategy is evident in the link Boesak establishes between this story and the community of struggle. In his initial reflections on this story he argues that we ought not to regard the story of Cain and Abel as either remote from or irrelevant to us today.

> The story of Cain and Abel is a story about two types or kinds of people. It is a very human story that is still being enacted today. This story does not tell us in the first place what happened once upon a time; rather, it tells us about something that happens today. Because this story is a human story, we

---

1 Boesak makes a point of relating his sermon to the Dutch and European context but his own South African context is clearly predominant. See also, for example, Boesak, 1977, where he argues that 'theology must engage itself in the *black* experience, an experience shared by, and articulated by the community' (p. 16). Later he says the point is 'not whether theology is determined by interests, but whether it is being determined by the interests of the poor and the oppressed, or by those of the oppressor' (p. 85).

find very human elements in it and elements from our own human history (p. 148).

Boesak's second interpretative strategy, then, is to advocate a common humanity connecting this 'very human story' with 'our own human history'. This identity and commonality between story and reader are what enables understanding to take place, and what bridges the hermeneutic gap between 'then' and 'now'. However, expressing this connection in these general, universal terms is not sufficient. Boesak goes on to make it quite clear that his specific concern is in the connection between the situation of struggle within the text and the context of struggle in South Africa.

Thirdly, it should be quite clear by now that Boesak's focus is on the text. He reads the final form of the 'Cain and Abel' story with careful attention to its literary characteristics. In addition, he not only reads the text as a self-contained story but also as part of the Christian canon.

But there are a number of features of Boesak's mode of reading which are not clear. As Boesak does not articulate a clear methodology underlying his mode of reading it is not clear *why* Boesak adopts this particular mode of reading.[1] As well it is not clear whether the focus for Boesak is on the struggle of the *characters* within the narrative or on *real people* who are represented in the narrative.[2]

We turn now to the relationship between Boesak's mode of reading and the struggle for liberation in South Africa. Throughout his reading he allows the story to speak to us today: his concern is not 'what happened once upon a time' but rather that 'it tells us about something that happens today'

---

1 I do not think that Boesak's focus on the text is simply a question of audience. Carlos Mesters' retelling of the exodus story, which is based on the sociological hypotheses of Norman Gottwald and others, is an excellent example of presenting such socio-historical interests to the people (Mesters, 1988). In other words, if Boesak was particularly interested in preaching from behind the text he could use a similar presentation. A more likely reason for this focus might relate to how Boesak sees his work in relation to the tradition within which he stands.

2 In his discussion of Cain's punishment Boesak makes the following aside: 'in that day, after all, human beings were more primitive than we are' (p. 150). Leaving aside the problems with the word 'primitive', it is not clear what time period Boesak is referring to here. Does 'in that day' refer to the time when the story was written or the primeval setting?

(p. 148). The link between the text and the liberation struggle today is based on two factors: first, a general commitment to read the text from within *a particular situation of struggle*, and second, *an analogy of struggle* which links the present South African situation of struggle with a past situation of struggle, a situation of struggle which is located *in the text*.

Reading Behind-the-Text

Mosala's reading of the 'Cain and Abel' story explicitly arises out of his response to Boesak's reading of the story (Mosala, 1987: 22-23). My concern at this stage is not to examine Mosala's critique of Boesak's reading but to construct from his own comments his reading of the 'Cain and Abel' story.

Having briefly summarized Boesak's reading of the 'Cain and Abel' story, Mosala briefly outlines his own reading. He argues that

> there is ample evidence to suggest that the Davidic monarchy, which forms the historical backdrop of the J-story we encounter in Genesis 4, inaugurated a relentless process of land dispossession of the village peasants in Israel. What the story as it stands now seeks to do is to validate this landlessness of the village peasants on the ground—hardly convincing—that their harvest was not an acceptable offering to the Lord.
>
> On this issue of an acceptable or a non-acceptable offering to the Lord, a critical biblical hermeneutics of liberation would have immediately thought of the question of tribute exaction by the ruling classes of the Israelite monarchy from the village peasants. This perspective would have raised the question of the class struggle in monarchic Israel and how its reality is signified in a discursive ideological textual practice such as Genesis 4 represents.
>
> There is also evidence that village peasants often resisted encroachments on their *nahalahs*—their inherited or family lands (2 Kgs 21). While no indication of their victories exists in the texts of the Bible, except in the New Testament (Matt. 21.33ff.), it is reasonable to believe that the death of Abel may stand for one such victory. But of course the text comes to us from the hands of the ruling class and thus one could hardly expect a textual celebration of that death. The class and ideological commitments of Genesis 4 are unequivocal. This fac-

tor, however, is not immediately obvious to the reader. It requires a reading that issues out of a firm grounding in the struggle for liberation, as well as a basis in critical theoretical perspectives which can expose the deep structure of a text (pp. 22-24).

Mosala articulates a clear methodology which underlies his mode of reading. His interpretative strategies are clear. His initial strategy as far as the text is concerned is to use historical-critical methods to determine the text and its context. For Mosala the important consequence of applying these methods is that they place the text in its socio-historical setting, which in this case is the monarchic period. With the identification of this setting Mosala then moves into a historical-materialist analysis of the text.

And here we see Mosala's focus. It is on the historical-materialist context behind the text of which the text itself is a product.[1] Mosala's materialist method incorporates two related interpretative strategies: it inquires into the material conditions of the text (which includes an analysis of the nature of the mode of production, the constellation of classes necessitated by that mode, and the nature of the ideological manifestations arising out of and referring back to that mode of production) and the ideological conditions of the text (including the class origins of the text and the class interests of the text). Underlying these inquiries is the recognition that the Bible is a site of specific historical-cultural class conflicts (Mosala 1986: 187).

Not only are these two related strategies applied to the text, they are also applied to the biblical reader. Inseparable from the material and ideological conditions of the text are the material and ideological conditions of the 'biblical reader', and these need to be investigated in similar terms (p. 187).

---

1 Mosala's choice of this particular sociological method is quite deliberate. Mosala offers a detailed critique of the ideological and political agendas accompanying the historical-critical methods and other sociological methods. 'The essence of this objection is not that the sociological approaches employed by biblical scholars should not have had an ideological and political agenda. On the contrary, the plea is for an open acknowledgment of the class interests that are being represented and thus an acknowledgment of at least the social limitation of the methods' (Mosala, 1986: 30).

The point that is being made here is that the ideological condition and commitment of the reader issuing out of the class
circumstances of such a reader are of immense hermeneutical significance. The biblical hermeneutics of liberation is
thoroughly tied up with the political commitments of the
reader. This means that not only is the Bible a product and
record of class struggles, but it is also a site of similar struggles acted out by the oppressors and oppressed, exploiters
and exploited of our society even as they read the Bible.

Those, therefore, that are committed to the struggles of the
black oppressed and exploited people cannot ignore the history, culture, and ideologies of the dominated black people as
their primary hermeneutical starting point. There can be no
Black Theology of liberation and no corresponding biblical
hermeneutics of liberation outside of the black struggle for
both survival and liberation. Such a struggle, however,
requires being as clear about issues in the black community
as possible (pp. 196-97).

We now turn to the relationships between Mosala's mode of
reading and the liberation struggle today. There are three
major links: first, a general commitment to read the text from
within *a particular situation of struggle*; second, *an analogy of
struggle* which links the present South African situation of
struggle with a past situation of struggle, a situation of struggle which is located *behind the text*; and third, *an analogy of
method* which applies a similar method of historical-materialist analysis to the present South African situation of struggle
as to the analysis of the text and situation of struggle behind
the text.

Readings and the Liberation Struggle

My analysis of the two readings can now be taken further as
we compare and contrast Boesak's and Mosala's respective
modes of reading.

An important similarity is their common commitment to
read the Bible from within the community of struggle in
South Africa. A related similarity is the important role the
analogy of struggle plays in their readings. In other words,
their common commitment to the liberation struggle in South
Africa provides an interpretative strategy which links the

situation of struggle within or behind the text with their own situation or struggle.

In summary, both Boesak and Mosala use an analogy of struggle to link a past struggle with their present struggle. But they differ on where this past struggle is to be located. For Boesak, the focus is the struggle portrayed within the text, a struggle which we have access to by a careful reading of the final form of the text from the perspective of the struggle for liberation. For Mosala the focus is the struggle behind the text, a struggle which the text in most instances masks and to which we only have access by a historical-materialist reading of the text from the perspective of historical-materialist understanding of the struggle for liberation. For Mosala the actual past situation is of secondary importance while the method of analysis itself is foregrounded.[1]

I will now briefly outline some of the implications of the discussion so far. In other words, I will outline why it is that such analysis matters, particularly in the South African context.

Grounds for dialogue

I would claim that the similarities between Boesak and Mosala, specifically their common commitment to read the Bible from within the South African community of struggle and the fact that this commitment shapes their reading strategies, albeit differently, are sufficient grounds for dialogue concerning their differences.

More importantly, I would suggest that such dialogue is not only possible but also vital in the South African context, particularly among those who are committed to reading the Bible and within and for the struggle for liberation in South Africa. Among those sharing such a commitment are those who adopt a variety of modes of reading the Bible. At this time when the 'Prophetic' voice of the Church is under attack by both 'State Theology' and 'Church Theology',[2] dialogue

1 I have argued elsewhere that this is also the central link between Norman Gottwald's work and liberation struggles today (G.O. West, 1987).
2 I use these terms as they are used in *The Kairos Document*. Briefly, 'State Theology' is the theology of the South African apartheid State which 'is simply the theological justification of the status quo with its racism, capitalism and totali-

among those who share a commitment to the struggle for liberation in South Africa is vital. Among those committed to reading the Bible within the community, with their differences, there are not only sufficient grounds for such dialogue and critique, but, I would claim, necessary grounds.[1]

So it is with a clear recognition of the important similarities in their modes of reading that I now turn to some of the questions that the differences in their modes of reading raise.

A question of strategy

An obvious question would be whether a particular commitment to a particular community of struggle demands not only a commitment to reading the Bible from within and for the community of struggle but also certain interpretative strategies. This is what Mosala is advocating in his analogy method, as is clear when he argues that 'The fundamental objection that is being raised in this thesis against the biblical hermeneutics of black theology is that not only does it suffer from an "unstructural understanding of the Bible" but, both as a consequence and as a reason, it also suffers from an "unstructural understanding" of the black experience and struggle' (Mosala, 1987: 20).[2] Although Mosala is here offering a critique of Boesak's mode of reading, he is not calling into question Boesak's commitment to the community of struggle. 'The problem is basically one of "contradiction". It has nothing to do with the difficult area of the interface between personal existential commitments and structural-ideological locations as well as frameworks of political activity. It is not enough to be existentially committed to the struggles of the oppressed

tarianism. It blesses injustice, canonises the will of the powerful and reduces the poor to passivity, obedience and apathy' (p. 6). 'Church Theology' is in a limited, guarded and cautious way critical of apartheid. 'Its criticism, however, is superficial and counter-productive because instead of engaging in an in-depth analysis of the signs of our times, it relies upon a few stock ideas derived from Christian tradition and then uncritically and repeatedly applies them to our situation' (p. 11). *The Kairos Document* moves towards a 'Prophetic Theology', a theology which 'speaks to the particular circumstances of this crisis, a response that does not give the impression of sitting on the fence but is clearly and unambiguously taking a stand' (p. 18).

1 I am not using these words as logical terms.
2 The phrase 'unstructural understanding' is taken from Norman Gottwald. See below.

and exploited people. One has also to effect a theoretical break with the assumptions and perspectives of the dominant discourse of a stratified society' (p. 26).

More specifically with respect to Boesak's mode of reading, which Mosala calls 'this existential appropriation of the Bible', he argues that

> To the extent... that this existential appropriation of the Bible by Boesak is founded on questionable historical and theoretical grounds it must be asserted in agreement with Hugo Assmann, contrary to Boesak, that there is a need to reject a 'fundamentalism of the Left' composed of short-circuits: attempts to transplant biblical paradigms and situations into our world without understanding their historical circumstances. It is equally false to state that the whole biblical framework, with its infinite variety of paradigms and situations, is an adequate basis for establishing a satisfactory dialectics of hermeneutical principles (p. 104).

Mosala also cites Norman Gottwald, who makes a similar point to Assmann when he argues that

> ...while invoking biblical symbols of liberation, liberation theologians seldom push those biblical symbols all the way back to their socio-historic foundations, so that we can grasp concretely the inner-biblical strands of oppression and liberation in all their stark multiplicity and contradictory interactions... A thinness of social structural analysis and a thinness of biblical analysis combine to give many expressions of liberation theology the look of devotional or polemical tracts... The picking and choosing of biblical resources may not carry sufficient structural analysis of biblical societies to make a proper comparison with the present possible. Likewise, those most oriented to biblical grounding for liberation theology may lack knowledge or interest in the history of social forms and ideas from biblical times to the present, so that unstructural understanding of the Bible may simply reinforce and confirm unstructural understanding of the present (p. 5).

Mosala recognizes that interpreters like Boesak are clearly correct 'in detecting glimpses of liberation and of a determinate social movement galvanised by a powerful religious ideology in the biblical text'. However, he argues, 'It is not the existence of this which is in question. Rather, the problem

being addressed here is one of developing an adequate hermeneutical framework which can rescue those liberative
themes from the biblical text. This task will not be successfully
performed by a denial of oppressive structures which frame
what liberative themes the text encodes' (p. 28).[1] In other
words, modes of reading like that of Boesak's, 'existentialist
uses of the Bible in the struggle for liberation',

> cannot be allowed to substitute for a theoretically well-
> grounded biblical hermeneutics of liberation. The reason for
> this is that while texts that are against oppressed people may
> be coopted by the interlocutors of the liberation struggle, the
> ideological roots of these texts in oppressive practices mean
> that the texts are capable of undergirding the interests of the
> oppressors even when used by the oppressed. In other
> words, oppressive texts cannot be totally tamed or subverted
> into liberative texts (p. 18).

So like Terry Eagleton's 'revolutionary cultural worker', biblical interpreters in the community of struggle must not only be
'projective' and 'appropriative' but also 'polemical' in their
reading of the Bible (p. 21).

But are Mosala's interpretative strategies the only ones we
ought to use in the South African context or struggle? Certainly there are those interpreters in the community of struggle who argue that the text, or more of it than Mosala would
accept, does not mask but in fact reflects the struggle behind
the text. For example, Gunter Wittenberg argues that 'during
the Solomonic era theologians responded in different ways to
the challenges posed by the political dispensation. Theologians
at the court were eager to legitimize Solomon's rule and to
develop a state theology.' But, he continues, 'This "theology
from above" was, however, challenged by a resistance theology "from below" both in Israel and Judah' (Wittenberg, 1988:
16). More significantly, Wittenberg argues that the primeval
history (Gen. 2–11) is not 'an effort in royal theology' but in
fact the opposite, 'it is an unmistakable critique of the

---

1 Mosala argues that 'Biblical scholars have always been aware of the tendency in
   biblical literature to use older traditions to address the needs of new situations',
   but that until recently they have not recognized the cultic-ideological origins of
   the texts of the Bible. In other words, 'The issue that has not been faced squarely is
   what kind of additions [and whose] are they' (Mosala, 1986: 185-86, 195).

Jerusalemite state theology' (p. 14).[1] He uses the 'Cain and
Abel' story as an example. Following B. Oded and Gottwald he
argues that the genealogy of Noah 'reflects the basic division
between the city and the countryside. The key variables,
according to Gottwald, in discriminating the two contrasting
forms of socio-political life are political dominion versus political decentralization, and social stratification versus social
egalitarianism' (p. 15). Wittenberg continues, 'While state
theology in Jerusalem has a city perspective, the author of the
primeval history leaves no doubt about where his sympathies
lie. His perspective is the perspective of the Judean "people of
the land"' (p. 15).

> This basic contrast is also highlighted in the story of Cain
> and Abel. Abel is the prototype of the Judean herdsman
> while Cain, after the murder of his brother, wanders
> towards the east and becomes the founder of the city, just
> like Nimrod in the genealogy of Ham. Cain is the ancestor of
> Lamech, the prototype of a man of violence, who boasts that
> he will revenge every wrong done to him not sevenfold but
> seventy-seven fold (Gen. 4.24). The message of the Yahwist is
> clear. Violence and the upheaval in societies emanate from
> the strong man, the builder of cities and empires (p. 16).

Clearly Wittenberg here addresses Mosala on his own terms,
using a similar mode of reading.

But is there a *'theoretically well-grounded* biblical hermeneutics of liberation' which could support something like
Boesak's mode of reading?[2] An attempt at such a answer
might develop along post-critical lines in a literary, canonical,
or a metaphoric/symbolic direction. Nothing like this has yet
emerged from biblical interpreters in the South African community of struggle.[3]

---

1   Wittenberg agrees with Crüsemann and others that the 'Yahwistic' primeval his-
    tory originally had no literary connection with the patriarchal narrative. 'Gen.
    2–11 is an independent literary work and has to be interpreted on its own.' 'If this
    is correct', he continues, 'then we need to ask whether Brueggemann and others
    are right when they claim that the "Yahwistic" primeval history is "an effort in
    royal theology"' (p. 14).
2   The italics are mine.
3   But see for example J.S. Croatto's *Exodus: A Hermeneutics of Freedom*. Croatto,
    who bases his mode of reading on the work of Paul Ricoeur and Hans-Georg
    Gadamer, summarizes his mode of reading as follows: 'we can speak of a circu-
    lar dialectic between event and word, and, by the same token, between kerygma

However, whether or not modes of reading similar to that of Boesak's have *a theoretically well-grounded* biblical hermeneutics of liberation, they do have a biblical hermeneutics of liberation, a hermeneutics which I have attempted to sketch. Given the existence of these two modes of reading, there are a number of other important questions which arise out of their differences.

A question of tradition

There is the question of the interpreter's relationship with the Christian tradition. What are the implications of embracing these respective readings for the ecclesiastical traditions in which we stand? For example, it is extremely unlikely that a significant group like the African Independent Churches would ever embrace Mosala's social scientific, historical-materialist reading of the Bible but would probably be receptive to Boesak's final form, canonical, and Christian reading of the Bible. In their booklet, *Speaking for Ourselves*, they write: 'We read the Bible as a book that comes from God and we take every word in the Bible seriously'. 'Some people will say that we are therefore "fundamentalists". We do not know whether that word applies to us or not but we are not interested in any interpretation of the Bible that softens or waters down its message... We do not have the same problems about the Bible as White people have with their Western scientific mentality' (p. 26). In other words, what are the implications of Boesak's affirmation of the biblical tradition and Mosala's suspicion (perhaps even rejection) of the biblical tradition for these and other interpretative groupings?[1]

A question of class

A related question concerns the extent to which these respective readings are accessible to the people, or more importantly,

---

and situation, between the biblical word on liberation and our processes of liberation. But a hermeneutic reading of the biblical message occurs only when the reading *supersedes the first contextual meaning* (not only that of the author but also that of the first readers). This happens *through the unfolding of a surplus-of-meaning disclosed by a new question addressed to the text*' (p. 3).

1 See Cady (1986) for an illuminating discussion on aspects of this discussion with particular reference to feminist readings of the Bible.

the extent to which such readings emanate from the people. Recent research into the ways in which a cross-section of 'ordinary' South African people read the Bible suggest that hermeneutically these ordinary interpreters are closer to Boesak's mode of reading than they are to Mosala's. One could argue that a final form or literary reading, whether it is precritical, fundamentalist or post-critical, is a more egalitarian reading, whereas a socio-scientific reading is produced by a new middle class, elitist, social scientific 'priesthood'.[1] And yet research also shows that there is a considerable openness among ordinary interpreters to historical and sociological perspectives (Draper and West, 1989). Mosala himself argues that black interpreters like Boesak and others 'have been surpassed by the largely illiterate black working class and poor peasantry who have defied the canon of Scripture, with its ruling class ideological basis, by appropriating the Bible in their own way using the cultural tools emerging out of their struggle for survival' (Mosala 1986: 184). Unfortunately, Mosala does not elaborate on this.

The role of the 'organic intellectual' is obviously a question which arises here. Many of the middle class involved in contexts of liberation find Gramsci's conception of organic intellectuals helpful. Gramsci views organic intellectuals as leaders and thinkers directly tied into a particular community of struggle primarily by means of institutional affiliations. Organic intellectuals combine theory and action, and relate popular culture and religion to structural social change.[2] Clearly the roles of such organic intellectuals would differ substantially within the two modes of reading. For example, the role of Carlos Mesters in *God's Project*, a sociological

1 In outlining the shift within Latin American theology between 'two lines' of liberation theology, one essentially a middle-class product and the other essentially the product of the 'common people', Segundo notes that in the former 'the *social sciences* are used in a way similar to the use theology made of philosophy in past centuries. The social sciences provide the theologian who wants to carry out a de-ideologizing task with valuable cognitive tools, but tools which . . . are beyond the grasp of the majority of people' (Segundo, 1985: 28). Here, and in the rest of his essay, Segundo captures the complexities and the tensions of these 'two lines'. Although the 'two lines' do not correspond exactly with my two modes of reading there are some relevant connections.
2 See Hoare, 1971, particularly pp. 3-23. See also G.O. West, 1982: 121.

retelling of the Bible story which is based on the work of Norman Gottwald and others, is substantially different from that of Ernesto Cardenal in *The Gospel of Solentiname*, the recorded commentary of *campesinos* discussing various biblical texts.[1]

A question of truth

A related question concerns the truth claims of the respective readings. One could argue that the truth of a reading which focuses on what is behind the text is the social scientific evidence which supports that reading, but what kinds of truth claims could one make concerning literary, canonical, or metaphoric/symbolic readings? Or should we go further and argue that none of these kinds of truth really matters but that what we need to do is to accept 'a practical and communal knowledge, which tests the truth of a position [or reading] by asking whether and how it might apply to the practice—that is, the history—of the community'? (Dean, 1986: 272).[2] Such questions and other related questions will need to be discussed and analysed in our South African context.

Grounds for challenge

I suggested in my introduction that this discussion has implications not only for our own context of struggle but also for biblical studies generally.

As literary and sociological modes of reading are among the most dominant modes of reading in biblical studies many of the issues raised here are pertinent to the wider debate.

However, the most important challenge arises from Boesak's and Mosala's commitment to reading the Bible from within and for a particular community, the community of struggle, the community of the poor, the powerless, and the oppressed in South Africa. Biblical studies has never been 'neutral' or 'objective', something which the poor, the power-

---

1 The former is an English translation, translated in South Africa, of Carlos Mesters' work. The illustrations, which form an integral part of the presentation, have been adapted for the South African context.
2 Here William Dean is putting forward the argument of Richard Bernstein's *Beyond Objectivism and Relativism: Science, Hermeneutics, and Praxis* (Philadelphia: University of Pennsylvania Press, 1983).

less, and the oppressed everywhere have long recognized. The challenge from the South African context of struggle is, first, to affirm that one does and should have commitments in reading the Bible and, secondly, to argue that these commitments should be shaped by the poor, the powerless, and the oppressed.[1]

Conclusion

In conclusion, I realize that many central questions are still unanswered. For example, are these two modes complementary? Are they opposed? These are questions yet to be addressed and answered by those committed to reading the Bible in the South African context of struggle. Of course, as attempts to liberate and to humanize the same people through the same Christian faith, they should be considered as complementary. Nevertheless, they are based on different presuppositions, they have different strategies and their methods are not easily compatible. Perhaps the only thing we can take for granted is that reading the Bible from within and for the struggle for liberation is profoundly alive in our country, although taking different forms. It is my hope that these different forms will prove to be convergent.

But in trying to focus attention on the important modes of reading which shape our struggle my aim has been not only to provide an analysis of different reading methodologies. My purpose has also been to challenge. The challenge is to move away from the notion of biblical studies as the pursuit of disinterested truth to something more human and transformative, something which is shaped by a self-critical solidarity with the victims of history.[2, 3]

---

1   I would be concerned to express this call in both socio-political and existential terms, along the lines drawn by Cornel West in his 'Introduction' in West, 1982.

2   The similarities between this conclusion and Segundo's conclusion are deliberate (Segundo, 1985: 29). The phrase 'solidarity with victims' is taken from Matthew Lamb's excellent work by that title. See Lamb, 1982.

3   I gratefully acknowledge those whose comments have shaped this essay, particularly the staff and post-graduates in the Department of Theological Studies in the the University of Natal, and Stephen Fowl, an editor of this volume.

BIBLIOGRAPHY

African Independent Churches, *Speaking for Ourselves*. Braam-
    fontein: Institute for Contextual Theology, n.d.
Assmann, H. *Theology for a Nomad Church*. Maryknoll, N.Y.: Orbis,
    1983.
Bernstein, B. *Beyond Objectivism and Relativism: Science, Hermeneu-
    tics, and Praxis*. Philadelphia: University of Pennsylvania
    Press, 1983.
Boesak, A. *Black and Reformed: Apartheid, Liberation and the
    Calvinist Tradition*. Johannesburg: Skotaville, 1984,
    pp. 148-57.
—*Comfort and Protest: Reflections on the Apocalypse of John of Pat-
    mos*. Philadelphia: The Westminster Press, 1987.
—*Farewell to Innocence: A Social-Ethical Study of Black Theology and
    Black Power*. Johannesburg: Raven, 1977.
Cady, L.E. 'Hermeneutics and Tradition: The Role of the Past in Juris-
    prudence and Theology', *HTR* 79 (1986), pp. 439-63.
Cardenal, E. *The Gospel in Solentiname*. New York: Orbis Books, 1976.
Croatto, J.S. *Exodus: A Hermeneutics of Freedom*. Maryknoll, N.Y.:
    Orbis Books, 1981.
Crüsemann, F. 'Die Eigenständigkeit der Urgeschichte. Ein Beitrag
    zur Diskussion von den "Jahwisten"', in J. Jeremias and
    L. Perlitt (eds.), *Die Botschaft und die Boten. Festschrift
    für Hans Walter Wolff zum 70. Geburtstag*. Neukirchen-
    Vluyn: Neukirchener Verlag, 1981.
Dean, W. 'The Challenge of the New Historicism', *JR* 66 (1986), pp. 261-
    81.
Draper, J.A., and West, G.O. 'Anglicans and Scripture in South
    Africa', in F. England and T.J.M. Paterson (eds.), *Bounty
    in Bondage*. Johannesburg: Ravan, 1989.
Eagleton, T. *Walter Benjamin, or Towards a Revolutionary Criticism*.
    London: Verso, 1981.
Gottwald, N.K. *The Tribes of Yahweh. A Sociology of the Religion of
    Liberated Israel, 1250–1050 BCE*. London: SCM, 1980.
Hoare, Q., and Smith, G.N. (eds.). *Selections from the Prison Notebooks
    of Antonio Gramsci*. London: Lawrence and Wishart, 1971.
The Kairos Document: Challenge to the Churches, Second Edition.
    Braamfontein: The Kairos Theologians, 1987.
Lamb, M.L. *Solidarity with Victims: Toward a Theology of Social
    Transformation*. New York: Crossroad, 1982.
Mesters, C. *God's Project*. Cape Town: The Theology Exchange Pro-
    gramme, 1988.
Mosala, I.J. *Biblical Hermeneutics and Black Theology in South
    Africa*. Ph.D. Thesis, University of Cape Town, 1987.

—'The Use of the Bible in Black Theology', in I.J. Mosala and B. Tlha-
    gale (eds.). *The Unquestionable Right To Be Free*. Johan-
    nesburg: Skotaville, 1986.
—'Social Scientific Approaches to the Bible: One Step Forward, Two
    Steps Backward', *Journal of Theology for South Africa* 55
    (1986), pp. 15-30.
Nolan, A. *God in South Africa: The Challenge of The Gospel*. Cape
    Town: David Philip; Zimbabwe: Mambo Press; London:
    Catholic Institute for International Relations; Grand
    Rapids: Eerdmans, 1988.
Oded, B. 'The Table of Nations (Genesis 10)—A Sociocultural
    Approach', *ZAW* 98 (1986), pp. 19-31.
Segundo, J.L. 'The Shift within Latin American Theology', *Journal of
    Theology for South Africa* 52 (1985), pp. 17-29.
Tracy, D. *Plurality and Ambiguity: Hermeneutics, Religion, Hope*. San
    Francisco: Harper and Row, 1987.
West, C. *Prophesy Deliverance: An Afro-American Revolutionary
    Christianity*. Philadelphia: The Westminster Press, 1982.
West, G.O. 'An Analysis of the Relationship Between Norman
    Gottwald's Sociological Reconstructions of Premonarchic
    Israel and Liberation Struggles Today' (Unpublished
    Paper, Sheffield University, 1987).
Wittenberg, G.H. *King Solomon and the Theologians*. Pietermar-
    itzburg: University of Natal Press, 1988 (= 'King Solomon
    and the Theologians', *Journal of Theology for South Africa*
    63 [1988], pp. 16-29).

DO OLD TESTAMENT STUDIES
NEED A DICTIONARY?

Philip Davies

I had better start with an apology for any misunderstanding
there may be about the topic. I am not going to talk about the
Classical Hebrew Dictionary, nor even about primary languages like Hebrew or English. My topic is a metalanguage,
the language of biblical scholarship. In fact, what I am ultimately investigating is the *nature* of biblical scholarship—and
in this context, Old Testament scholarship. What does biblical
scholarship have in common with other kinds of scholarship,
on the one hand, and what does it have with other biblically
related pursuits which are not scholarship, on the other hand?
Even to approach this topic on a broad front is well beyond a
short paper such as this one, and so I have chosen to focus on
the *language* of biblical scholarship as one particularly important and useful aspect. Examining the language not only
involves concrete data, but also responds to the philosophical
view that analysis of language is the only way to analyse
thought. According to this philosophy, language is seen not as
reflecting the real world, but as *constituting* the world, or, better, constituting *worlds*. This view of language has dominated
most recent work on parable, of course, and is therefore no
stranger to biblical scholarship itself. In the light of such an
understanding of language, or metalanguage, or discourse
(for the terms are often used interchangeably), it is reasonable
to ask what kind of world is constituted by the language of biblical scholarship, and what is the relationship of this world to
other worlds created by other forms of discourse, such as non-
academic biblical study or non-biblical scholarship.

One basic way of describing relationships between languages is through a dictionary, in which words and phrases in one language are given their correspondences in another. In the second part of this essay I shall offer some sample entries for such a dictionary. But first, I offer some comments about the language of biblical scholarship. As I have said, I am confining my remarks to Old Testament scholarship, and indeed, I do not prejudge the issue of whether Old Testament and New Testament scholarship exhibit the same dialect.

Academic Bibspeak

I begin with an obvious point about the genesis of the language of biblical scholarship, which I shall call Academic Bibspeak. It has a mixed character, in which at least three main components can be identified. First, biblical terms and concepts—'prophets', 'wisdom', 'sin', 'salvation', 'righteousness', 'covenant', 'holiness', 'God'. Second, terms drawn from the discourse of Christian doctrine and ecclesiology—the 'theology' of books, persons and authors in the Old Testament (and of the Old Testament itself!), prophets 'preaching' or 'exercising a ministry', 'piety' (in the Psalms, for example), 'worship' in the Temple. Most obvious among these elements is the term 'Old Testament' itself. Third, Academic Bibspeak also uses terms and concepts from other critical disciplines—text criticism, structuralism, historical criticism, social-science modelling.

Now each of these sets of terms belongs to a language or type of language—biblical, Christian, critical—which has its own distinct way of construing the world—or, if you like, constitutes its own distinct world. And when Academic Bibspeak takes over these terms it inevitably imports some elements of these worlds into its own world. For example, in using the word 'prophet' scholars are adopting a biblical classification of a function or type of person. But scholars who deal with such social functions recognize the total inadequacy of such a term for social description. 'Prophets' can be 'true' or 'false', and essentially the only qualification a prophet has for being so regarded is that the Old Testament calls a person one. To argue *in other terms* what a prophet is involves first and foremost abandoning the term 'prophet' and replacing it by, for example, 'intermediary'.The terms 'tribe', 'covenant', and 'Gentile' also carry special biblical resonances. The 'tribes' of Israel are not tribes in any non-biblical, i.e. anthropological, sense. Parallels drawn to the biblical covenant are not with Hittite 'covenants' but with Hittite *treaties*. 'Gentile' accepts a distinction which makes no sense in any world which is not Judaeo-centric.

Likewise with Christian terminology; 'messiah', 'the Fall narrative', 'salvation' are terms impossible to subtract from the world-view of Christian doctrine; they inevitably import the categories and values of that religion. The use of the term 'God' with a capital letter implies a belief in one god and, I think most would agree, implies the god of Christianity. Must biblical *scholarship* be monotheist, even deist? Finally, the use of critical terminology implies an acceptance of a world-view which rejects supernatural explanation and privileged access to knowledge, and which affirms natural cause and effect, the autonomy of texts, the value of sociological modelling, and so on. Functionally, it can also be said to be non-theist: divine activity does not play a role in critical language.

The problem arising from the adoption of the terminology and conceptuality of three other languages into Academic Bibspeak is simply this: have they been assimilated into a language which exhibits its own (reasonably) coherent world-view, or have they resulted in a language which has no clear world-view of its own, but drifts in and out of three different world-views? And if the latter (as I believe is the case), is such drifting deliberate or unconscious? If deliberate, the difficulty lies with the practitioner; if unconscious, the language itself is the disease.

The socio-religious factor

One way to approach the questions just raised is by considering Old Testament study from a sociological point of view (in however elementary a fashion). I don't know whether there is any other language with the same sort of composition as Academic Bibspeak. It may be claimed that other academic discourse is equally mixed. Whether this is true or not (and I doubt that it really is), the question of the status of the language we use is a matter for our own concern. What we need is a clear understanding among ourselves of what kind of world-view we as biblical scholars express, or wish to express through our language. Such a consensus has not come into being, however, and indeed the problem of language itself has scarcely been raised, let alone debated. One reason for this, I propose, lies in the social status of biblical studies, where one can see a relationship of biblical study to other academic subjects and to non-academic biblical studies which parallels the linguistic relationship and may very well reinforce it.

The socio-religious aspect of the problem itself has two dimensions. First, academic study of the Bible—or at least what is claimed to be academic study—is taught in both universities and seminaries (or theological colleges, in British parlance), and these two types of institution are not themselves necessarily devoted to the same description of reality, at least insofar as that reality is the object of academic study. The two types of institution would not in the last analysis want to pursue academic study for the same ends and would not want the same kind of language in which to express that study. The second dimension is that even in the university sector biblical scholarship is pursued, and the subject taught, largely by persons who are Christian, and most of these ordained. The Old Testament is studied mostly by, and taught mostly by, people who in admittedly varying ways and to varying extents, accept biblical values for themselves.

Neither of these sets of circumstances is to be deplored in itself. Religious denominations are entitled to train their ministrants and the holding of religious beliefs does not in itself render any person unfit for scholarship. But these considerations do not efface the problem, though they often provide a convenient pretext for complacency. If one were to ask why a practising orthodox Muslim might not be employed to teach Islam in a British university one might very well be told that his religious beliefs would inform his academic work and that he would be promoting his religion rather than analysing it critically. Are Christians exempt from this, especially when they are ordained? The problem is that Muslims do not have an equivalent of Academic Bibspeak in which the elements of Islamic doctrine can be blended in with critical terminology so as to disguise the fact that the critical work is conducted in Islamic categories, with Adam and Jesus as prophets, the Quran as word of God and the five pillars of Islam adopted into the vocabulary of the *analysis* of Islam. If it is true (as it is to me at least) that Old Testament scholarship has hitherto been essentially male, white, Western and Christian, then the feminist, black and Third World challenges to the traditions of our craft—and especially its language—do not go far enough, at least insofar as these operate within the boundaries of Christianity.

Academic Bibspeak in the university system in Britain and many other countries belongs where Old Testament scholarship is found, namely in faculties or departments of divinity or theology. That means, of course, Christian theology, since when any other theology becomes included in the curriculum the terms 'religious studies' or 'comparative religion' are used. The ethos in which academic Old Testament study takes place is religious if not confessional. This is a unique situation for an academic discipline, and it is buttressed by external as well as internal prejudices. Many if not most of our fellow academics in other disciplines, and nearly all of our own students, take it for granted that theology/biblical studies is rather different from other subjects in the way it is pursued. Colleagues are benignly suspicious of academic Bible study: a Sheffield University pro-vice chancellor (the equivalent of an American vice-president) once asked, on a visit to our department, whether it was possible to do research in biblical studies. On another occasion, the British Secretary of State for Education stated publicly that a university lecturer in theology who 'lost his faith' should not expect to be entitled to insist on his tenure.

Prospective students, too, usually tell me that they want to do Biblical Studies to strengthen or inform their religious (Christian) faith with more knowledge. This is a reasonable aim in life, but what is odd is that they assume that a British university is a normal place to expect to do this. And why not? In many Western countries everybody assumes that. Germany is the other extreme: the German system does not yet pretend that theology in the university is *not* at the service of the Church.

Hence it appears that the ambiguities of Academic Bibspeak persist at least partly because they are needed in order to allow colleagues in seminaries and in universities to speak the same language (even when the two institutions know perfectly well that they exist to serve different ends); they permit students to pursue a religious quest in the belief that they are being academic at the same time; and they also permit what is a religiously-based discipline, theology, to justify itself as a critical discipline. The ambiguities of the language of biblical scholarship are, then, sustained by the ambiguity of biblical scholarship in the academic community, as a branch of a peculiar discipline called 'theology' which—unlike other disciplines—has for its content not a body of data but an unverifiable theory, and which can mix descriptive and prescriptive language without too much difficulty.

Now, I do not overlook the immense benefits biblical scholarship enjoys by virtue of this privileged status. Without the external prejudices, particularly of our students, most of us who teach the subject would be out of a job. The number of people who want to study the Old Testament out of sheer intellectual curiosity is very small. It is an enormous pity, but there we are. It seems that the Bible is interesting as 'word of God' but otherwise rather boring. In Britain at least, it is necessary to explain on nearly every occasion, even to the most intelligent lay person, that one can be a biblical scholar without professing any religious commitment. It would not however seem to be in our interests to change the socio-religious circumstances; the price to pay, nevertheless, may be that we shall never be practising in a truly critical environment. The only other obvious alternative is to persuade people that the Bible is something which is intellectually rewarding in its own right, a proper object for academic curiosity, and that its treasures are open for the general public to marvel at. As far as I can see, novels, television, radio and the cinema occasionally treat the Bible in this way (as well as the opposite at other times!); why don't biblical scholars? The answer: a large number of us don't really believe in the (non-Christian) religious value of the Bible anyway.

What is a critical language?

I am not going to give a full definition of a critical language. That is itself a major task. However, I shall assume that all academic biblical scholars wish to think of themselves as being critical. I shall just put forward one essential requirement. It seem to me a basic principle that a critical language cannot adopt the terminology and conceptuality of its subject matter. If one is using biblical terms to analyse the Bible itself one cannot possibly avoid a biblical solipsism. Interpreting scripture by scripture is good rabbinic doctrine and good Reformation doctrine, but very bad academic criticism. The starting point, it seems to me, of all biblical criticism is a criticism of its language: in other words, a determination to *impose* a non-biblical language upon the subject matter and not to take over the terms that the subject matter gives. As I said earlier, it is impossible to take over the terms without also taking over something of the concepts. And to the extent that one builds biblical concepts into one's academic discourse, one will to that extent end up with a Bible criticized according to biblical canons. I observe that this technique widely passes for scholarship, and I ponder whether it is more dangerous than out-and-out fundamentalism because its closedness is concealed, even from the practitioner, who thinks (s)he is describing when in reality (s)he is only paraphrasing.

This basic requirement (not a definition!) of criticism, that one should use coherent categories of analysis, language and conceptuality which are not those of the subject matter itself, seems to me to drive a very sharp wedge between both the critical and the confessional contexts in which biblical scholarship operates, one which makes me personally very sceptical about the extent to which compromise between the two is possible. Critical Bible study must start somewhere other than the Bible; it must have not a biblically-prompted agenda, but its own agenda of inquiry. It must end up with its own answers to its own questions, and not with a sort of targum, with biblical categories transferred into a modern idiom. There is a possible objection to this requirement, which is an objection indeed often heard, from conservative scholars who dabble in hermeneutics, that wherever one starts from will be as subjective as if one starts from the Bible itself, and that objective criticism is a myth. That is both true and obvious. Nevertheless it both misses the point and gives the argument away. For the point is not about subjectivity versus objectivity. It is about circularity. To use a simple metaphor, it is about whether the subject matter is a hard currency or a soft one, whether it can be exchanged or not into another currency. If a currency cannot, it has no value. Studying Marxist thought in Marxist categories is equally uncritical, and the end result will always be the same: inbreeding generates freaks. Critical judgments are arrived at by describing one system in terms of a second and *independent* system. Hence, feminist criticism of the Old Testament *and indeed, biblical criticism of feminism*, both fulfil this basic requirement. This does not mean that the *result* of either or both is critical. That judgment involves further criteria. On the other hand, to analyse the Bible in terms of Christian doctrine does not seem to me entirely to fulfil the requirement insofar as the one system is derived in large part from the other. However, because they are by no means identical, an impression of critical operation can be given. Biblical scholars will readily, and rightly, claim that Christian doctrine very often distorts biblical language in much the way that films notoriously distort novels ('you've read the book, now believe the doctrine!').

By way of clarification of the issue I offer two illustrations. The first is a recent review by Walter Brueggemann of some Jeremiah commentaries, which appeared in the journal *Interpretation*. Having criticized the work of Holladay, Brueggemann turned his attention to Robert Carroll and William McKane.[1] Carroll is accused of a 'defiant pugilism', of a 'negative, abrasive relation to the literature', which regards the Deuteronomistic redactor of Jeremiah as uncritical, unthinking and intolerant. McKane is reproached for his refusal to follow the 'claim' that the book of Jeremiah is the 'word of the Lord' since McKane declares that 'all language is human language'. Carroll is seen as resisting the values of

---

1 W. Brueggemann, 'Jeremiah: Intense Criticism/Thin Interpretation', *Int* 42 (1988), pp. 268-80; W.L. Holladay, *Jeremiah* (Hermeneia; Philadelphia: Fortress, 1986); R.P. Carroll, *Jeremiah* (OTL; London: SCM, 1986); W. McKane, *Jeremiah* (ICC; Edinburgh: T. and T. Clark, 1986).

much of the text, while McKane is seen as being wilfully indifferent to them. Brueggemann protests that the interpreter cannot 'dismiss the claim of the text, but must see what the claim means'. (The claim is, I understand, that the book of Jeremiah is the 'word of God'—though whether the book itself makes that claim I doubt: the opening reads 'words of Jeremiah'.) Now, my impression is that both scholars have taken the claims of the text seriously enough, but with different results: McKane has concluded that any claim to divine origin cannot mean anything to a critical interpreter, or mean anything in critical language. Carroll, on the other hand, has examined the claims of the text and decided he doesn't like them. For Brueggemann neither of these strategies is good enough: for him not only is attending to them an indispensable task of responsible interpretation, but attending to them means affirming them. The values of the text are there, it seems, in order to be co-opted. Brueggemann's justification for this is that the interpreter ought to 'be reflective of a double loyalty to the scholarly community and the community of faith'.

This claim, which Brueggemann articulates and practises with much more passion and much more subtlety than the very many interpreters who would agree with him, at least confirms that he shares my view of the socio-religious status of biblical scholarship. I also concede that the language of biblical scholarship permits Brueggemann this dual nationality, for it does not oblige the user to declare him or herself in allegiance *as a scholar* to one rather than the other. I am suspicious of the notion of scholarship which regards itself equally at the service of academia and ecclesia. How far is it compatible to 'attend to' (i.e. affirm, uphold) the 'claim of the text' and conduct a critical analysis of the text? Ultimately, if not immediately, there will be conflict. How will it be resolved? Brueggemann gives an answer: loyalty to the 'community of faith' will prevail, because Brueggemann will not allow the interpreter the freedom to be indifferent to or even to reject the 'claims' of the literature being studied. 'Attend to' is a worthy entry in the vocabulary of Academic Bibspeak because it disguises what it really means, and prompts one to ask whether freedom to agree or disagree is a value of

Brueggemann's 'community of faith'. I doubt, nevertheless, that Brueggemann would assent to the implications I have drawn from his words. If so, the fault lies with his language rather than his principles, and it is language rather than principles—far less individual scholars—that I am criticizing. Quite possibly Brueggemann is a victim of Academic Bibspeak. Let us therefore concentrate on the kind of interpretation he advocates. Is it not critical? An enormous number of people find it thus, as well as stimulating, well-written and scholarly. Nevertheless, I suggest the following definition of the kind of writing Brueggemann appears to endorse:

> A type of literature, oral or written, which has its starting point in a fixed canonical text, considered the revealed word of God by the author and his audience... an activity which finds its locus in the religious life of the community...

This sentence is very slightly adapted from Gary Porton's definition of midrash.[1] Midrash is a non-critical exercise addressed to a religious community in which its scriptures are interpreted in such a way as to make their meaning relevant to that community. What is criticism, then? Criticism is an exercise which assigns *a priori* no privilege to the values of the text over the values being used to analyse it. I could add that by using for criticism criteria which can easily apply to other literature also, and by using canons of historiography which can be applied to non-biblical history, criticism aims not only to understand the Bible by reference to the world, but the world by reference to the Bible, a task beyond the range of midrash.

By way of a second illustration I offer an extract from a much-used academic text book:

> [On Zephaniah:] He denounced the sins both cultic and ethical that Manasseh's policy had allowed to flourish as a prideful rebellion against Yahweh which had invited his wrath (e.g. chs. 1:4-6, 8f., 12; 3:1-4, 11). Announcing that the awful Day of Yahweh was imminent (e.g. ch. 1:2f., 7, 14-18), he declared that the nation had no hope save in repentance (ch. 2:1-3), for which Yahweh had offered one last chance (ch. 3:6f.).

1 G. Porton, 'Defining Midrash', in *The Study of Ancient Judaism*, ed. J. Neusner (New York: Ktav, 1981), p. 62.

> [On Jeremiah:] Savagely attacking the idolatry with which
> the land was filled, he declared it an inexcusable sin against
> the grace of Yahweh who had brought Israel from Egypt and
> made her his people (ch. 2:5-13)... While pleading with
> Judah, he also hoped for the restoration of Israel to the fam-
> ily of Yahweh (chs. 3:12-14; 31:2-6, 15-22).
>
> Into this ferment of resurgent nationalism, and yet of
> anxiety, the Deuteronomistic law fell like the thunderclap of
> conscience... [1]

To render this into a reasonably objective and critical comment upon the biblical texts (which furnish the sole basis for
the report, as the references convey) would require considerable recasting. At the very least, one would reserve judgment
on the reliability of the poetry in the books of Zephaniah and
Jeremiah as objective social analysis, one would not presume
to make the reader's own value-judgments for him or her,
and one would refrain from speculation designed to enhance
the biblical appeal. Such a recasting might run something like
this:

> The book of Zephaniah criticizes what it sees as cultic and
> ethical practices which may have been encouraged in the
> reign of Manasseh. They are presented as amounting to
> rebellion against the deity Yahweh and inviting his anger.
> An imminent 'day of Yahweh' is threatened, which can be
> averted only by 'repenting' of these practices, for which
> Yahweh had given one further opportunity.
>
> The book of Jeremiah strongly attacks the worship of
> deities other than Yahweh, claiming that it amounts to a
> 'sin' against the 'grace' of Yahweh who, as his worshippers
> believed, had once brought the nation out of Egypt and
> adopted it. Jeremiah is represented as pleading with the
> nation and looking forward to its return to the cult of Yah-
> weh.
>
> It was at this time, when apparently the royal policy
> aimed to assert independence of the Assyrian monarch,
> that, according the book of Kings, a law-book (possibly a ver-
> sion of the book of Deuteronomy) came to be found in the
> Jerusalem temple, providing, it seems, a convenient pretext
> for a change in the organization of the national cult.

---

1 J. Bright, *A History of Israel* (London: SCM, 1980), p. 299.

Sample Entries in a Dictionary

The final part of this essay consists of some excerpts from a book provisionally entitled *A Critical Dictionary of the Old Testament*. The aim of the entries is to represent extremely *conservative* scholarship (unlike the *TDOT*)—that is, to be content with describing as objectively as language can be what we appear to know with good reason, and to disregard any radical speculation or unwarranted inference from the literature. Terminology used by the Bible itself is as far as possible either avoided or carefully glossed, and the same is true of terminology hallowed by Christian and Jewish tradition. In the past some of this language has had the effect of making the Bible too *familiar* ('congregation', 'angel', 'redeem'), while at other times unnecessarily *mystified* ('ark', 'psalm', 'covenant'). Terms implying value judgments are obviously rejected, like 'false prophet' and 'idolatry'.

OLD TESTAMENT

A collection (strictly collections) of writings composed in Palestine in the Persian and Hellenistic periods, subsequently adopted by two religions, Judaism and Christianity, as all or part of their canon of scripture. Both traditions find in this literature a body of belief which legitimates their respective religion, with attendant implications for critical scholarship. Also called Hebrew Bible, though the two corpora are not identical in arrangement, and the original languages of the literature included Aramaic.

The canon itself dates from about the 1st or 2nd century CE. Like most other religious literature known to us, it contains myths, ethical teaching, poetry (including erotic poetry) and various kinds of narrative, including historiographical and quasi-historiographical. The contents reflect as a whole the ideals (admittedly quite varied) of the scribal classes of the élite of the city of Jerusalem in the Persian province of Yehud, drawing—to an extent which remains disputed—on sources from the earlier (Iron II) kingdoms of Judah and Israel. No straightforward correspondence between this literature and the ancient societies of these kingdoms, or of Yehud, ought to be drawn without corroborative support from archaeology, since several such inferences have in the past turned out on the evidence of archaeology to be erroneous (see PATRIARCHS, CONQUEST, DAVIDIC EMPIRE, YAHWISM).

THEOLOGY
Any kind of ideology concerned with the existence and activity of deities. When in narrative form may also be known as MYTHOLOGY.

ISRAEL
(a) A probably fictitious entity supposedly composed of the elements of two nation-states formed in Palestine during the Iron II period under the kings David and Solomon. It is probable that these two royal figures are based on historical characters, but extra-biblical confirmation is still awaited. Israel is said to have been made up of twelve or perhaps thirteen 'tribes' and have originated outside Palestine—contrary to the best archaeological evidence available.
(b) The name given to a kingdom centred in the Ephraimite hill-country of Palestine between the end of the 10th and the end of the 8th centuries BCE, possibly deriving its name from a group mentioned in the MERNEPTAH STELE.

CANAANITES
In the Hebrew Bible, counterpart to the fictitious twelve-tribe 'Israel' (see ISRAEL (a)), supposedly the indigenous people of Palestine 'driven out' by this Israel and used negatively to define 'Israel' as a distinct ethnic and religious group. Outside this ideological framework, the term can only mean 'inhabitants of Palestine', strictly speaking including what the Hebrew Bible calls 'Israel'.

COVENANT
The term is used in modern English only of biblical treaties and tax-free donations. Applies in particular to a theoretical analysis of the structure of Judaean religion in which the deity and the people were connected through the sort of political treaty well-known over a long period in the ancient Near East. This theory, prominent in the book of Deuteronomy, became so fashionable that other covenants were proposed by

the compilers of the Hebrew Bible, many of which are simply promises by the deity without any conditions (e.g. to Noah, Abraham, David, Phinehas). The covenant theory of religion has remained an important element in Judaism and Christianity (see COVENANT, NEW).

SYNCRETISM
Amalgamation of deities. The Old Testament offers a number of names for the deity or deities it presents—Yahweh, Yahweh Sebaoth, El, Elohim, El Elyon; others have been suspected to underlie personal or place names, like Shelem or Ṣedeq. Also other deities' characteristics, but without their names, can be transferred to a deity with another name—e.g. as with Ba'al. Hence the Old Testament shows widespread evidence of syncretism, to the point where it ends up with only one deity, addressed by title or epithet rather than name (Lord, King of Kings, Highest, Ancient of Days, Elohim).

The reason for this development is hardly debated by scholars, perhaps because of a latent belief among them that it came about by some form of divine revelation. One possible explanation is the establishment of the Persian province of Yehud as a small temple-society around a single city (Jerusalem) in the 6th century BCE; since the usual ration of public deities in the ancient Near East was one god per city, one god for the province of Yehud may have evolved naturally, though not without a great deal of influence from Iranian religious ideas (see SATAN, ANGELS, UNIVERSALISM, DUALISM, ESCHATOLOGY, LAW [DIVINE]).

MONOTHEISM
Belief in existence of one deity only. Often claimed to be a doctrine in the Old Testament and widely assumed by scholars to be preferable to a cult of many deities, for reasons unconnected with critical scholarship. See also SYNCRETISM.

PROPHET
Widely used of any person called *nābî'* in the Hebrew Bible; also of the eponyms of the books in the LATER PROPHETS or of any other authors of parts of this section—i.e. Deutero-Isaiah, Trito-Isaiah, Deutero-Zechariah. Prophetic individuals may

be historical or fictional, a pseudonym or a collective, and it is often impossible to tell for certain which of these options obtains any one case (e.g. Isaiah, Ezekiel, Malachi). It is possible that some of these persons (where historical) functioned as one or other kind of intermediary in ancient Judaean or Israelite society, but the heavy editorial activity apparent in the literature precludes any serious investigation of this possibility (see PROPHECY).

ON MODELS AND METHODS
A Conversation with Robert Morgan

Anthony C. Thiselton

I

From among the variety of recent studies which examine the general area of biblical interpretation, one of the most honest and wide-ranging books which concentrates specifically on questions of *method* is Robert Morgan's book *Biblical Interpretation* (Oxford University Press, 1988), written in collaboration with John Barton. Much of this work is devoted to arguing for the inadequacy of a purely historical paradigm in biblical studies. In more positive terms it is all gain to engage in a fuller and more serious interaction with other disciplines, both theological and non-theological. In particular the paradigm of literary study constitutes a 'breakthrough' in terms of the reader's appreciation of the text. Surrounding these more specific questions is a larger one about the standpoint of the interpreter and of the interpretative community. Robert Morgan writes, 'The constructive aim of this book is to make explicit a model for bridging the gulf between critical scholarship and religious faith' (p. 25). On one side, he argues, we cannot retreat from a public academic agenda and from wrestling with issues of general 'theory' which reflect the places at which human modernity stands. On the other side, we cannot overlook the fact that the Bible concerns human religion.

In order to come to terms with some of these issues in more detail, it is worth stating more precisely some of the positive and negative theses which Robert Morgan advocates. First, one of the most important theses of the book concerns the crucial distinction between historical methods and historical aims. Morgan writes, 'The step from using historical *methods* to defining the *aims* of biblical scholarship in exclusively historical terms sets it at odds with the interests of most other readers and students of the Bible' (p. 171). Morgan reiterates the point in his final conclusion, 'The polemic implied here is directed...against the uncritical assumption that the inevitable prominence of historical *methods* in studying these ancient texts means that historical *aims* are the only ones that are respectable' (p. 287). It is quite correct to assume that, in order to reach a mature understanding of most biblical texts, the process of critical historical reconstruction must go on. Morgan illustrates this point with reference to the history of biblical interpretation. The same point might have been made on the basis of a theory of meaning. Meaning cannot be restricted simply to the linguistic signs of the text, since it comes into being by interaction between these signs and the processes of life in which they are embedded. This principle is well expressed by Werner G. Jeanrond. He writes, 'The individual meaning of linguistic expressions is not determined solely by the choice of words, or by the way in which the sentence is structured, but also by the context in which an expression is embedded. This embedding comes about through the linguistic context on the one hand, and, on the other, through the situation of communication which is also constitutive of meaning.'[1]

It is one thing to allow historical reconstruction to serve questions about the meaning and function of the text. But, as Morgan rightly insists, it is quite another thing to reduce the entire status and function of the text to that of a tool for the purpose of historical reconstruction. This is simply to make the biblical writings rather like a second-class version of some of the standard books on biblical history which were written by John Bright, F.F. Bruce, and many others. Morgan floats the hypothesis that the use of the German word 'tasks' (*Aufgaben*) may have allowed the distinction between 'methods'

1 Werner Jeanrond, *Text and Interpretation as Categories of Theological Thinking* (Dublin: Gill and Macmillan, 1988), p. 76.

and 'aims' to become blurred in the work of such thinkers as Wrede and Wellhausen.

Here, however, Morgan is judicious in disentangling the respective roles played by the different aims of different biblical interpreters. It is a theme of his book that 'Some disagreements about what the Bible means stem not from obscurities in the texts, but from the conflicting aims of the interpreters' (p. 8). But there is a place, he rightly argues, for differences of aim. In the context of the work of Reimarus, for example, we may wish to re-examine the biblical material in terms of its status as a witness to certain miracles or to the event of the resurrection. But this is only one particular way among others of looking at the function of biblical texts. The more we allow this one particular way to monopolize our attention, the more we allow a rift to develop 'between the rational methods and conclusions of biblical scholarship and the way that believers use their scriptures to inform and nourish religious faith. The task of theological interpretation is to heal that rift, and hold together faith and reason' (p. 174).

We shall pursue in due course some of the further issues which arise from what Morgan regards as the undue monopoly and isolation of the historical paradigm. He rightly questions, for example, a widespread hermeneutical assumption that the sequence of tasks for the biblical interpreter is first to engage in historical reconstruction and then, after this, to engage in theological evaluation or application. Rather, the interpreter needs to make an imaginative leap towards what we think the text is getting at, drawing on our whole experience of reality, and then historical scrutiny, some measure of objectivity and 'critical distance' follows as part of a checking process (p. 183; cf. p. 184). Further, 'historical research on the Bible is also a tangle of competing hypotheses. Few command sufficiently general assent to bear the weight of the theological constructions placed upon them' (p. 196). Because often one generation will call into question the conclusions of another, when theological application follows historical reconstruction 'the great syntheses of theological interpretation have collapsed with depressing regularity' (p. 192).

In the face of this multitude of problems, while not abandoning the historical paradigm, Morgan urges that these problems are 'eased by the switch to a literary paradigm for biblical interpretation. Modern literary interpretation tolerates and even encourages a greater variety of valid "readings" than an exegesis which is more tightly bound to the authorial norm' (p. 198). This allows the biblical writings to illuminate the great diversity of human experience. The literary paradigm allows for a wide range of approaches, but in principle, Morgan argues, it is capable of rejuvenating Christian theological interpretation. In contrast to the historical paradigm, in much literary work 'the primary aim has been to elucidate ... texts, not to reconstruct what they refer to. Meaning and reference have been distinct' (p. 206).

Morgan offers an illuminating survey of examples of these literary approaches from the work of Robert Lowth in the eighteenth century to the present day. In the course of this survey he makes the perceptive observation that 'throughout the history of the Church and Synagogue the most impressive theological interpretations of their Bibles have taken up the best rational insights available, not declared war on them' (p. 214). Up to the 1920s the emphasis in literary studies was mainly on the historical and philological; after I.A. Richards and T.S. Eliot the so-called New Criticism focused on the autonomy of the text or individual work of art; the 1960s ushered in a period after the New Criticism when structuralism, post-structuralism, and a variety of approaches were explored.

Two fundamental points which Morgan makes in the course of this survey are convincing. First, something like a 'breakthrough' (Morgan's word, p. 221) occurred in the shift of focus away from past events and traditions as such to the impact of texts upon present day hearers and readers. The claim is supported by selective considerations of aspects of the work of E.M. Good, Robert Alter, Alan Culpepper, Dan Otto Via, J.D. Crossan, and Robert Tannehill, among others.

A second point is worth noting in Morgan's argument which is, to my mind, beyond question. Ironically the point emerges most strikingly in Morgan's discussion of structuralist approaches to New Testament interpretation. It is ironic, because he is in process of paying to biblical structuralists a fairly left-handed compliment, with which I also sympathize.

He says of this movement, 'It has contributed very little to understanding the Bible' (p. 219), and 'It has probably been more successful in the social sciences than in literary criticism' (p. 144). Nevertheless, Morgan maintains, those who have explored structuralism have been right to do so, for it is part of the contemporary intellectual world with which biblical scholars need to interact. At its best, for example, it raised broader questions about whether the meaning of life depended 'more upon our place in social systems than our place in historical tradition' (p. 255).

II

So far I have been following Morgan's major theses fairly closely, and expressing broad agreement with them. His language about the inadequacy of an exclusively historical paradigm is so well balanced and so carefully guarded that it is difficult to disagree with its general thrust. But now some queries begin to emerge. First, while the very broad contrast between a historical and literary paradigm is straightforward and memorable, is there not a much wider network of models and choices, some of which criss-cross and overlap, especially in terms of how positively or how negatively they may relate to concerns within communities of religious faith? Rather than aim for a shift of emphasis between two paradigms, might not a more constructive task be the welding together of a more comprehensive hermeneutical model which seeks to draw on the strength of each approach while avoiding its distinctive weaknesses?

Rather than drawing mainly on a bi-polar conceptual contrast between a historical and a literary paradigm, it might be helpful to begin with the fourfold distinction popularized by M.H. Abrams in his book *The Mirror and the Lamp*. A text, he points out, can be related to the world in one or more of four different ways. First it can be seen as the expression of the author who produced it. If I am looking at Romans 5 or 1 Corinthians 15, I can look 'behind' the text to the mind of Paul, or, still further back, to the circumstances and experiences to which Paul reacted in producing the texts. This model is often criticized contemptuously as resting on the genetic fallacy, that meaning is to be explained in terms of what produced it; but, as we shall see when we turn to Schleiermacher, the focus of this model is not necessarily orientated exclusively towards the past, nor does it necessarily ignore what a text is designed to do or to set in motion.

Second, we can approach a text in terms of what it is about: its subject-matter or its content. In the Passion narrative this object of reference may be a chain of events; in a theological argument in the epistles it may be a set of theological ideas. The weakness of this model is that it may be taken to imply a didactic fallacy; that the purpose of all texts is to provide information about events or ideas. But it need not be understood in this way. Similarly of all models it most readily lends itself to decontextualization—to the conceptualizing of some 'content' independent of the context in which it was articulated. But again, this rests on an abuse, not a use, of this model, and this approach has a rightful place among the others.

Third, texts may be seen as part of a wider body of literature in which each text performs a different role in relation to a network of texts. Brevard Childs and others have explored how levels of meaning may change, depending on whether we have in view an early oral unit, the role within a chapter, book, or redactional scheme, or its broader canonical context. If there is any fallacy involved in this model, it would be that in theory a chain of inter-textuality could remain indefinitely unrelated to the everyday world. But in practice, as we have seen, especially in the light of Werner Jeanrond's comment, the contexts of texts cannot be abstracted entirely from some context of situation.

Fourth, there is the reality of what occurs, to use Ricoeur's language, 'in front of' the text. Here we are concerned with its effects on the reader. Morgan correctly notes both the importance of reader-response theory in literary studies and also that it is a fundamental concern in any community of religious faith. A key question for a pastor or leader of a study group is: what does this text *do*? The great merit of reader-response theory is that it focuses attention on the reader's own engagement with the text and his or her own activity. In Norman Holland's terminology, what 'personal transaction' does the present reader have with the text? In Todorov's language, how does a text get us to construct an imaginary world? The emphasis falls upon a contemporary temporal process of the reader's forming expectations, looking forward, looking back, having his or her expectations revised or frustrated, and re-creating new ones.

Nevertheless, within this fourth category, as well as in the other three, there is room not only for a greater or lesser emphasis on the author, context of situation, or historical considerations, but also for an enormously wide range of approaches which criss-cross and overlap a general bi-polar distinction between a historical and a literary paradigm. For example, some versions of reader-response theory focus on the implied reader envisaged from within the horizons of the author or the text; others focus more directly on the creative activity of the actual or contemporary reader. In addition to this, there are also other kinds of classificatory grids which also cut across a basic history/literature distinction. In hermeneutical theory, for example, we may distinguish between five or more working models: the Romanticist model of Schleiermacher, Dilthey and Betti; the existential, de-objectifying, or self-involving model of Bultmann, Via, and others; the so-called ontological model exemplified in Gadamer; socio-critical models which operate in Marxist, feminist, and liberation hermeneutics; and semiotic or speech-act models which seek a more comprehensive theoretical basis. But a broad contrast between historical and literary paradigms makes the classification of most of these models in these particular terms problematic.

To select two of the classic examples: Schleiermacher is usually thought of as representing a historical and reconstructionist model in the classic form. Yet a close study of Schleiermacher's volume, *Hermeneutics: The Handwritten Manuscripts*, proves beyond question that Schleiermacher's hermeneutical concerns were broader, more complex, and far more subtle than that, and I do not have in mind the kind of theological considerations addressed by Morgan in his excellent survey of historical scholarship in the first half of his book. In Schleiermacher, the task of New Testament introduction is that of 'placing us in the position of the original *readers* for whom the New Testament authors wrote'.[1] So the point of departure for questions about the use of the Bible in the Church is the specificity of the *reading* situation to which the biblical writings were first addressed.[2] Schleiermacher, far from being obsessively pre-occupied with the role of the author and with historical reconstruction, actually recognized well ahead of his time that whether we regard 'psychological' interpretation relating to the author as a higher priority or whether we regard 'grammatical' interpretation relating to texts and to language as 'higher' depends entirely on judgments and purposes of *interpretative strategy*.[3]

A second example concerns the use of existentialist or self-involving models. Morgan introduces his discussion of Bultmann under the heading of questions about the history of traditions, and of Via under the general heading of literary study of the Bible. But in both cases the root issue has to do with the role of de-objectification in biblical interpretation. While the general usefulness of a broad distinction between a historical and a literary paradigm is not denied, we raise the question of whether it might not be even more useful, more suggestive, and more precise, to draw on networks of sub-categories of the kind to which we have alluded.

III

A very brief consideration of a second and closely-related point may serve to take the issue further. While Morgan clearly recognizes the varying and uneven value of the literary paradigm for communities of faith, it might be of help to spell out still further some key theological issues in this area in comparable detail to that which marks Morgan's earlier and helpful discussion of the value and limitations of various uses of the historical paradigm. Simply to restrict our attention to one example for illustrative purposes, there can only be an extraordinarily ambivalent relation between theologies of scripture within communities of faith and the many different versions of reader-response theory which emerge in literary criticism.

1 F.D.E. Schleiermacher, *Hermeneutics: The Handwritten Manuscripts* (Eng. tr.; Missoula: Scholars Press, 1977), p. 38 (my italics).
2 Schleiermacher, *Hermeneutics*, p. 103.
3 Schleiermacher, *Hermeneutics*, pp. 99-100.

Communities of faith are concerned with levels of operative engagement between the reader and the text. Theologically, the function of texts is to allow the reader to expand his or her relatively self-centred horizons in which persons or things are seen as objects within a network of personal or corporate hopes and interests to a wider and less self-centred perspective. In religious terms this means that for texts to be effective, the reader must be willing to some extent to be vulnerable and open to change. In reader-response theory there is therefore a welcome focus in upon adjustments and revisions of the reader's expectations and projected world. According to such theorists as David Bleich, the reader's deepest feelings may be transformed; while according to Norman Holland his or her very identity, or the corporate identity of a reading community, may be either shaped or affirmed.

Nevertheless, this model poses at least three potential difficulties in many communities of faith. First, all this now moves from a hermeneutical model of human 'understanding', which for Schleiermacher and his successors was primarily an *epistemological* category, to a model of 'reading' which has a *pragmatic* rather than an epistemological focus. But traditionally texts have been seen in communities of faith fundamentally as vehicles of truth, often also as vehicles of revelation. Traditionally they are perceived as providing a basis in truth for the changes of orientation and attitude which may take place in interaction with the text. Some of the more radical versions of reader-response theory are philosophically closer to Richard Rorty's view that 'hermeneutics is not "another way of knowing"... It is better seen as another way of coping.'[1]

Second, most versions of reader-response theory emphasize that the reader makes an active contribution to what constitutes meaning. But the notion that so much depends on what the reader contributes does not seem to fit easily with a theology of divine gift and grace, as this theology is perceived to function in many communities of faith. Admittedly any reflective theology of grace will include the recognition that the appropriation of grace entails human transformation and

1 Richard Rorty, *Philosophy and the Mirror of Nature* (Princeton: Princeton University Press, 1980), p. 356.

change; but this is usually seen to rest on the appropriation and renewal of some kind of given which is foundational in the community. Most communities of faith would have difficulty with Robert Crosman's conclusion to his essay 'Do Readers Make Meaning?' when he asserts: 'Meaning is made precisely as we *want* it to be made, and as usual we want different things'.[1] To quote the memorable aphorism of Stanley Fish, 'The reader's response is not *to* the meaning, it *is* the meaning'.[2]

Third, where effect is separated from corporate reflection upon the reading process, or where there is pessimism about the discovery of shared beliefs about meaning, the individual becomes isolated, and separated from processes of corporate reflection on the text. Wolfgang Iser, for example, writes: 'In view of the irreconcilability of effect and explanation, the traditional expository style of interpretation has clearly had its day'.[3] Yet, as Werner Jeanrond points out, even Iser shares in the process of explaining how a reader can contribute to the process of filling the blanks which belong to texts.[4] The use made of Iser's model by Susan Wittig for parable interpretation illustrates further its value and limitations in relation to the expectations of communities of faith, as well as its significance in New Testament interpretation.[5]

Morgan touches on the work of Iser and then on the use which Via makes of Iser's work. He rightly urges that in biblical studies we must engage with this kind of work because we must participate seriously in the intellectual debates of the day, including interdisciplinary studies of theory, and also because we must explore the kind of pluralism which such approaches imply (pp. 258-63). But whereas in the first half of his book he was concerned to draw attention to the effects of various uses of the historical paradigm both for the academic world and for communities of faith, in the second half we also

1 S.R. Suleiman and I. Crosman (eds.), *The Reader in the Text* (Princeton: Princeton University Press, 1980), p. 164.

2 Stanley Fish, *Is There a Text in this Class?* (Cambridge, Mass.: Harvard University Press, 1980), p. 3.

3 Wolfgang Iser, *The Act of Reading* (London: Routledge & Kegan Paul, 1978), p. 10.

4 Jeanrond, *Text and Interpretation*, pp. 106-107.

5 Susan Wittig, 'A Theory of Multiple Meanings', *Semeia* 9 (1977), pp. 75-104.

need a further exploration of the effects of various uses of the
literary paradigm, if the whole argument is to fulfil its aim of
making 'explicit a model for bridging the gulf between critical
scholarship and religious faith' (p. 25).

IV

A third and more important set of questions concerns Morgan's observation about the relation between faith and criticism, and the use of the notion of 'human religion' as a bridge-
building and mediating concept in this context. First of all, it
seems entirely right and extremely important to call in question the popular assumption that the appropriate *sequence* in
biblical studies is first to try to arrive at some supposedly
value-neutral historical reconstruction and then as a second
part of the process to try to arrive at some kind of theological
evaluation, interpretation, or application. Morgan rightly
insists on an essential balance between history and hermeneutics (p. 182), but he questions whether the interpretative
process follows the sequence popularly assumed to be appropriate. He writes, 'As theological interpreters we make an
intuitive jump to what we think the text is getting at, and then
see if it will stand up to the cool rational scrutiny of our
historical judgment' (p. 183). In different words: 'It is commonly assumed that ... theological interpretation should
follow historical and exegetical research: first see what the
text meant, then (perhaps) what it means. But this model of
objective scholarship, taking the Bible reader to the end of the
line and then handing over to "application" or the religious
appropriation of scripture is unsatisfactory. Historical
conclusions are uncertain, and historical work is never
complete ... The key is to recognize that historical research
and theological interpretation are in principle different
tasks ...' (p. 184).

All this raises at least three issues. The first concerns the
respective roles of the interpreter as reader and as critic. A
careful distinction is drawn by Robert Fowler in his helpful
essay, 'Who is "the Reader" in Reader-Response Criticism?'[1]

---

1 Robert Fowler, *Semeia* 31 (1985), pp. 5-23.

As readers we allow ourselves to be mastered by the text. The text has its way with us. We feel what we are meant to feel, and enter the text's projected world, for the reader's relation to the text is one of immediacy in which the whole person is affected. But the role of critic reverses the epistemological direction of flow. The critic scrutinizes the text or object, consciously distances himself or herself from it, and creates a high enough level of abstraction to ask: what is going on here? The critic looks at the text from outside it; the reader accepts its invitation to enter its world.

To *begin* with what the critic perceives must inevitably reduce and restrict the area and nature of encounter with the text. We cannot dispense with the critic's role; but critical detachment and checking *follows* the immediacy of engagement. Uncritical reading encourages naivety; criticism alone encourages a pre-occupation with theory. What we need, Fowler asserts, is *both* 'readerly passion' *and* 'critical distance'.[1]

Second, all this is expressed, although not exactly in the same terms, with great sensitivity and balance by Schleiermacher. Schleiermacher's concerns about intuitive rapport and sympathetic imagination bring us close to Morgan's comments about human religion as a bridge-building term of understanding. Schleiermacher believed that what he regarded as the 'feminine' intuitive perception of meaning is at least as fundamental as what he called the 'masculine' work of comparison and deduction. In his short writing, *The Celebration of Christmas*, written in 1805, he depicts the women of the household expressing the spirit of Christmas in reminiscences of experiences and in Christmas music, while the men partly miss the point by engaging in a theological debate about the incarnation. He writes, 'Divinatory knowledge is the feminine strength in knowing people; comparative knowledge, the masculine...[2] 'By leading the interpreter to transform himself, so to speak, into the author, the divinatory method seems to gain an immediate comprehension of the

1 Fowler, 'Who is "the Reader"?', p. 9.
2 Schleiermacher, *Hermeneutics*, p. 150.

author as an individual. The comparative method proceeds by subsuming the author under a general type.'[1]

It would be over-simple to correlate these two modes of understanding entirely with Schleiermacher's respective concern for the particular and for the general, or to relate them isomorphically to his distinction between psychological and grammatical (linguistic) hermeneutics. His hermeneutical system is subtle and complex. But he does stress that it is the interplay and interaction between these processes which is decisive, and he shows that we should achieve little or nothing if we simply began with comparative, scientific, and cerebral processes in isolation from a larger vision of the whole. The critical dimension comes into play only as part of a larger and longer process of understanding.

Third, Morgan's careful and sensitive tracing of historical factors in the development of modern biblical studies helps us to appreciate why in practice these two tasks have become identified respectively with what amounts to two traditions, or to two communities, of interpretation. In one community an academic and historical agenda tends to determine the angle of approach; communities of faith often feel a need to provide a different agenda. Morgan shows, equally convincingly, that some or even perhaps most biblical specialists have attempted to remain members of both communities, but also that some degree of tension has often been a more characteristic outcome than synthesis, at least in the long run. It is important to note, as Morgan does, that dual commitments to academic objectivity and to social, political, or religious action constitute a problem not only for some biblical specialists, but also for many Marxists, Freudians, and academics working in such areas as sociology, social policy, psychology, and politics (pp. 24-25).

In an essay published in 1982 under the title, 'Academic Freedom, Religious Tradition, and the Morality of Christian Scholarship', I attempted to explore these points in some detail, arguing that moral constraints arise on both sides and in both communities on the basis of loyalties and commitments to more than one community. It is perhaps equally simplistic and mistaken either to see the academic community as

1 Schleiermacher, *Hermeneutics*, p. 150.

always freeing the Bible from the shackles of church doctrine, or to see the church as always having a monopoly of 'religious' truth. In agreement with the spirit of Morgan's stress on interdisciplinary dialogue, I explored the relevance of Max Black's philosophical work on the morality of scholarship, Charles Taylor's discussion of neutrality in political science, and Alan Montefiore's *Neutrality and Impartiality*, among other works, to try to elucidate part of what is involved in being citizens of more than one community.[1]

Morgan believes that some fundamental bridge-building can be achieved by making more use of the 'middle term' of human religion in biblical interpretation rather than surrendering either to theological language about 'the God whom we worship' (p. 24) or to exclusively empirical language about historical events, situations, and institutions. He writes, 'The middle term which links reason (rational methods) and faith (religious understanding of the Bible) is a theory of religion which can make sense of the historian's empirical data without denying the truth of a religion's own claims' (p. 198). In his introductory chapter he makes the promise: 'It is Schleiermacher's re-orientation of theology which provides the key to our later discussions...The re-orientation towards reflection on religious and human existence has provided the basis for most modern attempts to interpret the Bible theologically' (p. 32).

There is much to be said in support of this central thesis, although there is also one point of difficulty which he may perhaps not have fully addressed. From the point of view of hermeneutics, several positive points may be affirmed. As Morgan points out, in Reformation theology, Luther, Calvin and Zwingli all insisted that knowledge of God and knowledge of humankind are inseparable (p. 30). They protested against the scholasticism of late mediaeval theology. Second, Schleiermacher's hermeneutics drew both from the pietism of his youth and from Reformation theology to a larger extent than has often been recognized. As Morgan rightly insists, his thought is not simply the product of Enlightenment rational-

---

1 A.C. Thiselton, 'Academic Freedom, Religious Tradition, and the Morality of Christian Scholarship', in M. Santer (ed.), *Their Lord and Ours* (London: SPCK, 1982), pp. 20-45.

ism, nor is it derived from Romanticism alone. Schleiermacher was concerned to combine 'loyalty to the tradition with
openness to new knowledge' (p. 33). He was concerned to take
account of historical contingency, particularity and uniqueness, but within a framework of scientific concern about the
general and universal. Similarly he placed emphasis on the
creative role of sympathetic imagination and intuitive rapport
alongside the critical function of rational comparison and scientific testing. Dilthey developed these principles in terms of
the interpreter's putting himself or herself into the shoes of
the author or text. Understanding is achieved only when the
interpreter enters the dynamic flow of life which allows a re-
living or re-experiencing of what gave rise to the text. Emilio
Betti, the twentieth-century representative of this approach in
hermeneutics, argues that this model has much to offer to all
disciplines in the humanities. Indeed, in the face of competing
ideologies and party-slogans it has much to offer to human
society as a whole. Nothing is more important, Betti urges,
than patience, tolerance, and genuinely mutual understanding between persons as persons, rather than the adoption of
'positions' or ideologies before such understanding begins or is
reached. All this accords with Morgan's call for openness, and
for a positive recognition of the role of religion as a given part
of human life. On both sides interpreters need to remain open
to what may be unexpected or difficult, whether from the
standpoint of religious experience and institutional religion or
from the standpoint of the supposed regularities perceived
only by empirical observations of data.

Morgan argues that the *methods* used by academic communities and by communities of faith will be the same, but
that there will be differences of *context* and *goals* in interpretation (p. 36). 'The concordat between faith and reason by
which this combination of rational methods and religious
interests has been achieved hinges on the concept of
"religion"' (p. 39). But Morgan's recognition of the decisive
significance of context and goal raises a question about the
adequacy of the same language about religion, when different
goals are at issue. When we were considering reader-reponse
theory in the context of the literary paradigm, we pointed out
that for many communities of faith texts were perceived as

vehicles of truth as well as vehicles of transformation. A parallel issue emerges here. Most communities of faith regard biblical texts as vehicles of *address*, rather than simply as records of witness, sources of information, or instruments of change. Paul Ricoeur's work on Old Testament modes of discourse as manifestations of meaning may serve to illuminate the point. In his essay 'Hermeneutic of Revelation', Ricoeur identifies five modes of discourse in the biblical writings: in narrative discourse God is named as an actor in founding events for a community; in prophetic discourse, language often takes the form of a first-person address in which the voice of God stands behind the voice of the prophet; in prescriptive language, God is the giver of law; in wisdom discourse God may often be hidden, but may also address humans in boundary situations; in hymnic discourse the reader addresses God in a second-person 'you'.

All this poses a dilemma. It is a convention in most universities to retain a level of critical abstraction which speaks more readily of how a biblical writer or tradition may be seen to have conceived of God, rather than of 'God' as an active agent, as one who addresses the reader through the text, or as an addressee. Does the concept of human 'religion' help to solve the problem of how biblical texts can be allowed, as Bultmann would put it, to constitute an address *from* God rather than someone's thought *about* God? Is there an ambivalence in Morgan's approach here? Is it perhaps even an unavoidable ambivalence which many of us cannot help but share as members of more than one community? Morgan speaks critically of 'the believer's insider talk of "God whom we worship"' as language which, at least in the university, does not accord with the language of a wider and more pluriform culture (p. 25). Yet he also sympathetically notes that 'a theologian cannot, like a historian, rest content with having described someone else's religion' (p. 73). He comments, 'Many biblical scholars are believers, and therefore speak in both languages' (p. 25).

What may be doubted, therefore, is whether it can ever be comfortable to be a member of both communities, each of which imposes different, and sometimes seemingly incompatible, moral and linguistic obligations. This is why, while I share

Morgan's view that the notion of human religion as a middle term can take us positively some distance along the road towards a building of bridges, in the end there is no way of avoiding the tension which is imposed when a single individual feels loyalties to both communities. In an essay entitled 'Theology as a Discipline of a Modern University', Donald MacKinnon argues: 'It should not be easy to be a theologian in a modern university'. The pressures and tensions of being at once committed and open, of being questioned so that one is always discontent and still looking for further light, make the academic theologian 'a rootless man, restless and awkward, ill at ease with himself'.[1]

V

There is space only very briefly to touch on a fourth main area which may be open to question, namely the theory of meaning which seems to be generally presupposed in Robert Morgan's book. Morgan is entirely correct to claim that meaning is more than a semantic property of the text. He writes, 'Meaning is better seen as the product of an interaction between two or more people' (p. 6). But does this entail the further proposition that 'texts, like dead men and women, have no rights, no aims, no interests'? 'They can be used', he writes, 'in whatever way readers or interpreters choose. If interpreters choose to respect an author's intentions, that is because it is in their interest to do so' (p. 7). 'The text itself is passive' (*ibid.*).

We need to break down this claim into several components to see that some are true while others may be open to question. What is true, first, is the claim that interpretative communities have enormous power to set up expectations and aims which will largely determine a semantic or semiotic agenda: what counts as meaning, or what seems to be the 'literal' or 'natural' meaning emerges from within the horizons and standpoint of a given community and tradition. This can be established from two different angles of approach. One is that of the philosophy of language. We may cite, for example, the

---

1   T. Shanin (ed.), *The Rules of the Game: Cross-Disciplinary Models in Scholarly Thought* (London: Tavistock Publications, 1972), pp. 170, 172.

work of such writers as John R. Searle to the effect that no supposedly 'natural' meaning is entirely context-free from the assumptions and expectations which surround it.[1] The other angle of approach which corroborates this claim about the role of interpretative communities is the flood of literature which now comes under the heading of socio-critical hermeneutics. As Habermas expresses it, language is a medium of domination and social force. It seems to legitimate relations of organized power. The work of Habermas on 'interest' would contribute a useful commentary on some features of biblical interpretation both in some academic communities and in many communities of faith. As we may recall, Marxist and feminist hermeneutics have explored such areas.

A second valid aspect of the theory of meaning which Morgan seems to presuppose is the role of interpretative decision or strategy in posing and answering questions about meaning. There is perhaps no need to elaborate this point. We earlier noted that even at the beginning of the nineteenth century Schleiermacher himself noted that whether we deem 'psychological' questions about the author or 'grammatical' questions about the text to be 'higher' depended entirely on our interpretative agenda and strategy. Morgan rightly argues that many of the tensions which arise in biblical interpretation owe their origin to decisions which have been made about 'different kinds of framework of interpretation within which the Bible is read today' (p. 22). In current literary theory the work of Stanley Fish, to which we earlier referred, establishes the far-reaching effects of interpretative strategies and decisions.

A more problematic element in Morgan's approach to meaning is an over-readiness perhaps to give hospitality to what Jonathan Cohen has called a *de facto* theory of meaning.[2] For *de facto* theories of meaning, language is a pattern of *events*. Meaning is conveyed as it is perceived to have been conveyed, whether it ought to have been so perceived or not. By contrast *de jure* theories of meaning can easily be carica-

1 John R. Searle, 'Literal Meaning', in *Expression and Meaning: Studies in the Theory of Speech Acts* (Cambridge: Cambridge University Press, 1979), pp. 117-36.

2 L. Jonathan Cohen, *The Diversity of Meaning* (London: Methuen, 1966), pp. 24-94.

tured as depending on clear linguistic *rules* which are supposedly prescriptive, and are therefore, it may be argued, more
likely to concern logic rather than ordinary language. But a
softened and more convincing version of this concern about
pattern and constraint will draw attention to the role of conventions, customs, human traditions, and the mutual interdependence of language and life in both ancient and modern
language-situations as systems of reference for interpretation.
On this basis it may be difficult to follow Morgan all the way in
giving a relatively maximal role to communities of interpretation and, by contrast, a relatively minimal role to the author
and the author's situation. As Roman Jakobson and others
have insisted, meaning is not simply a product of the relation
between an author and his or her addressee; it is also constrained by such additional factors as context, contact, code,
and message.

The inter-relationship between language and life which
generates and constrains meaning concerns *both* the relationship between the text, the author, and the historical language-
community or implied reader *and* relationships between the
text and the interpretative language-community to which the
modern reader belongs. But here two points need to be made.
First, the text is not simply 'passive', except perhaps in a relatively unimportant *de facto* sense. Even where there are
degrees of polyvalency of meaning, the injunction 'He who has
ears to hear, let him hear' does not mean 'go and make what
you like out of this'. But Morgan's suggestion that we should
be reluctant to assess the relative propriety of different interpretative *goals* risks too open and unconstrained an approach
at this point. Second, from the standpoint equally of theories of
meaning and of Christian theology, any tendency towards a
docetic disembodying of the text from the language-situation
entails missing part of the context which contributes to
meaning, authenticity of meaning and meaning-effect.
Because language-systems and codes are inseparable from
speech-acts, acts of speaking or of writing remain part of the
historical flow of human life and human tradition. But this
brings us back to our first query. From the standpoint of theories of meaning it may not be entirely helpful to suggest an
organization of interpretative models and methods which

turns primarily on a bi-polar distinction between a historical and literary paradigm, even though this basic contrast helps us to see some valuable points.

Nevertheless Morgan has carefully balanced his more positive comments about the historical paradigm with admitted reservations about certain versions of a literary approach. Such qualifications will also be reflected in many communities of faith. While Calvin may have insisted that meaning is *simplex*, other religious writers distance themselves from the analogy of 'mathematical theorems which present exactly the same idea to every person' (John Newton, *Cardiphonia*). Newton compares the biblical writings to a mirror (2 Cor. 3.18) in which 'the longer we look, the more we see' (*ibid.*). Morgan has left room for such a perspective within communities of faith.

FOUR OR FIVE THINGS TO DO WITH TEXTS
A Taxonomy of Interpretative Interests

Mark G. Brett

Introduction

Modern biblical research has frequently been marked by conflicts about method, but in recent years these conflicts have been particularly intense. On the one hand, seminal ideas deriving from neighouring disciplines have been shown to be fruitful in biblical studies, and some of these ideas have apparently undermined the methods which are native to the discipline. On the other hand, the native methods of source, form and redaction criticism have recently been subjected to severe criticism by biblical scholars who could not be accused of an excessive commitment to exotic fashions.[1] In short, our methodological options seem to be expanding, and the defence of new proposals has often been accompanied by an attack on older methods. But not all of these attacks have been necessary; one does not always need to annihilate the opposition. In the discussion that follows I would like to make a few suggestions about how some competing approaches might learn to co-exist peacefully.

My most basic point is that any talk about method should be preceded by an analysis of interpretative *interests*; a 'method' will only be coherent if it is guided by a clearly articulated question or *goal*. A goal like 'understanding the text' is too

---

1 See, for example, R.N. Whybray, *The Making of the Pentateuch* (JSOTSup, 53; Sheffield: JSOT, 1987); W. Richter, *Exegese als Literaturwissenschaft* (Göttingen: Vandenhoeck & Ruprecht, 1971).

vague to be of any real use in resolving methodological disputes. The notion of 'understanding' includes too many different things.[1]

In referring to interests and goals I mean to speak naively about the most explicit aspects of scholarly intentions. The concept of scholarly 'interests' is itself ambiguous in some respects, since it can include deeper, less explicit motives like building a career or gaining power. More positively, Habermas has also described an 'emancipatory cognitive interest' which seems to have more to do with the ethical use of knowledge than with the narrower concerns of this paper.[2] But here we are restricting ourselves to the more or less explicit and immediate goals of interpretation. In speaking of *interpretative* interests I mean to narrow the focus and thereby gain some conceptual clarity.

Biblical critics now have a wide range of interpretative interests, and some of these, I suggest, may be compatible even though they are perceived to be in conflict. In order to develop this suggestion in detail, I shall have to locate the older interests, like those in genre or authorial intention, within a wider framework. The resulting taxonomy of interests will not lead to an all-embracing and unifying method. On the contrary, when the differences between the various interests become clear, then a diversity of methods would seem inevitable. But questions of method can only be explored fruitfully when the prior discussion about interests has achieved some clarity. This paper, therefore, sets out to make a contribution to the clarification of interests. Its analysis will be informed by some basic technical vocabulary which derives from neighbouring disciplines but no special importance need be attached to the specific terms used; they are simply tools of analysis. If in the long run they obscure more than they clarify then they may be replaced.

---

1 See W.G. Runciman, *A Treatise on Social Theory. Vol. 1: The Methodology of Social Theory* (Cambridge: Cambridge University Press, 1983).
2 See J. Habermas, *Erkenntnis und Interesse* (Frankfurt: Suhrkamp, 1968) [tr. J.J. Shapiro, *Knowledge and Human Interests* (Boston: Beacon, 1971)]. On the ethical evaluation of interpretative interests, see further the paper in this volume by Stephen Fowl.

1. *Emics and the Intentions of Authors*

It should be quite uncontroversial to say that an individual communicative act has to be understood 'in context'. Difficulties begin to arise, however, as soon as one begins to specify the relevant features of a context; the context of a communicative act is clearly multi-layered. At the widest levels of context, human interaction takes place within economic, technological and cultural systems. Within the cultural domain, communicative interaction is mediated by symbolic and linguistic systems.

Traditional humanistic scholarship, with its characteristic interest in individual authors from the distant past, has focused first on the narrowest level of context—the ancient language (without yet conceiving of language as a 'system', a point taken up below). This focus, however, was not primarily motivated by an interest in the language as such but by an interest in the specific ideas of authors which were expressed *by means of* the language. This is not to deny the obvious fact that humanistic scholarship has produced grammars and lexicons, i.e. handbooks on languages as such, but these were more often considered tools in the service of the more basic interest in individual communicative acts; the intention of an ancient author was the primary focus.

Individual communicative acts take place, however, not only within the context of a specific language but also within the context of an historical situation. Hence, in the humanistic tradition, the process of understanding an author or editor began with an analysis of grammar, and was supplemented with hypotheses concerning political, geographical or social 'background', in order to produce an interpretation of an individual communicative act. This brief account of humanistic scholarship and its primary goal, although incomplete, will be sufficient for our present purposes. Our main concern, here, is to locate humanistic scholarship within the broader conception of research which is provided by the social sciences.

With the rise of the social sciences, the task of understanding an 'author' (social scientists would speak more technically of a social 'agent' or 'actor') began to be reformulated. Where a humanistic scholar might allude to selected elements of political, geographical or social background, the social scientist would stress that these elements were themselves part of economic, environmental, technological and social sytems. Any individual agent needed to be understood within the context of these wider systems which constrained or enabled an individual's action. In effect, the basic claim of the social sciences was this: we can only understand individuals if we understand not simply the grammar of their language but also the 'grammars' of the techno-environmental or socio-economic systems which constrain or enable their life.

This basic idea departs from traditional humanistic scholarship in that it proposes a different conception of the relationship between the individual and the corporate. Individual action or 'agency' is seen to be significantly constrained by corporate realities. Hence, the focus of the social sciences has generally shifted away from understanding individual human actions, or individual intentions, towards providing accounts of social *inter*action within the broader contexts of socio-cultural, economic and environmental systems.[1] To speak metaphorically once again, social scientists have been seeking to discover the 'grammar' of these broader systems.

So far we have ignored the differences between the various schools of social science, but the main point in this section depends upon a distinction between two main strands of social scientific endeavour. Here we should be clear that the detailed questions of method are being left to one side; following Pike, Harris, Runciman and others, we need to draw a distinction between two different kinds of interest—'emic' and 'etic'.[2] We shall deal first with emics, since this kind of interest stands closer to traditional humanistic scholarship.

Emic social science is concerned with describing events, meanings, symbols, or processes *from the native's point of view*. In more humanistic terms the main task here would be to provide an account of ancient beliefs and practices in terms

---

1 Whatever one might think about their methods, form critics had already moved towards this kind of interest by trying to identify the specific social institution which formed the 'locus in life' of reconstructed oral traditions. In developing their modest style of social description, form critics have tended to eschew larger explanatory theories about societies as systems.

2 The origin of these terms (in phon*emic*s and phon*etic*s) is discussed below in section 2.

that derive from the ancient authors themselves. This is the task that is sometimes (and less precisely) described as 'understanding the text in its own terms'.

Emic interpretation could well provide the grounds for a more amiable alliance between humanistic exegetes and social scientists. Although their focus is different (the former more individualistic and the latter more social), their interests are not only compatible but also complementary. This complementarity becomes evident when one considers the process by which anthropologists develop their interpretations of foreign cultures. One of the central problems for emic description is the reliability of individual 'informants'. Even assuming the sincerity of an informant, knowledge of a particular culture or society is never distributed evenly over every one of its members. The information provided by individual informants will be coloured by their own perspective. In practice, field anthropologists try to use a number of informants, checking their information from as many angles as possible. The whole picture can only be built up from a large number of individual communicative acts. But in the course of assessing these *individual* communicative intentions anthropologists are acting like humanistic scholars.

There are, however, special difficulties in using 'informant reports' from the distant past, and in this respect field anthropologists are in a much stronger position than humanistic scholars. The social scientist is able to collect any number of informant reports whereas the biblical scholar is restricted to the available historical evidence. Biblical scholars are also at a disadvantage in so far as this historical evidence for Israelite culture comes primarily from *written* historical records. The problem here is not just that biblical records might be dominated by a particular cultural perspective (e.g. of those Israelites who believed that Yahweh alone was the only divinity worthy of worship). The additional problem is that 'the native point of view' may be expressed as much by actions and practices as it is by spoken or written communication. The field anthropologist has access to all these dimensions whereas the biblical scholar is largely restricted to written communicative acts; these become the narrow basis for inferences about ancient Israelite cultural systems. In this respect the narrow focus of much humanistic biblical scholarship is entirely justified; whenever biblical scholars attempt to move beyond the scope of their written evidence (by, for example, reconstructing oral traditions, social practices or institutions behind the text) their hypotheses are inevitably weakened by the paucity of direct evidence.

One need not, however, infer that it is impossible for biblical scholars to distinguish critically between more and less probable hypotheses about the non-literary dimensions of Israelite culture. The point is simply that biblical scholars will almost always have less direct evidence to work with than the field anthropologist who is also interested in emics.

2. *Etics*

Etic scholarly interests are of an entirely different kind. Here the over-riding goal is to provide the best scientific explanation of the subject matter, and this might well entail the use of concepts and explanations which are entirely foreign to the social actors being studied. The recent works of Gottwald and Frick[1] provide the clearest examples of this kind of study; they explain Israelite origins and the rise of the Israelite state primarily in terms of the ancient environment and economy. Such materialist explanations were entirely unknown in ancient Israel itself, but that is beside the point. Gottwald and Frick are not guided by the concerns of emic description. Even if their own materialism could be decisively refuted, the methodological point would stand. Etic historical explanations need to be defended before the bar of the modern sciences, not before the bar of ancient Israelites.

This point can be most simply demonstrated by returning to the roots of the distinction between emics and etics. The distinction was first formulated by the linguist Kenneth Pike as a

---

1 N.K. Gottwald, *The Tribes of Yahweh* (Maryknoll: Orbis, 1979); F. Frick, *The Formation of the State in Ancient Israel* (The Social World of Biblical Antiquity, 4; Sheffield: Almond, 1985). Gottwald's version of scientific Marxism is well known in biblical studies, but among literary critics there is a range of less deterministic Marxisms. See the helpful introduction by Michael Ryan, 'Political Criticism', in *Contemporary Literary Theory* (ed. G.D. Atkins and L. Morrow; London: Macmillan, 1989), pp. 200-13.

tool for the analysis of human action. He derived the terms
from the linguistic disciplines of phonemics and phonetics:
phonemics describes the significant differences between the
sounds of speech *as perceived by native speakers in their own
linguistic system*; phonetics attempts to describe rigorously all
the sounds of human speech irrespective of whether particular native speakers would describe their language in these
terms. For example, the validity of terms like 'labial' or
'dental', and so on, does not depend on these words being part
of everyday conversation. Given the comprehensive goal of
phonetics the use of a scientific 'meta-language' (i.e. an analytical language of which native speakers need never be
aware) becomes unavoidable. By analogy, modern historians
may need to use scientific meta-languages. For example, they
may possess information about economic processes which was
unavailable to ancient authors. The use of this information in
historical explanation is entirely justified. If it seems that
ancient societies lacked the concept of an economy it by no
means follows that they were never influenced by economic
forces, just as if they lacked the concept of malaria it by no
means follows that they could never have died from it.[1] Such
modern conceptions only become anachronistic where the
goal of inquiry is an emic one.[2]

1 Runciman, *Treatise on Social Theory*, vol. 1, p. 13.
2 One further clarification of emics is appropriate at this stage. J.W. Flanagan has
   recently reviewed a number of anthropological studies which draw the emic/etic
   distinction in slightly different ways. He seems to prefer the view of Holy and
   Stutchlik who speak of the domain of 'notions' (the concern of emics) as opposed to
   the domain of 'actions' (analysed by etic observation). This distinction has at
   least the virtue of terminological simplicity, but there is a danger here of conflat-
   ing 'ontological' questions with methodological ones. In speaking of two separate
   domains of data Flanagan is pushed into discussing ontological questions like
   the following: do segmentary lineage systems exist 'in native heads', or are they
   part of objective and observable social structure? Whatever one might think about
   this theoretical issue, it is a mistake to think that only etic studies can have
   recourse to the domain of actions. Even if it were true, for example, that lineage
   systems are primarily 'in native heads', the *evidence* for this claim is not derived
   from an internal examination of native minds. The evidence can only come
   from a study of action—including communicative interaction. Contrary to some
   opinions on the subject, the distinction between emics and etics should not be confused with a distinction between observable human actions and unobservable
   mental notions. Neither interpretative interest can avoid using 'observable' evidence.

In the light of the preceding discussion, humanistic scholars may be tempted to think that the distinction between emics and etics is a matter that is best left to social scientists. The study of literary genres, however, raises precisely the same issue. It is difficult to believe, for example, that ancient Israelites themselves distinguished between the vast numbers of literary genres now proposed by critical scholars to describe the biblical literature. Our scepticism at this point need not, however, restrict the careful comparison of texts undertaken by form critics and others. Credulity is only stretched when form critics attribute their elaborate taxonomies to the conscious processes of communicative interaction in ancient Israel.

Some recent arguments conerning apocalyptic literature provide convenient examples of this point. John Barton has argued that during the period of the second temple the authors of apocalyptic literature would not have seen any distinction in genre between their own texts and the revered texts of the ancient prophets. The audiences who accepted these apocalypses would, similarly, have recognized no such distinction.[1] In other words, although prophecy was an emic genre, apocalypse was not. If Barton is right, then it follows that the modern debate about the rise of apocalyptic literature should be undertood as an etic enterprise. It is indeed difficult to demonstrate that the original authors and audiences saw this material as a distinctively new and different type of literature. In fact, an explicit consciousness of such novelty would probably have undermined the strategy of pseudonymity.

Having re-stated this argument from Barton's *Oracles of God*, it will be instructive to turn to his work on method,

---

See J.W. Flanagan, *David's Social Drama* (JSOTSup, 73; The Social World of Biblical Antiquity, 7; Sheffield: Almond, 1988), esp. pp. 88-108; L. Holy and M. Stuchlik, *Actions, Norms and Representations* (Cambridge: Cambridge University Press, 1983). See also the work of Clifford Geertz who takes for granted the views of Wittgenstein and Ryle in so far as they reject the explanatory value of mental events (*Interpretation of Cultures* [New York: Basic Books, 1973], e.g. pp. 6-12, 17, 91, 96-97, 214-16). Cf. also M. Harris, 'History and Significance of the emic/etic Distinction', *Annual Review of Anthropology* 5 (1976), pp. 329-50; R. Feleppa, 'Emics, Etics and Social Objectivity', *Current Anthropology* 27 (1986), pp. 243-55.

1 J. Barton, *Oracles of God* (London: Darton, Longman & Todd, 1986), e.g. pp. 9, 122, 129, 201.

Reading the Old Testament. In this work one of the central theses is this: 'it is impossible to understand any text without at least an implicit recognition of the genre to which it belongs'.[1] But does he mean emic or etic genre? This is not clear. He has, however, himself implied that in order for the original audiences to understand an apocalypse they did not need to see the text *as an apocalypse*. On the contrary, they would have seen apocalypses as prophecy. It is clear that we *now* understand classical prophecy to be a different kind of literature from the apocalypse, but this fact has very little bearing on the emic interpretation of *either* classical prophecies *or* apocalypses: the classical prophets were not aware of apocalyptic literature (since it did not yet exist) and the original authors and audiences of apocalypses thought of these works as prophecies. The implications of Barton's arguments on genre require, it would seem, further clarification. In any case, the distinction between emics and etics is directly relevant to the older humanistic concern with genres.

3. *Synchronic Interests*

If the preceding argument has any validity, then a number of points follow. First, interpreters will need in the future to be much clearer about the nature of genre classifications; emics and etics need to be distinguished. Second, the 'historical' character of emic genres needs a much closer analysis. In developing this second point about genre, it will be useful to distinguish between synchronic and diachronic interests generally. I hesitate to introduce these terms since although they are already widely familiar they are understood in different ways. Nevertheless, a clear grasp of this distinction as it was originally formulated will help to illuminate the general argument that different interpretative interests can peacefully co-exist. I shall, therefore, first discuss the original distinction between synchronic and diachronic interests in linguistics and then return to the issue of genre.

---

1   J. Barton, *Reading the Old Testament* (London: Darton, Longman & Todd, 1984), p. 16.

The distinction was formulated by F. de Saussure in the widely influential account of his lectures, *Cours de linguistique générale* (1916).[1] He argued that the all-too-easy conflation of synchronic and diachronic interests in linguistics was especially damaging to synchronic studies, i.e. those studies which seek to illuminate the language used by any particular community of native speakers at a particular time. In one sense Saussure gave methodological priority to the 'state' or 'system' of a language at a particular time when he argued that 'the synchronic viewpoint... is the true and only reality to the community of speakers'.[2] In rough paraphrase: only synchronic interests can illuminate the native point of view. At first glance, this argument might seem to deny the significance of history, but such an impression of Saussure's work would be mistaken. Saussure's structural linguistics should not be simply conflated with the anti-historical sentiments found in the writings of some literary and anthropological structuralists.

Saussure defended his position by discussing numerous examples of how words can change their meaning over the course of time, i.e. diachronically. Take, for example, *necare* which in classical Latin means 'kill' but in fourth- and fifth-century vulgar Latin means 'drown'. Although diachronic study is quite justified in recognizing a connection between these two meanings, Saussure argues that what we have here is evidence for distinguishing between two different linguistic systems. A fourth-century speaker of Latin would usually be unaware of the earlier meaning of *necare*, and the classical meaning is indeed irrelevant to the synchronic point of view (just as English speakers do not need to be familiar with Romance or Germanic etymologies before becoming competent speakers of English). Each linguistic system would have a number of words clustered around the concept of death, and it is the specific *cluster* of available lexical items which is relevant to synchronic studies of Latin. Accordingly, Saussure could even argue that 'a loan word no longer counts as such

---

1 F. de Saussure, *Cours de linguistique générale* (ed. C. Bally and A. Sechehaye; Paris: Payot, 1916). Our citations are from the translation of the 3rd edn (1931) by W. Baskin, *Course in General Linguistics* (Glasgow: Collins, 1974).
2 De Saussure, *Course*, p. 90; cf. p. 81.

whenever it is studied within a system'.[1] For the most part, in other words, native speakers of a particular linguistic system need never recognize a word borrowed from another language *as a loan word*. This point corresponds to the main thesis that native speakers need never know the earlier history of their 'own' language.

This is not to deny, of course, that native speakers may be fully conscious that they are using foreign words or at times display an interest in the history of the words they use. We have, for example, numerous biblical examples of personal names being explained in the text itself—the phenomenon of 'folk etymology'. But even in this kind of case, the methodological point still stands: the native point of view, expressed by folk etymologies, need not constrain the diachronic explanations offered by a modern linguist. For example, the folk etymology for the name 'Samuel' offered in 1 Sam. 1.20 could well have been applied at an earlier time to the name 'Saul'. Folk etymologies (like genealogies) are best used as evidence for a native point of view at the time of composition. When we say that folk etymologies are often 'mistaken', this is a shorthand way of saying that modern diachronic semantics has provided us with a more exacting analysis of the development of a word's usage. Folk etymologies can, nevertheless, be of great significance for emic description.

A second kind of objection to Saussure's argument has to do with loan words. Once again, one need not deny examples of the *conscious* use of a foreign word; such usage may have some special emic significance within specific speech situations (one thinks, for example, of the social credit gained in some circles by demonstrating one's facility with foreign languages). But whatever special significance is attached to a loan word its meaning will often not be reducible simply to the meaning of that word in its foreign context. For one thing, the introduction of a foreign word into a linguistic system will affect the configuration of lexical items in the same 'semantic field'.[1] Indeed, with repeated use the explicitly 'foreign' status of the word will usually fade in the course of time.

Before we examine a specific example of a synchronic interest in the study of biblical Hebrew, it may be helpful to digress slightly and describe an anthropological example where the basic issue at stake is the same. Consider, for example, the use of horse-drawn hansom cabs in present day New York City. A synchronic anthropologist would insist, for example, that one must not account for the use of such vehicles in the present day by explaining their invention and the original contexts of their usage; as a cultural artefact, their 'meaning' or significance has changed. The contemporary use of hansom cabs should be understood as serving the function of nostalgia or 'retrospective sentiment'.[2] This example makes clear that there is no denial here of the fact that hansom cabs do indeed have a history, or that 'natives' may be very interested in their history. It is just that in their original setting, hansom cabs *could not have served the function of nostalgia*. The explanation is synchronic rather than diachronic. That is to say, phenomena are explained within the context of the contemporary society, rather than within the context of some earlier society in which, for example, there was a different 'cluster' of the means of transport.

If there is a conflict between synchronic and diachronic interests it is not because one is 'historical' and the other is not; synchronic studies focus on serial slices of history, treating each slice as a systemic whole. In biblical studies, however, there has been an unfortunate clash between historical-critical research and studies of the 'final form' which purport to be synchronic. Some scholars interested in the received form of the Masoretic text have rightly pointed out that hypotheses about the pre-history of a text (e.g. the sources and oral traditions which lie behind it) do not necessarily illuminate the present shape of the literature. A literary source, like a hansom cab, may mean something quite different when it is edited

---

1 The notion of a semantic field refers to the collection of lexical items in a linguistic system that are associated with a specific concept. See further J.F.A. Sawyer, cited below.

2 M. Harris, *The Rise of Anthropological Theory* (London: Routledge & Kegan Paul, 1969), p. 166.

together with other sources or traditions. It does not follow from this, however, that synchronic interests can only be directed at the final form.

This kind of point has been made, but also obscured, by J.F.A. Sawyer in his comprehensive study of words for salvation in the Hebrew Bible. In this study Sawyer opts, in a self-consciously arbitrary way, to study the whole of the Hebrew text as if it were the product of 'masoretic Hebrew': 'how the masoretes themselves understood the text should be the subject for semantic analysis'.[1] Whatever sense can be made of this goal it is important to recognize that it does not exclude *other* goals for synchronic semantics. Sawyer rightly points out that

> The language of the OT... originated in various distinct contexts, and therefore no field which takes in the whole of OT Hebrew could satisfactorily be used as a guide to any one historical situation.[2]

By working on the semantic field of words for salvation in the final form of the Masoretic text Sawyer has avoided the historical changes to the field of salvation during the biblical period. Thus, although the size of the field was enlarged over time (e.g. *pṣh* and *prq* are probably loan words from Aramaic[3]), Sawyer's chosen goal has not constrained him to describe the field at any one time during the biblical period. He has conflated final form study with a synchronic interest, but it need not have been so. A study which attempted to reconstruct the Hebrew spoken in Jerusalem during the latter half of the ninth century BCE would have been equally synchronic.

On the whole, Sawyer's monograph uses the term 'synchronic' in a way that is consistent with Saussure's usage. A number of other critics, however, use the term analogically, suggesting that the final form of the biblical text is itself a system and that any diachronic dimensions behind the text (redactions, sources, or oral traditions) should be neglected by

---

1 J.F.A. Sawyer, *Semantics in Biblical Research* (Studies in Biblical Theology; London: SCM, 1972), p. 11.

2 Sawyer, *Semantics*, p. 41. Cf. also p. 114: 'The [OT] corpus is not a representative cross-section of the Hebrew language at any one time'.

3 Sawyer, *Semantics*, p. 42.

'synchronic' interpretation. I would argue that this analogy of 'text as system' confuses Saussure's distinction between *langue* (a linguistic system) and *parole* (communicative acts made possible by the linguistic system). The fruitfulness of Saussure's notion of a synchronic interest will be lost if the analogy is allowed to persist.[1] For example, properly synchronic studies of genre could be highly significant, and it is to this issue that we once again turn.

Although form critics have attempted to trace the history of biblical genres, very few studies have sought to reconstruct the genres that may have been available in a specific period of Israelite history. It is often said, for example, that genuine 'history writing' only arose during the period of the monarchy; before this period, narratives which refer to the past should be understood as 'legends'. But if this is the case, a synchronic implication can be drawn for the pre-monarchic period: the distinction between legend and history writing was not an emic distinction. No native Israelite of this period would have made this distinction since history writing did not yet exist. If as critics we describe legends by using Gunkel's classic division, legend *as opposed* to history writing, then we should be clear that this is an etic distinction. Assuming the consensus about the beginnings of history writing, it may have become an emic distinction only after the rise of the monarchy.

Consider now the period during which 'history writing' came to be, whenever that may be dated. J. Van Seters has recently argued that the Deuteronomistic Historian produced

---

1 Most recently, Robert Morgan has contributed to the eclipse of Saussure's notion by citing a description of synchronic interpretation as a universalizing attempt to 'flatten out the past into a great synchronic mush'. The force of Saussure's work is, however, precisely in the opposite direction: he is attempting to preserve historical differences. Cf. R. Morgan with J. Barton, *Biblical Interpretation* (Oxford: Oxford University Press, 1988), p. 261.

  We should perhaps point out here that deconstructionist literary critics have joined forces with sociolinguists in insisting that Saussure's *langue* is an ideal construction. This criticism of Saussure has been absorbed by linguists, and it does not justify the deconstructionist penchant for unrestrained etymological interpretation. Such playful etymologies actually obscure semantic *differences*, and no more damaging criticism could be uttered against a deconstructionist than that. See J. Lyons's remarks on 'the fiction of homogeneity' in his *Language and Linguistics* (Cambridge: Cambridge University Press, 1981), pp. 24-27; A. White, 'Bakhtin, Sociolinguistics, and Deconstruction', in *The Theory of Reading* (ed. F. Gloversmith; New York: Barnes & Noble, 1984), pp. 123-45.

the first genuine history of the 'Western' tradition. But this claim presents a logical puzzle: if this really was the first example of its type, then the original audience could not have recognized it as such. To be a literary 'type' there would need to be more than one example, but in this case there could only be one example since this was, according to Van Seters, the first one of its type.[1] To put the point more generally, works which embody generic innovation are less determinate with respect to their emic genre. This is especially the case if one includes audience expectation in the notion of emic genre;[2] audiences may well recognize a literary novelty, but they cannot recognize such novelty *as an example of a determinate genre*. These are just some of the implications that could be drawn from properly synchronic studies of genre.

4. *Diachronic Interests*

The essential nature of a diachronic interest will be evident from the preceding discussion, but one would need to distinguish between emic and etic diachronic interests. The works, already mentioned, by Gottwald and Frick clearly provide examples of diachronic etics. The historical 'trends' that they purport to have found can properly be judged by scientific communities, not by the theories and conceptions of the native communities in ancient Israel. But what of diachronic emics?

Given our account of synchronic interests, the idea of a diachronic emic interest would seem, at first glance, to be inconceivable; Saussure, for example, did not discuss the idea. I would suggest, however, that diachronic emics is indeed possible, and many histories of Israelite tradition could be fitted under this heading. Recently, for example, in *David's Social Drama* J.W. Flanagan has provided us with what he calls 'a genealogy of ancient notions' which extends from the pre-

---

1 J. Van Seters, *In Search of History* (New Haven: Yale University Press, 1983). Cf. E.D. Hirsch, *Validity in Interpretation* (New Haven: Yale University Press, 1967), p. 64: 'Anything that is unique cannot, with respect to those aspects which are unique, be a type'.

2 Hirsch provides a comprehensive account of genre that ties it both to authorial intention and to the notion of audience expectation (*Validity in Interpretation*, see esp. p. 86).

Yahwist worship of El to the priestly Yahwism of Chronicles.[1]
One might well argue that such an extensive diachronic
sweep was not actually available to any one ancient Israelite
community; for the pre-monarchic worshippers of El, priestly
Yahwism did not yet exist, while for the priestly Yahwists of
post-exilic times, El was simply another name for Yahweh.
Yet at some stage in between these diachronic extremes there
must have been cultural agents who forged the link between
El and Yahweh. At each of these stages, the native view of the
divinity was in all likelihood quite different, and similarly, at
each stage the perception of Israel's past was quite different.

What I have said above about anthropological fieldwork is
also relevant at this point: the knowledge of a culture is not
distributed evenly over all of its agents. Diachronic emic studies, however, attempt to trace the transitions of native notions
through time. They begin to approach the character of etics in
that they move beyond any single native perspective, but they
do not attempt to translate native notions into scientific meta-
languages. We therefore need to qualify Saussure's view
stated above: 'the synchronic viewpoint... is the true and only
reality to the community of speakers'. Yes, emic studies should
first pursue synchronic slices of history, but communities
which extend through time are the bearers of mutable traditions, and diachronic emic studies explore this mutability.

What I am proposing, then, is that histories of Israelite tradition can be understood as diachronic emic description
(histories of religion or tradition could also be treated from an
etic perspective, so our more technical term is clearer in this
case). But writing histories of Israelite tradition is not the only
possible task for the biblical historian with emic interests. Even
after the biblical traditions were transformed into relatively
'immutable' scripture, they were read and commented on by
successive generations. The history of exegesis can, therefore,
also be understood as part of diachronic emic description.
What is being studied in *emic histories of reception* are the
various native interpretations of scripture through the ages
(raising the question, native to what community?). But in this

1 Flanagan, *David's Social Drama*, esp. the summary on pp. 258-59.

case the primary evidence will be the commentaries and not the biblical literature itself.

5. *Interests in Texts as Such*

We have seen that biblical texts can be used as evidence for native points of view (emics), and as evidence in scientific comparisons and explanations of those points of view (etics). But it is also possible to be interested in texts as such. Here I have in mind especially literary discussions, for example, of plot, character, point of view, theme, scene, repetition, metaphor, style, organic unity, contradiction, indeterminacy, and so on, all of which may be carried on without direct reference to an authorial intention or original audience. Some literary concepts would seem to be inherently intentional, like satire, but many literary critics explicitly reject the idea that authorial intention should be held up as a regulative norm for all interpretation. Some, like the New Critics, defended this on the grounds that literary works are qualitatively different from ordinary communicative actions. Others, like structuralists and post-structuralists, reject any boundary between literary and non-literary language. I would argue, along with the latter group, that it is possible to have an interest in texts as such, even when the language has no obvious 'literary' qualities.

In order to make this discussion more concrete, let us return as an example to Saussure's influential book discussed above. This work was not actually prepared for publication by Saussure himself, and indeed, a critical edition has recently been produced which, on the basis of scattered notes and other sources, attempts to be more faithful to Saussure's intentions. After pointing this out, a leading authority in linguistics goes on to say, 'It is, however, the *Cours* as originally published, that has been of historic importance'.[1] In other words, modern linguistics has been decisively influenced by a book that is relatively autonomous of its author. A biographer of Saussure will take more notice of the critical edition. But linguists who were

1 J. Lyons, *Semantics*, vol. 1 (Cambridge: Cambridge University Press, 1977), p. 231.

more interested in the truth content of the *Cours* have sub-
jected the ideas of the historic *text* to critical examination, and
the discipline has moved on. In short, the idea of examining
the objective content of a text is both intelligible and logically
separable from any hypotheses about its author.[1]

This argument has been rigorously defended by Karl Popper. In his influential account of scientific argument, Popper
has argued that objective knowledge should not be conceived
of as the product of individual scientists. Individual work is too
often reducible to the idiosyncrasies of personal biographies for
this to be the case. Rather, objective knowledge only comes to
light through the rigorous processes of falsification, i.e. critical
interaction. One of the implications of this idea is directly relevant to the present discussion: Popper has concluded that
objective knowledge exists independently of any particular
knower; indeed, it exists in texts and computers rather than in
human minds. This argument includes a distinction between
three 'worlds':

> first, the world of physical objects or physical states; sec-
> ondly, the world of states of consciousness, or mental states,
> or perhaps behavioural dispostions to act; and thirdly, the
> world of *objective contents of thought*, especially of scientific
> and poetic thoughts and works of art.[2]

'Thought' is here understood as a public and objective content
contained in texts, rather than as an individual's mental act of
thinking. It is only within 'world three' that a researcher's
thoughts can begin to be objective; it is only there that the scientific community can 'correct those prejudices which are the

---

1 Contra James Barr, the idea that texts might have 'intentions' is not an indefensi-
ble anthropomorphism. See Barr, 'Childs' Introduction to the Old Testament as
Scripture', *JSOT* 16 (1980), pp. 13-14. One should concede to Barr, however, that
Brevard Childs' work does at times amount to an infelicitous attempt to combine
emic interests with an interest in texts as such. See further my doctoral work, *The
Canonical Approach to Old Testament Study* (PhD thesis, University of Sheffield,
1988).

2 K. Popper, *Objective Knowledge* (Oxford: Oxford University Press, 1972), p. 106.
One should not infer that each 'world' attracts a peculiar set of interests. See R.
Rorty, 'Texts and Lumps', *New Literary History* 17 (1985), pp. 1-16; L. Dannen-
berg and H.H. Müller, 'Wissenschaftstheorie, Hermeneutik, Literaturwissenschaft', *Deutsche Vierteljahrschrift für Literaturwissenschaft und Geis-
tesgeschichte* 2 (1984), pp. 177-237.

unavoidable consequence of his peculiar mental history'.[1] The details of an ideological habitat 'always play a part in the short run',[2] but they can be purified, according to Popper, in the fires of critical interaction which leave their deposit in world three.

Biblical scholars will be familiar with the recent wave of studies which distinguish between the meaning of a text on the one hand, and the intention of its author on the other. Some historical-critical scholars have found such a distinction unintelligible, but I think it is clear that Popper at least would find the distinction not just intelligible but essential; indeed, he is willing to rest his argument for the objectivity of science upon it. Scholars guided by emic interests are concerned that interests in biblical texts as such will produce interpretations which no ancient author would have intended. This is a proper concern of emics, but need it restrict other interpreters with more 'objective' literary interests? I would suggest not. It is instructive to see that Popper has also addressed this issue. He emphasizes that the linguistically formulated contents of 'world three' give rise to new and unexpected problems which were not part of the author's consciousness.[3] This is an essential feature of objective scientific criticism.

This kind of argument has long been associated with New Criticism, although other schools of literary theory would also assent to it. The New Critics were concerned to eliminate from the study of literature all facts which they considered to be irrelevant or 'extrinsic' to the text (for example, both an author's intention and the details of an author's biography were considered extrinsic). The proximity of this view to Popper's is striking, and it is noteworthy that New Criticism was advanced under the label of 'objective' criticism. John Barton

1 K. Popper, 'The Sociology of Knowledge', in *The Sociology of Knowledge* (ed. J. Curtis and J. Petras; London: Duckworth, 1970), pp. 555-66.
2 K. Popper, 'The Logic of the Social Sciences', in *The Positivist Dispute in German Sociology* (ed. T.W. Adorno *et al.*; London: Heinemann, 1976), p. 96.
3 Popper, *Objective Knowledge*, pp. 74, 118-19, 148. A similar idea has been advanced by the anthropologist Jack Goody with respect to the unforeseen cognitive consequences of literacy. Goody argues that writing is not simply objectified speech; rather, it allows distinctive forms of problem-raising and problem-solving not to be found in oral cultures. See Goody, *The Domestication of the Savage Mind* (Cambridge: Cambridge University Press, 1977), and my own discussion, 'Literacy and Domination: G.A. Herion's Sociology of History Writing', *JSOT* 37 (1987), esp. pp. 20-24.

has provided us with a helpful account of this literary movement, and he has rightly argued that New Criticism has been
very influential in biblical studies even when it has not been
explicitly invoked. Barton himself, however, seems to think
that it is only 'extrinsic' factors like authorial intention and
historical context that can provide us with determinate
meanings of texts; without these factors texts in themselves
would be indeterminate.[1] We would be left with just a variety
of readings and no way of resolving their differences.

It should be clear, however, that authorial intentions and
historical contexts do not arrive on the critic's desk ready-
made; they have to be reconstructed. And at least emic reconstruction is dependent on textual evidence. Accordingly, one
would have to say that interests in texts as such have an epistemological priority, even if they leave us with a whole range
of equally possible readings. In practice, however, the prospect
for emics is not so bleak. After surveying the range of possible
readings of various biblical texts, the critic with emic interests
may suggest that a particular *configuration* of readings (e.g. of
texts considered Priestly or Deuteronomistic) makes best
sense in a specific historical situation, and the foundations of a
hypothesis about authorial intention can thereupon be laid.
But to argue in advance that all readings must come supplied
with authorial intentions and historical backgrounds would
surely restrict the development of fresh insights even in emic
studies.

Conclusions

I have described five different interpretative interests,
although some might argue that interests in texts as such
should be understood as merely exemplification of etic interests. The list is not exhaustive, and others may wish to refine it.

---

1 Barton, *Reading*, p. 188. Such indeterminacy is, of course, deplored by Barton but
   celebrated by deconstruction. The most intelligible introductions to this literary
   movement are those by C. Norris, *Deconstruction: Theory and Practice* (London:
   Methuen, 1982), and J. Culler, *On Deconstruction* (Ithaca: Cornell University
   Press, 1982). See also the influential essays reprinted in D. Lodge (ed.), *Modern
   Criticism and Theory* (London: Longman, 1988).

The analysis of intention, for example, is as yet incomplete.[1] Yet the discussion should demonstrate that the recent plurality of interests in biblical studies need not be a cause for alarm. Conflicts inevitably arise when critics believe that they have discovered the only valid method of biblical study, but the discipline would be better served if we pursued our interests in relative independence and compared our results in a spirit of openness. Different interests might well provide results that bear fruit in unintended ways; at least Popper would lead us to expect this. It would be a pity if we became bewitched by the dream of an all-inclusive method; we will all suffer if logically separable tasks come to be subjected to a totalitarian regime. Being clear about our own interests would at least bear the fruit of separating apparent conflicts from genuine ones.[2]

1 In speaking of 'intentions' one should at least distinguish between motives, communicative content, and illocutionary forces, but this would require another paper to explicate. I have begun the task in my thesis, *The Canonical Approach to Old Testament Study*, pp. 77-87. It is the study of motives, for example, which seems to be the primary focus for the 'critique of ideology', an etic interest.

2 Ben Ollenburger has rightly pointed out, for example, that interests in texts as such need only conflict with diachronic ones when a critic moves on explicitly to deny the redactional development of a text. His analogy is apt: 'a description of a table may be considered adequate, given some set of interests, even if it does not refer to the molecular structure of the wood that composes it. But no such description can simply claim that there are no molecules hidden in the wood ('What Krister Stendahl "meant"—a Normative Critique of "Descriptive Biblical Theology"', *HBT* 8 [1986], p. 98 n. 33).

THE ETHICS OF INTERPRETATION
or
WHAT'S LEFT OVER AFTER
THE ELIMINATION OF MEANING

Stephen Fowl

What do biblical scholars do when they interpret the Bible? Ask most scholars and they will tell you that the aim of interpretation is to uncover, elucidate or explicate the/a meaning of the text.[1] How do they do this? By rigorously and systematically applying some form of interpretative practice or method. Behind each of these practices and methods stands some theory about what meaning is and how it is to be attained. Even when it is recognized that few scholars actually reflect on the theories underlying their practice, the quest for meaning necessarily relies on some account of what it is you are looking for. The assumption that biblical interpretation is involved with determining meaning logically depends on at least one of these theories being right. For even if you hold that there are several meanings to a text, this supposition is still supported by a single theory which must explain what these meanings are and how to get at them.

According this scenario it is not difficult to see that the power of an interpretative theory is directly related to its ability to answer the question of what the meaning of the text is. Yet, depending on where you do your interpretation, what

---

1 Lest anyone think I am creating a straw person, I would direct them to look at the way the term 'meaning' is used in John Barton's recent article, 'Reading the Bible as Literature: Two Questions for Biblical Critics', *Literature and Theology* 1 (1987), pp. 135-63. I use Barton as an example because he is one of the most hermeneutically sophisticated and self-reflective biblical scholars in Britain.

counts as meaning varies tremendously.[1] It is no secret that
what counts as meaning in Sheffield most certainly does not
count as meaning in every other university. This would not
bother someone like me, writing in a volume celebrating Biblical studies in Sheffield, if there were some way to show that
Sheffield is right and those who do things differently are
wrong. What is so distressing is that there do not seem to be
any defensible criteria by which one could argue the case
either for Sheffield or against. As Jeffrey Stout notes, we really
have no way of adjudicating between competing conceptions
of textual meaning.[2] Without criteria for resolving the question of what the meaning of a text is, we are unable to develop
an adequate theory of interpretation.

> If interpretation is a matter of discovering meaning, and is
> therefore bound to run amuck when informed by mistaken
> assumptions about what meaning is, then literary criticism,
> religious studies, classics, history [and biblical studies]—in
> short, all disciplines involving the interpretation of texts—
> will consist largely in failure to deliver the goods.[3]

This in itself would not be bothersome if, as in the natural
sciences, we could say that we were moving forward by systematically removing error. Failure would be tolerable if it
were leading to increased probability of success. But in the
case of developing a theory of textual meaning without a clear
conception of what meaning is, we do not even know what
'success' would look like.

Given this state of affairs, I would like to propose that we in
Biblical studies give up discussions of meaning and adopt
Stout's position of dissolving disputes about meaning by expli-
cating these disputes in terms of interpretative interests.[4] In

---

1   See Stanley Fish's various arguments for this point in *Is There a Text in This
    Class? The Authority of Interpretive Communities* (Cambridge: Harvard Uni-
    versity Press, 1980); cf. also his 'Anti-Professionalism', *New Literary History* 17
    (1985), pp. 89-117.
2   See 'What is the Meaning of a Text?', *New Literary History* 14 (1982), pp. 1-12. To
    those familiar with this essay it will be evident that my debt to Stout in this essay
    goes well beyond the passages cited.
3   Stout, 'What is the Meaning of a Text?', p. 1.
4   Richard Rorty makes a similar proposal in 'Texts and Lumps', *New Literary
    History* 17 (1985), pp. 1-16. See also Steven Mailloux, 'Rhetorical Hermeneutics',
    Critical Inquiry 11 (1985), pp. 620-41. As Mark Brett indicated in the previous

the rest of this essay I would like to indicate what Biblical studies might look like in this light. I then plan to explore some of the residual issues and consequences of adopting this pragmatist position. Finally, I will raise the question of whether the institutions which sustain professional Biblical studies are capable of resolving these issues. My first task, then, will be to elaborate and qualify what Stout's proposal entails for Biblical studies.

The reason we cannot agree on what the meaning(s) of a text are, Stout proposes, is that our concerns with textual meaning are confused. The source of this confusion is the term meaning itself.[1] Of course, most of us can use the term meaning in informal conversations with relative ease and clarity. This is because in these informal conversations the contexts in which the term meaning is used are so clearly circumscribed (or capable of circumscription in the course of the conversation) that the term poses no impediment to discussion. The problem arises when we move to formal discussions of meaning as such. Here the term meaning is not so clearly circumscribed. Take, for example, discussions about a theory of meaning.

> What is a theory of meaning a theory of? Evidently, it may be a theory of any number of things. A question of the form, 'What is the meaning of x?', retains all of the ambiguity of its central term but none of the grammatical features that... would diminish its tendency to confuse.[2]

Stout's remedy for this confusion is to eliminate it at its source. That is, we should eliminate talk of meanings in favour of other terms that will both suit our interpretative interests and be precise enough to put a a stop to futile discussions. To do this, Stout suggests that we employ a form of explication in regard to the term 'meaning' which has its roots in

essay in this book, interests can be of varying types. Like him, I an concerned for the moment with interests one might have in interpreting (taken in a narrow sense) the Bible.

1 See John Lyons' description of the various meanings of 'meaning' in *Semantics* (Cambridge: CUP, 1977), vol. 1, pp. 2ff.
2 Stout, 'What is the Meaning of a Text?', p. 3.

the work of the philosopher W.V.O. Quine.[1] That is, 'We fix on the particular functions of the unclear expression that make it worth troubling about, and then devise a substitute, clear and couched in terms to our liking, that fills those functions'.[2] 'Good explication… tells us how to translate theories from familiar but confusing idioms into idioms better suited to our purposes.'[3] When explication is applied to a term like meaning, the result is that instead of answering our questions about meaning, we replace our present question—what is the meaning of this text?—with different questions.[4]

Instead of talk about meanings we would, for example, claim that we are interested in an author's intentions—what he or she intended to do in writing a certain text. The notion of intention would require further explication, but once this is done, it would then be possible to perform all of the tasks necessary to display this intention without ever having recourse to the term 'meaning'. For example, to the best of our abilities, we can describe what Luke's communicative aims were in presenting Jesus in the way he does.[5] The reading this interpretative interest yields can be evaluated in terms of the adequacy of the way the task has been defined and in terms of the way the task is carried out.

On the other hand, we may decide that we are interested in something else. We may, for example, be interested in a text's contextual connections to the material or gender-based means of its production. Having defined this interest closely enough we can then perform the necessary analysis and come out with some sort of answer. There is, however no need to cloud the issue further by calling the result of this interest 'meaning', particularly when it is done at the expense of other

---

1   See Stout, 'What is the Meaning of a Text?', pp. 2ff. Quine's views on explication are laid out in *Word and Object* (Cambridge, Mass.: Harvard University Press, 1960), pp. 258ff.

2   See Quine, *Word and Object*, p. 260.

3   Stout, 'What is the Meaning of a Text?', p. 2.

4   See Mailloux's comment, 'The solution to the realist/idealist debate in hermeneutics is not, then, the proposal of still another Theory. The way to answer the realist/idealist question "Is meaning created by the text or the reader or by both?" is simply not to ask it, to stop doing Theory' (p. 628).

5   Of course, this does not entail that all of the methods currently used to do this are adequate to the task.

interpretative interests. The obvious example of such interpretative gerrymandering is E.D. Hirsch's position in *Validity
in Interpretation* that only an account of an author's intention
can be called 'meaning' and everything else has the status of
'significance'.[1]

A rejection of Hirsch's claims, however, need not entail a
rejection of the existence of meanings in some sort of ontological sense (if this is felt to be important). It could at some time
be divinely revealed to NT scholars that textual meaning can
only be attained by reading NT texts in the light of the rules
laid out in Graeco-Roman rhetorical manuals. In that event,
we should not need to change our interpretative practices. We
should just have to say that we are interested in things other
than textual meaning and continue with what we were doing.
Indeed, according to this scenario, meaning might be the least
interesting and useful thing to pursue.[2]

There may, however, be some who would wish to claim that
while no single interpretative interest can lay claim to meaning at the expense of any other interest, the term 'meaning'
should be bestowed on that reading which synthesizes all or
most of these interests into some sort of macro-reading—a
reading that looks at a text from all or several possible angles.[3]
This may also go under a description like 'full understanding'.
There is no reason, however, to think that substituting a word
like 'understanding' for 'meaning' will solve any problems.

Further, there are good reasons for thinking that such a
synthesis is not generally possible. Most of the interpretative
interests we adopt are exclusive of other interests. The reading
which one yields is likely to contradict a reading based on

---

1 See his *Validity in Interpretation* (New Haven: Yale University Press, 1967).
   Hirsch revised this position somewhat in subsequent works (cf. 'Meaning and
   Significance Reinterpreted', *Critical Inquiry* 11 [1984], pp. 202-25). For powerful
   critiques of his revised position see Rorty, 'Texts and Lumps', and Lutz Dannen-
   burg and Hans-Harald Müller, 'On Justifying the Choice of Interpretive Theories', *Journal of Aesthetics and Art Criticism* 43 (1984), pp. 7-16, with a reply by
   Hirsch on pp. 89-91.
2 Stout presents a somewhat similar scenario ('What is the Meaning of a Text?',
   pp. 4f.).
3 Perhaps the great fictional example of this is Morris Zapp's desire to produce a
   series of volumes covering all of the possible ways of reading Jane Austen's
   works. See David Lodge, *Changing Places: A Tale of Two Campuses*
   (Harmondsworth: Penguin, 1979).

another. If this were not the case, we would not have such confusion about the term 'meaning' in the first place. For example, a reading of Lk. 8.19-21 within the context of the gospel as a whole would indicate that Jesus thought of his family members as faithful disciples. One would, at least, have to say that Mary was one of those who listened well (8.18) and should be considered as one of those who heard the word of God and did it (cf. Lk. 1.38; 2.19).[1] A reading based on an earlier form of that tradition, Mk 3.28ff., would indicate that Jesus had a negative attitude towards his family, who, for their part, were unsure about Jesus' mental stability. If we are interested in what the earliest traditions thought, the Marcan reading will be important evidence. If we are interested in some phase of this tradition's reception, then both texts along with other data might be relevant, but this would be a third interest altogether and not a synthesis of both into one. This is not to say that scholars must confine themselves to simplistic interests. Our interests can be quite complex and detailed as long as they are precisely formulated. There is, however, no reason to assume that complexity should be a criterion of meaning.

There may indeed be cases when several normally independent interests overlap sufficiently to allow them to be combined into a larger interpretative picture. This, however, is the contingent result of the text under consideration and the particular interests we bring to it. It is not evidence that several interests can be brought together into a unified theory of meaning that will not beg all the questions that first led us to eliminate talk of meaning. Nor should such coincidences encourage us to argue that interests capable of such syntheses are preferable to those interests which are not.

Eliminating talk about meaning by explicating it in terms of interpretative interests should not lead us to think that we have now resolved all of our interpretative disagreements. Should such a state ever be reached, those of us who make a living by interpreting texts will need to look for other means of

---

1 It may well be the case that Jesus' positive evaluation of Mary is based on her discipleship and not her maternal role (cf. 11.27-28). Nevertheless, the contrast with the Marcan evaluation of Mary is still quite strong.

support. Rather, the aim of explicating meaning in terms of interpretative interests is to try to make some of our most intractable disagreements about meaning disappear by indicating that they are not really disagreements about the same thing. Our disagreements about what the meaning of a text is have largely been verbal ones.[1] What we once thought to be one topic, is really several topics. The more we seem to differ on any particular topic the more likely it is that we are not discussing the same topic at all. 'Identification of a common subject matter for divergent theories requires numerous shared beliefs about the nature of the subject matter. Too much divergence ceases to be divergence altogether: it merely changes the subject.'[2] Once we have recognized this, we can proceed to deal with a much more manageable set of disagreements of a much more substantive nature.

It seems to me that there will be three particular areas where disagreement will remain. The first will be in terms of how we formulate our interpretative interests. Once we forego the use of a term like meaning to characterize our particular interpretative interests we should not assume that all talk of interpretative interest will be equally coherent. For example, I may claim that my interest in reading Philippians is to uncover Paul's intention. This interest itself, however, is potentially as confusing as claiming that I want to uncover the meaning of Philippians.

Do I want to uncover the communicative aims of the person who wrote the epistle? If so, I will need to have a knowledge of the linguistic conventions of the situation that is addressed in the epistle, or, at least, Paul's perception of that situation, and what, if any, mutual knowledge is presupposed between Paul and the Philippians.[3] On this view of intention, the text of Philippians will be the primary piece of evidence.

---

1 See Stout, 'What is the Meaning of a Text?', pp. 5-6.
2 Stout, 'What is the Meaning of a Text?', pp. 5-6.
3 These are basically the criteria of successful communication presented in Geoffrey Leech's *Principles of Pragmatics* (London: Longman, 1983).

On the other hand, Paul's intention may also be construed in terms of his motives for writing the epistle.[1] In this case I would need to rely on a picture of the inner workings of Paul's psyche. His conversion experience might be a relevant place to start.[2] Those things which are left unsaid will be as important as what is said.[3] I will need to know something about the history of Paul and the history of his relationship with the Philippians. Having sorted through the evidence, I am then faced with another set of interpretative options. I could try to explain the evidence in terms that would have been recognizable to Paul and the Philippians. On the other hand, I might employ interpretative models from modern social sciences in order to give an explanation of Paul's intentions. In this case, Paul's own description of his intentions need not be taken at face value.

These are just two ways of explicating the notion of intention in regard to a particular Pauline epistle. Clearly, there are other ways of doing this. My aim is not to opt for one over the other. Rather, I simply want to show that once we have eliminated talk of meanings we will still have disagreements about how we formulate our particular interpretative interests. As with the explication of meaning, the more precision we inject into this discussion the more interests we are bound to end up with. We will also be better able to evaluate the results of any particular reading once we are clear about what the reading is actually trying to achieve.

A second level of expected disagreement is in terms of interpretative practice. Given a particular, clearly defined, interest, we may still have disagreements about the readings generated by that interest. Disagreements of this sort will generally be about what is to count as evidence and how we are to read that evidence. Unlike debates about meaning, explication will not be of use to us here. Once we have agreed

---

1   In making this sort of distinction between motives and intentions I am following Mark Brett's work in this area in his 1988 Sheffield PhD, 'The Canonical Approach to Old Testament Study'.

2   See for example, S. Kim, *The Origin of Paul's Gospel* (Grand Rapids: Eerdmans, 1981). While Kim begins his interpretation of most of Paul's writings from the Damascus road experience (and, incidentally, tends to reduce them to that experience), he is not very precise on what his actual interests are.

3   This seems to be one of Roland Barthes' favourite aphorisms.

that we are talking about the same thing, we have reached the point of genuine disagreement. Unfortunately, there is no single method for resolving these disputes. Rather we must rely on rhetorical argumentation, the ability to narrate an account that makes comprehensive sense of the recognized evidence while at the same time accounting for the strengths and weaknesses of alternative views.[1]

Without going into too much detail, and at the risk of being simplistic, I will try to give a concrete example of the way such a disagreement might be resolved. That renowned exegete of the last century, J.B. Lightfoot, and I have shared a similar interest in the phrase μορφὴ θεοῦ in Phil. 2.6. This interest could be characterized as the desire to understand how a relatively competent, koine-Greek-speaking, Philippian Christian of the first century would have read this phrase.[2] (Of course, Lightfoot never would have formulated his interest in this way in his own lifetime. I think, however, that could we resurrect him and educate him in the critical discourses of the twentieth century, he would agree that this is what his interest was. Since we cannot know the truth of this matter one way or another, I simply ask my reader to imagine that this reconstruction is accurate for the purposes of my example.) Given this common interest, it is clear that Lightfoot and I disagree on what the answer to our common question should be. Lightfoot based his reading of μορφή on the way the term is used in Plato and Aristotle. In these texts the word is linked with such terms as οὐσία and φύσις and describes the 'attributes of the Godhead'. I, on the other hand, rely on the way the term μορφή is used in the New Testament, Septuagint and the Sibylline Oracles, and especially the way the phrase μορφὴ

1 These are basically the criteria proposed by Alasdair MacIntyre for resolving epistemological crises in science. 'When an epistemological crisis is resolved, it is by the construction of a new narrative which enables the agent to understand *both* how he or she could intelligibly have held his or her original beliefs and how he or she could have been so drastically misled by them. The narrative in terms of which he or she at first understood and ordered experiences is itself made into the subject of an enlarged narrative' ('Epistemological Crises, Dramatic Narrative and the Philosophy of Science', *The Monist* 60 [1977], p. 455).
2 See J.B. Lightfoot, *St. Paul's Epistle to the Philippians* (r.p. Lynn, MA; Hendrickson, 1981), esp. pp. 127ff. For my reading of this passage, see *The Story of Christ in the Ethics of Paul* (JSNTSup, 36; Sheffield: JSOT Press, 1990).

θεοῦ is used in *Corpus Hermeticum* 1.12.14. Here the μορφή of God refers to the visible appearance of God.

By relying on classical uses of μορφή, Lightfoot was simply following the standard philological practice of the day. He did this better than almost anyone else. Nevertheless, by making recourse to more recent theories of synchronic semantics, I think I can convincingly argue that Lightfoot's philological methods are inadequate to our common task. For a synchronic understanding of μορφή (which is what we are both after) Plato and Aristotle are not relevant pieces of evidence. The LXX and *Corpus Hermeticum* 1.12.14 are relevant pieces of evidence. Provided I have not misrepresented the way μορφή is used in these texts, I can reasonably claim that my dispute with Lightfoot should be resolved in my favour.

To support his reading, a reconstructed Lightfoot (or a devoted follower) would have to show that nineteenth-century philological methods are, in fact, superior to those of synchronic semantics for answering this question. Failing that, he could show that my reading of the relevant evidence was faulty and that these texts actually support his original reading of μορφή. Until a Lightfoot supporter can do this, however, our disagreement will remain resolved in my favour.

While this may be a very common type of disagreement, the sort that much exegesis tries to resolve, it may not be the most important disagreement that is left over once we have eliminated meaning. Having recognized that no one interpretative strategy can lay claim to meaning at the expense of other strategies, we are left with the question of which interpretative strategy to adopt in any particular situation. There seem to be at least three possible ways of answering this question. None of these answers, however, exists in abstraction from the social and political arrangements within which one does one's interpretation. That is, any answer to the question, 'What sort of interpretative interest should I adopt in any particular situation?', can only be coherent within a particular social and political context in which interpretation takes place. What I would like to do in the rest of this essay is to describe what some of the possible responses to the question, 'What particular interpretative interest should I adopt?', might be, and how these answers gain their coherence and arise out of certain political arrangements. Let me say here, however, that my aim is not to give an exhaustive taxonomy of answers to this question. Rather, I simply wish to show the close connection between the resources available for answering this question and the political constitution of the context in which one interprets the Bible.[1]

Having recognized that the term 'meaning' has effectively worked to obscure the plurality of interpretative interests, one could go further and view the maintenance of plurality as a worthy end in and of itself. In fact, those who have argued most strongly against granting any particular interest epistemological privilege have generally supported the view that we should encourage a plurality of interests.[2] As Stout urges, 'Let us then celebrate the diversity of interpretations as a sign that our texts are interesting in more ways than one. The only alternative would be to have texts that weren't.'[3]

Given an interpretative task, pluralists can perform it more or less adequately and rationally argue that one performance is better than another performance of the same task. Their only desire is that they be free to pursue any interpretative task that interests them. For pluralists, the only criterion for pursuing an interpretative interest is that it is interesting to sufficient numbers of interpreters to sustain its practice. There will of course be practical limits to this, but they are simply practical.

The pluralist position is most completely embodied in those sorts of interpretative institutions whose primary (or sole) aims are focused on providing a forum in which as many interests as possible can be pursued. Such an institution would provide the occasions and the means for otherwise separate interpreters to validate their interpretative practice in conversation with other like-minded interpreters.

---

1 The term 'political' here is not used with reference to contemporary partisan politics, but to designate the types of arrangements which people form in order to enact certain practices and achieve certain goods.
2 Stout makes this point on pp. 6ff. Richard Rorty makes similar points in 'Texts and Lumps' (see esp. pp. 13ff.). Readers of Foucault will want to note here that interests do not simply arise in an organic fashion. They reflect and sustain various configurations of power.
3 Stout, 'What is the Meaning of a Text?', p. 8.

Within such an institution one could and should engage in discussion about how well its activities conform to its basic pluralist convictions. Discussions of this nature would focus on questions such as: Is the forum provided as open as is practically possible? Whose interests are recognized as sufficiently interesting to be discussed? Who can contribute to such discussions? Whose discussions get wider exposure through publication? All these questions raise ethical and political issues related to the openness of the forum provided and sustained by an institution whose primary commitment is to interpretative pluralism.[1]

The one question that such an institution could never answer, on other than practical grounds, is whether its members should pursue one interest in preference to another. In fact, the continued existence of an institution committed to interpretative pluralism may depend on this question never being asked.[2] To ask such a question would be to betray the fundamental convictions of the pluralist and whoever asked this question would either have to withdraw it or remove themselves from the institution before asking it. I take it that most of the professional institutions to which biblical scholars belong—SBL, SOTS, SNTS, CBA, etc.—are examples of bodies with the commitment to pluralism I just described.[3]

---

1   Cornel West directs insightful and sophisticated forms of these general questions to the sort of philosophical and cultural pluralism espoused by Rorty. See 'The Politics of American Neo-Pragmatism', in *Post-Analytic Philosophy*, ed. J. Rajchman and C. West (New York: Columbia University Press, 1985), pp. 259-75. For a more direct attack on the coherence of pluralism in literary studies see Ellen Rooney, 'Who's left Out? A Rose by Any Other Name is Still Red; Or, the Politics of Pluralism', *Critical Inquiry* 12 (1986), pp. 550-63, and Mary Louise Pratt, 'Interpretive Strategies and Strategic Interpretations: On Anglo-American Reader-Response Criticism', in *Postmodernism and Politics*, ed. J. Arac (Minneapolis: University of Minnesota Press, 1986), pp. 26-54.

2   In her analysis of Stanley Fish's view of interpretative communities Pratt realizes a similar point. 'The question of what constrains and constitutes interpretive communities is apparently too uncomfortable to ask. The answer, it would seem, is the shape of the rest of the community's social and material life' ('Interpretive Strategies', p. 51).

3   In spite of its name the Catholic Biblical Association has certainly maintained a pluralist stance. See, for example, P. Perkins, 'The Theological Implications of New Testament Pluralism', *CBQ* 50 (1988), pp. 5-23, esp. pp. 5, 14. Upon closer examination, it may turn out that these institutions are really fragmented and not pluralist. In spite of this, I think that their aims are basically pluralist and my comments are based on that assumption.

In addition to the pluralists, there may be those who, while willing to accept that there is no epistemological difference between interpretative interests, wish to argue that there are reasons of an ethical or political nature for adopting one (or several) interpretative interests at the expense of others. There are actually two separate ways of arguing this point and I will briefly sketch them in turn.[1]

I shall call the first position, for lack of a better name, the social responsibility view. This position begins from the view that no interpretative activity takes place in a vacuum. Few, of course, would dispute this. The social responsibility position, however, goes further. It claims that not only do interpreters play a role in often obscure interpretative institutions, but that interpreters (or the institutions which sustain their practices), as interpreters, play some relevant role in society at large. Within this role, interpreters have certain responsibilities to society.[2] Given these responsibilities, it is not hard to imagine that the pursuit of certain interpretative interests could be seen as ethically or politically bad because they would in some way inhibit the interpreter from fulfilling her or his social responsibilities. Hence, they should not be pursued.

As opposed to the pluralist's sole criterion for pursuing an interest—that it is interesting—criteria such as social justice and well-being are invoked as those that should guide an interpreter's or an institution's choice of interpretative interests. Within an institution supporting biblical interpretation the question would always be raised as to how any particular interpretative interest will aid society's quest for justice and well-being. The institution would then have to order its practice accordingly.

1　I should, perhaps, note here that while there are those who advocate positions similar to those I will now sketch, they do not begin from the position that these are issues raised by the elimination of meaning from a statement of the aims of interpretation. Indeed, their discourse is as likely to be as infected with this term as anyone else's. In spite of this, I will use them as concrete examples because they more than others resemble the positions I am trying to describe.

2　This is roughly the position argued by Virginia Held in 'The Independence of Intellectuals', *Journal of Philosophy* 80 (1983), pp. 572-82. This article, and the replies by Richard Rorty, 'Postmodernist Bourgeois Liberalism', pp. 583-89, and Alasdair MacIntyre, 'Moral Arguments and Social Contexts', pp. 590-91, respectively represent the three basic answers to the question of what is left over after the elimination of meaning which I will discuss.

Recently, Elisabeth Schüssler Fiorenza has presented a form of this social responsibility view in her 1987 Society of Biblical Literature presidential address, 'The Ethics of Interpretation: Decentering Biblical Scholarship'.[1] Schüssler Fiorenza begins by noting that biblical interpretation has started to rely on rhetoric as a central part of its critical practices. Schüssler Fiorenza's view of rhetoric

> rejects the misunderstanding of rhetoric as stylistic ornament, technical skills or linguistic manipulation, and maintains not only 'that rhetoric is epistemic but also that epistemology and ontology are themselves rhetorical'.[2]

Having noted the rise of rhetoric, Schüssler Fiorenza goes on to note that

> Since the sociohistorical location of rhetoric is the public of the *polis,* the rhetorical paradigm shift situated biblical scholarship in such a way that its public character and political responsibility become an integral part of our literary readings and historical reconstructions of the biblical world.[3]

Presumably, Schüssler Fiorenza's point is not that it is only the adoption of rhetoric that establishes the social responsibility of biblical studies. The social responsibility of biblical scholars must depend on their already established role in society. The adoption of rhetoric simply helps them to see that role and its responsibilities in a new light or to see that previous practices may have worked to obscure the social role of biblical scholarship. In other words, I do not take it that her aim is to argue for the social responsibility of biblical scholars from scratch using the 'new rhetoric'.[4] Rather, hers is a call to rec-

---

1   *JBL* 107 (1988), pp. 101-15. I am grateful to Professor Schüssler Fiorenza for making this article available to me prior to its publication.
2   Schüssler Fiorenza, p. 102. The citation within this citation is from Richard Harvey Brown, *Society as Text* (Chicago: University of Chicago Press, 1987), p. 85.
3   Schüssler Fiorenza, 'The Ethics of Interpretation', p. 102.
4   The phrase 'the new rhetoric' comes from the book *The New Rhetoric*, by C. Perelman and L. Olbrechts-Tyteca (Notre Dame: University of Notre Dame Press, 1966). The phase can be taken as a means of designating a wide variety of critical practices which emphasize 'the social aspect of language which is an instrument of communication and influence on others' (*The New Rhetoric,* p. 513). See also Willhelm Wuellner, 'Where is Rhetorical Criticism Taking Us?' *CBQ* 49 (1987), pp. 448-63.

ognize a responsibility that has always been there, but sub-jected to the previously dominant models of interpretation.

Nevertheless, having described the social role of biblical scholarship, Schüssler Fiorenza makes the following pre-scription for the SBL:

> In short, if the Society were to engage in disciplined reflec-tion on the public dimensions and ethical implications of our scholarly work, it would constitute a responsible scholarly citizenship that could be a significant participant in the global discourse seeking justice and well-being for all.[1]

Here, explicitly, justice and well-being are invoked as the ends to which the SBL should order its interpretative interests if it is to fulfill its social responsibilities. The logical result of this ordering is that the pursuit of some interests, while epistemo-logically as sound as the pursuit of any other interest, will be seen as ethically or politically irresponsible and not worthy of our attention.[2]

For this viewpoint to be applicable to an institution commit-ted to interpretative pluralism such as the SBL, two elements are crucial. First, a case must be made that there is something like a global *polis* of which all the members of the SBL are members by necessity. Without such a *polis* the notion of criti-cal responsibility loses most of its bite. For if a pluralist SBL is just one of the several fragmented institutions interpreters participate in, then their responsibilities become much more circumscribed and fragmented. In short, an interpreter's responsibilities are relative to her or his communal alle-giances. This point is made aptly by Richard Rorty. In response to Virginia Held's charge of social irresponsibility directed at intellectuals, who by their very interests marginalize themselves, Rorty notes:

> One cannot be irresponsible toward a community of which one does not think of oneself as a member. Otherwise run-away slaves and tunnelers under the Berlin Wall would be

---

1 Schüssler Fiorenza, 'The Ethics of Interpretation', p. 115.

2 'The rhetorical character of biblical interpretations and historical reconstruc-tions, moreover, requires an *ethics of accountability* that stands responsible not only for the choice of theoretical interpretive models but also for the ethical conse-quences of the biblical text and its meanings' (Schüssler Fiorenza, 'The Ethics of Interpretation', p. 15).

irresponsible. If such criticism [of social irresponsibility] were to make sense there would have to be a supercommunity one *had* to identify with—humanity as such.[1]

If there were such a supercommunity, then, it is theoretically possible that an interpreter's responsibility to a pluralist institution such as the Society of Biblical Literature would come into conflict with his or her larger responsibilities to the supercommunity. To act responsibly in such a case the interpreter would have to subject her or his pluralist aims to her or his larger responsibility to this *polis* or supercommunity.

Secondly, such a supercommunity would have to depend on a Rawlsian view of justice as an ahistorical trans-cultural virtue recognizable by all rational people.[2] This is because the supercommunity's ability to sustain a 'global discourse seeking justice and well-being for all' depends on justice being some one thing that we all can recognize. If this turned out not to be the case, global discourse would simply dissolve into intractable arguments about what constitutes justice—arguments which would be much like those arguments associated with meaning. On such a scenario, it would be impossible to argue that one interpretative practice would serve the pursuit of justice any more than alternative interests.

Only with these two elements firmly established could biblical scholars whose primary allegiance was to an institution committed to interpretative pluralism order their interests in a way that would fulfil their global responsibility to pursue justice. In fact, without a supercommunity, it is not clear that biblical scholars, as interpreters, have any social responsibilities at all. Schüssler Fiorenza's prescriptions, however, simply presuppose that these two elements are firmly established.

It would be churlish of me to criticize a presidential address for not thoroughly examining the inadequacies of its presuppositions. Rather, I merely wish to point out that for Schüssler Fiorenza's ethics of interpretation to have any relevance for a pluralist interpretative institution such a the SBL there must be something like Rorty's supercommunity *and* Rawls' con-

---

1   Rorty, 'Postmodernist Bourgeois Liberalism', p. 583, responding to Held's argument in the article cited in n. 23.
2   See John Rawls, *A Theory of Justice* (Oxford: OUP, 1972).

cept of justice. Of course, these are two things that are not firmly established. Rawls' significant contribution to a theory of justice can hardly be said to have won the day.[1] Further, the article from which Rorty's mention of a supercommunity comes is itself a stinging attack on just these two elements. Finally, very few who have read the works of Jean François Lyotard or Alasdair MacIntyre or assorted others could believe in the sort of global *polis* necessary for Schüssler Fiorenza's position.[2]

The mention of MacIntyre leads me to introduce another way of addressing the interpretative plurality left over after the elimination of meaning. I shall, for the sake of convenience, call this view the communal or collective position.[3] This position shares with the social responsibility position the view that while no interpretative interest could claim epistemological privilege, there may be ethical reasons for pusuing one interest over another in a particular situation. This position, however, refuses to accept the two elements essential to the social responsibility position outlined above—a global *polis* and an ahistorical, trans-cultural, universally recognizable notion of justice. This refusal is fundamentally rooted in the recognition that the dream of moral philosophy since the Enlighten-

1 As one might expect, a work as large and significant as *A Theory of Justice* has occasioned a host of critical reponses. See for example, Michael Sandel, *Liberalism and the Limits of Justice* (Cambridge: CUP, 1982) and Alasdair MacIntyre, *After Virtue* (Notre Dame: University of Notre Dame Press, 2nd edn, 1984), esp. ch. 17; also see *Whose Justice? Which Rationality?* (London: Duckworth, 1988) for an account which grounds notions of justice firmly within specific historical traditions of enquiry.

2 Jean François Lyotard, *The Postmodern Condition: A Report on Knowledge* (tr. G. Bennington and B. Massumi; Minneapolis: University of Minneapolis Press, 1985); and MacIntyre, *After Virtue*.

3 In his criticisms of the work of Robert Bellah *et al.* in *Habits of the Heart*, Fredric Jameson shows how a term like 'community' can become a pious platitude, 'an absent, yet powerful, empty conceptual space', if not given concrete social and historical specification. See 'On *Habits of the Heart*', *South Atlantic Quarterly* 86 (1987), p. 546. This is correct. To some degree, I suspect that my own use of the word 'community' is open to similar criticisns. While acknowledging the need for notions of community to be given concrete specifications, my aim here is simply to outline the general sort of communal configuration necessary for any community to have the moral resources to answer the question of which interpretative interest to pursue. The issue of whether that community (or collective) should be Marxist, Green or ecclesial is one that would have to be developed in greater detail than I can go into here.

ment—to establish ethical reasoning on ahistorical universal
truths of reason to which all rational people would be
reponsible—is an illusion.[1]

Rather than continue the quest for universal foundations
for moral reasoning, the communal view would suggest that
the reasons for adopting one interpretative interest over
another lie in particular historical communities. These communities would be based on shared convictions about the goods
and ends they are to pursue and on 'shared dispositions edu-
cated in accordance with those beliefs'.[2] Such a community
will have a provisionally specified *telos* to which its life and
practices are directed, to which its members are responsible by
virtue of their communal commitments.[3]

Within a community constituted on these grounds a notion
such as justice would no longer be an abstract ahistorical concept. Rather, it would receive specification and embodiment in
concrete discussions and practices within the community.
Having specified what justice is and how biblical
interpretation is relevant to attaining it, such an
interpretative community could then order its interpretative
interests towards achieving such an end in any particular
situation.[4]

---

1 See MacIntyre, *After Virtue*, esp. chs. 4, 5 and 6.

2 MacIntyre, 'Moral Arguments and Social Contexts', p. 591.

3 See also Jameson's point that 'What is wanted, then, is the reinvention, for late-
   industrial society, of a new form of the utopian project. . .' ('On *Habits of the
   Heart*, p. 563). The pluralist may well respond to this by noting that for an institution whose primary end is the maintenance of pluralism, the best practices to pursue are those which enhance the prospects of pluralism. Someone holding the
   communal position would have to agree. They would, however, simply note that
   such a pluralist institution could never entertain an ethical discussion about
   which interpretative interests to pursue without betraying their pluralist convictions. One may also raise the question of whether a group of people whose sole connection is their shared practice of biblical interpretation and the shared disposi-
   tion towards pluralism actually constitute a community in the first place. I am
   taking this last observation from points made by L. Gregory Jones in 'Alasdair
   MacIntyre on Narrative, Community and the Moral Life', *Modern Theology* 4
   (1987), pp. 53-69.

4 The specification of a communal *telos* within which biblical interpretation is a
   relevant practice is, however, only the first step in the ethical debate regarding the
   adoption of a specific interpretative interest in a particular situation. This debate
   will also require a critical account of the particular situation in which the interpretative community finds itself as well as the exercise of practical reasoning.

For MacIntyre, the paradigm of such a historical comunity is the Aristotelian *polis*. In MacIntyre's view such communities of coherent moral discourse were evident in various forms down to the Enlightenment, but are now absent from the scene.[1]

A community like this is open to the charge of sectarianism or totalitarianism if one of its ultimate goods is not a critical openness to the various discourses of a pluralist society. In fact, this community may well encourage the existence of a pluralist interpretative community such as the SBL. This is because the interpretative results of a pluralist community could be seen as potential resources which this community could adopt and use to serve its own purposes on its own terms.[2]

Briefly, then, these are some of the responses one might make to the elimination of meaning from the discourse of biblical interpretation. There is obviously much more to be said about the constitution, strengths and weaknesses of these various political arrangements in which these issues may be addressed. The aim of this essay is simply to introduce the notion that the ethical issues of interpretation cannot be resolved in abstraction from the political nature of the contexts in which they are addressed.

Even after a superficial introduction, however, it is clear that what is an ethical issue within one type of context will not be an issue in others. Which ethical issues are left over after the elimination of meaning will depend on a variety of factors, none of which is directly related to theories of interpretation.

Practical reason will operate to order a community's interpretative interests in accord with its specified ends in a particular situation.

1 Recently, however, several Christian ethicists have argued that the church might prove to be the modern-day manifestation of Aristotle's *polis*. The most obvious case is found in the extensive writings of Stanley Hauerwas. If this is to be the case, the notion of 'church', however, will need greater specification. See also MacIntyre's own suggestions in the last chapter of *After Virtue* entitled: 'After Virtue: Nietzsche *or* Aristotle, Trotsky *and* Saint Benedict'.

2 In addition, see Cornel West's comment, 'Despite the limitations, Rorty's neopragmatism can serve as a useful springboard for a more engaged, even subversive, philosophical perspective. This is so primarily because it encourages the cultivation of critical attitudes toward all philosophical traditions' ('The Politics of Neo-Pragmatism', p. 270).

Rather, such factors will be related to the political constitution of the contexts in which interpretation takes place.[1]

1   I am grateful to Andrew Adam, Mark Brett, Michael Cartwright, Stanley Hauer-
    was, Greg Jones and Ken Surin for their numerous insightful comments. I am
    also indebted to those members of the SBL's Structuralism and Exegesis Section
    who responded to an earlier draft of this paper.

CONTRIBUTORS

Dr Loveday C.A. Alexander is Lecturer in New Testament in the University of Sheffield.

Dr Mark G. Brett received his Ph.D. from the University of Sheffield and lectures in Old Testament at Lincoln Theological College.

Professor F.F. Bruce founded and was the first Professor in the Department of Biblical History and Literature in the University of Sheffield. He subsequently became John Rylands Professor of Biblical Criticism and Exegesis (now Emeritus) in the University of Manchester. He now lives in Buxton, Derbyshire.

David J. Chalcraft is a graduate in Biblical Studies in the University of Sheffield and is currently a research student in the faculty of Social Studies at Oxford University.

The Revd Professor Bruce D. Chilton was a Lecturer in the University of Sheffield from 1976 to 1985. He is currently Bernard Iddings Bell Professor of Religion and Philosophy and Chaplain at Bard College, Annandale-on-Hudson, New York.

Professor Ronald E. Clements was one of the first persons to receive a Ph.D. in Biblical Studies from the Univesity of Sheffield. He is currently Samuel E. Davidson Professor of Old Testament Studies at King's College, University of London.

Professor David J.A. Clines is Professor of Biblical Studies in the University of Sheffield.

Dr Philip R. Davies is Senior Lecturer in Biblical Studies in the University of Sheffield.

Dr Stephen E. Fowl received his Ph.D. from the University of Sheffield and is Assistant Professor of Theology at Loyola College, Baltimore, Maryland.

Professor David M. Gunn was Lecturer and Senior Lecturer in the Department of Biblical Studies in the University of Sheffield from 1970 to 1984, and is now Professor of Old Testament, Columbia Theological Seminary, Atlanta, Georgia.

The Revd Canon Colin J.A. Hickling, formerly of King's College, London, is Vicar of Arksey and Honorary Lecturer in the Department of Biblical Studies in the University of Sheffield.

Dr Andrew T. Lincoln is Lecturer in New Testament in the University of Sheffield.

Dr Stanley E. Porter received his Ph.D. from the University of Sheffield and is Assistant Professor of Greek at Biola University, La Mirada, California.

The Revd Canon Professor John W. Rogerson is Professor and Head of the Department of Biblical Studies in the University of Sheffield.

The Revd Dr Anthony C. Thiselton was Stephenson Fellow, Lecturer and Senior Lecturer in the Department of Biblical Studies in the University of Sheffield from 1970 to 1985, and is now Principal of St John's College in the University of Durham.

Dr Laurence A. Turner received his Ph.D. from the University of Sheffield and lectures in Old Testament at Avondale College, Cooranbong, New South Wales.

Dr Barry G. Webb received his Ph.D. from the University of Sheffield and lectures in Old Testament at Moore Theological College, Sydney, New South Wales.

Gerald West is a research student in the Department of Biblical Studies in the University of Sheffield and Lecturer in the Department of Theological Studies in the University of Natal, South Africa.

Dr K. Lawson Younger received his Ph.D. from the University of Sheffield and lectures in Old Testament at LeTourneau University, Longview, Texas.

INDEX OF AUTHORS